GEOGRAPHY AND CHANGE

David Flint, Corrin Flint and Neil Punnett

Hodder & Stoughton
A MEMBER OF THE HODDER HEADLINE GROUP

Acknowledgements

The authors and publishers would like to thank the following for permission to reproduce copyright materials in this book:
The Daily Telegraph, Figures 7.3 and 7.4; European Schoolbooks, *Global Issues: World Population*, Figures 2.6 and 2.7; *The Guardian*, Figures 19.4 and 20.3; Helicon Publishing Ltd, *Atlas of the Environment 2ed*, Don Hiurichsen and Geoffrey Lean, Figure 2.3; *The Independent*, Figure 10.9; Oliver & Boyd, *Population Geography*, Hazel Barrett, Figures 3.5, 3.6 and 3.7 and *World Studies 8–13*, D Hicks and M Steiner, Figure 6.11; Ordnance Survey, Figures 11.4 and 32.2; Oxford University Press, *British Agriculture*, Brian Ilbery, Figure 15.7; Overseas Development Administration, *Overseas Development Newsletter*, Figure 7.8; Population Concern, *1995 Datasheet*, Figures 1.3–1.7; Yorkshire Dales National Park, *Dales '94*, Figure 20.6.

The authors and publishers would also like to thank the following for permission to reproduce photos in this book:

Dan Addelman, Figure 7.10; Penni Bickle, Figures 27.1 and 29.2; J Allan Cash, Figures 11.11, 12.2, 17.1, 22.22, 26.2 and 30.9; Celtic Picture Library, Figure 11.12; Simon Dack, Figure 10.8; Eye Unbiquitous, Figures 2.5, 12.1 and 28.7; G S F Picture Library, Figures 13.6 and 13.8; Robert Harding Picture Library, Figures 12.8 and 22.23; Impact, Figure 29.5; James Davis Worldwide Photographic Travel Library, Figures 1.1, 13.9 and 13.10; Hulton Deutsch, Figures 11.20 and 12.11; Life File Photo Library, Figures 5.8, 27.2, 31.5 and 31.8; Panos Pictures, Figures 6.4, 7.7 and 16.4; Edward Parker, Figures 8.2 and 27.10; Photoair, Figure 12.6; Science Photo Library, Figures 9.9, 10.1, 10.3, 12.10, 13.1, 15.13, 20.1, 21.8, 21.9, 22.20, 23.1 and 27.9; Still Pictures, Figures 13.16 and 21.10; C M Taylor, Figures 30.6 and 30.7; Topham Picturepoint, Figures 9.8, 15.10, 22.15 and 23.8; Trip, Figures 2.1, 5.4, 6.7, 7.1, 10.15, 13.2, 15.16, 17.2, 18.4, 19.5, 19.7, 20.2, 22.21, 23.9, 23.10, 24.1, 24.2, 24.3, 25.11, 28.1, 28.6, 29.3 and 30.3; University of Dundee, Figure 14.13; Stewart Weir, Figures 11.4, 15.14, 18.3, 26.7, 27.3, 27.7, 27.8, 29.6, 30.10, 31.2, 31.3 and 31.4.

All other photos supplied by the authors.

Every effort has been made to trace and acknowledge copyright holders, but if any have been overlooked the publishers will be pleased to make the necessary arrangements.

All inside artwork by Martin Berry and Oxford Illustrators Ltd.

British Library Cataloguing in Publication Data
Flint, David
  Geography and change
  1. Geography
  I. Title II. Flint, Corrin III. Punnett, Neil
  910

ISBN 0 340 64786 8

First published 1996
Impression number 10 9 8 7 6 5 4 3 2 1
Year   1999 1998 1997 1996

Copyright © 1996 David Flint, Neil Punnett, Corrin Flint

All rights reserved. No part of this publication may be reproduced or transmitted in any form or by any means, electronic or mechanical, including photocopy, recording, or any information storage and retrieval system, without permission in writing from the publisher or under licence from the Copyright Licensing Agency Limited. Further details of such licences (for reprographic reproduction) may be obtained from the Copyright Licensing Agency Limited, of 90 Tottenham Court Road, London W1P 9HE.

Typeset by Fakenham Photosetting Ltd, Fakenham, Norfolk.
Printed in Malaysia for Hodder & Stoughton Educational, a division of Hodder Headline Plc, 338 Euston Road, London NW1 3BH by Times Offset(M)Sdn Bhd.

Contents

Introduction	**4**
Population Change	**7**
1 People and development	7
2 Population growth and change	13
3 Birth and death	19
4 Population and resources	23
5 Migration	26
6 Trade links	33
7 Aid links	40
8 Transnational companies	46
Change in the Physical Environment	**49**
9 Volcanoes and earthquakes	49
10 Weathering and soils	57
11 Rivers	69
12 Coasts	78
13 Highland glaciation	84
14 Weather and climate	93
Change in the Countryside	**108**
15 Agricultural change in more economically developed countries	108
16 Agricultural change in less economically developed countries	120
17 Leisure and tourism	124
18 Migration to the countryside	131
Changing Resources	**134**
19 What are resources?	134
20 Mineral resources	139
21 Forest resources	147
22 Energy resources	154
23 Pollution	170
Industrial Change	**181**
24 Types of industry	181
25 Industrial growth and development	184
26 Industrial location	191
Changing Urban Environments	**197**
27 Housing	197
28 Changing communities	204
29 Shops and services	208
30 Transport in towns	213
31 New towns	218
32 Pressures on the urban fringe	223
Country Fact Files	**226**
The UK	226
Spain	229
The USA	231
Thailand	234
Glossary	**236**

Introduction

Why geography and change?

This book is about the world, and the ways in which it is changing. All over the world people are coping with different types of change. In some places the change is caused by human activity such as the building of a new motorway or out-of-town shopping centre. In other places the change is the result of a combination of physical and human processes such as a rise in sea level or an increase in population. We are all affected by changes and this book will explore:

- how things are changing;
- why things are changing;
- what issues are involved in the changes;
- the effects of the changes.

Change at different scales

Change takes place on a range of different scales. Local changes affect people in relatively small areas. These might include the building of a bypass around a traffic bottleneck or the sinking of a well to provide clean water for people in a semi-desert region. Regional changes affect larger parts of countries. These might include changes such as the opening of a new oilfield or the redevelopment of a declining industrial area. National changes affect whole countries and include things like an increase in famine or the development of high-technology exports. Finally, there are international changes which affect large parts of the world. Events such as global warming, acid rain and population growth are all international changes, as are international political agreements or large-scale wars.

Changes in different places

The book focuses on change in different parts of the world. Many of the case studies are drawn from the UK and as such will include examples with which you may be familiar. To that end one of the Fact Files towards the end of the book provides an up to date summary of some key data on the UK. However the authors are also keen to use examples from another, larger economically more developed country, namely the USA. So, for example there are US examples on migration (Chapter 5), energy (Chapter 22), pollution (Chapter 23), industrial growth and development (Chapter 25) and transport (Chapter 30). It is intended that these examples will permit comparisons between the UK and the USA. Similarly examples from Spain, one of the UK's European partners, are featured in relation to agriculture (Chapter 15), tourism (Chapter 17) and industrialisation (Chapter 26). There is also a Fact File on Spain towards the end of the book. In this way both European and world wide case studies of change have been incorporated in the book.

Thailand has been chosen as a good example of a less economically developed country. Thailand is a country of extremely rapid change, and some of these changes are highlighted in relation to migration (Chapter 5), aid (Chapter 7), weathering and soils (Chapter 10), agriculture

(Chapter 16), tourism (Chapter 17) and industrial growth and development (Chapter 25). The fourth Fact File contains up to date information on Thailand. In this way you will be able to compare developments in the UK, Spain and the USA with those in Thailand and other economically less developed countries.

Change and issues

By definition, change means that things do not stay the same. The problem is that some changes, such as a rise in standards of living, are good, whilst others such as an overall increase in world poverty are not. However, most changes are not so easy to categorise as 'good' or 'bad'. This is because changes affect different people and environments in different ways. For example, the building of an out-of-town shopping centre may be welcomed by people with cars who can park close to the shops but it may not be popular with people living near the new centre, where roads may become crowded and dangerous due to the extra traffic. Thus changes give rise to *issues*, which are often about how resources such as land, water, soil or minerals should be used. Geographers can help to identify, analyse and clarify these issues.

Behind each change and each issue is a set of decisions about how resources will be developed and how changes will be managed. So it is important to understand how individual people and groups of people make decisions, and what factors influence the decision-making process. You will have the chance to examine the effects of different people's attitudes, values and beliefs throughout this book. But you also need to think about your own ideas about changes and issues. Which of the people and groups in the book do you agree with? Are your views based on evidence and logic or on emotion? How do you make up your mind about issues? How much are you influenced by parents, friends, the media? Remember, it is important to see other people's points of view even if you do not agree with them.

Population Change

Chapter 1: People and development

What is development?
How can development be measured?
How does development affect people in different parts of the world?

This unit looks at the idea of development and, in particular, what it means for people in countries around the world. The unit includes ideas about standards of living and quality of life.

What is development?

Over the last 200 years, people in the more economically developed countries of the world have expected their *standard of living* to rise. From time to time this rise has been halted by war and economic recession but, in general, people in most of the more economically developed countries have enjoyed better living standards. Similarly, the recent improvements in living standards in less economically developed countries like Singapore and South Korea suggest that other countries can achieve higher living standards. This is especially true if they have developed their industries, as Figure 1.1 shows.

Until the 1970s, countries which had not developed industries were called *'undeveloped'* or *'underdeveloped'*. This was a Western view. It suggested that there was a need for those countries to change and raise living standards, implying that the correct way to do this was to establish more industries.

In the 1960s poorer parts of the world were described as *'Third world'*. This term was used to distinguish poorer countries from the countries of the *'First World'*, which were rich capitalist countries like the UK, USA and Japan and the *'Second world'* which comprised the Communist countries of eastern Europe.

Today, poorer nations are most often known as

Figure 1.1 Central Singapore

'Less Economically Developed Countries' (LEDCs), implying that there is potential for future change, while wealthier nations are described as 'More Economically Developed Countries' (MEDCs).

Many people have tried to define what is meant by 'development' and Figure 1.2 gives some examples.

Figure 1.2 Definitions of development

> '...the cumulative perceptible increase in the material standard of living for a rapidly increasing proportion of the population.'
> BW Hodder, geographer
>
> 'Development is growth plus change; change in turn is social and cultural as well as economic, and qualitative as well as quantitative.'
> United Nations
>
> 'The progressive elimination of poverty, equality and unemployment within the context of a growing economy.'
> W Todaro, economist
>
> ''Development' must imply a change for the better. All the arguments about 'development' really centre around the questions: better for whom, in what way and how do we know?'
> F Thomas, economist
>
> 'The building of a society in which all members have equal rights, and equal opportunities; in which all can live at peace with their neighbours without suffering or imposing injustice, being exploited or exploiting; in which all have a gradually increasing basic level of material welfare before any individual lives in luxury.'
> J Nyerere, former president of Tanzania

1. (a) Use Figure 1.2 to make a list of all the different elements that make up development.
   (b) Write your own definition of development.
   (c) Compare your definition of development with that of other people in the class. In which areas do you agree? Where do you disagree?

So development is not simply about economic progress. It involves an improvement for an increasing percentage of population in aspects of life such as prosperity, health care and education. Development also involves justice and peace.

How can we measure development?

In the past, purely economic features were used to measure a country's development. The most common method was **per capita gross national product (per capita GNP)**. This is calculated by dividing the total value of all goods and services produced by a country by the population. Figure 1.3 shows how per capita GNP varies from country to country and Figure 1.4 gives the world picture.

Figure 1.3 Per capita GNP for some countries, 1993

	US $
Ghana	430
Mali	300
Nigeria	310
Kenya	270
Zimbabwe	540
South Africa	2900
USA	24 750
Mexico	3750
Brazil	3020
Saudi Arabia	7780
India	290
Malaysia	3160
Singapore	19 310
Thailand	2040
UK	17 970
Spain	13 650

Per capita GNP has serious drawbacks as a means of measuring development, because:

- accurate data are often hard to obtain;
- much production in poorer countries is for **subsistence** and is not taken into account in the statistics;

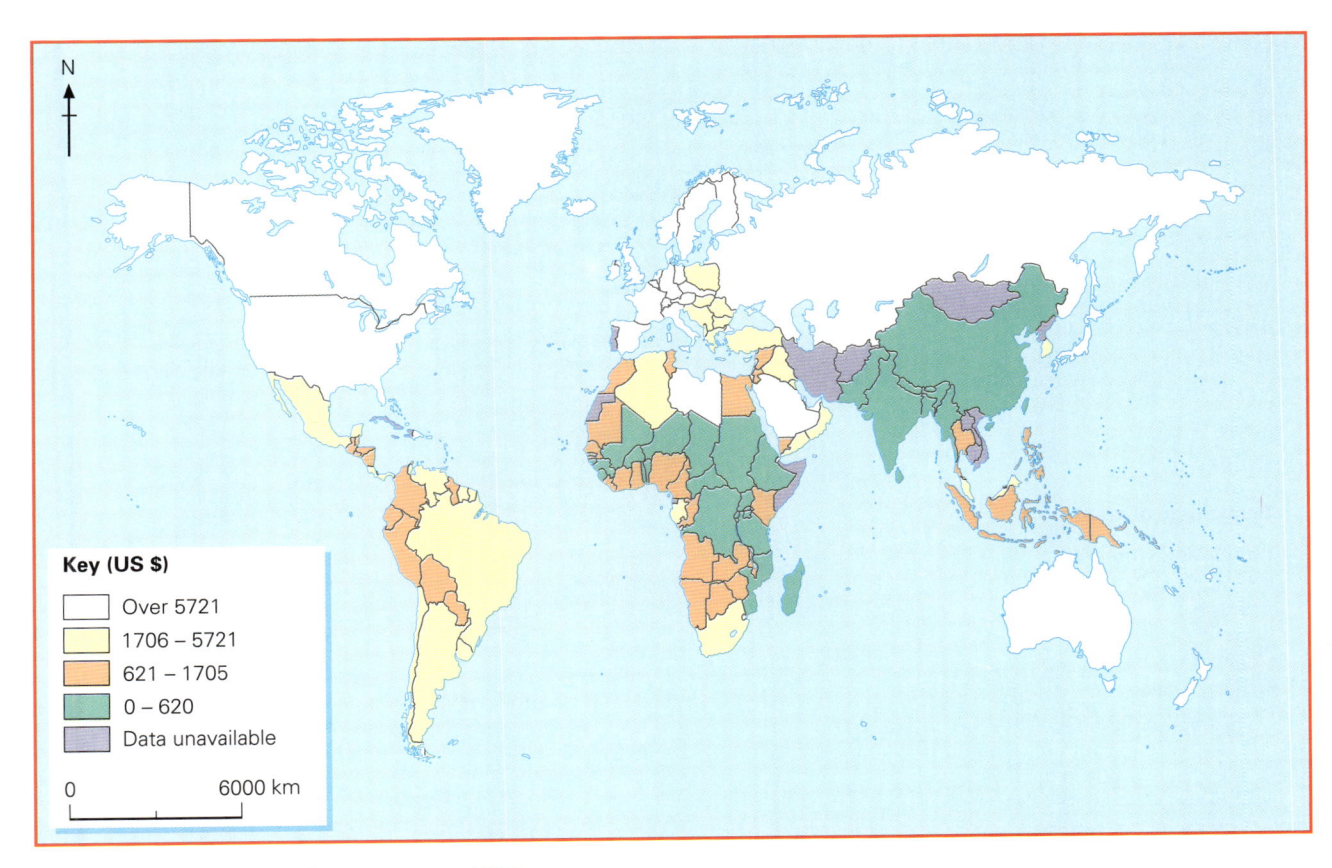

Figure 1.4 World GNP per capita, 1993

- currency rates change from day to day so it is hard to put a value on goods and services in any one currency;
- per capita GNP conceals important internal differences. For example, the per capita GNP for Brazil is US $ 2920 but 10 per cent of the population possess 60 per cent of the country's wealth. So the average per capita figure is meaningless.

Because per capita GNP on its own is a poor measure of development, and because development includes broader ideas of social, political and material well-being, other indicators can be used. Figure 1.5 shows one such indicator.

In the 1980s, a new indicator of development was calculated, called the **Physical Quality of Life Index (PQLI)**. This composite indicator comprised the factors of **life expectancy**, **infant mortality** and **adult literacy**. For each of these criteria, countries were placed on a scale of 0–100 with 0 the worst and 100 the best. Each of the three criteria has the same weighting and their average gives the PQLI. Figure 1.6 shows world PQLI values. On the map, an index figure of 77 represents the basic minimum for human need and over 90 represents a high level of well-being.

2. Look at Figures 1.4, 1.5 and 1.6. Which one gives the 'best' picture of development according to your definition? Give the reasons for your choice.
3. Read the description of an economically developing country in Figure 1.8. On the basis of this description, and referring to Figure 1.5, decide which countries on the list in Figure 1.7 are 'economically developing'.
4. Which single set of statistics in Figure 1.7 best separates LEDCs from MEDCs? Give reasons for your answer.

People and development

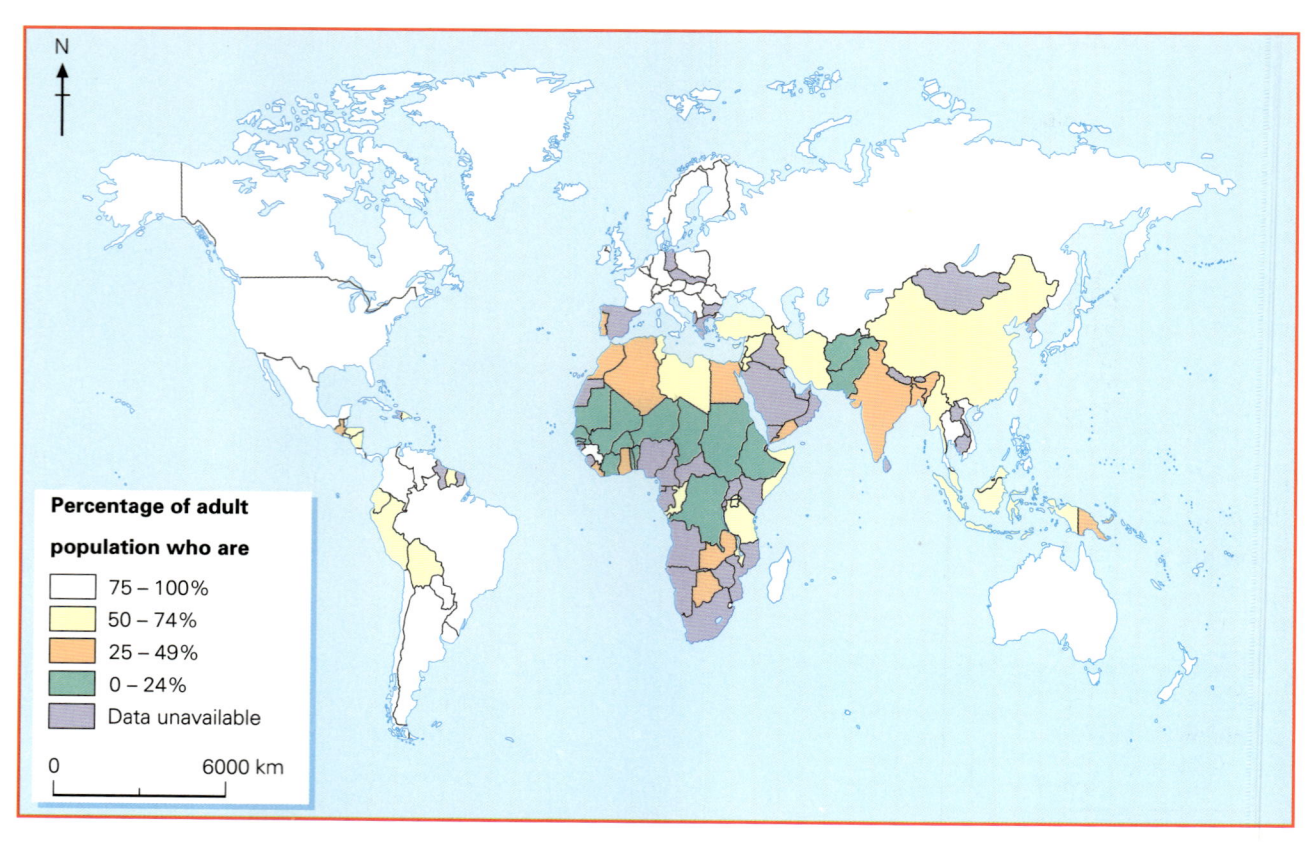

Figure 1.5 World adult literacy rates, 1993

Figure 1.6 World PQLI values, 1993

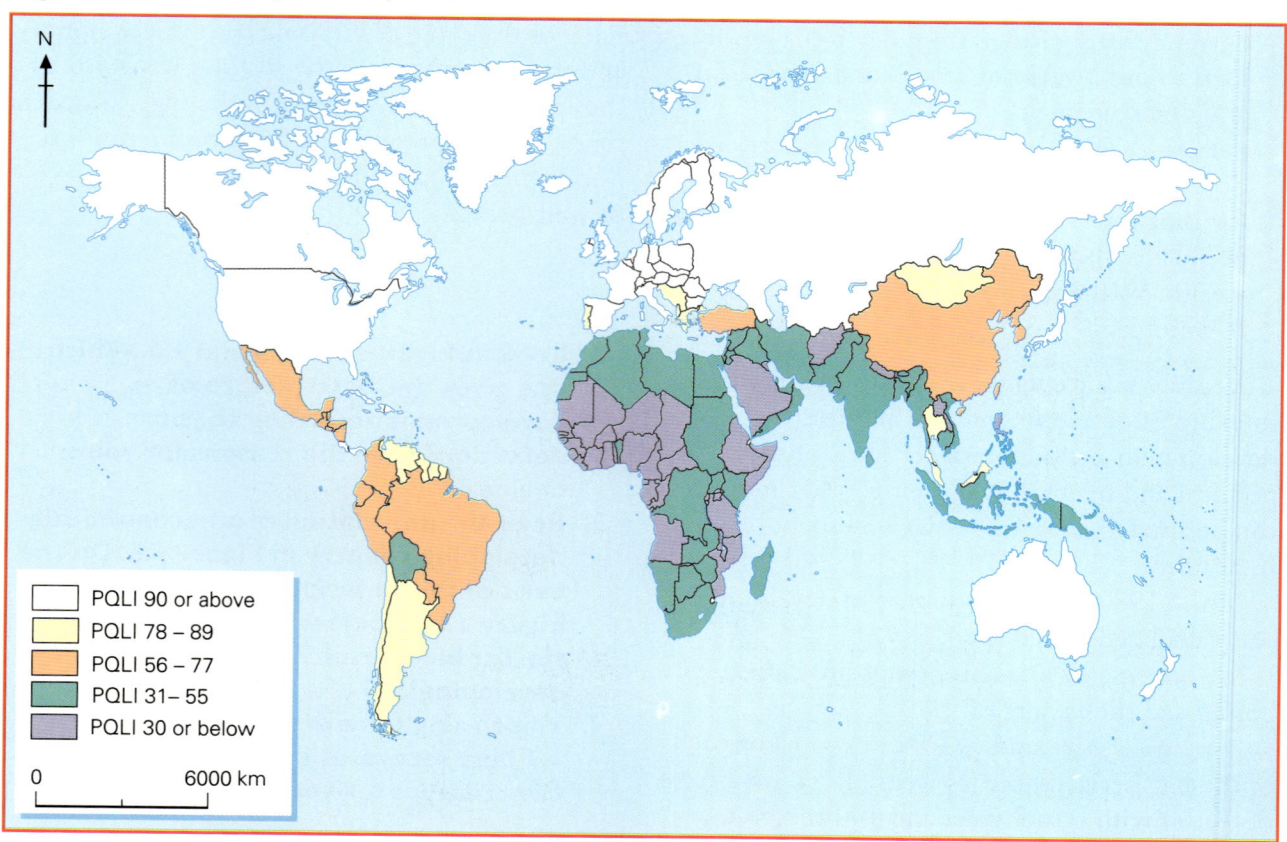

10 Population Change

Figure 1.7 Measuring development

Country	Number of people per doctor	% of workforce in agriculture, fishing and forestry	Population increase (%)	Life expectancy (years) M = male F = female	Infant mortality (% of babies who die before one year per 1000 live births)	% of population over 15 who can read and write	% of total population with access to safe water
Argentina	370	13	1.3	M68 F75	15	95	74
Australia	400	3	1.5	M74 F80	7	99	97
Bangladesh	6500	57	2.5	M53 F53	108	35	51
Brazil	1000	29	2.1	M64 F69	57	81	72
China	1000	74	1.3	M69 F73	27	70	not known
Egypt	1320	34	2.5	M60 F63	57	48	66
India	2460	63	2.1	M60 F61	88	48	37
Japan	610	7	0.5	M76 F82	5	99	99
Nigeria	7990	45	2.2	M51 F54	96	51	52
Saudi Arabia	660	49	4.9	M64 F68	58	62	88
UK	300	2	0.2	M73 F79	8	99	99
USA	420	3	0.9	M73 F80	8	99	99

Figure 1.8 Description of an LEDC

- A high percentage of the population working in agriculture;
- a low per capita GNP;
- a high rate of population growth;
- low life expectancy and a high rate of infant mortality;
- many people to each doctor;
- a low rate of adult literacy;
- poor access to supplies of safe water.

Points to remember about 'development'

- It is often unwise to label whole countries as 'economically developing' because within nations there may be small groups of people who are rich and powerful.
- Development is a broad idea that is difficult to define and harder still to measure but is useful when thinking about inequality in the world.
- Development is based on the idea of **interdependence**, that is that all countries depend on each other. What happens in one part of the world affects all of us. For example, a severe frost in Brazil may damage the coffee crop and cause the price of coffee to rise in supermarkets all over the world.

5. Figure 1.9 shows some of the most common attitudes towards people in developing countries. Work in pairs and discuss each view. Write down the aspects of each statement with which you agree and disagree. Compare your results with those of other pairs.
6. Over the period of a week, collect cuttings from local and national newspapers on the theme of developing countries. For each cutting (a) identify the attitude of the writer towards developing countries and then (b) compare this with Figure 1.9. (c) How far do they agree or disagree?

People and development

Figure 1.9 Attitudes towards LEDCs

'People in developing countries are there to supply us with raw materials and food like tea, bananas, coffee and iron ore. They enjoy the simple life working on the farms or in the mines and they buy our cars, tractors, and other manufactured goods.'

'Lots of people in poorer countries still live in straw or mud huts. They have been left behind. But with our help they can soon have fast food, discos, and lots of cars.'

'There's no hope for them. Everything there is in a desperate state with floods, droughts, famines, and earthquakes. People are dying like flies and I suppose they will expect us to help them out again ...'

'People in developing countries fund 85 per cent of their own development and some have made a lot of progress.'

'Developing countries have avoided many of the problems facing richer countries such as crime, unemployment and pollution.'

Summary

- Different terms are used to describe the rich and poor countries of the world.
- Development is a complex idea.
- It is difficult to measure development.
- Development is based on the idea of interdependence.
- Individuals and groups have different attitudes towards LEDCs.

Population Change

Chapter 2 Population growth and change

How and why is world population growing so rapidly?

This unit examines the rate of world population growth, and how this varies around the world.

Growth and more growth

The world's population has grown from 500 million in 1650 to 2500 million in 1950 and then to 5600 million in 1994. This is a very rapid rate of growth; around the world, 130 people are born every minute of every day! Each year, there are an extra 70 million people in the world (see Figure 2.1), and the total world population doubles every 30 years! This growth is very recent and is one of the most important challenges facing people all over the world. The problem is that as population growth increases, the earth, which has to provide the resources to feed and house all these people, is not getting any bigger. In fact we are making it more difficult to support life on earth by polluting the air, seas and land and by mismanaging the world's resources.

Figure 2.1 Children in a developing country

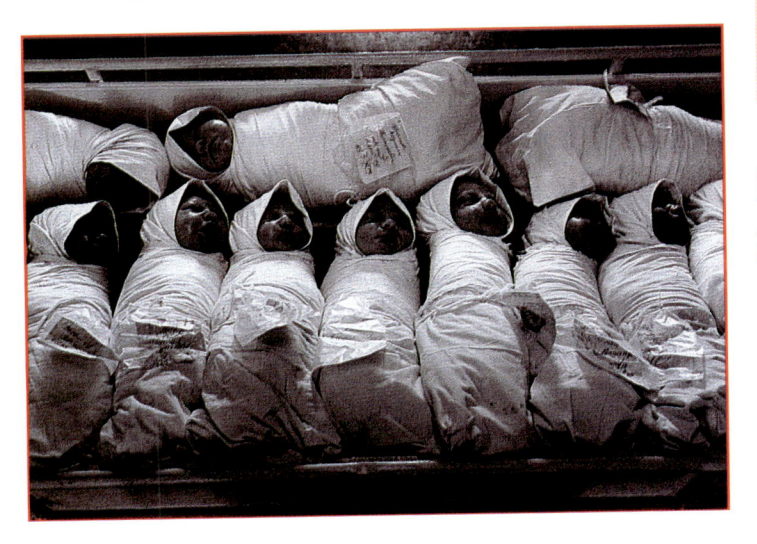

Figure 2.2 World population growth

Year	Total world population (millions)
1650	500
1700	600
1750	750
1800	900
1850	1200
1900	1700
1950	2300
1980	4000
1994	5600
2010	8000

1. Figure 2.2 shows the total world population change from 1650 to 1994, with the United Nations estimate for the year 2010. Draw a line graph to show these changes.
2. In 1700 the world's population was 600 million. How many years did it take to double this number? When is the 1980 population total expected to double?

Different places, different population growth

The figures for world population growth are only average figures for many different countries. They conceal big differences between different parts of the world. Figure 2.3 shows how the rate of population growth varies world-wide.

Figure 2.3 World population growth and the North–South divide

North/more economically developed

Countries in North America, Europe, Russia, Japan, Australia and New Zealand

- These countries are called more economically developed countries (MEDCs)
- Has 80 per cent of the world's income
- Has 25 per cent of the total world population
- Has 25 per cent of the world's population increase each year
- Most people have enough to eat
- On average a person can expect to live more than 70 years
- Most people are educated at least through secondary school

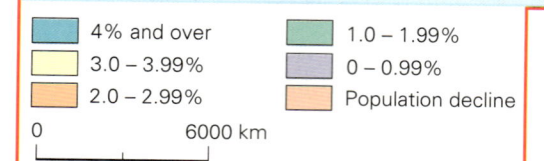

South/less economically developing

Countries of Asia, Africa and Latin America

- These countries are called less economically developed countries (LEDCs)
- Has 20 per cent of the world's income
- Has 75 per cent of the total world population
- Has 75 per cent of the world's population increase each year
- 20 per cent or more of the people suffer from hunger and malnutrition
- A person can expect to live about 50 years
- 50 per cent of the people have little chance of much formal education, especially females

Legend:
- 4% and over
- 3.0 – 3.99%
- 2.0 – 2.99%
- 1.0 – 1.99%
- 0 – 0.99%
- Population decline

0 ———— 6000 km

Most of the MEDCs are rich, whilst most of the LEDCs are poor. Figure 2.3 shows some of the other differences between rich and poor nations.

3. A low population growth rate is one of 1 per cent or less per year. Growth rates of over 2 per cent per year are high. Name four countries with low growth rates and five countries with high growth rates.
4. Is population growth fastest in more or less economically developed nations?
5. Write a paragraph called 'Living in an unequal world', using Figure 2.3 to write a summary of the main features of MEDCs. Contrast these features with the main features of LEDCs.

Why is world population growing so fast?

One explanation for rapid population growth is that fewer people die each year. Deaths are measured by the **death rate**, a figure which gives the number of deaths for each 1000 of the population. In Thailand the death rate in 1995 was seven per 1000, but only 45 years ago, in 1950, it was nineteen per 1000. Improvements in medicine and hygiene (clean water and sanitation) have reduced death rates all over the world.

A second reason for rapid population growth is the large number of babies born each year. This is measured by the **birth rate**, which is the number of births for every 1000 of the population. In 1950, the birth rate in Kenya was 65; in Thailand it was 47 and in Britain, it was 16. In 1995, Kenya's birth rate was 47, compared to 16 in Thailand and only 13 in Britain. So Kenya's population is growing rapidly, because the birth rate is only falling slowly whilst the death rate is falling much faster.

14 Population Change

Should countries be trying to reduce the birth rate?

Some experts argue that there are already too many people in the world. They say that people, especially in the poorer countries, are having too many children and that they should reduce the birth rate. However, many of these experts are from wealthier nations and they sometimes fail to see that children bring major benefits to people in developing countries, as Figure 2.4 shows. Figure 2.4 also shows how children can be a burden to people in the developed countries.

Figure 2.4 Children – burden or benefit?

Poorer countries

In less economically developed countries like Indonesia, children are a benefit in many ways.

- They collect wood for fuel and fetch water – jobs that can take hours each day.
- They look after the animals. Cattle and water buffalo in Indonesia need green fodder mixed with rice stalks every day. This has to be cut from the fields, gardens and river banks. Cattle owners without enough children of their own to do these jobs pay other children.
- They help with farming from the age of eight.
- Some, especially girls, help with cleaning, cooking and weaving baskets and mats to sell, as well as looking after younger brothers and sisters.

Richer countries

- Toys, clothes, books, bikes, computer games, watches, CDs and videos are all expensive. As children grow older they want more of these.
- Most children stay on at school until they are at least sixteen, so parents have to buy uniforms and equipment, as well as paying for extra lessons like music and supporting children in the home.
- Larger families need larger houses, which may lead to higher rents and mortgages and bigger telephone and fuel bills.

Population growth and change

Figure 2.5 A family planning poster in China

> 6. Use Figure 2.4 (page 15) to explain why people in some poorer countries may want more rather than less children.
> 7. The governments of some poorer countries like China, Thailand and Indonesia have tried to persuade people to have fewer children by initiating **family planning programmes** (see Figure 2.5). They are aimed at reducing the pressure to find food, jobs and houses for a growing population. These are some of the ways in which countries have tried to reduce their birth rate:
> (a) creating more jobs for women;
> (b) raising the age at which people are allowed to marry;
> (c) teaching men and women to read and write;
> (d) providing better health care for babies and women.
> Explain why each method might encourage people to have fewer children.

Are people spread evenly over the world?

The world's population is not spread evenly over the land surface. As Figure 2.6 shows, in particular areas like India, the UK and Germany, lots of people are crowded together in relatively small areas of land. Such places have a high **population density**, which is the number of people per square kilometre (km²). In other places, like North Africa, where there are relatively few people, population densities are low.

> 8. Study Figure 2.6.
> (a) Name ten countries with a population density over 100 people per km².
> (b) Name eight countries with a population density below ten people per km².
> (c) Eighty per cent of the world's population live on 20 per cent of the land. Suggest some reasons why it would be difficult for people to start living on the other 80 per cent of the earth's land surface?

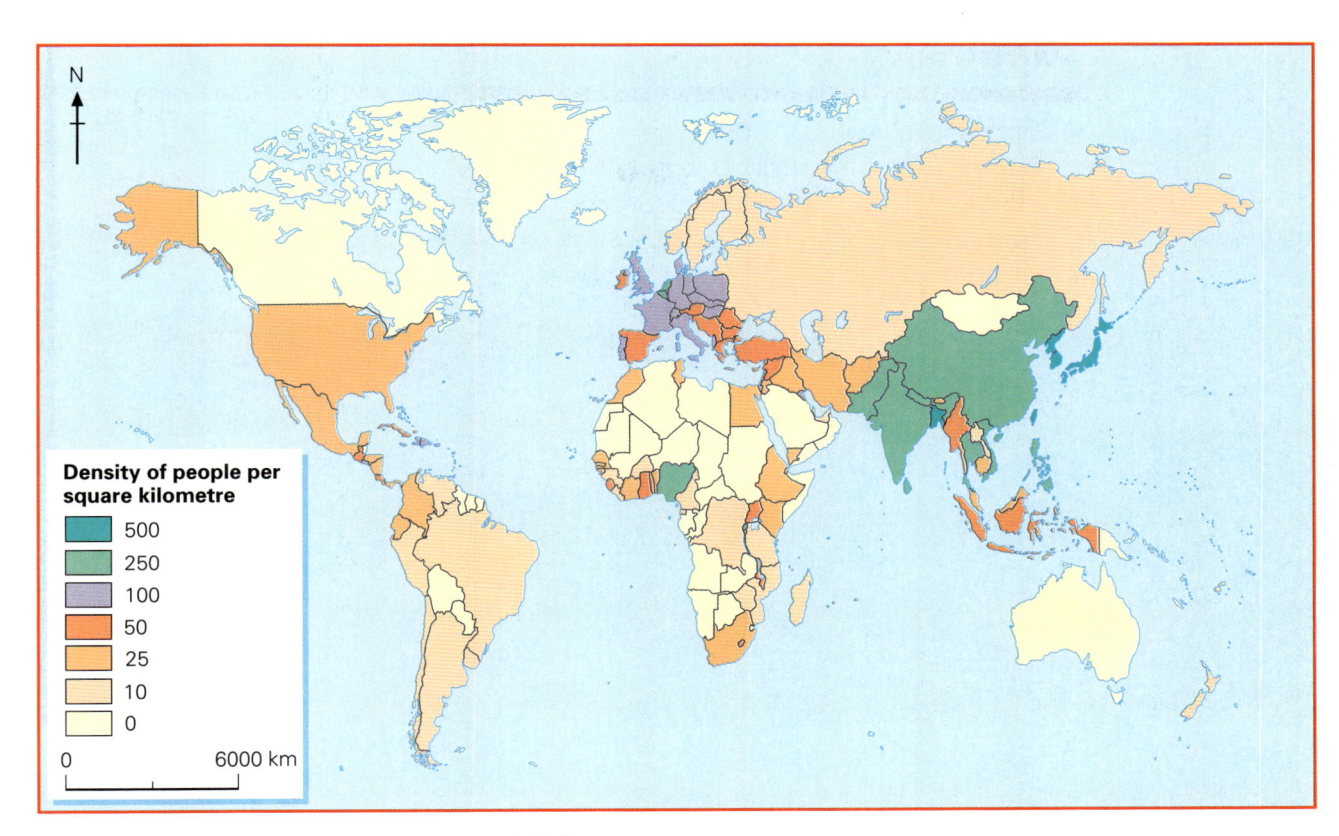

Figure 2.6 World population density, 1994

Density of people per square kilometre:
- 500
- 250
- 100
- 50
- 25
- 10
- 0

0 — 6000 km

9. Look at Figure 2.7 which shows how the distribution of the world's population is expected to change.
   (a) What percentage of the world's population lived in Asia and Oceania (the Pacific area) in 1960? What is the percentage expected to be in 2025?
   (b) How is the percentage of the world's population living in MEDCs expected to change between 1950 and 2025?
   (c) Overall, which parts of the world are expected to become more important in terms of world population by 2025?

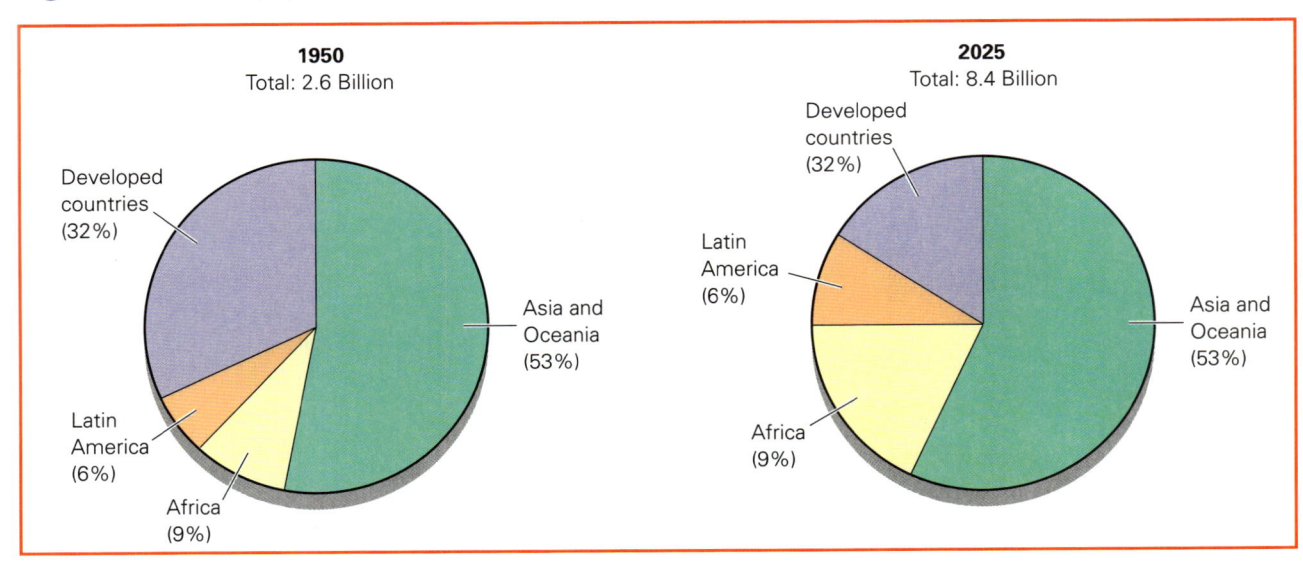

Figure 2.7 World population in 1950 and 2025

1950 — Total: 2.6 Billion
- Developed countries (32%)
- Asia and Oceania (53%)
- Latin America (6%)
- Africa (9%)

2025 — Total: 8.4 Billion
- Developed countries (32%)
- Latin America (6%)
- Asia and Oceania (53%)
- Africa (9%)

Population growth and change   17

Summary

- World population is growing rapidly.
- Population growth is fastest in poorer countries.
- Children can be a benefit or a burden.
- Some governments try to influence the birth rate in their countries.
- Population density varies considerably from place to place.

Chapter 3: Birth and death

How and why have birth and death rates changed over time?
What are the effects of these changes?

This unit examines the factors affecting birth and death rates in relation to the Demographic Transition Model. It uses case studies to highlight these changes and considers their implications.

The Demographic Transition Model

The **demographic transition model** of population change is shown in Figure 3.1. This model is also called the **population cycle**. It is based on the changes in birth and death rates and total population over many years in MEDCs like the UK and the USA.

The demographic transition is divided into four stages:

Stage One (the 'high stationary stage')

At this time, countries have high birth rates and high death rates, so population growth is slow.

The birth rate is high because:

- people do not have access to birth control or family planning;
- many children die young so parents have lots of children to ensure that some survive;
- children are needed for the work they do, for example, fetching water;
- some religious groups such as Moslems, Hindus and Roman Catholics encourage large families.

The high death rate is due to:

- diseases, such as typhoid, polio, cholera;
- relative lack of doctors, nurses, hospitals and medical care;
- lack of clean water or sewage disposal which encourages the spread of disease.

Figure 3.1 The Demographic Transition Model

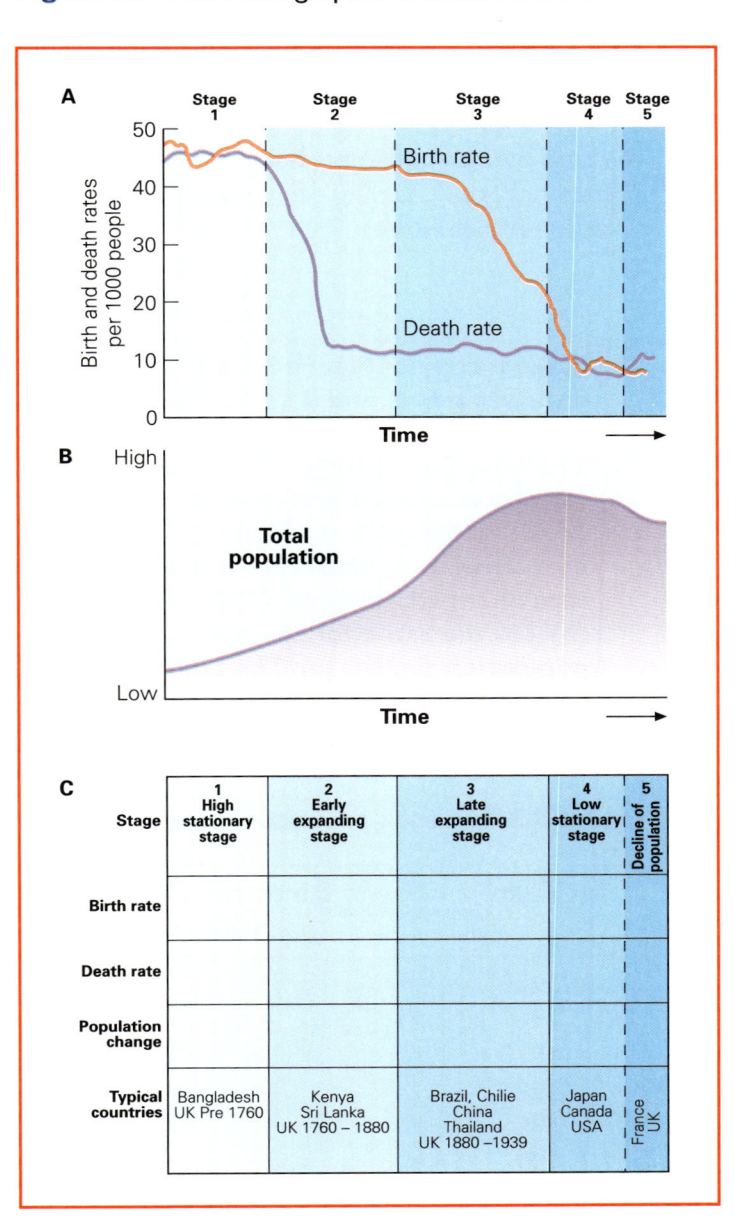

Stage two (the early expanding stage)

This stage has a falling death rate but the birth rate remains high, creating rapid population growth.

The death rate falls because:

- medical care improves with better drugs, vaccinations and more doctors and nurses;
- people have access to a safer water supply and better sanitation;
- there is an increase in food production.

Stage three (the late expanding stage)

When the death rate remains low and the birth rate starts to fall, population growth slows down.

The fall in the birth rate is due to:

- rising living standards which bring a desire for material goods such as television sets and cars and fewer children;
- better medical care, which means that fewer children die, and families no longer need to be so large;
- a wider availability and use of family planning;
- improvements in women's rights, making them freer to follow careers rather than having a large family.

Stage four (the low stationary stage)

Both birth and death rates are low so population growth is very slow.

Some writers suggest that there may be another stage to this model. In this stage, birth rates fall below rising death rates. So the total population actually decreases, as in Scandinavia, where more people are dying than are being born.

The rise in the death rate may be due to:

- the increase in deaths from diseases like cancer and heart disease which correlates with a rise in living standards.

---

1. Make a copy of Figure 3.1 and use the data in parts A and B to complete the table in part C.
2. Thailand Case Study
   (a) Draw a graph and plot the birth and death rate data from Figure 3.2 to show how Thailand's birth rate and death rate changed between 1950 and 1993.
   (b) Do the same for the total population figures for Thailand from Figure 3.2.
   (c) Write a paragraph describing the changes in Thailand's birth rate, death rate and population between 1950 and 1993.
   (d) Read Figure 3.3, then explain why Thailand's birth rate dropped between 1950 and 1993.
   (e) How far does Thailand seem to follow the demographic transition model? Which stage do you think it is at now?

Figure 3.2 Thailand's population change

Year	Birth rate (per 1000)	Death rate (per 1000)	Total population (millions)
1950	47	19	20
1960	44	13	26
1970	35	9	35
1980	28	8	47
1990	16	7	56
1993	15	7	58

Figure 3.3 Family planning in Thailand

Until 1960, Thailand had a policy of encouraging people to have lots of children – a **pro-natalist policy** – to increase the country's workforce. However, since 1960 the policy has changed to one of reducing the population by discouraging people from having children – an **anti-natalist policy**.

In 1970 the Thai Government introduced the National Family Planning Programme of the Ministry of Health. This programme consisted of:
- establishing information and education programmes to inform people about contraception;
- establishing 8000 health centres providing free contraception;
- using advertising to encourage people to have two children or less;
- training paramedics, called 'barefoot doctors', and midwives to provide basic health care in all parts of the country. These people were chosen from local villages, so they were trusted.

These factors have also helped Thailand to reduce its birth rate so rapidly:
- there are no religious or cultural objections to contraception;
- women have equal status and education to men, so begin family planning earlier to avoid having children too soon in their careers;
- infant mortality is falling so more babies survive, making couples less likely to have so many children;
- Buddhism, the main religion in Thailand, stresses individual freedom of action, so women can choose whether or not to have children.

Important facts about the demographic transition model

- It is based on the experience of MEDCs, but there is no guarantee that poorer countries will follow the same pattern.
- The fall in the death rate in the UK took place over 150–200 years, but the fall in poorer countries is much more rapid because sophisticated medical knowledge is now available.
- The fall in the birth rate in the UK was achieved by factors such as the desire for higher living standards, but this may not be true of some developing countries.
- Even when birth rates do fall in poorer countries like India, China and even Thailand, millions of adults are still likely to become parents which means that population growth will continue.

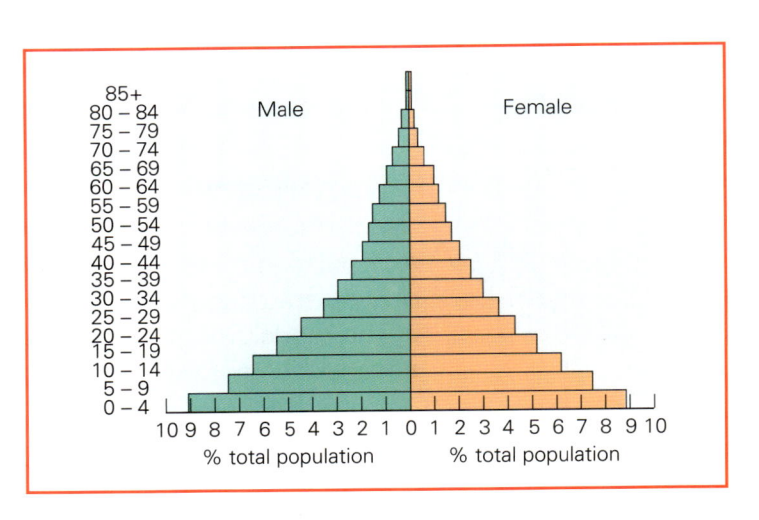

Figure 3.4 Population pyramid of Malawi, 1989

Population pyramids

Changes in birth rate, death rate and life expectancy (the average number of years a person can expect to live) bring changes in the **population structure** of a nation. This population structure is usually shown as a **population pyramid** (see Figures 3.4–3.7) and

Birth and death 21

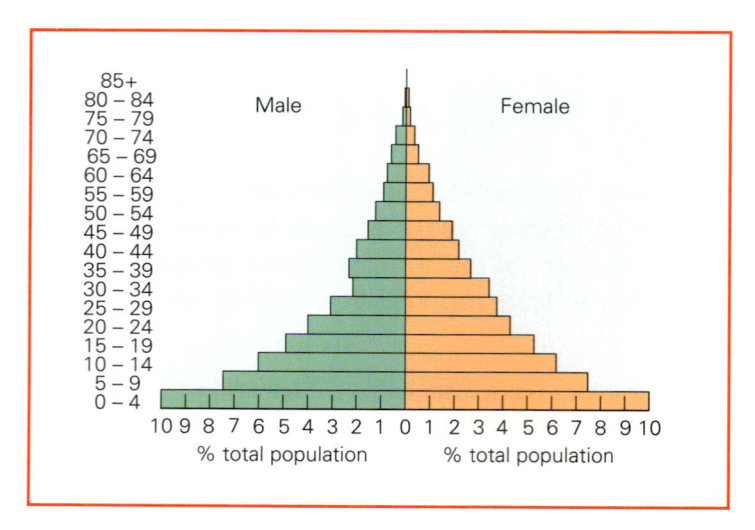

Figure 3.5 Population pyramid of Guatemala, 1989

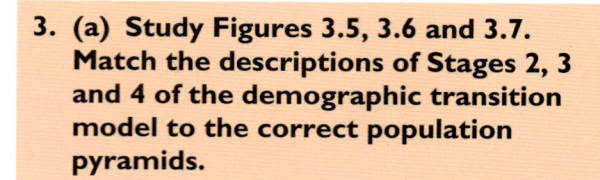

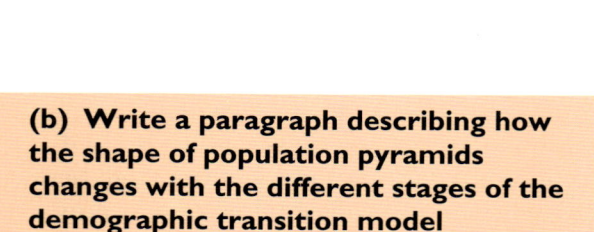

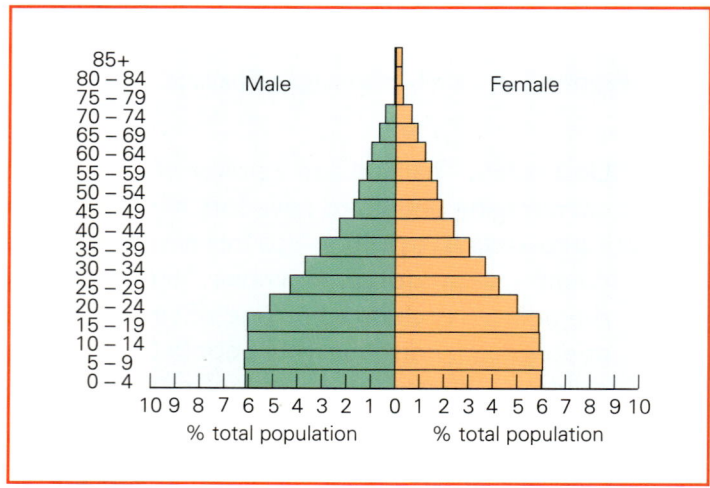

Figure 3.6 Population pyramid of Thailand, 1989

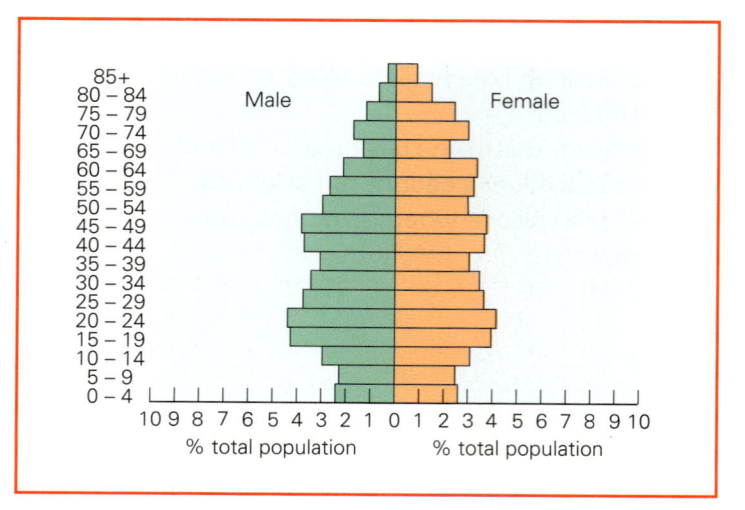

Figure 3.7 Population pyramid of West Germany, 1989

sometimes as an age-sex pyramid. Population pyramids show the population in five-year age groups and by gender.

Countries at different stages of the demographic transition have different shaped population pyramids, as Figures 3.5–3.8 show. For example, Malawi (at Stage 1) has a pyramid that is very narrow at the top and very broad at the base. This is because the death rate is high and few people survive to old age, and the birth rate is high, meaning that there is a large number of children under five years of age.

3. **(a) Study Figures 3.5, 3.6 and 3.7. Match the descriptions of Stages 2, 3 and 4 of the demographic transition model to the correct population pyramids.**

(b) Write a paragraph describing how the shape of population pyramids changes with the different stages of the demographic transition model

Summary

- Population changes are described in the demographic transition model.
- Different countries are at different stages in relation to the model.
- The model may not be applicable to poorer countries.
- Population pyramids reflect changes in birth and death rates.

22 Population Change

Chapter 4: Population and resources

Are there too many people in the world? Is there a population problem or a resource problem?

This unit looks at the links between population growth and the world's resources.

Are there too many people in the world?

In 1798 the British Reverend Thomas Malthus was one of the first people to believe that the earth's resources could only support a limited number of people. He wrote a book called *Essay on the Principle of Population* in which he said that food supplies only increased at an arithmetic rate (the straight line on Figure 4.1) but that population grew at a faster geometric rate (the curved line on Figure 4.1), so Malthus argued that, eventually, there would be too many people for the world's food supply. This would lead to disasters such as famine, disease and war, which would reduce population numbers. Malthus called these disasters **positive checks** on population growth. He also argued that people should try to limit their numbers by **preventative checks** such as later marriages or deciding to have fewer children (Malthus did not believe in birth control, partly because there were no reliable methods in 1798).

> 1. (a) What were Malthus's 'positive checks?' (b) What were his 'preventative checks'?
> 2. Copy Figure 4.1. The dotted line shows what happens when population grows faster than the food supply. Continue the population line on the graph to show what Malthus thought would happen after famine, disease and war.

In fact, the world population crash predicted by Malthus has never happened. He was writing in the eighteenth century, before both the Agricultural and Industrial Revolutions, which vastly increased people's ability to produce more food and other goods. However, there are still experts who believe that, in time, Malthus will be proved to be right because more and more of the earth's resources are being used up. Other experts disagree and argue that progress in technology will allow us to continue increasing production.

How many is too many?

Every minute of every day 18 people around the world die as a result of diseases caused by hunger. Every year, from 1990 to 1995, 20 million people died as a result of hunger and

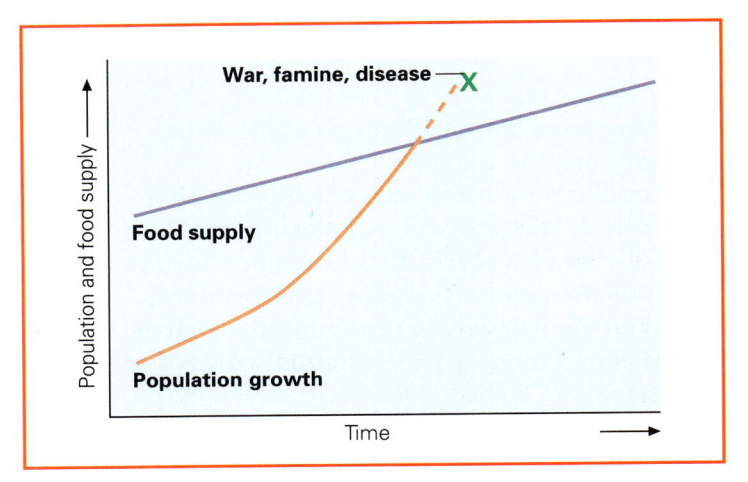

Figure 4.1 World population and food supplies, as predicted by Malthus

malnutrition. In the last six years more people in the world have died from hunger than were killed in all the wars, revolutions and murders in the last 150 years! Worse still, the problem of hunger is becoming more acute. For example there is now 10 per cent less food per person in Africa than there was ten years ago. So there are people who were hungry before they were born, hungry when they were born and are hungry all their lives. In 1960 there were 360 million hungry people in the world. By 1994 this had risen to 620 million so, despite years of efforts to end hunger, more people are suffering and dying than before.

Enough for everyone?

Experts have proved that there is enough food in the world at present to feed over 7 billion people, many more than the current population of 5.6 billion. Even with over 6 billion people projected for 2000, the earth could still provide enough grain to give every person a daily diet of 3000 calories, which is roughly what the average person in the USA consumes.

So why are poor people in less economically developed countries hungry?

Food is very unevenly shared around the world and this is part of the cause of hunger.

The 25 per cent of the world's people who live in the richer countries of the North eat half of all the world's food. In other words, they eat 25 per cent more calories than they need! They have to spend huge sums of money on diets and health farms to lose weight! In contrast, millions of people in poorer countries die of starvation. Solving the world's food problems depends partly on increasing the poorer countries' share of the world's food and increasing food production in these poorer countries (see Chapter 16). Other solutions involve land reform and a switch from growing cash crops for export to food crops for domestic consumption.

Food is just one example of the world's **resources**. These resources are not shared equally around the world. The richer countries of the north use their wealth and power to control the world's resources for their own benefit. This fact leads some experts to argue that there are not too many people in the world at all. They say that the real problem is one of resources and wealth and the richer countries who control the resources are responsible for the hunger in poorer countries.

What are overpopulation and underpopulation?

A country is said to be **overpopulated** when it has too many people depending on its resources and available technology. Technology is a factor because it allows increased production from an existing resource. A country is not necessarily overpopulated because its population has risen to 50, 80 or 200 million. It can only be overpopulated in relation to its resources. Hence, countries like Ethiopia and Bangladesh are described as overpopulated because they do not have enough food, minerals, energy resources and industrial development to provide for their populations. Famine, war, poverty and disease make this situation worse. Other countries, like Australia, Zambia, Israel and Singapore, feel that they need to increase their population in order to develop their resources and raise living standards. These countries are described as **underpopulated**. In theory, there is an ideal population size for each country, based on its resources and technology. This is called the **population optimum**, but, in practice, this is very hard to calculate.

---

3. Why have the predictions of Malthus not come true?
4. Explain why some experts believe that there is not a world population problem but rather a world resource problem. In your answer refer to: (a) the problems of world hunger; (b) the unequal shares of world food; (c) the unequal control of the world's resources.

5. Make a list of things that people in the North could do to: (a) reduce the amount of the world's resources they use, for example, reducing the amount of packaging of goods; (b) reduce the pollution they cause, for example, use public transport instead of private cars.

6. Explain what is meant by the terms overpopulation, underpopulation and the population optimum.

7. How would you describe the balance between population, resources and technology in: (a) the UK; (b) India; (c) Thailand; (d) Spain; (e) the USA?

Summary

- Thomas Malthus first raised the idea of positive and preventative checks to population growth.
- Ideas about the merits or drawbacks of population growth have to be linked to resources and technology.
- World hunger has more to do with control of resources than with population.
- Overpopulation, underpopulation and the population optimum are ideas applied to the links between population, resources and technology.

Chapter 5: Migration

Why do people migrate?
What are the effects of migration?

This unit examines different types of migration, and their causes and their effects on both the areas that people leave and those to which they migrate.

What is migration?

Migration is the movement of people from place to place. There are many different types of migration but the most important are:

- **international migration**, which takes place between countries, and can be: voluntary, for example, Turkish guest workers to Germany or Mexicans to the USA; or forced, for example, the movement of African slaves in the eighteenth century to the USA and the Caribbean;
- **internal migration**, which takes place within a country, and can be: from rural areas to towns, for example, from villages in Thailand to Bangkok; or, for example, from cities to villages in the UK;
- other migrations from cities include seasonal movements, such as the movement of Mexican workers to the USA at harvest time.

International Migration

Emigrants are people who leave a country, usually in search of a better job or lifestyle. **Immigrants** are the people who arrive in another country. In the 1960s there was a major movement of people from the poorer parts of Latin America, especially Mexico, into the southern states of the USA. Sometimes these people went to work on North American farms at harvest time, or in new factories in California and Texas, while others went to work as cleaners or housemaids in cities like Los Angeles and San Diego. The rapid pace of economic growth in the southern USA, especially in California and Texas, lasted into the 1970s. There were many job opportunities, particularly those that were not wanted by the US workers because they were hard, dirty, badly paid or demanded long hours.

The Mexicans were seen as 'guest' workers and it was thought that they would stay for a few years and then return home. As a result, the Mexicans lived in very poor housing conditions. In the 1970s and 1980s, a world recession began to affect the USA. Both agriculture and industry grew more slowly and unemployment started to rise. Local people began to resent the Mexicans and other immigrants (from the Caribbean) who they saw as competing for their jobs. Laws were passed in the 1980s, making it much harder for people to migrate to the USA and, as Figure 5.1 shows, arrests of illegal immigrants increased sharply.

Figure 5.1 Figures for the arrest of illegal immigrants in the USA

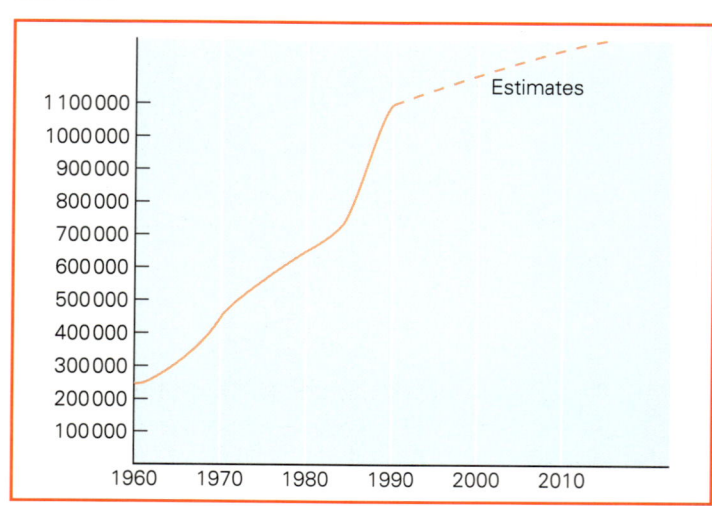

26 Population Change

Across the river and into the States

GATEWAYS
El Paso, Texas

Concha Robles de Villegas is a typical inhabitant of the frontier land that lies between the US and Mexico. It is a world of shared loyalties, divided families, economic self-sufficiency, and mixed and blurred customs, cultures and laws.

Carmen and Rodriga have just crossed the Rio Grande illegally from Mexico. They are going shopping at J C Penney's, the American store. They say it sells cheaper, better quality trainers than those sold in their home town.

El Paso is where the First World meets the Third. Only a small river divides them.

"There isn't any work in Mexico," says Hernandez. "That's why the frontier is the way it is." He is not exaggerating. Unemployment in Mexico runs at 40 per cent. Another 20 per cent of adults are estimated to be underemployed. Mexico's population stands at about 85 million, of which 40 million are under 18 years of age. In El Paso, 69 per cent of the inhabitants are of Mexican origin.

In a survey published last March, the Rand Corporation of California estimated that some 135,000 Mexicans emigrate illegally every year. There are 12.4 million Mexicans in the US.

Figure 5.2 Article from *The Guardian*

Figure 5.3 Californian views on Mexican immigrants

Many Mexicans still seek work in the USA (Figure 5.2). Some manage to enter illegally and it is estimated that there may be up to 8 million illegal workers in the USA, half of whom are Mexican.

'More people speak Spanish in California than English. It is not right.'

'The Mexican food, music, and culture dominate southern California.'

'Mexicans will work for very low wages so they take our jobs.'

'Mexican children dominate in our school and, for my children, it's like going to school in another country.'

'Mexicans take all the cheap houses as soon as they come on the market so we don't stand a chance.'

'The Mexicans have taken over whole parts of the city with their own shops, restaurants, cafes and bars. It's just like being in Mexico.'

'I could not make a profit on my farm if I didn't have Mexicans to pick the lettuces for low wages.'

'Thank goodness the Mexicans are willing to do the dirty jobs like emptying the trash bins.'

Migration 27

1. Look at Figure 5.1. How many immigrants were arrested in: (a) 1960; (b) 1970; (c) 1980; (d) 1990?
2. Look at Figure 5.2.
   (a) Why did Carmen and Rodriga claim to have entered the USA illegally?
   (b) What percentage of Mexico's population are: (a) unemployed? (b) underemployed? (c) Explain the difference.
   (c) What percentage of Mexicans are aged 18 or under? How many people is this?
   (d) How many Mexicans emigrate illegally every year?
   (e) Why can so many Mexicans still enter the USA illegally?
3. Use Figure 5.3 to write a paragraph entitled 'Why Californians are worried by Mexican immigrants', explaining their fears.
4. Write a paragraph describing and explaining the problems Mexicans face when they arrive in the USA. Mention factors such as prejudice, the high cost of housing and being forced to live in ghettos.

Internal migration

Moving from the countryside to towns

In many developing countries, such as Thailand, there is a large-scale movement of people from the countryside into towns and cities. This migration is generally a combination of negative **push factors**, which drive people away from the land (such as poor pay for farm work), and positive **pull factors** (such as better job prospects), which attract them to other areas. Some of these factors are shown in Figure 5.5, which summarises why people leave the Roi-et region of north east Thailand and move to Bangkok.

Figure 5.4 Mexican market in Los Angeles, USA

Figure 5.5 Migrants' views on leaving north east Thailand

'I earn a lot more money in Bangkok than I did in Roi-et.'

'If left Roi-et because farming was so hard on the thin and sandy soil. We were very poor.'

'We farmers regularly faced droughts then floods and there is very little irrigation so in the end I had to give up farming.'

'I came to Bangkok for better housing and other services like education and health care.'

'Over 90 per cent of the people in Roi-et are farmers. There are no other jobs.'

'There is a lot more choice of jobs in Bangkok, from taxi driving to working on building sites or in factories.'

'Bangkok is more exciting than Roi-et. There's lots of night life and plenty of shops.'

'Roi-et is very isolated from the rest of Thailand. We were too far from the market to farm profitably.'

'Flats in Bangkok are expensive but they are better than our house in Roi-et.'

5. Use Figure 5.5 to make two lists, one of 'push' factors operating in rural Thailand and one of 'pull' factors operating in Bangkok.
6. Migration is never a simple process. There is always a mixture of push and pull factors. In general, there are more push factors in rural Thailand and more pull factors in cities like Bangkok. However, there also are 'obstacles' that the migrants have to overcome. Work in pairs to make a list of these obstacles, such as the high cost of housing in the city.

Problems facing new arrivals in cities

In developing countries like Thailand, millions of people have already migrated from the countryside to the town. But when they arrive in the cities, their problems may just be starting. Many of the newcomers feel intimidated by the sheer size of the city. Some also find it difficult to adapt to the faster, busier pace of urban life. Other changes to which newcomers have to adapt include the importance of cash as the means of survival and, in some cases, language, religious or cultural differences. In short, many new arrivals in developing cities like Bangkok may feel frightened, bewildered and homesick.

Migration

Top nations receiving savings from workers abroad

	US $ millions
Pakistan	3.5
Egypt	3.0
Portugal	3.0
India	2.8
Italy	2.7
Poland	2.7
Turkey	2.0
Greece	1.6
Philippines	1.5
Spain	1.4
Morocco	1.2
South Korea	1.0
Thailand	1.0

The Guardian, 14 June 1991

Figure 5.6 Figures for selected countries of income from migrants

What are the effects of rural to urban migration?

Internal migration affects both rural areas (the origin) and urban areas (the destination).

Effects on the area of origin

Once people start to leave permanently an area like north-east Thailand a downward spiral starts. As more people leave so there are fewer farmers and fewer customers for local shops and services. So even more services decline and then may close. Roads deteriorate even further and isolation and poverty may increase as only old people remain because they are unable or unwilling to move. This process is shown in Figure 5.7.

As people migrate away from remote rural parts of countries like Thailand there is a reduction in population pressure on the land. Farmers are no longer forced to cultivate the poorest land but are able to concentrate on more fertile areas. However, the migrants tend to be the younger, more progressive members of the population and rural areas cannot afford to lose these enterprising people.

Most migrants send back money to their relatives who may still be living in rural areas. This money can be vital to the survival of families in remote areas. For example, many men from north east Thailand work on construction projects in Saudi Arabia and other Middle Eastern countries. The money they send back to their wives and families allows them to enjoy a high standard of living. Figure 5.6 shows which countries received most payments from their people working overseas in 1993.

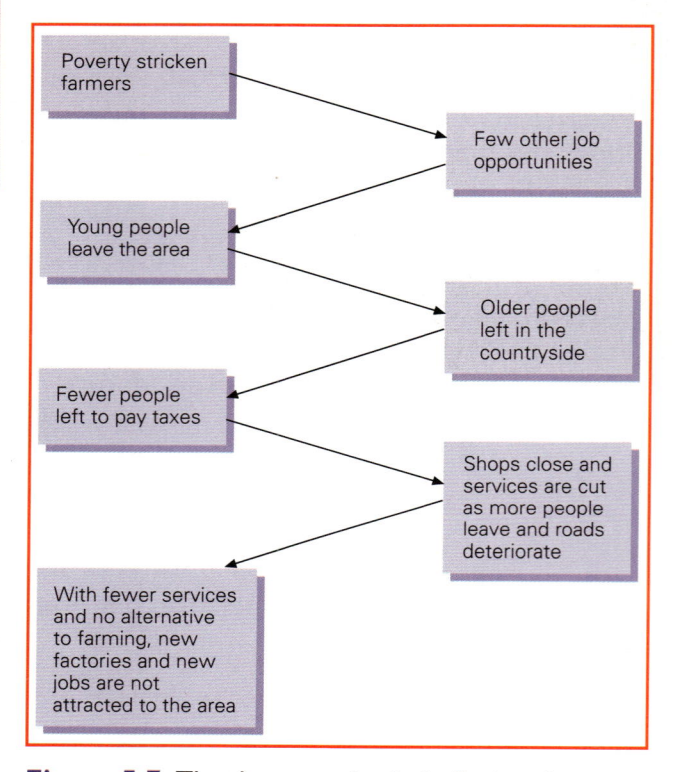

Poverty stricken farmers → Few other job opportunities → Young people leave the area → Older people left in the countryside → Fewer people left to pay taxes → Shops close and services are cut as more people leave and roads deteriorate → With fewer services and no alternative to farming, new factories and new jobs are not attracted to the area

Figure 5.7 The downward spiral of migration

7. Look at Figure 5.6.
   a) Which four countries received most in payments from their workers overseas?
   b) What do the figures show about the importance of overseas workers to the economy of their countries?
8. Study Figure 5.7 and suggest at least three ways in which a government could try to halt this downward spiral. For example, they might consider building new roads to improve accessibility.

30   Population Change

Figure 5.8 Poor conditions in a shanty town, Thailand

Effects on areas of arrival

Each week, the arrival in Bangkok of 2000 people from the countryside in search of work clearly causes problems. There is a severe housing shortage throughout the city, and most new arrivals have to live in shared, cramped flats. Others, unable to find or afford even this, are forced to build their homes in shanty towns (Figure 5.8). Most shanty towns have no piped water supply, electricity or sewage drainage so conditions for families living there are harsh.

The massive influx of people from the countryside also puts a severe strain on Bangkok's health and education services, as well as the public transport.

In all developing countries the migration of people from the countryside has caused towns to grow and grow. In most places, the largest towns (which are often capital cities, like Bangkok or Cairo) attract most immigrants. The speed of urban growth is so rapid that most towns are unable to cope, resulting in overcrowding, unemployment and poverty. However, many migrants feel that these conditions are better than those they left in the countryside.

Figure 5.9 shows the main problems faced by men and women who migrate to Bangkok.

> 9. Look at Figure 5.9.
>   a) What was the biggest problem for male migrants?
>   b) What was the problem for most female migrants?
> 10. Write a paragraph describing the main difficulties in moving to Bangkok faced by:
>   (a) women (b) men.
>   (b) people who move from towns in to the countryside.

Migration 31

Problem	Men (of total per cent surveyed)	Women (of total per cent surveyed)
Housing	41	43
Work	25	13
Could not find a place for education or job training	37	60
Difficulty in getting along with people	15	21
Bad environment (for example, crime and theft)	6	12

Figure 5.9 Problems facing migrants in Bangkok

Summary

- There are different types of migration.
- People migrate as a result of a combination of 'push' and 'pull' factors.
- People moving between countries bring changes both to the countries they leave and those to which they move.
- Rural to urban and urban to rural migration affect both rich and poor countries but in different ways.

Chapter 6 Trade links

In what ways are people in more economically developed and less economically developed countries linked?
What is interdependence?

This unit examines how people in developed and developing countries are connected through trade and aid.

World trade

Richer MEDCs depend on imports of minerals, food and raw materials like tin, coffee and cotton from poorer LEDCs. In return, the poorer countries have to buy most of their manufactured goods, such as cars, machinery and computers, from the richer countries. This is because 90 per cent of the world's manufacturing industry is located in MEDCs like Japan, the USA and the countries of the European Union (EU). For example, 20 per cent of Britain's exports go to developing countries and include goods like buses sold to Zambia and tractors to Pakistan. In return, 30 per cent of Britain's tin imports come from Malaysia and 20 per cent of the copper imports come from Zambia. Britain, like most developed countries depends on trading with the rest of the world to maintain the living standards of its people (see Figure 6.1).

Is there a problem with world trade?

The pattern of world trade today dates back to nineteenth-century *colonial* times. LEDCs still tend to concentrate on producing raw materials such as tea, timber and metal ores. A survey of 120 developing countries showed that raw materials make up 100 per cent of exports for 20 countries; 85 per cent of exports for another 74 countries and 50 per cent for the other 26 countries (see Figures 6.2 and 6.3). In return, these poorer countries buy manufactured goods from more economically developed nations. The problem is that the value of raw material exports has declined whilst the value of manufactured goods has increased.

Figure 6.1 Depending on ourselves?

Figure 6.2 World trade figures, 1994

A Countries whose exports are dominated by agriculture	
Country	Per cent of total exports from agriculture
Somalia	98.4
Mali	88.7
Burkina Faso	85.1
Sudan	83.6
Madagascar	82.4
Burundi	81.5
Malawi	80.1
Tanzania	77.2
Honduras	77.1

B Countries whose exports are dominated by mining and minerals	
Country	Per cent of total exports from mining and minerals
Libya	99.6
Brunei	97.0
Saudi Arabia	96.0
Congo	91.1
Angola	84.5
Gabon	83.1
Niger	79.7
Algeria	73.8
Bolivia	73.6

C Countries whose exports are dominated by manufactured goods	
Country	Per cent of total exports from manufactured goods
Bermuda	100.00
Japan	99.5
Barbados	99.2
Macao	98.5
Austria	98.4
Malta	98.0
Sweden	97.7
Italy	97.1

1. Look at Figure 6.2.
   (a) On a world map shade in red all the countries with over 70 per cent of their exports coming from agriculture.
   (b) Now shade in green all those countries with over 70 per cent of their exports from mining and minerals.
   (c) Now shade in yellow countries where over 90 per cent of their exports come from manufactured goods.
   (d) Describe the pattern of exports shown on your map including the general location and type of countries whose exports are dominated by: (i) raw materials; (ii) manufactured goods.

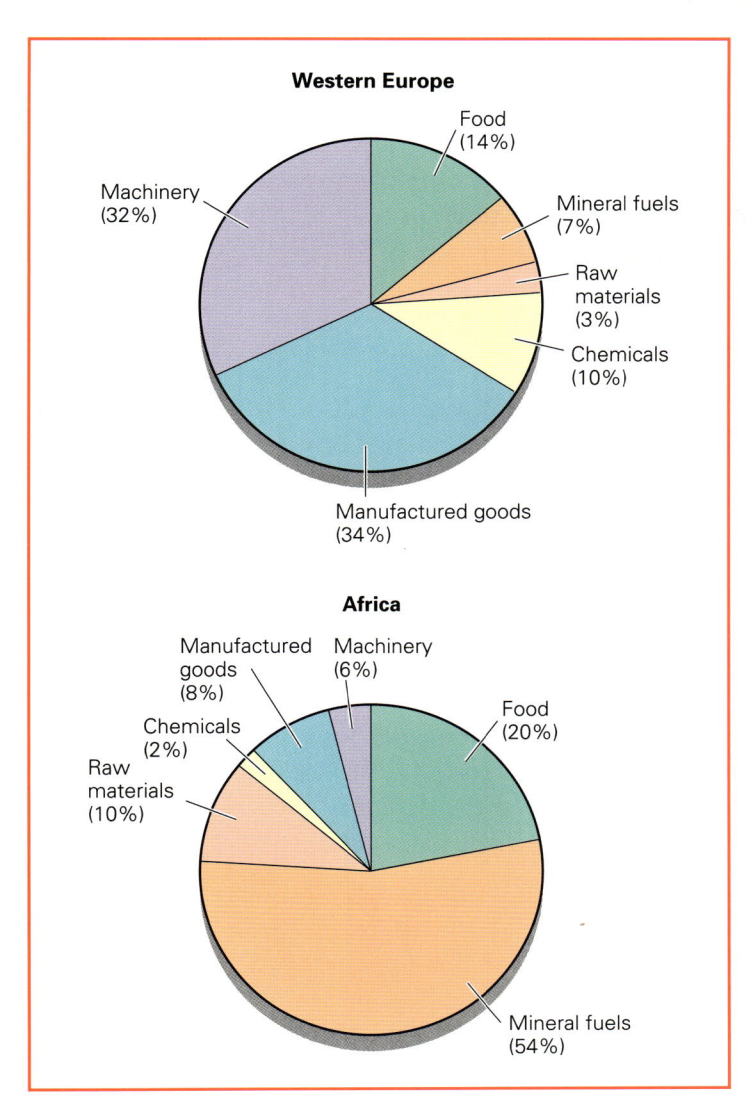

Figure 6.3 Exports from Europe and Africa

Western Europe:
- Food (14%)
- Mineral fuels (7%)
- Raw materials (3%)
- Chemicals (10%)
- Manufactured goods (34%)
- Machinery (32%)

Africa:
- Manufactured goods (8%)
- Machinery (6%)
- Chemicals (2%)
- Raw materials (10%)
- Food (20%)
- Mineral fuels (54%)

> **2. Look at Figure 6.3 and write a paragraph comparing the exports of Western Europe with those of Africa.**

Tanzanian trade

Tanzania's trade illustrates some of the challenges facing developing countries. Although Tanzania gained its political independence 30 years ago, it has still not gained its economic independence. For example, Tanzania produces tea for export to Britain (see Figure 6.4). A tea picker can expect to earn 200 Tanzanian shillings for a six day week, barely enough to buy the basic necessities of life. From the plantation, the tea goes to a state processing plant and it is then exported. Although the tea is processed in Tanzania, financial control remains firmly in Britain. The price paid for Tanzania's tea is fixed at the London Tea Auction, which is dominated by a few large firms from more economically developed countries. Prices are kept very low and, for every packet of tea sold, Tanzania gets less than 20 per cent of the price. From this must come the money to cover all the costs of planting and caring for the plantations, processing and transport to the port. Experts estimate that Tanzania would need to get 50 per cent of the retail price to cover these costs. Figure 6.5 shows what happens to the rest of the profits from tea.

Figure 6.4 Tea picking in Tanzania

Figure 6.5 What happens to the profits from the sale of a packet of tea in Britain?

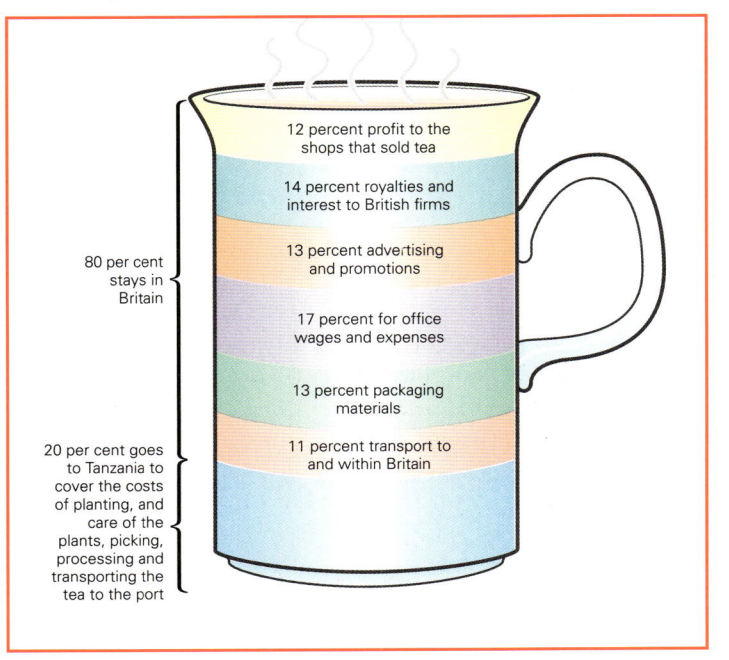

80 per cent stays in Britain:
- 12 percent profit to the shops that sold tea
- 14 percent royalties and interest to British firms
- 13 percent advertising and promotions
- 17 percent for office wages and expenses
- 13 percent packaging materials
- 11 percent transport to and within Britain

20 per cent goes to Tanzania to cover the costs of planting, and care of the plants, picking, processing and transporting the tea to the port

Trade links 35

Why does Tanzania continue selling at a loss?

Despite the low price, Tanzania continues to grow and sell tea, for two reasons. Firstly, Tanzania needs the foreign currency earned by these exports and secondly, Tanzania cannot afford to abandon its investment in the tea plantations, factories and ports. Rather than close down the whole system, Tanzania continues to sell tea at a loss in the hope that the price will rise. As Edward Nyrege, a Tanzanian tea manager, says *'If you are hungry and you need money to buy food, you will sell your tea even if the price is very low.'*

> 3. **Write a memo to the President of Tanzania as if you were a member of a team responsible for future economic planning. Outline why Tanzania earns so little from its tea exports.**
> 4. **Outline the main advantages and disadvantages to Tanzania of the following strategies for increasing earnings from tea.**
>   **(a) reducing tea production to try and force up world prices (a shortage would increase prices);**
>   **(b) forming a World Tea Producers League for tea producing countries, to try to agree to limit output in order to get higher world prices;**
>   **(c) selling tea direct to UK supermarkets rather than through the London Tea Auction (need for packaging, advertising, etc.).**
> 5. **Can you suggest any other ways in which Tanzania might increase its income from tea exports?**

The terms of trade

One problem with the pattern of world trade is that the poverty of LEDCs is the result of a system which allows raw material prices to be controlled by MEDCs. But low prices for raw material exports like Tanzania's tea are only half the story. The other half concerns the **terms of trade**. MEDCs produce most of the world's manufactured goods, and can set the price of these goods. So countries like Tanzania get the worst of both worlds – earning a low price for its exports and paying a high price for its imports. The situation has become even worse in the recent past, as the price of tea has fallen by two-thirds over the last ten years. The terms of trade have turned against Tanzania.

The OPEC case

In the case of one raw material, oil, LEDCs have managed to break the control of the more economically developed nations over prices. In 1973 the Middle East War led to a four-fold increase in oil prices when supplies were cut off to the USA and Europe. The resulting shortage drove up prices in just a few weeks. Because OPEC (Organisation of Petroleum Exporting Countries) controlled 85 per cent of the world's oil exports and because MEDCs cannot do without oil, prices rose. OPEC's success in forcing up prices is the dream of most raw material exporters. But it is very unlikely that countries exporting products like tin, iron ore, cotton or tea will be able to follow the OPEC example. Oil is unique because the industrial economy of wealthy countries depends on it. This is not true for bananas, tea, coffee, cocoa or other such raw materials. Higher oil prices have made a few countries, like Saudi Arabia, very rich, but they have also made things worse for poorer countries that also need oil and have to pay the new higher prices.

The arms trade

Many LEDCs spend large amounts of their export earnings on buying tanks, planes and other arms. This spending of scarce resources on military security is at the expense of providing the basics of life, such as food, health care and education. The arms are purchased from MEDCs, which produce 95 per cent of the world's weapons. Many LEDCs are small; for example, 62 have populations of less than 1 million and 36 of these have a population of under 200 000. Because they are small they feel insecure and hence buy arms to guarantee their security. Figure 6.6 shows some of the choices facing governments in LEDCs. More and more

Figure 6.6 Economic choices of LEDCs

Figure 6.7 A soldier in Rwanda, Africa

arms (see Figure 6.7) are being sold to poorer nations, which then have less to spend on agriculture, health, education, etc. On page 38 Figure 6.8 shows how the world's spending on arms has grown and Figure 6.9 shows what some people in poorer countries think of this spending.

6. Explain why the terms of trade have worsened for LEDCs.
7. (a) Explain how OPEC managed to break the system of price control dominated by MEDCs.
   (b) Why has this had serious consequences for LEDCs?
8. Use Figures 6.6 and 6.8 to list the main arguments against spending money on weapons. Make particular reference to alternative spending.
9. Look at Figure 6.9. What are the arguments in favour of an LEDC having a strong defence programme?

Trade links 37

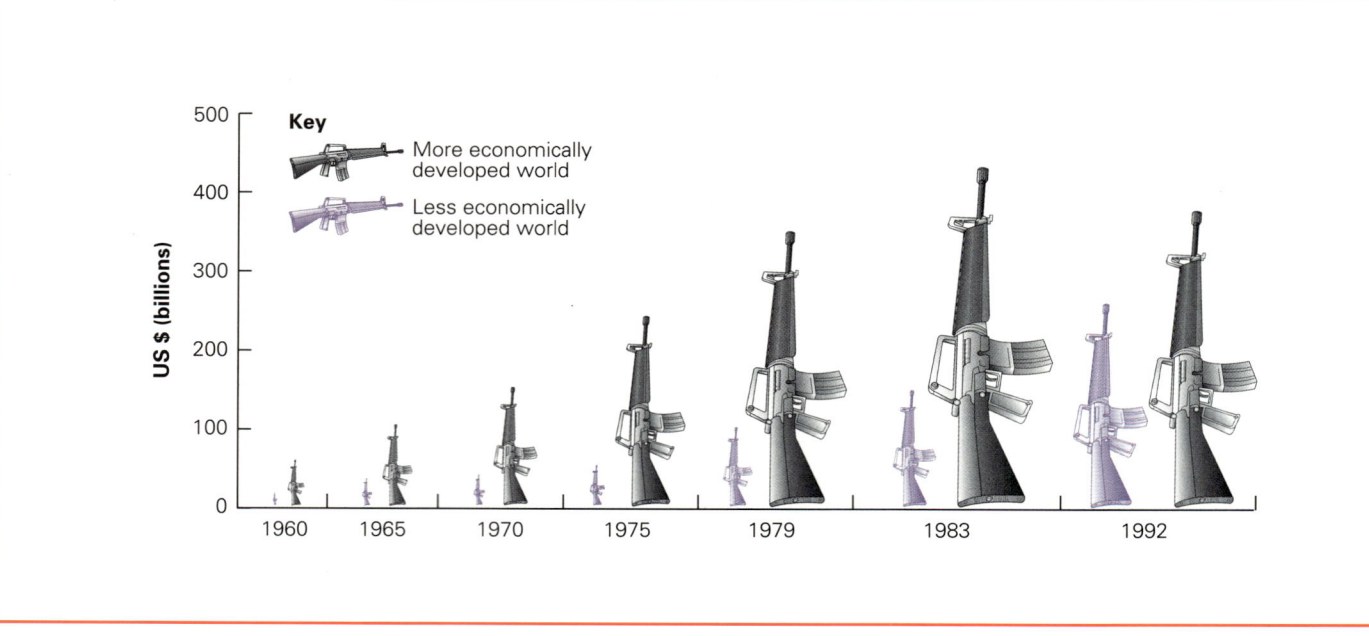

Figure 6.8 World spending on arms, 1960–1992

Figure 6.9 Views of people from LEDCs on their nations' expenditure on arms

'Spending more on the military only makes our problems worse not better.'

'Every gun, every plane is really depriving poor people of food, water and medicines.'

'We need to tell people that the arms race is a waste of resources.'

'More arms only make the world a more dangerous place.'

10. Look at Figure 6.10.
    (a) Explain what the diagram shows in terms of people's needs and how these change with increasing wealth.
    (b) Suggest some countries which might be at the different levels in the diagram and give reasons for your choices.
11. Do you think MEDCs should cut down on their export of arms to LEDCs? What are the arguments for and against this policy?

38 Population Change

Figure 6.10 All I want …

Summary

- All countries depend on trade.
- World prices for raw materials are kept low by more economically developed countries.
- World prices for manufactured goods are kept high by more economically developed countries.
- Only in the case of oil have a few producing countries been able to increase the price.
- Spending on arms by less economically developed countries reduces the amount of money available for education, health, agriculture, etc.

Trade links 39

7 Aid links

Chapter

What is aid?
Who supplies aid?
Who benefits from aid?

This unit examines the flow of aid from more economically developed countries to less economically developed countries and looks at the positive and negative effects of aid on progress.

Who needs aid?

The 75 per cent of the world's population who live in LEDCs have to survive on just 20 per cent of the world's wealth. Aid is one way in which the inequality between MEDCs and LEDCs might be bridged. However, the flow of aid from developed countries to developing countries is only one-fiftieth as big as the flow of profits from developing countries into developed countries. Despite receiving aid, LEDCs finance 85 per cent of their development themselves.

What is aid?

Some aid is short-term help, sent to countries after disasters such as floods, earthquakes and civil wars (see Figure 7.1). This aid is often in the form of tents, food, medicines and water purification equipment. However, some aid is more long-term, such as financial loans, equipment or the help of technical advisers, doctors or teachers.

Figure 7.1 US aid lorries in Sudan

40 Population Change

Types of aid

There are four main types of aid.

- **Multilateral aid** goes from the donor country (usually a more economically developed nation such as the USA, Japan or the UK) to the LEDC, through an international agency such as the World Bank.
- **Bilateral aid** goes directly from the donor to the receiving country.
- Loans from commercial banks.
- Aid from charities and other non-governmental organisations.

About 30 per cent of aid from Britain is multilateral, reaching LEDCs through the European Development Fund and the World Bank. The other 70 per cent of British aid is bilateral. Figure 7.2 highlights some of the advantages and disadvantages associated with each type of aid.

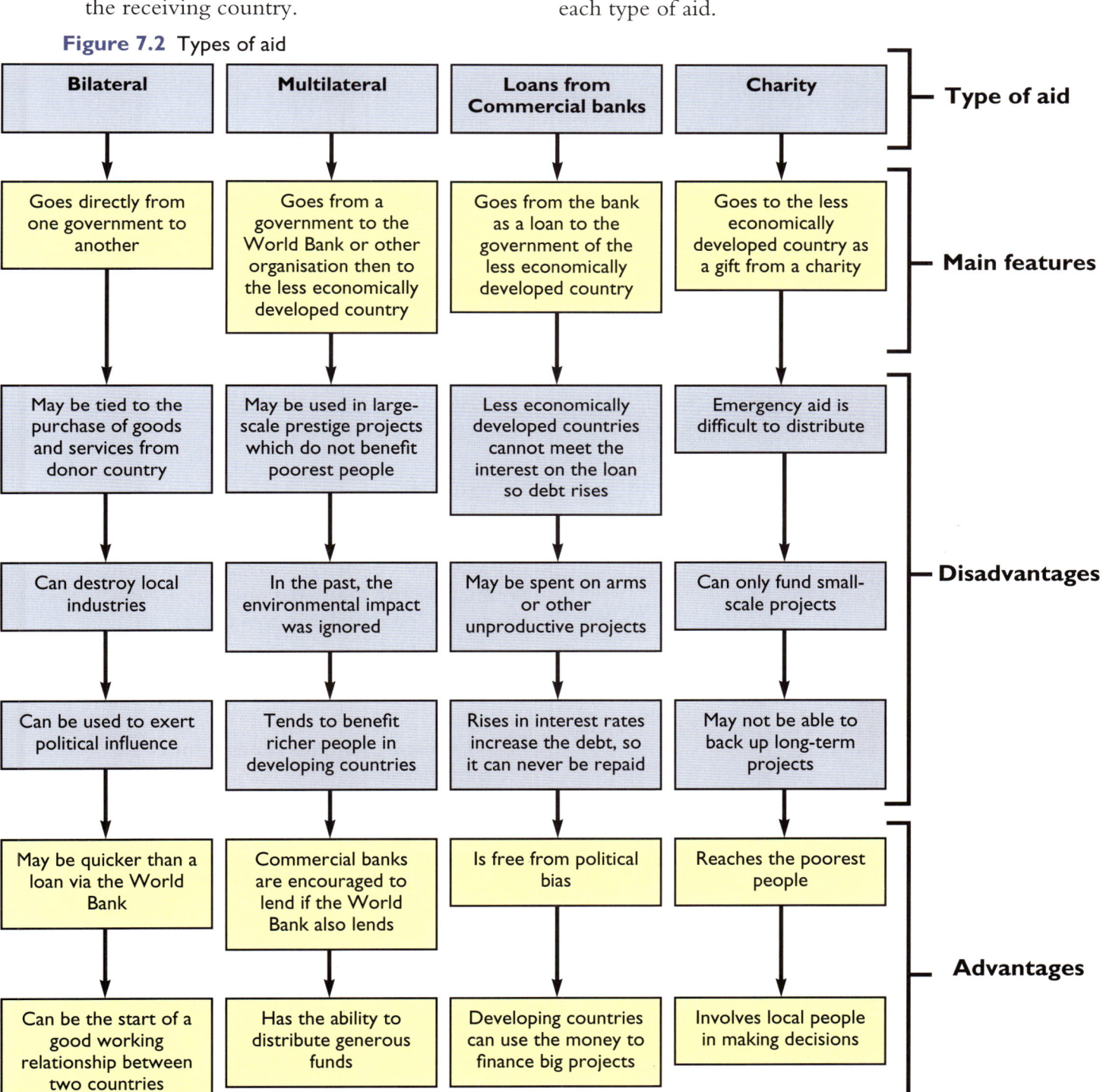

Figure 7.2 Types of aid

Bilateral	Multilateral	Loans from Commercial banks	Charity	**Type of aid**
Goes directly from one government to another	Goes from a government to the World Bank or other organisation then to the less economically developed country	Goes from the bank as a loan to the government of the less economically developed country	Goes to the less economically developed country as a gift from a charity	**Main features**
May be tied to the purchase of goods and services from donor country	May be used in large-scale prestige projects which do not benefit poorest people	Less economically developed countries cannot meet the interest on the loan so debt rises	Emergency aid is difficult to distribute	**Disadvantages**
Can destroy local industries	In the past, the environmental impact was ignored	May be spent on arms or other unproductive projects	Can only fund small-scale projects	
Can be used to exert political influence	Tends to benefit richer people in developing countries	Rises in interest rates increase the debt, so it can never be repaid	May not be able to back up long-term projects	
May be quicker than a loan via the World Bank	Commercial banks are encouraged to lend if the World Bank also lends	Is free from political bias	Reaches the poorest people	**Advantages**
Can be the start of a good working relationship between two countries	Has the ability to distribute generous funds	Developing countries can use the money to finance big projects	Involves local people in making decisions	

Aid links

1. Use Figure 7.2 on page 41 to describe the four main sources of aid available to LEDCs. Point out the main advantages and disadvantages of each.

Who gives what?

Figures 7.3 and 7.4 show which countries give most aid. Figure 7.3 simply shows the value of aid in billions of pounds, and Figure 7.4 shows that aid as a percentage of the country's GNP. In other words, Figure 7.4 shows what countries can afford to give. The United Nations has been urging MEDCs to devote one per cent of their GNP to aid. But, as Figure 7.4 shows, only Norway and Saudi Arabia achieve this target. This means that insufficient aid is reaching less economically developed countries, and the wealth gap between them and more economically developed countries is widening.

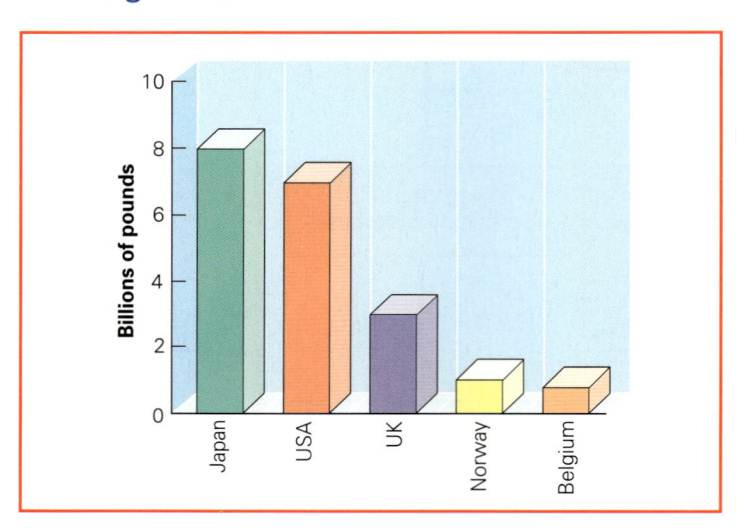

Figure 7.3 Aid donors, 1992

Figure 7.4 Aid donors as a percentage of GNP

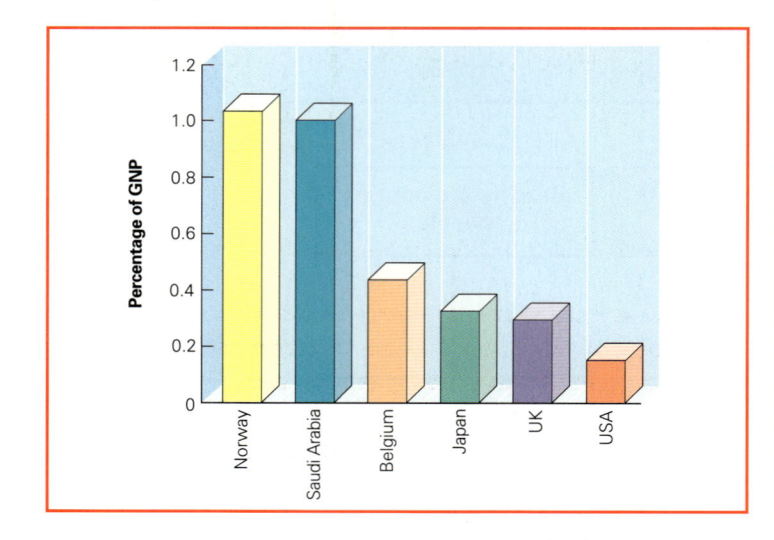

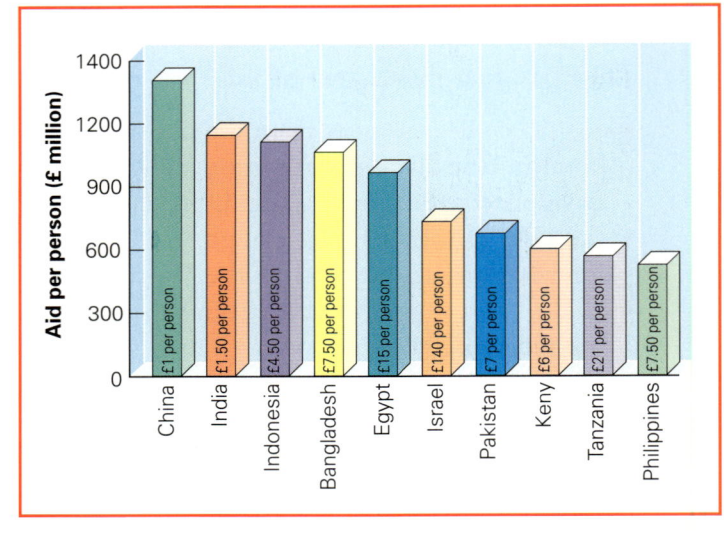

Figure 7.5 The ten countries receiving the most aid, 1992

2. Study Figures 7.3, 7.4 and 7.5. Write a newspaper report of about 150 words entitled 'The truth about world aid'. Aim for a punchy, journalistic style and include the following points:
   - which countries give most;
   - which countries give most as a percentage of GNP;
   - which countries receive most aid in total;
   - which countries receive most aid per person.

3. Work in pairs and discuss the following questions. Make notes and then compare your ideas with those of other groups in the class.
   (a) Should Britain try to solve its own economic problems before it gives aid to LEDCs?
   (b) Can Britain afford to give more aid?
   (c) Does Britain have a moral obligation to help people in LEDCs when there is a natural disaster such as a famine?

Population Change

Figure 7.6 The leakage of aid

THE LEAKAGE OF AID...

Half of all aid is tied to buying goods from the donor country

Aid is used to build naval or air bases for foreign governments

Spending on weapons

One third of all aid is used to repay interest on loans

Corruption in donor and recipient countries

Spending on prestige projects

Cost of administering the aid

The remaining aid is a slow trickle that does not always reach the neediest people

What happens to aid?

Aid from donor countries does not always reach the poorest people in LEDCs. This is because some of the aid 'leaks' away, as Figure 7.6 shows.

Figure 7.7 Tractor donated in aid, Zimbabwe

4. Study Figure 7.6, then explain why not all the aid given to developing countries benefits the people who need it most.
5. Look at Figure 7.7. The tractor was made in Britain and given as aid. Some people argue that this is not the type of technology needed by Zimbabwe. Can you suggest why they say this?

Aid links

Figure 7.8 Article from *Overseas Development*

TURKS AND CAICOS:
Islanders see new tourist project as basis for sound economic development

The eight main islands in this British dependency southeast of the Bahamas possess few useful natural resources. Their 7,500 inhabitants subsist largely on imported food.

Fresh water is in short supply, the annual rainfall of about 600 mm must be carefully collected and used. Natural vegetation is mostly twisted scrub, cactus and wiry grass; thick slabs of limestone protrude everywhere, baked in usually unclouded sunshine.

Until quite recently these islands relied on the salt industry, which finally collapsed in the early '70s. Today they are not economically viable.

Lobsters and shellfish offer a modest export for local fishermen. Tourism, with a few small hotels – at present supplies neither the revenue needed to balance the budget, nor significant employment.

Agriculture – despite possibilities on North Caicos, which has some fresh water – can never amount to a large industry.

This situation puts emphasis on the development of tourism. A lovely climate, beautiful beaches suited to water sports and diving, a friendly people – these are the assets TCI can offer. A large potential market lies at their doorstep – Americans who want to "get away from it all" for a while.

The drawbacks of tourism are known and accepted. But the islanders feel they can cope with an increased number of visitors. The alternatives they see, as already manifested, are:
- emigration to the Bahamas and elsewhere, chiefly by skilled younger people; and
- "begging" the British Government for development capital and budgetary aid.

As a spokesman put it to us: "We want to build up a firm economy so we don't have to rely on handouts.'

In 1979 the head of Club Méditerranée, one of the world's leading tourist firms, told the TCI Government he was prepared to establish a holiday village on 70 acres of land purchased at Grace Bay on Providenciales (usually called Provo), one of the main islands of the Caicos chain.

Club Méditerranée would spend US $12 million building the village, which would accommodate 600 guests and 100 employees. The condition was that TCI would provide the improved infrastructure – mainly an extension to allow the airport to handle larger planes for package tours, but also better roads and assistance towards electricity and water supplies.

An agreement was reached. The project, it was evident, would benefit the islands generally – both socially and economically. Revenues from it would include landing fees, departure tax, hotel bed tax and customs duties on imported goods: these are expected to more than cover additional recurrent costs and so strengthen the budget.

When Club Med is established, the islanders assert, other business will follow. It will serve as a catalyst to attract more tourist and other industry, not only to Provo but to the other islands as well.

Throughout the islands at least a thousand new jobs are needed over the coming decade. And without expansion of the tourist industry there would be few prospects of achieving this – let alone solving the existing problems of unemployment or under-employment.

Under the Club Med project, apart from local people directly involved, benefits will spill out to shops, restaurants, taxi-drivers and boatmen, for example.

Those who will be either directly or indirectly employed immediately are estimated to number about 200. Over a five-year period such employment is expected to have spread to some 600 people.

Consultants Wallace Evans and partners, of Penarth, will supervise construction of the infrastructure required to support the Club Med project. This infrastructure, supplied under an ODA grant of £3.95 million, involves:
- Airfield runway and apron sufficient for two 200-seater aircraft; terminal buildings; runway lighting and generator; fire station and equipment.
- Roads from airfield to Club Med site: from jetty to airfield, for goods brought by sea; to Blue Hills, home of many locals who will be employed at the Club.
- Building customs and immigration accommodation.
- Public utilities – electricity supply improvement, and a loan toward a desalination plant so the Club will not affect local water supplies.

And the TCI Government are confident that, once these facilities are available, other tourist developments will follow – so that the islands will become self-supporting.

Overseas Development, 15 February 1988

Aid in action – the case of the Turks and Caicos Islands

There are many different types of aid but not all are equally effective. Figure 7.8 is an extract from the magazine *Overseas Development*, produced by the Overseas Development Administration (ODA), the British government agency which controls the flow of aid to LEDCs. The article describes a proposal for an aid project in the Turks and Caicos islands, a small group of islands in the Caribbean which are a British dependency.

Figure 7.9 Criteria for 'real' aid (to benefit the poorest people)

The best projects:

- reduce the gap in income between rich and poor people;
- conserve the environment;
- use simple, local technology;
- involve local people in all aspects of the scheme;
- focus on small-scale projects;
- give local people new skills;
- help communities to work together.

Figure 7.10 Children playing in Thailand

6. Read Figure 7.8 and draw up a table showing: (a) the reasons given for the choice of tourism as the main development; (b) the benefits claimed for the project.
7. The criteria that people now use to assess aid projects are shown in Figure 7.9.
   (a) How far does the Turks and Caicos scheme in Figure 7.8 fit in with these criteria?
   (b) Do you think it should have gone ahead?

Summary

- Aid is one way of reducing the inequality between the rich and poor parts of the world.
- There are many different types of aid.
- Aid can benefit both donor and recipient countries.
- Good aid projects are those which involve local people in decision making, and target help to those people in most need.

Aid links

8 Transnational companies

What are transnational companies?
How do transnational companies operate?
Do transnational companies benefit people around the world?

This unit looks at the growth and key features of large global companies. It looks at how these powerful companies operate in theory and in practice.

What are transnational companies?

Large companies with branches in many countries are called **multinationals**, **supernationals** or **transnationals**. In this book the term transnationals is used. Transnational corporations (TNCs) have their headquarters in one country (usually a MEDC) and branches in many LEDCs. Firms like Exxon, Unilever, Ford and MacDonalds are all transnational companies which link people in both more and less economically developed countries.

Size

Transnational companies are very big. As Figure 8.1 shows, their turnover is often larger than the Gross Domestic Product (GDP) of some countries.

International character

Transnationals try to locate each element of production in the country where it will be most profitable. Hence, research work is concentrated in MEDCs, which have many universities and where information and skilled labour are available. Manufacturing is located in countries where wages are low, trade unions weak and the government offers high *incentives* to new firms.

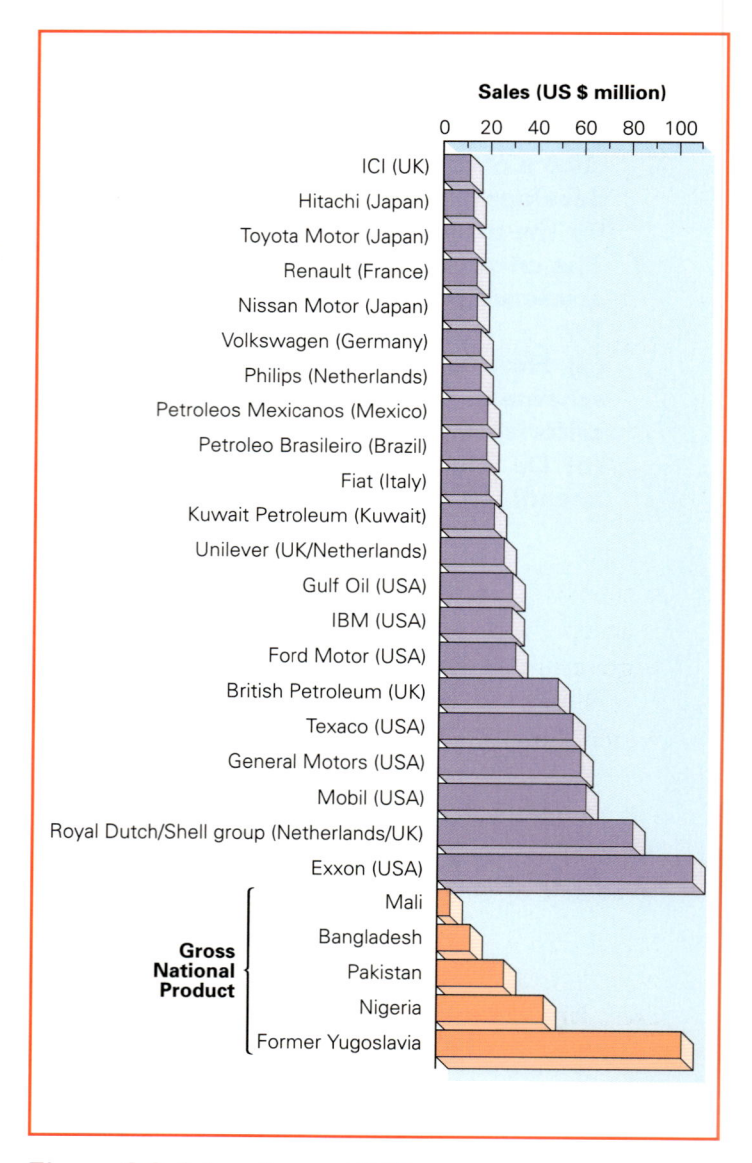

Figure 8.1 Sales of some TNCs

Sales (US $ million)
0 20 40 60 80 100

- ICI (UK)
- Hitachi (Japan)
- Toyota Motor (Japan)
- Renault (France)
- Nissan Motor (Japan)
- Volkswagen (Germany)
- Philips (Netherlands)
- Petroleos Mexicanos (Mexico)
- Petroleo Brasileiro (Brazil)
- Fiat (Italy)
- Kuwait Petroleum (Kuwait)
- Unilever (UK/Netherlands)
- Gulf Oil (USA)
- IBM (USA)
- Ford Motor (USA)
- British Petroleum (UK)
- Texaco (USA)
- General Motors (USA)
- Mobil (USA)
- Royal Dutch/Shell group (Netherlands/UK)
- Exxon (USA)

Gross National Product
- Mali
- Bangladesh
- Pakistan
- Nigeria
- Former Yugoslavia

46 Population Change

Integration

Some transnationals try to control all aspects of the process of production. So, for example, they may buy a sugar cane plantation, sugar refineries, road haulage companies, shipping and marketing companies. In this way, the company can control the sugar from the field to the supermarket shelf. This process of acquiring companies is called **vertical integration**.

Other transnationals follow a policy of **horizontal integration**, in which they buy a wide range of very different companies. The aim is to spread the risk so if one company is unsuccessful, the transnational will be compensated for any losses by its other companies that do well. For example, the Boeing company make aircraft but they also own potato and wheat farms. Gulf Oil produces petroleum but also grows sugar, sells cigars, makes paper and even owns a New York ice hockey team.

Transnationals and less economically developed countries

Transnationals, with their headquarters in MEDCs like the USA, Japan or Europe, are interested in expanding in LEDCs because:

- these countries have resources of minerals, timber, power or agricultural land;
- their trade unions are weak so workers will accept low wages;
- governments in LEDCs often offer incentives such as tax free periods;
- rich, powerful transnationals can often influence the political structure of a developing country.

Transnationals in theory and practice

Many developing countries, such as Mexico, are keen to attract transnationals. This is because these large, global companies can bring benefits such as:

- jobs in areas of high unemployment;
- training in industrial skills;
- advanced technology;
- higher wages for local people;
- the establishment of an industrial zone in countries where agriculture is the main source of employment.

Figures 8.2 and 8.3 illustrate the effect of US transnational companies opening new factories in Mexico.

1. Explain the differences between horizontal integration and vertical integration.
2. Read Figure 8.3.
   (a) Why was Dolores's father unable to get a job in the new factories?
   (b) Why is Mexico an attractive location for US companies?
   (c) How has the Mexican Government benefited from the transnationals?
   (d) Why is unemployment still greater than the jobs created by the transnationals?
   (e) Why do US transnational corporations in Mexico employ women rather than men?
   (f) How do the transnationals regard trade unions?
3. Write a paragraph explaining how far you think the US transnationals in Mexico have brought the benefits claimed.

Figure 8.2 US transnational company (*maquilladora*) in Tijuana, Mexico

Transnational companies 47

Figure 8.3 Effects of US transnationals on Mexico

Uncle Sam's jobs south of the border

TEN YEARS ago, when Dolores was 17, her family moved from rural Chihuahua to Mexico's booming border town of Ciudad Juarez. Her father had heard that there was work in the new factories which *los gringos* (the Americans) were building.

New factories there certainly were, but not enough to absorb the influx. Moreover, they did not want to employ Dolores's father. The advertisement specified: "We need female workers; older than 17, younger than 30; single and without children; minimum education primary school, maximum education secondary school; available for all shifts." Dolores's father remained unemployed. Dolores got a job.

Dolores is typical of the 100,000 women who work in the mainly US-owned assembly plants on the northern Mexican border. Since 1965, when the In Bond Border Industrialisation Programme began, the seven major border towns have swelled. Ciudad Juarez, a town of some 150,000 in the 1950s and early '60s, now has a population of 650,000.

Mexicans who can no longer scrape a living off the land come in search of work. The US companies come in search of cheap labour.

The Mexican and US governments arranged the *maquiladora* industrialisation programme to benefit both countries. The idea was to alleviate unemployment in Mexico and strengthen the economy, while enabling US transnationals to maximise profits.

The scheme has benefited the transnationals, which are exempted from the law which states that companies operating in Mexico must have a 51% Mexican share. Most *maquiladoras* are 100% US owned. Operating in Mexico is cheaper than in other less developed countries because it is so close to home, and transport costs are minimal.

By employing young women like Dolores who have never worked before, the companies are not reducing unemployment but creating a new workforce.

The personnel manager of one transnational explained his criteria for recruitment: "I choose people with elegant figures and thin hands because they are more agile ... I take physical appearance into account; you can tell if people are aggressive by the way they look, so I try to choose people who seem more docile and can be managed more easily." Mexican women will work for long, tedious hours assembling tiny components, whereas – as the American said: "It goes against a man's macho pride."

Mexican women are 40% more productive than their North American counterparts. Taught all their lives to submit to male authority, they rarely object to the conditions imposed upon them.

Dolores rises at 4 am to arrive at the factory for the 6 am shift. During her 8-hour day she will have one break of ten minutes, and one of 20. She will solder a minimum of 4,400 "resistors". The company organises competitions between production lines to see who can produce the most. When most of the lines have exceeded the minimum, the "standard" is raised. What was once the goal becomes the minimum.

The future of the *maquiladoras* looks bright. This year European and Japanese firms are opening subsidiaries on the Mexican border, and the Government is allowing some firms to operate farther inside the country.

Their ability to do so depends on a docile and submissive labour force. However, the very fact that women are now earning and working together means that the workforce is becoming less docile.

The Guardian, 15 May 1985

Summary

- Transnational corporations are very large companies with vertical or horizontal integration.
- Transnationals are interested in the resources, land, cheap labour and other attractions of developing countries.
- Transnationals do not always bring the benefits claimed for them.

Change in the Physical Environment

Chapter 9: Volcanoes and earthquakes

**What causes volcanoes and earthquakes?
What effects do volcanoes and earthquakes have on people?**

This unit describes the location of earthquakes and volcanoes, explores their causes and uses case studies to consider their effects.

Location of volcanoes and earthquakes

There are about 500 **active** volcanoes on earth and between 20 and 30 of these erupt each year. Volcanoes which have not erupted for some time, but have erupted in the past, are described as **dormant**. Those which have not erupted since prehistoric times are known as **extinct** volcanoes. Every continent has active volcanoes. They are located in long, narrow belts (see Figure 9.1). The Pacific Ocean is surrounded by over 100 volcanoes forming a 'ring of fire' (see Figure 9.1).

Figure 9.1 The world's active volcanoes

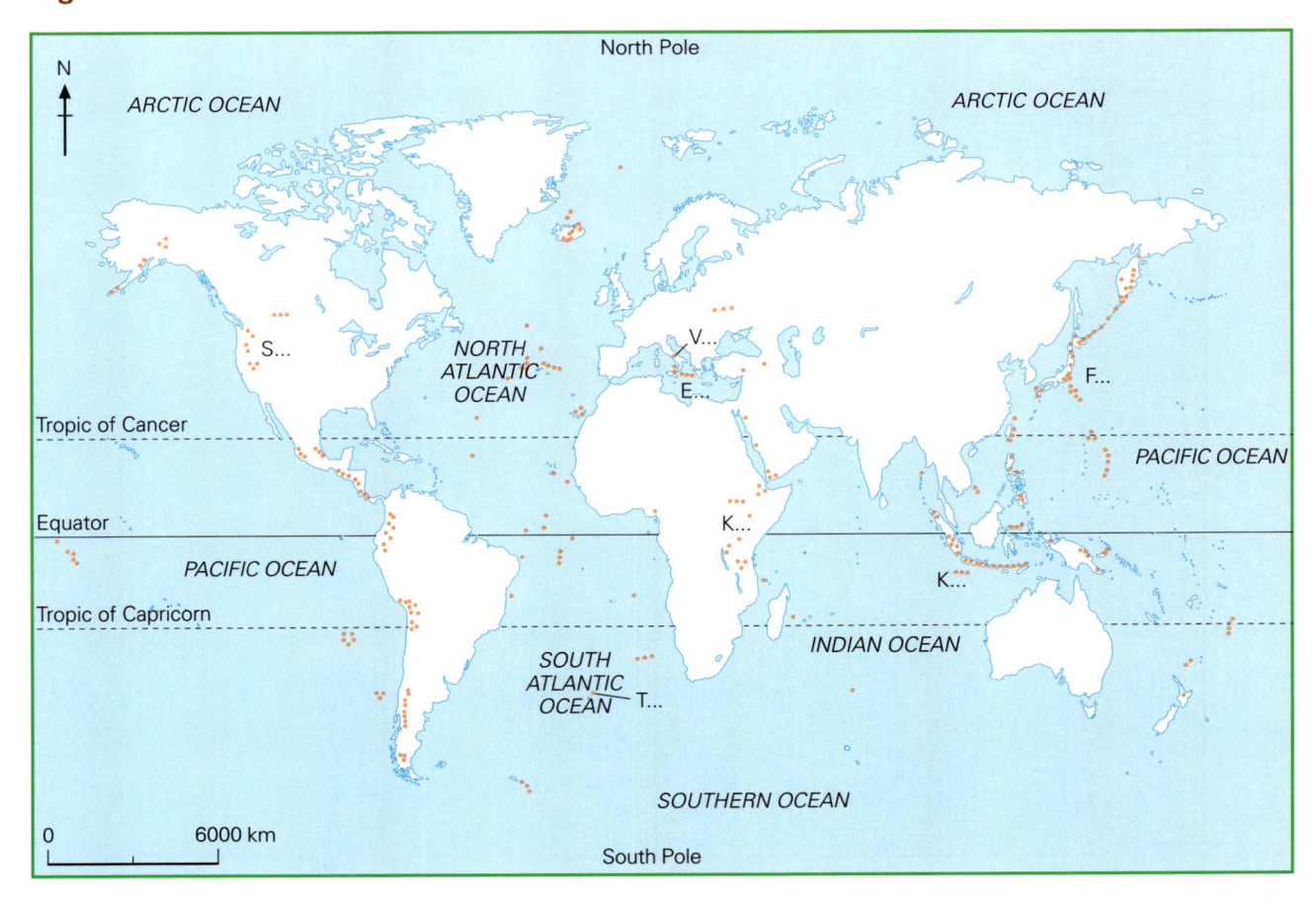

Volcanoes and earthquakes 49

What causes volcanoes and earthquakes?

Figure 9.2 shows the location of the world's earthquakes. By comparing Figures 9.1 and 9.2 we can see that many volcanoes and earthquakes are located in the same narrow belts around the earth, such as the 'ring of fire'. Geologists have discovered that the earth's crust is divided into a number of separate sections called **plates**. The plates move slowly across the planet at about the speed that your fingernails grow. The plates grind against each other with great force. As Figure 9.3 shows, most of the world's earthquakes and volcanoes are found at the edges of the plates.

There are two main types of plate margin; constructive and destructive (see Figures 9.4–9.6). Volcanoes and earthquakes occur at both types of margin. Constructive plate margins (see Figure 9.4) occur where new crust is formed. The **oceanic ridges** are constructive margins. Two plates are moving apart and **magma** rises to the surface from below. The Mid-Atlantic Ridge is an example. This is a range of volcanoes running in a narrow line beneath the middle of the Atlantic Ocean. In places, these volcanoes are so high that they reach the ocean surface to form islands, like Iceland. Constructive margins on land form **rift valleys**.

Destructive plate margins occur where crust is being destroyed. There are two types of destructive margin: subduction zones and collision zones. Subduction zones (see Figure 9.5) occur at the deep ocean trenches where the sea floor is pulled down as one plate slowly passes under another. The subduction zone is marked by earthquakes. As the oceanic crust plunges into the **mantle** it melts and rises to the surface where it erupts as **lava**. When this happens right out in the ocean, a chain of volcanic islands, called an island arc, is formed.

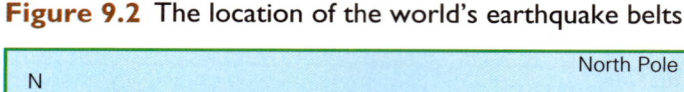

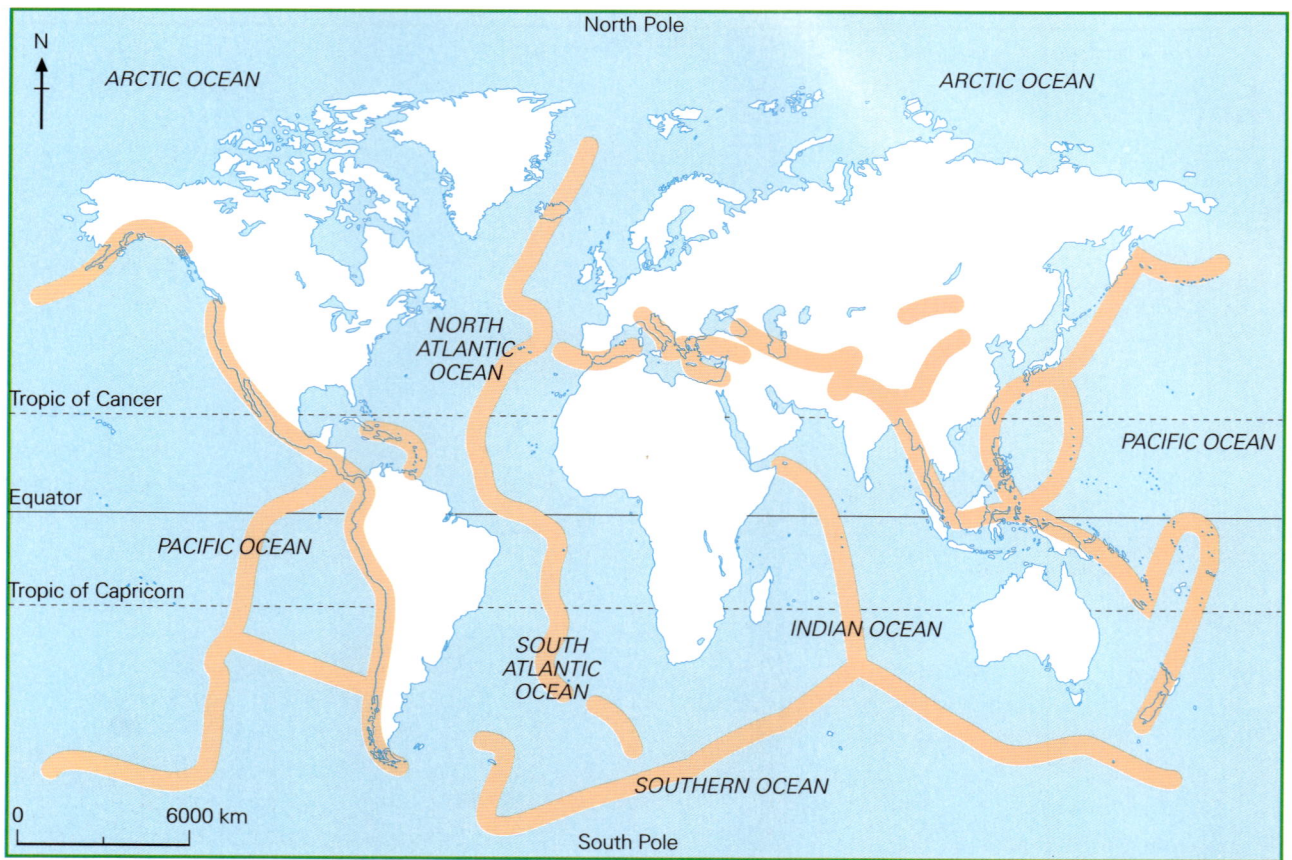

Figure 9.2 The location of the world's earthquake belts

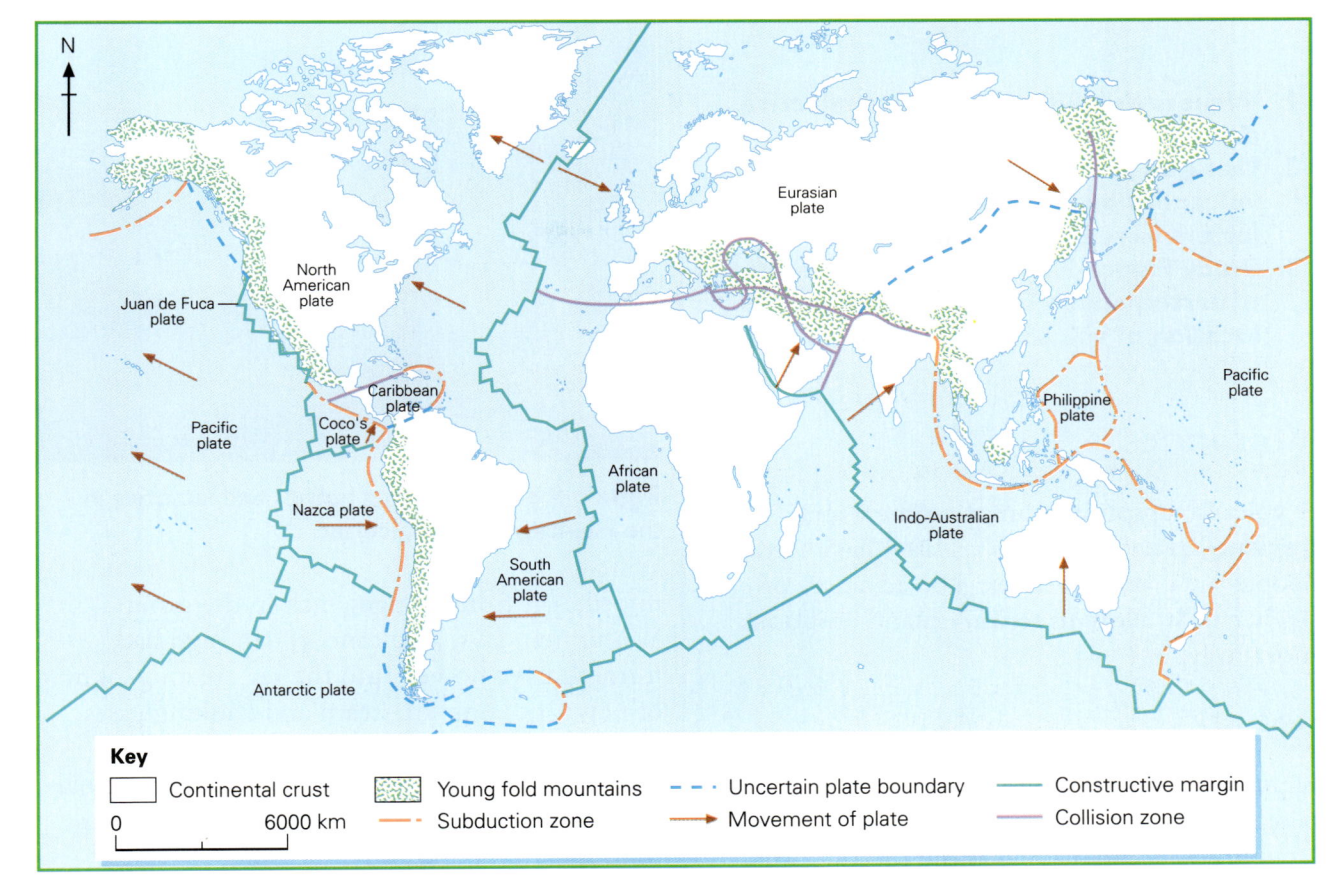

Figure 9.3 The position of the earth's crustal plates

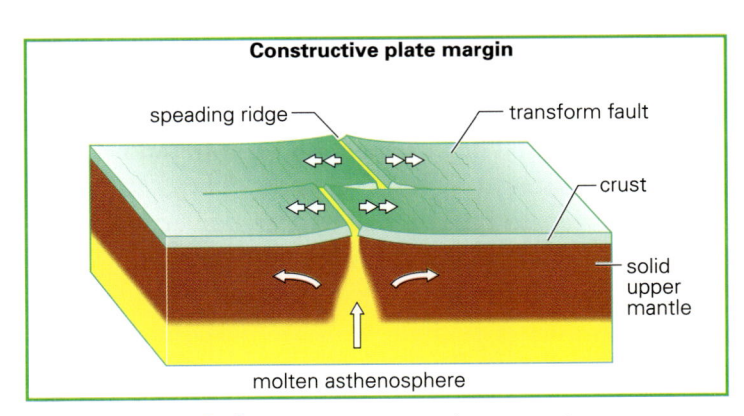

Key
- Continental crust
- Young fold mountains
- Uncertain plate boundary
- Constructive margin
- Subduction zone
- Movement of plate
- Collision zone

An example of a subduction zone is the Aleutian trench, where the Pacific plate passes beneath the North American plate. The Aleutian islands mark the island arc. Collision zones (see Figure 9.6) occur where two plates carrying continental crust collide. The **continental crust** crumples up to form **fold mountains**. An example is the Himalayan mountain range, formed where the Indo-Australian plate is colliding with the Eurasian plate.

Figure 9.4 A constructive plate margin

Figure 9.5 A destructive plate margin

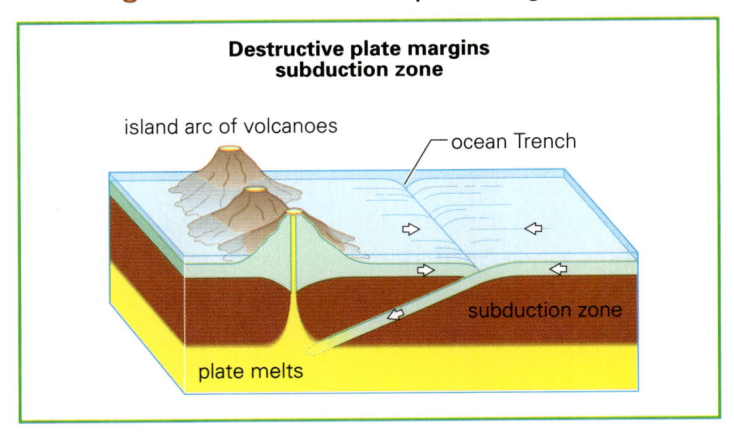

Figure 9.6 A destructive plate margin collision zone

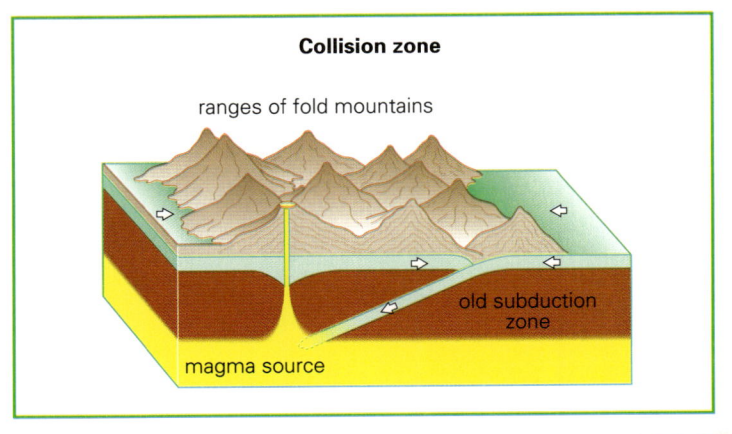

Volcanoes and earthquakes 51

1. What is the difference between active, dormant and extinct volcanoes?
2. Using an atlas to help you, name the volcanoes on Figure 9.1 for which first letters have been given.
3. Study Figure 9.2. How does the location of earthquakes compare with the location of volcanoes?

Volcanoes

A volcanic eruption is an awesome event. The tremendous natural forces released have terrified people since ancient times. The advances of science now allow us to understand eruptions more fully.

The Heimaey volcano

Heimaey is an island off the south coast of Iceland, on a constructive plate margin. In January 1973, Heimaey was the location for a major volcanic eruption. The calm of a cold winter's night was shattered by a vast explosion. The night sky was lit up by orange and yellow bursts of flame. Lava was thrown over 100 m

Figure 9.7 Heimay, Iceland

Figure 9.8 Lava burying houses and factories in the Heimaey volcano, Iceland

into the air from a huge crack in the ground. Within ten days, a volcano 180 m high had formed. Lava flowed into the sea creating 2 km² of new land. Smoke, steam and choking gases hung over the island. The lava threatened to engulf the town and harbour of Vestmannaeyjar (see Figure 9.7). The town depended upon its fishing harbour and fish-processing factories. Half of the town was evacuated. Soon several houses and factories were buried (Figure 9.8).

Although they were at first terrified by the eruption, the islanders refused to accept that the volcano was going to destroy their homes and their livelihoods. They cleaned ash off roofs and extinguished fires lit by hot fragments. They used bulldozers to build a wall to try to divert the hot lava flows. They also used high-pressure water hoses to cool the lava and slow its progress. A quarter of the town was destroyed, but only one person died. Today, Vestmannaeyjar is a thriving fishing port again and memories of 'the days of hell' have faded. Ash from the eruption has been exported for making building blocks.

The Pinatubo volcano

Mount Pinatubo is a volcano on a destructive plate margin on Luzon island in the Philippines. Mount Pinatubo had lain dormant for over 600 years when, on 2 April 1991, steam erupted from vents on the mountainside. Worried villagers called in scientists from the Philippine Institute of Volcanology. The scientists installed

52 Change in the Physical Environment

instruments and monitored the volcano. It soon became clear to them that Mount Pinatubo was going to erupt. They called for the evacuation of villages on and immediately around the volcano. A series of minor ash eruptions in early June led the scientists to extend the evacuation area to a 25 km radius.

Just after midnight on 15 June, the mountain began to eject deadly clouds of ash and gas heated to 1000° C. Ash was blasted 40 km up into the atmosphere. A series of increasingly strong earthquakes preceded a massive explosion at dawn which blew out the side of the mountain. The materials ejected by a volcano are called **pyroclasts**. The largest fragments erupted fell swiftly to earth as **volcanic bombs**. Soon the sky was black with ash, bringing darkness at noon. Ash and lava flowed nearly 20 km from the shattered peak, completely filling a 200 m deep canyon on the way (see Figure 9.9).

Despite the evacuations, the eruption of Mount Pinatubo killed nearly 900 people, mainly through **mudflows** and the collapse of roofs due to build-up of ash. The eruption laid waste to hundreds of square kilometres of land and destroyed crops. Over 1 million farm animals died, either through starvation because of loss of grass or through drinking contaminated water. 110 000 homes were destroyed and the final cost was £10 billion. Without the scientific monitoring and early evacuation many thousands more people would have died.

It was a disaster for the Philippines, but the eruption of Mount Pinatubo also had global effects. Twenty million tonnes of sulphur dioxide were ejected into the **stratosphere**, creating a cloud of fine dust which circled the whole planet within just 21 days. Pinatubo's dust cloud deflected 2 per cent of incoming sunshine, reducing global temperatures by 1° C for several years following the eruption.

Figure 9.9 The eruption of Mount Pinatubo volcano, Luzon Island, Philippines, 1991

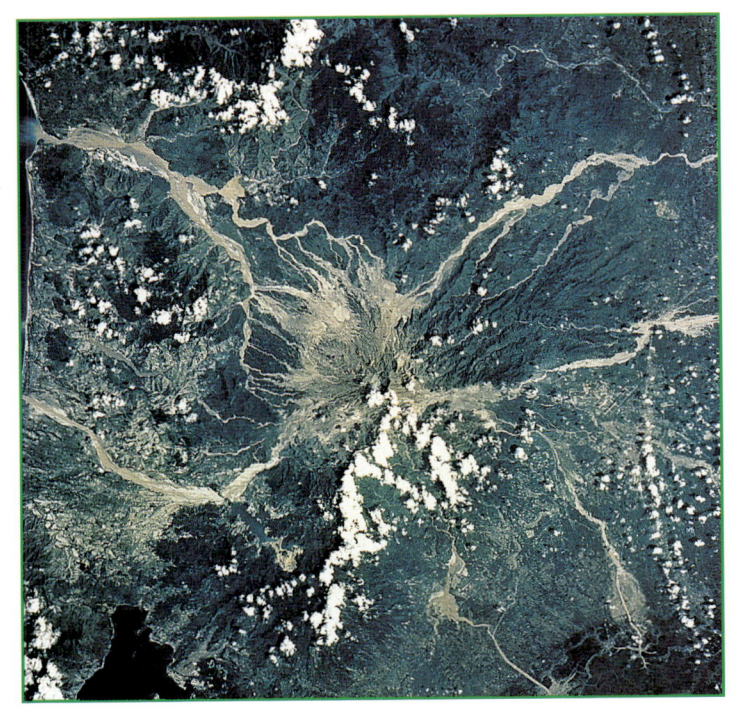

Figure 9.10 A composite cone

Types of volcano

Volcanoes tend to be conical in shape, but they can have a number of different forms depending upon the type of lava and ash erupted. Mount Pinatubo is an example of a composite volcano. This means that it is composed of alternate layers of lava and ash. Most volcanoes are of this type. Composite volcanoes have a gently sloping concave shape (see Figure 9.10).

Some volcanoes are formed almost entirely of lava. The shape of these volcanoes depends upon the type of lava which erupts. **Basic lava** flows easily and covers a vast distance. It produces very gently sloping volcanic cones called **shield volcanoes** (see Figure 9.11). An example is Mauna Loa in the Hawaiian Islands, which rises 9 km above the sea bed and has a diameter of

Figure 9.11 A basic lava cone

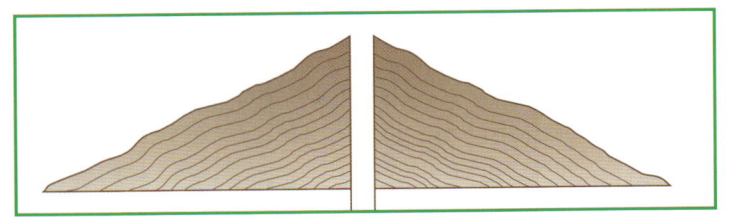

Volcanoes and earthquakes 53

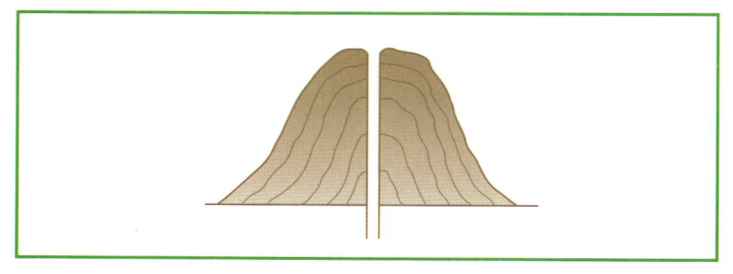

Figure 9.12 An acid lava cone

over 250 km at its base (the distance from London to Sheffield!). *Acid lava* is much thicker (viscous) than basic lava and does not flow very easily. Acid lava cones are very steep, with a much narrower base (see Figure 9.12). An example is the Puy de Dôme in the Auvergne region of France, which last erupted over 1 million years ago.

Sometimes the eruption of a volcano can be so explosive that the volcano itself is destroyed. This was the case in 1883 when the volcanic island of Krakatoa in Indonesia blew itself apart. Tidal waves, more correctly called *tsunamis*, were triggered off by the explosion and 36 000 people drowned. The massive eruption left only shattered remains of the volcanic cone – a *caldera* (see Figure 9.13). A caldera can also be produced by the process of collapsing. The vast caldera of Crater Lake in Oregon, USA, was produced in this way.

> 4. On an outline map of the world draw on the major crustal plate margins (Figure 9.3) and add the major areas of volcanoes and earthquakes.
> 5. (a) Where is Heimaey?
>   (b) How did the volcano threaten the town and harbour of Vestmannaeyjar?
>   (c) How did people try to combat the eruption?
>   (d) Use Figures 9.3 and 9.4 to help you explain why volcanoes are found on Heimaey.
> 6. (a) Where is Mount Pinatubo?
>   (b) How many people were killed in the eruption of Mount Pinatubo? What caused most of the deaths?
>   (c) How did the eruption of Mount Pinatubo affect the whole world?
>   (d) Use Figures 9.3 and 9.4 to help you explain why a volcano is found there.

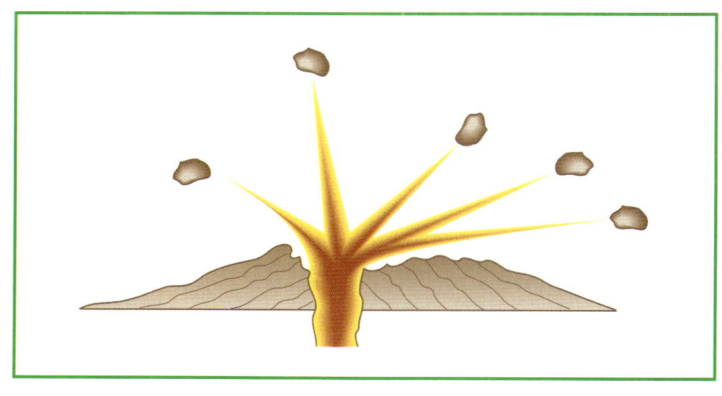

Figure 9.13 A caldera

> 7. Write definitions of: (i) viscous lava; (ii) acid lava; (iii) basic lava; (iv) pyroclast; (v) shield volcano; (vi) caldera; (vii) parasitic cone.

Earthquakes

Volcanic eruptions can kill large numbers of people (Figure 9.14), but there is usually enough warning for many others to escape. Earthquakes have killed many more people, largely because they occur without warning.

Earthquakes are caused by the release of stress which has built up within the earth's crust (Figure 9.14). Most earthquakes occur at crustal plate margins. The plates grind against each other with great force. However, the movement is not continuous but occurs as a series of jerks which cause earthquakes. The rocks break along a *fault line*, with horizontal and vertical movements on either side of the fault. Both pressure (pushing together) and tension (pulling apart) can produce faults.

An earthquake begins at a point within the crust called the *focus*. The point on the surface, directly above the focus, is called the *epicentre* (Figure 9.15). Shock waves move out from the focus: fast *primary waves* and slower *secondary waves* move out in all directions; but *longitudinal waves* travel only around the surface of the planet. Longitudinal waves are the major cause of destruction to buildings and loss of life. The energy generated by an earthquake is measured by the Richter Scale. The observed effects of an earthquake are recorded using the Mercalli Scale (Figure 9.16).

54 Change in the Physical Environment

Figure 9.14 Major eruptions and earthquakes

Earthquakes

Year	Location	Number of people killed
1906	San Francisco (USA)	740
1920	Kansu (China)	180 000
1923	Tokyo (Japan)	143 000
1935	Quetta (India)	60 000
1960	Agadir (Morocco)	12 000
1970	Northern Peru	70 000
1974	Northern Pakistan	10 000
1976	Tanghshan (China)	650 000
1980	El Asnam (Algeria)	20 000
1985	Mexico City (Mexico)	30 000
1988	Northern Armenia	50 000
1990	North west Iran	35 000
1993	Maharashtra (India)	10 000
1995	Kobe (Japan)	6000

Volcanic Eruptions

Year	Location	Number of people killed
1815	Tambora (Indonesia)	92 000
1883	Krakatoa (Indonesia)	36 000
1902	Mont Pelée (Martinique)	30 000
1965	Taal (Philippines)	1050
1980	Mount St Helens (USA)	61
1982	El Chichon (Mexico)	4000
1985	Armero (Colombia)	25 000
1986	Wum (Cameroon)	1700
1991	Pinatubo (Philippines)	890

The Kobe earthquake in Japan

In the hour before dawn the normally bustling Japanese city of Kobe was quiet on 17 January 1995. At 5.46 am, most of its 1.5 million inhabitants were still asleep. Suddenly, people became aware of a noise like a bomb exploding and the ground began shaking. Within seconds the shaking had become frighteningly intense, hurling people to the ground. A series of shockwaves lifted the ground over 50 cm. Cracks over 30 cm wide opened in the streets and buildings began to crumble and fall. The air was filled with the sound of breaking glass, falling masonry and terrified screams. Broken gas mains exploded into flames and fires spread. The fires raged throughout the day and into the following night. Over 11 000 buildings were destroyed. Mains water supplies were cut off.

Kobe, Japan's leading port, had been hit by an earthquake measuring 7.2 on the Richter Scale. The earthquake's epicentre was at Awajishima Island, 60 km south west of Kobe. Kobe was destroyed. 6000 people were killed and over 26 000 were injured, while 300 000 were made homeless. The cost of rebuilding Kobe was estimated at between $40 billion and $100 billion.

Japan had a high reputation for taking measures to prevent earthquake damage, but

Figure 9.15 Release of stress created by the subduction of the Cocos Plate beneath the North American Plate caused the Mexican earthquake of 1985 which killed 30 000 people

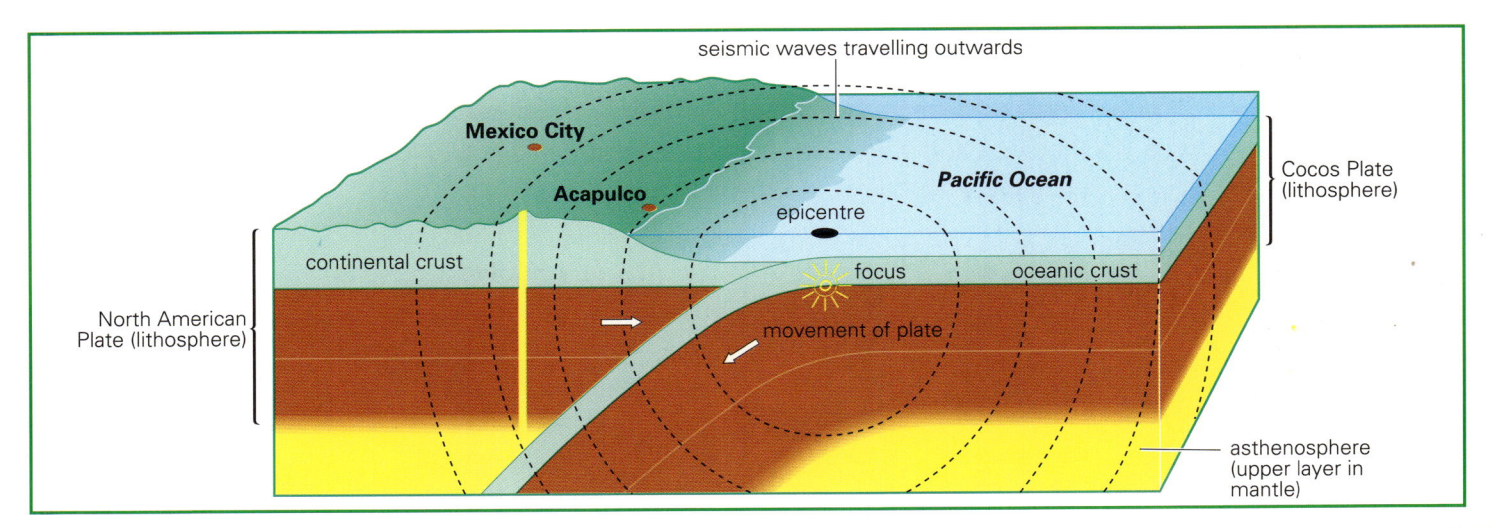

Volcanoes and earthquakes 55

Kobe had been overwhelmed. There was a clear relationship between the age of buildings and the degree of damage. Buildings constructed after 1981, when building standards were improved, survived better. There was strong criticism of the failure to improve the safety standards of older buildings, roads and bridges.

> 8. What causes earthquakes?
> 9. (a) How do the different types of earthquake shock wave differ?
>   (b) Which type of shock wave causes the greatest destruction during an earthquake? Why do you think this is?

Figure 9.16 The Richter Scale and Mercalli Scale for earthquakes

Mercalli Scale Intensity (degree of shaking)	Description of characteristic effects	Richter Scale Magnitude (total energy released)
I	Instrumental: detected only by seismographs.	2
II	Feeble: felt only by sensitive people.	
III	Slight: like the vibrations due to a passing light lorry.	3
IV	Moderate: like the passing of a heavy road vehicle; rocking of loose objects, including standing cars.	4
V	Rather strong: felt by most people; church bells ring.	5
VI	Most people frightened; windows broken; dishes fall out of cupboards.	
VII	Very strong: general alarm; walls crack; plaster falls.	6
VIII	Destructive: car drivers find it difficult to steer; masonry cracked; chimneys fall.	
IX	Ruinous: general panic; ground cracks appear and pipes break open.	
X	Disastrous: ground cracks badly; many buildings destroyed; landslides on steep slopes.	7
XI	Very disastrous: most buildings and bridges destroyed; all services (railways, pipes and cables) out of action; great landslides and floods; dams badly damaged.	
XII	Catastrophic: total destruction; objects thrown into air; ground rises and falls in waves; cracks open and close.	8

Summary

- Earthquakes and volcanoes can cause great damage and loss of life. Most occur close to the boundaries of the earth's crustal plates.

10 Weathering and soils

Chapter

What is weathering?
How is weathering caused?
What comprises different types of soil?
How does soil erosion occur?
What types of natural vegetation are there?
How have humans affected the earth's vegetation?

This unit explains weathering and describes the features of a limestone area. Different types of soil are compared and the causes and effects of soil erosion are considered through case studies. The earth's natural vegetation and how it is affected by human action are also explored.

Weathering

Figure 10.1 shows how a statue, erected in the fourteenth century in Cracow, Poland has been **weathered**. The atmosphere itself, rain and frost have attacked the rock of the statue over the years. The same effects can be seen on gravestones and buildings and on rocks in their natural locations.

There are three main processes of weathering: physical, chemical and biological.

Physical weathering

This is the physical break-up of rock, often by frost. Water seeps into cracks and joints in rock and, on freezing, it expands by 10 per cent and creates great pressure within the rock. Repeated freezing and thawing eventually splits the rock into jagged pieces. This is called **frost shattering**. Large amounts of these shattered rocks can be found in **scree slopes** in mountainous areas where frost shattering is, or has been, intense.

Extreme changes of temperature also cause mechanical weathering. In deserts, the blistering

Figure 10.1 Acid rain has damaged this stone sculpture on the roof of Cloth Hall in Crakow, Poland

heat of the day causes the rock's surface to expand and break away from the inner layers of rock. In the cool of the desert night the rock's surface contracts. As this happens daily, it will eventually cause the rock to crack. Pieces of rock drop off in layers, like the skin of an onion. This process is called **exfoliation**

Weathering and soils   57

Chemical weathering

Water causes chemical weathering. Rain water is slightly acidic and can dissolve certain minerals, such as calcium carbonate in limestone. Decaying plants and animals also produce acids which break down rocks.

Human actions have increased chemical weathering through the burning of coal, oil and gas. When they burn, they release sulphur dioxide as a gas. The sulphur dioxide combines with water and oxygen in the atmosphere to form dilute sulphuric acid or *acid rain*, which can harm plants, animals and buildings.

Biological weathering

Plants and animals can cause biological weathering. The roots of trees may grow into joints and cracks in rock and force the rock apart. Burrowing animals such as moles or earthworms also help to break down rock.

The processes of weathering, *erosion* and *deposition* can be viewed as part of a simple system (Figure 10.2) with inputs, storage and outputs.

> 1. Describe the type of weathering which you would expect to occur on: (a) bare rock exposed in the Sahara Desert; (b) a mountainside in the Lake District.
> 2. How have human actions increased chemical weathering rates?

Weathering in a limestone area

Limestone is vulnerable to chemical weathering. It contains large amounts of calcium carbonate from the remains of sea shells and coral. Rain water is slightly acidic and can dissolve calcium carbonate. Water containing dissolved calcium carbonate is called *hard water*.

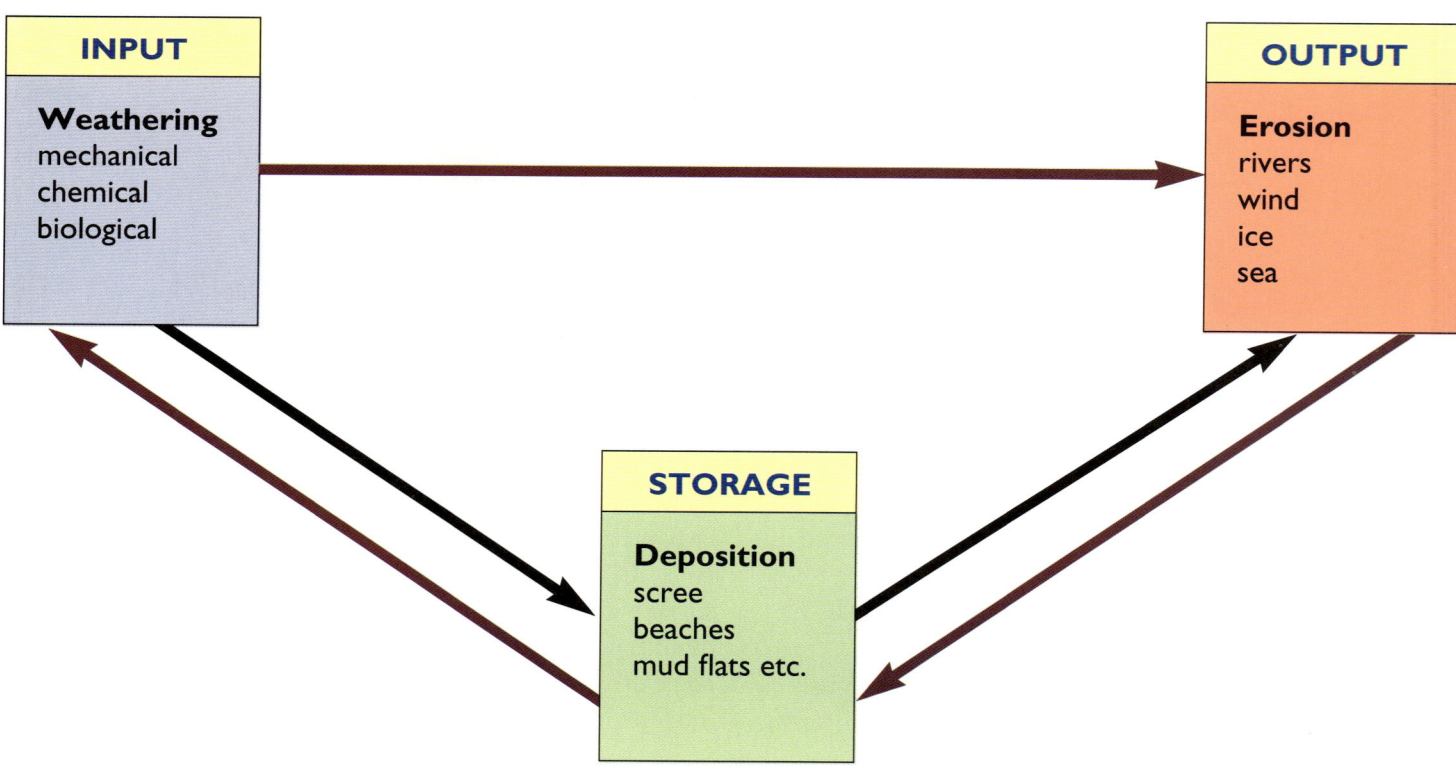

Figure 10.3 shows a carboniferous limestone landscape. Carboniferous limestone is particularly strong. The landscape is dry, with steep slopes and expanses of bare rock. There are few streams and most drainage is underground. Water enlarges the *joints* and *bedding planes* in the limestone to create *swallow holes* and *caverns* (see Figure 10.4).

In the Ingleborough area of North Yorkshire is the huge swallow hole called Gaping Ghyll. Gaping Ghyll is 111 m deep, plunging vertically

Figure 10.2 The weathering system

INPUT
Weathering
mechanical
chemical
biological

STORAGE
Deposition
scree
beaches
mud flats etc.

OUTPUT
Erosion
rivers
wind
ice
sea

58 Change in the Physical Environment

down into an enormous cavern. **Stalactites** hang from the roof of the cavern. They are formed by water dripping through the roof and re-depositing calcium carbonate. From the floor of the cavern **stalagmites** rise up. Sometimes a pillar is formed where a stalactite and stalagmite join together.

The land surface of a limestone landscape is often very irregular. Limestone pavements may develop where the soil has been washed away, revealing bare rock. The joints are enlarged by water to form grikes and the upstanding blocks are called clints. Deep **gorges** may be formed, either by the collapse of the roof of an underground cavern or by rapid river erosion in areas where the water table is higher, or was higher in the past.

> 3. Study Figure 10.4. Describe the following features and explain how they are formed: (a) swallow holes; (b) caverns; (c) stalactites and stalagmites; (d) limestone pavements, clints and grikes; (e) limestone gorges.

Figure 10.3 A carboniferous limestone landscape near Malham, North Yorkshire

Figure 10.4 A limestone landscape

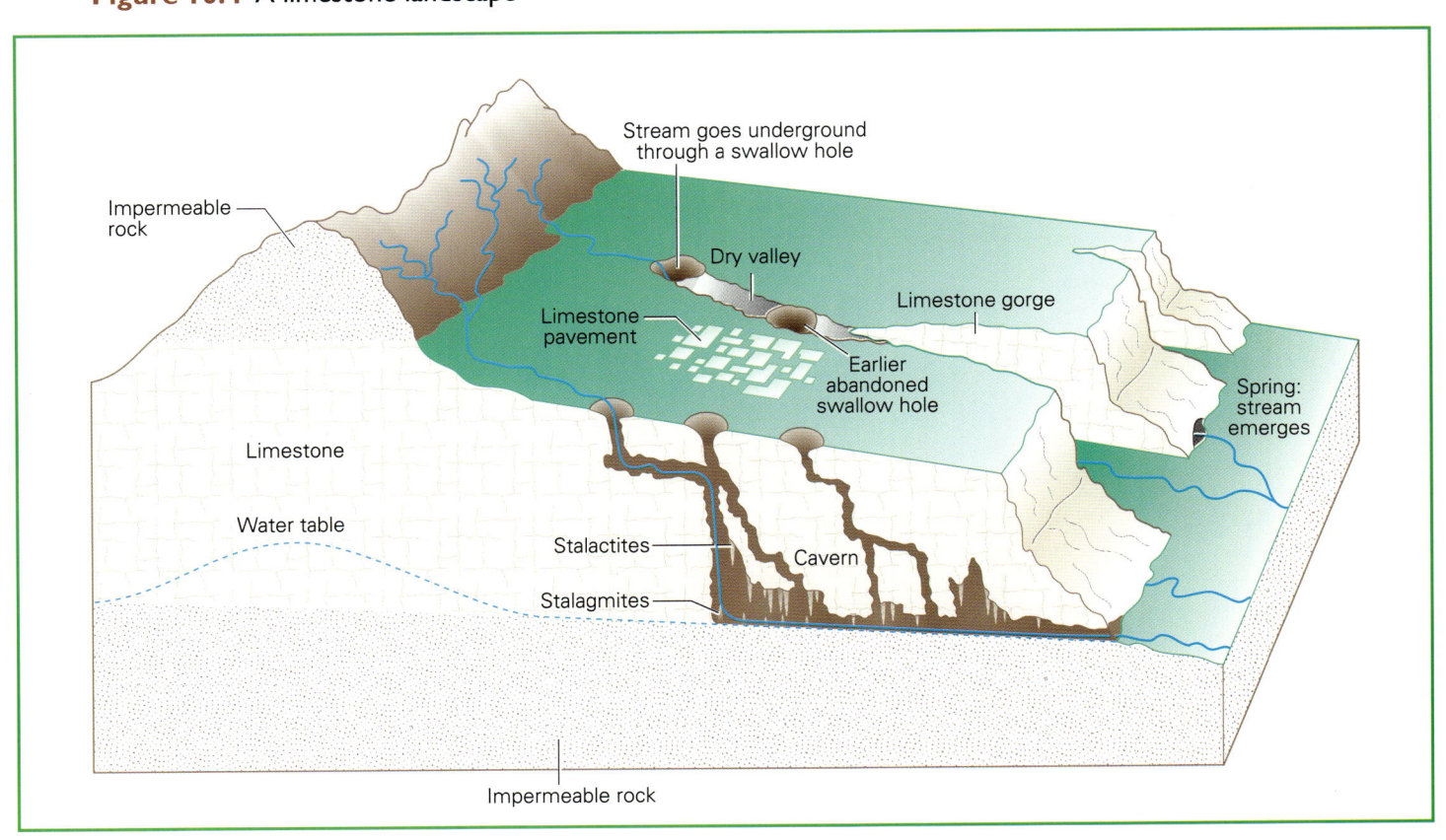

Weathering and soils

Figure 10.5 Rock particle sizes

Size of particle (mm diameter)	Type of particle	Texture of the soil
Less than 0.001	Clay	Very sticky; easily moulded into any shape
0.001–0.1	Silt	Not sticky; rolls easily between the hands
0.1–2.0	Sand	Not sticky; feels gritty
Greater than 2.0	Gravel	Not sticky; stony

Soils

Soil is a vital but fragile resource that we take for granted. Yet, without soil, farming and forestry would be impossible; almost all our food is obtained from crops grown in soil or animals grazing on crops.

Soil is made up of rock fragments, plant and animal matter, water and air. The rocks have been broken down by the process of weathering. Rock particles are classified according to their size (see Figure 10.5); the finest particles are clay, silt particles are larger, and sand is larger still.

Plant and animal remains build up on the surface of the soils of forest or heathland in cooler climates. Elsewhere, it is mixed into the soil by earthworms and broken down by soil organisms to form humus, an organic material which is vital for the fertility of the soil. This is decomposed into simple compounds which can be taken up by plants through their roots and used as food.

Figure 10.6 shows several layers within the soil. These layers are called soil horizons. The complete section of horizons from the surface to the parent rock is called a soil profile. Minerals within the soil may be washed down through the soil profile by water in a process known as leaching. In wet climates, leaching may be intense. Sometimes the leached minerals and organic matter are re-deposited in a lower horizon to form a thin, sheet-like layer rich in

Figure 10.6 A model soil profile

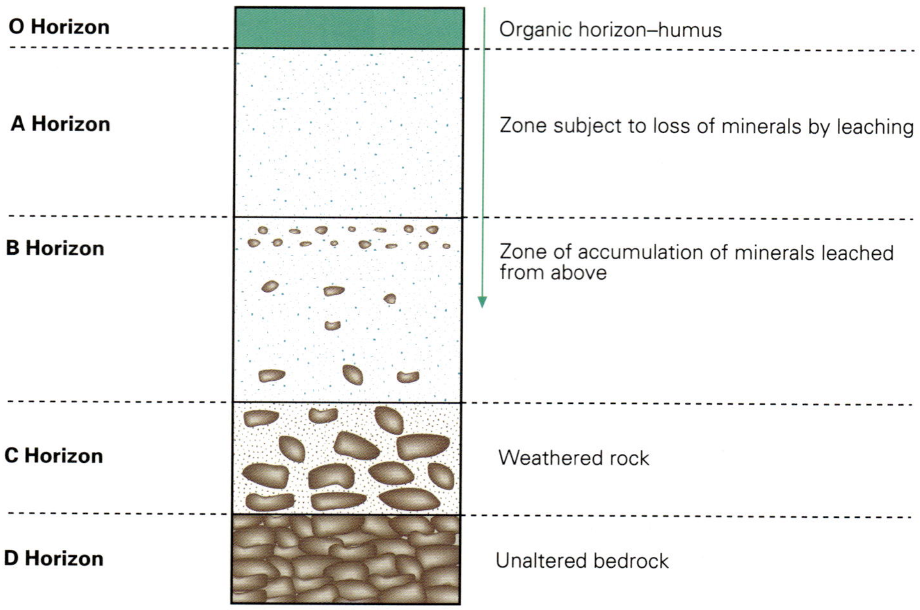

O Horizon	Organic horizon–humus
A Horizon	Zone subject to loss of minerals by leaching
B Horizon	Zone of accumulation of minerals leached from above
C Horizon	Weathered rock
D Horizon	Unaltered bedrock

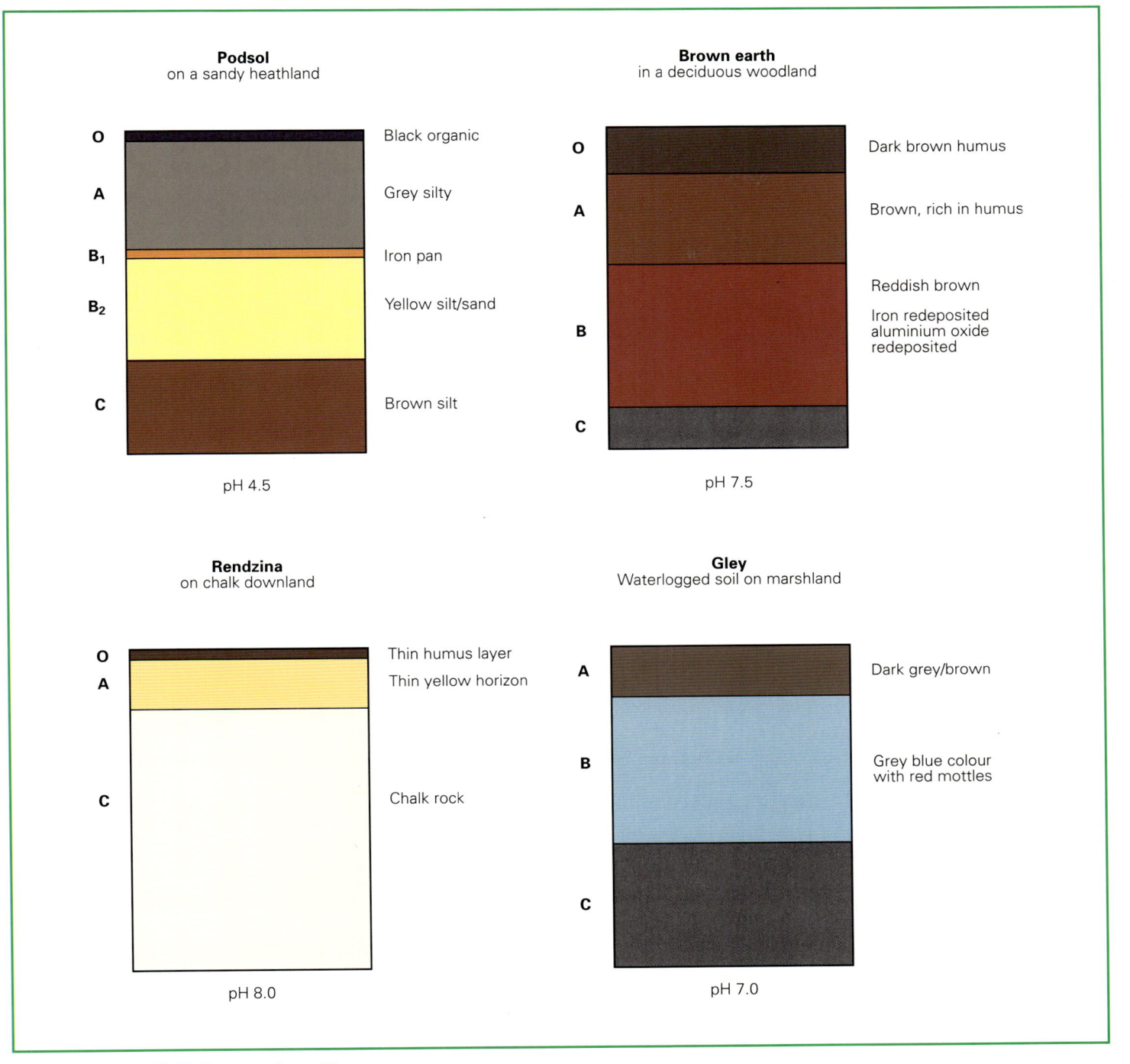

Figure 10.7 Four soil profiles

iron called an iron pan. The resulting soil is known as a podzol. It has a grey sandy upper horizon above the iron pan; yellow silt and sand lie beneath the iron pan, partly stained by re-deposited iron and aluminium oxides.

Soils can vary greatly within a small area. Figure 10.7 shows four soil profiles dug by students on fieldwork in Dorset. The first is a heathland podzol, the second a brown earth found in a deciduous wood, the third a thin rendzina soil found on chalk downland, and the fourth a waterlogged gley soil found in marshy land. The special features of each type of soil are explained on Figure 10.7. Notice how the soil acidity, measured on the pH scale, differs from a pH of 4.5 in the podzol to 8.0 in the rendzina. A neutral soil has a pH of 7.0; a pH above 7.0 is alkaline, below 7.0 is acid. The acidity of a soil is very important because most plants prefer neutral or slightly acidic soils (pH 6.5–7.0).

Weathering and soils 61

The European Soil Charter

The European Union (EU) prepared the European Soil Charter in 1990. This states:

- soil is one of the world's most precious assets. It allows plants, animals and humans to live on the earth's surface;
- soil is a limited resource which is easily destroyed;
- farmers and foresters must use methods which preserve the quality of the soil;
- soil must be protected against erosion and pollution;
- urban developments must cause minimum damage to adjoining areas.

In 1990 it was estimated that over 30 per cent of soils in the EU were moderately or severely damaged.

> 4. Why is soil: (a) vital; (b) fragile?
> 5. What is humus, how is it formed and why is it so important for plant growth?
> 6. Look at Figure 10.7.
>   (a) Why is the podzol more leached than the other soils?
>   (b) What effect have plants had on the brown earth?
>   (c) Why is the rendzina so thin?
>   (d) Why does the gley have such poorly developed horizons?

Soil erosion

The causes

Neglect of the soil has caused many problems in the past. When topsoil is eroded away, crop yields fall and eventually it may become impossible to grow any crops as the remaining soil turns to useless dust or is lost altogether. In the twentieth century, soil erosion caused by poor farming techniques has become especially severe.

No soil is free from erosion but the effects of it are worst in areas of high rainfall or drought. Heavy rain breaks up the topsoil and washes it away. Drought dries the soil into a loose powder which is blown away by the wind.

Farming practices which are particularly detrimental to the soil are:

- the removal of trees or hedgerows, which provide shelter for the soil and, through their roots, help to bind the soil particles;
- the ploughing of land on steep slopes, which often results in rain washing the loosened soil away. The water follows down the furrows and form **gullies**, which can erode large amounts of soil;
- overgrazing by animals causes a reduction in the amount of vegetation which binds and protects the soil.

Soil erosion in Britain

There is serious soil erosion in Britain. Soil scientists estimate that 44 per cent of the arable land of England and Wales is at risk of erosion.

Figure 10.8 shows flooding of a housing estate at Rottingdean in East Sussex on 7 October 1987. Over £1 million of damage was caused by the soil-laden water.

Soil erosion across the Sussex Downs in 1987 produced the highest losses of soil ever recorded in Britain. A single 9 ha field lost 270 tonnes of soil per hectare during that year, over one-tenth of the total soil in the field. Such a rate of loss is disastrous; soil only forms very slowly, at a rate of less than half a tonne per hectare per year. Soil suitable for farming may take over 6000 years to form.

Dry winters in Britain can mean that arable land is more vulnerable to soil erosion from the wind. In the spring, before the crops have grown strong, winds can blow away valuable topsoil. The rapid increase in the planting of winter cereals during the autumn, leaves fields bare during the winter months, drilled with cereals rather than ploughed. A ploughed field is less at risk from soil erosion, provided it has been ploughed along, rather than across, the contours.

Soil erosion in less economically developed countries

Figure 10.9 describes a natural disaster which is becoming all too common in LEDCs.

Figure 10.8 Flooding of a housing estate in Rottingdean, East Sussex on 7 October 1987

Deforestation allows soil erosion to occur. The soil is washed down slopes into rivers, where it chokes the channel and causes flooding. The deforestation of Nepal is causing soil losses of over 10 tonnes per hectare. As the soil is washed away, crop yields fall. On average, Nepalese farmers can grow only enough food to supply their families for eight months of the year.

Reforestation schemes are the key to controlling soil erosion in many areas. At Ed Debba, 500 km north west of Khartoum, northern Sudan, the River Nile flows through a fertile plain which it has itself created through regular floods depositing silt. The winds blow from the desert, carrying sand and blowing away the silty topsoil from the fields. This erosion threatens the wheat, maize, sorghum, beans, tomatoes and okra on which the area depends.

The Rome-based International Fund for Agricultural Development has supported a voluntary organisation called SOS Sahel in its efforts to combat the soil erosion and

Figure 10.9 Thai flood caused by overlogging

Thai flood 'caused by over-logging'

A vast heap of mud, sand and timber is all that remains of Katoon, a farming village of 300 families after devastating floods and landslides in southern Thailand. Katoon was obliterated in half an hour on the afternoon of 22 November, when days of heavy rain brought flash floods, and dislodged mud and sand from hills overlooking the valley of Phi Pun district.

The death toll from the floods in 12 southern provinces was 429 up to yesterday. The mud slides sent boulders and thousands of felled timber logs crashing into flimsy wooden houses, destroying the already flooded village and wiping out most of its population.

Villagers blamed the tragedy on illegal logging. Environmentalists say this eliminates natural shade needed for the growth of ground foliage that traps rainfall in the highlands during the monsoon. Deep red gashes mark the mountainsides of the once fertile valley of rice fields and orchards, now a wasteland, metres deep in mud and logs.

The Independent, December 1988

Weathering and soils

encroaching sand at Ed Debba by planting trees to act as shelter belts. Some 50 000 seedlings of the fast-growing mesquite tree have been planted. The mesquite can grow as much as four metres in a year and spreads out thickly. About 20 km of shelter belts have been planted, ranging in width from six to 24 m. The local farmers buy the seedlings and plant them, seeking advice from SOS Sahel if they need it. Although the young trees need irrigation, once they are established their roots tap the groundwater.

Ed Debba's shelter belts are protecting the soil from erosion, boosting yields, halting the encroaching sand dunes and providing much-needed shade from the desert sun.

Figure 10.10 summarises various methods of reducing soil erosion.

In Burkina Faso in West Africa farmers had traditionally placed lines of stones along the contours to trap **runoff** and reduce soil erosion. Many of the slopes were so gentle that it was too easy to place the stones *across* rather than *along* the contours, thus encouraging the erosion which the farmers were trying to prevent. The charity Oxfam provided a cheap solution (Figure 10.11): the water level on the hose allows the farmers to find the same level across the slope. Stone lines can then be laid along the contours. Although they take up 2 per cent of the available farmland, the stone lines can increase yields by up to 50 per cent. By trapping the runoff, this simple method re-supplies the water table and prevents the soil from becoming crusted and platy in texture, thus allowing plants to grow more easily. New stone lines can now be seen in countries surrounding Burkina Faso, including Mali and Niger.

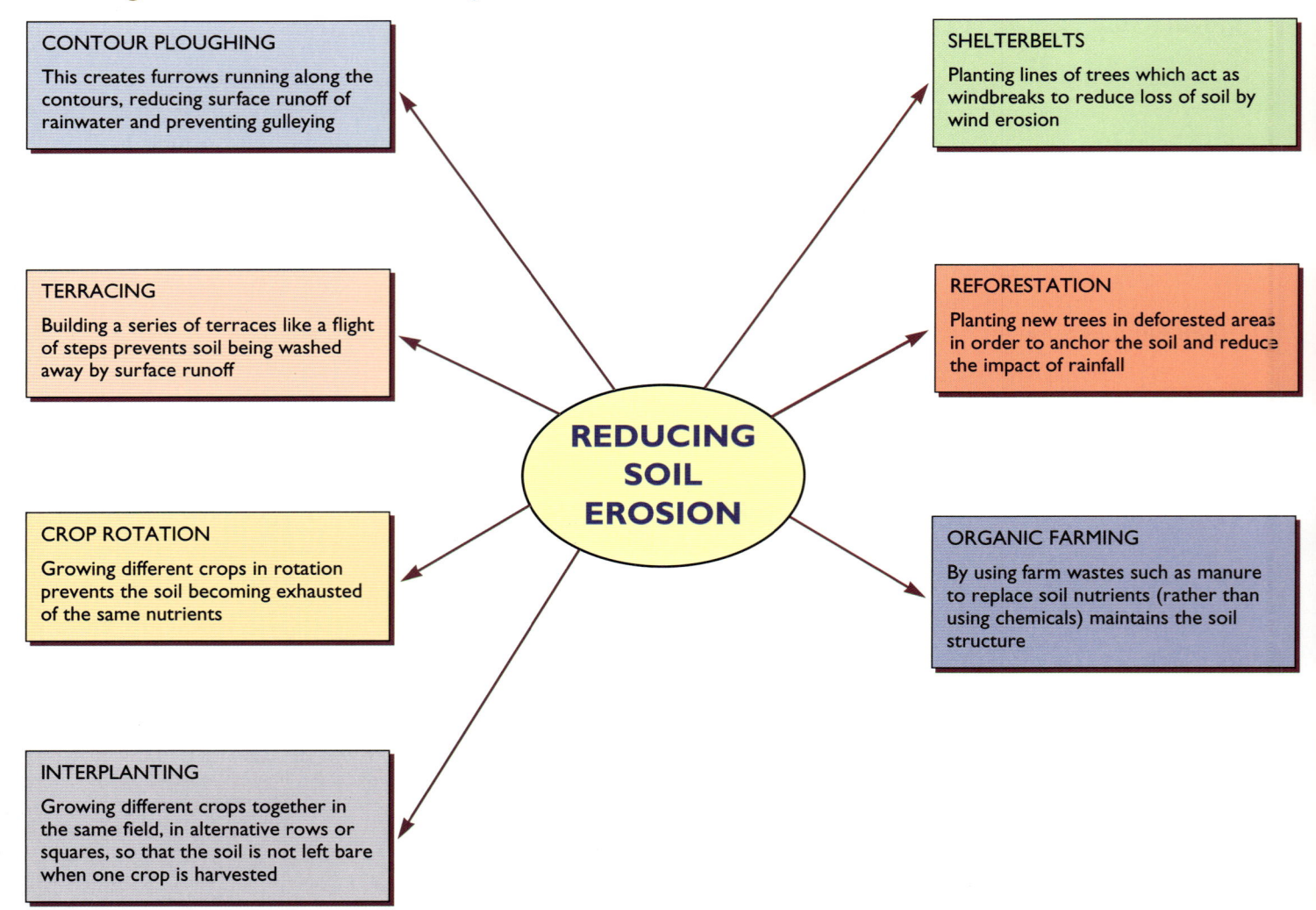

Figure 10.10 Methods of reducing soil erosion

REDUCING SOIL EROSION

CONTOUR PLOUGHING
This creates furrows running along the contours, reducing surface runoff of rainwater and preventing gulleying

SHELTERBELTS
Planting lines of trees which act as windbreaks to reduce loss of soil by wind erosion

TERRACING
Building a series of terraces like a flight of steps prevents soil being washed away by surface runoff

REFORESTATION
Planting new trees in deforested areas in order to anchor the soil and reduce the impact of rainfall

CROP ROTATION
Growing different crops in rotation prevents the soil becoming exhausted of the same nutrients

ORGANIC FARMING
By using farm wastes such as manure to replace soil nutrients (rather than using chemicals) maintains the soil structure

INTERPLANTING
Growing different crops together in the same field, in alternative rows or squares, so that the soil is not left bare when one crop is harvested

64 Change in the Physical Environment

Figure 10.11 Burkino Faso levelling tube

> 7. Design a pamphlet for farmers in Britain alerting them to the dangers of soil erosion, how it can be caused and the methods they should adopt to prevent it.
> 8. Use an atlas to describe the type of climate shared by the northern areas of Sudan and Burkina Faso.

Natural vegetation

Figure 10.12 shows the natural vegetation regions of the earth. These are the types of vegetation which would dominate the regions if humans had not interfered. Vegetation is closely linked with climate. It is a two-way relationship – climate influences the type of vegetation which, in turn, may influence the climate. For

Figure 10.12 A map of the world's natural vegetation

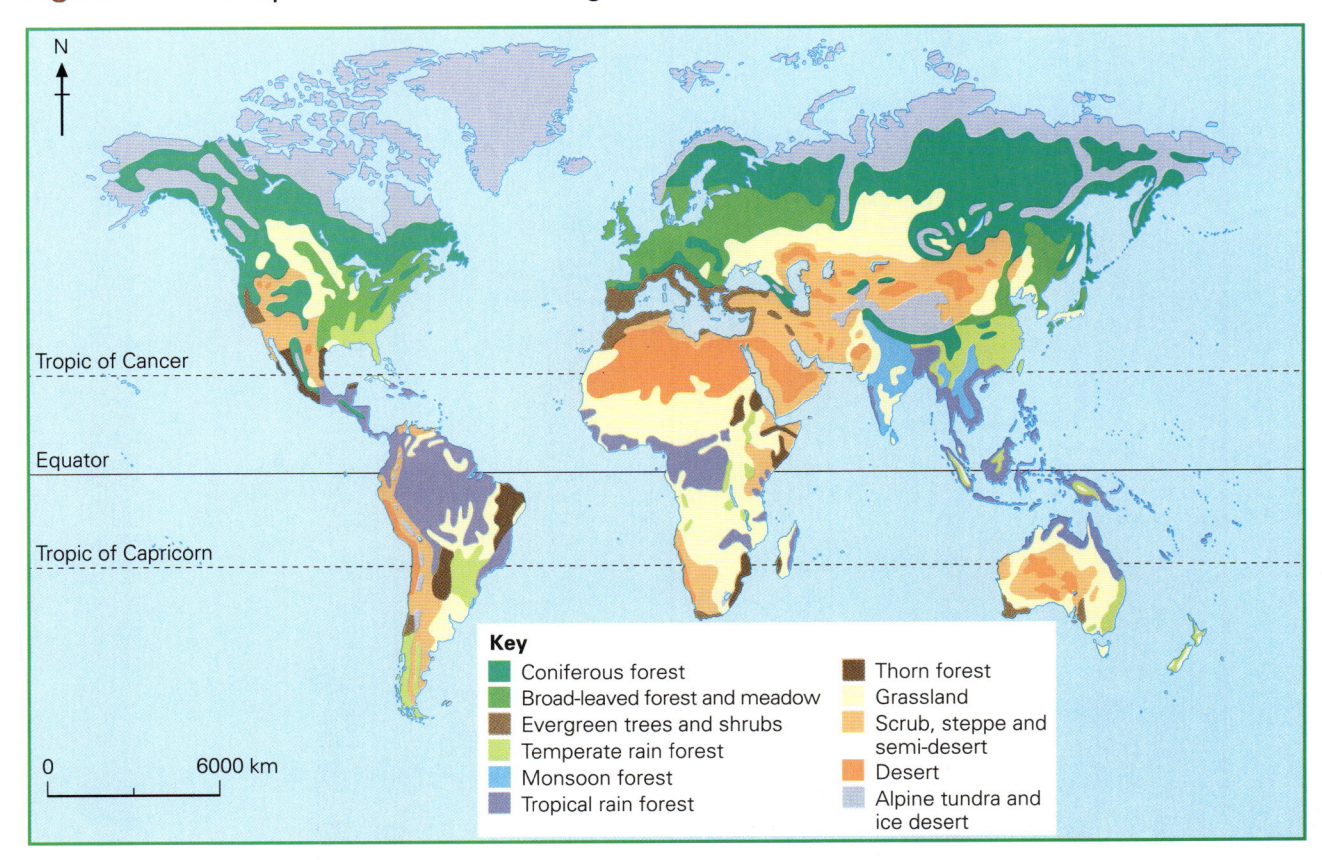

Key
- Coniferous forest
- Broad-leaved forest and meadow
- Evergreen trees and shrubs
- Temperate rain forest
- Monsoon forest
- Tropical rain forest
- Thorn forest
- Grassland
- Scrub, steppe and semi-desert
- Desert
- Alpine tundra and ice desert

Weathering and soils 65

example, forests add moisture to the atmosphere and can increase rain fall levels.

Evidence of human interference is apparent everywhere. The British Isles are shown on Figure 10.12 as part of the region of broadleaf deciduous forest. However, since 3000 BC or earlier the inhabitants of the British Isles have been clearing the forests so that today only tiny remnants of the natural vegetation survive in remote and isolated places. The forests which cover about 9 per cent of the British Isles are almost entirely planted by humans, either by the Forestry Commission as a crop or by landowners to serve local needs or simply to enhance their estates.

The process of forest clearance which deprived Britain of its natural vegetation is now being repeated in the equatorial rainforests, as described in Chapter 21.

Figure 10.13 The savanna landscape of Kenya showing grassland, acacia trees and wildlife

The vegetation of the savannas

Figure 10.13 shows an area of savanna grassland in Kenya. This beautiful parkland vegetation covers much of the earth's surface between the equatorial rainforests and the hot deserts.

The savanna climate poses special problems for plants (Figure 10.14) but the plants of the savanna have adapted to suit the climatic conditions. The dominant type of vegetation is grass, which is suitable for a savanna climate because:

- its narrow stems and blades lose little water from their surfaces, enabling the grasses to survive the long dry season;
- its narrow stems and blades also offer little resistance to strong winds, so that the plant is not broken by the wind;
- during the wet season it grows much more quickly than shrubs or trees;
- the light seeds are carried long distances by the wind.

Figure 10.14 Climate statistics for Tamale, Ghana

The tallest variety of grass in the savanna is elephant grass, which can grow to a height of over 4 m. Probably the most remarkable plant of the savanna is the baobab tree (Figure 10.15). Its trunk can be up to 8 m in diameter and the baobab's thick bark and its wood act like a sponge, storing water. The baobab is tough enough to survive the fires which often sweep the savanna. Another common tree of the savanna is the acacia (Figure 10.13), which loses its leaves during the dry season in order to reduce water loss. The acacia has very long roots which penetrate deep into the soil to tap groundwater.

During the dry season, many of the trees lose their leaves, becoming bare and stark. The grasses dry out and become yellow and parched. The start of the wet season renews the grass growth. The shrubs and herbs blossom and leaves appear on the trees again. Bulbs and tubers, dormant during the dry season, sprout and flower.

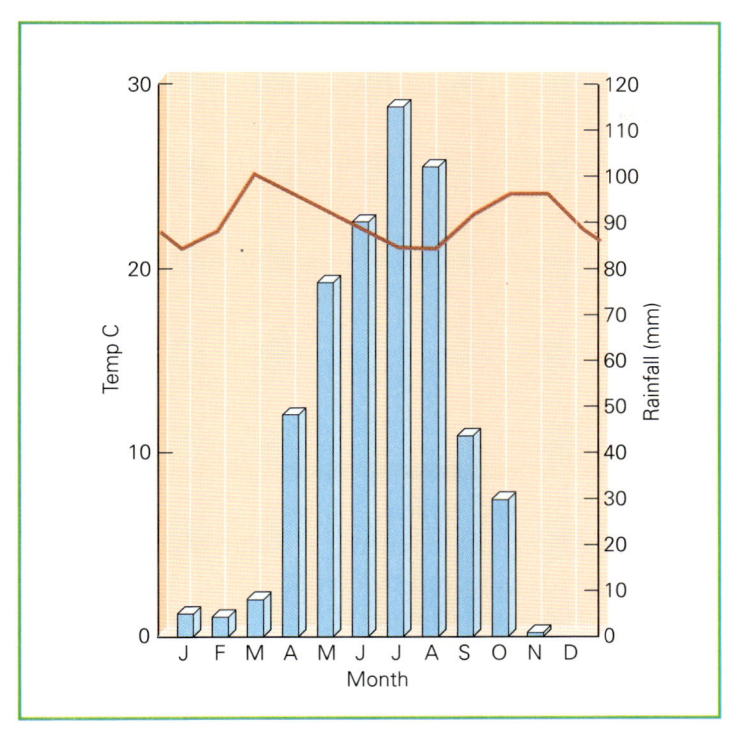

Figure 10.15 A baobab tree in Zimbabwe

Weathering and soils

The savanna climate becomes drier nearer the border with the hot desert. The grass cover is no longer continuous, shorter grasses grow in tussocks separated by patches of bare soil and trees and shrubs become much sparser.

9. (a) What is the natural vegetation of much of the British Isles?
   (b) Why is this type of vegetation now restricted to 'tiny remnants'?
10. (a) Study Figure 10.14. What are the main features of the savanna climate?
    (b) What problems does this climate pose for plants?
    (c) Give examples of how plants in the savanna have adapted to the climate.

Summary

- There are three types of weathering: mechanical, chemical, and biological.
- Limestone areas develop distinctive features because of chemical weathering.
- The world's natural vegetation has been greatly affected by human action.
- There is a two-way relationship between plants and climate.
- The plants of the savanna are specially adapted to withstand the long dry season.

11 Rivers

What is the hydrological cycle?
This unit studies the main components and links in the hydrological cycle, and examines the main features of river systems using an example from North Wales. The causes and effects of river floods are examined through case studies.

The hydrological cycle

Our planet's water system is known as the hydrological cycle (see Figure 11.1). Water circulates between the land, sea and air, and is stored in clouds, lakes, ice sheets and the oceans. Figure 11.2 shows that the oceans are by far the greatest store within the hydrological cycle, containing over 97 per cent of all the earth's water.

The hydrological cycle is self-contained. There are no major inputs or outputs. The amount of water within the cycle has been estimated as 1385 million km³. This sounds a vast amount of water, but, as Figure 11.2 shows, only a tiny fraction is available for human use.

> 1. What labels at points **a, b, c, d** and **e** would complete the systems diagram of the hydrological cycle in Figure 11.3?
> 2. Use Figure 11.3 to find the words which mean: (a) water seeping down into the soil and rocks; (b) water vapour turning to water droplets; (c) water moving through the soil; (d) water vapour given off by plants.
> 3. Study Figure 11.2. What percentage of the world's water is available for human use?

Figure 11.1 The hydrological cycle

Rivers 69

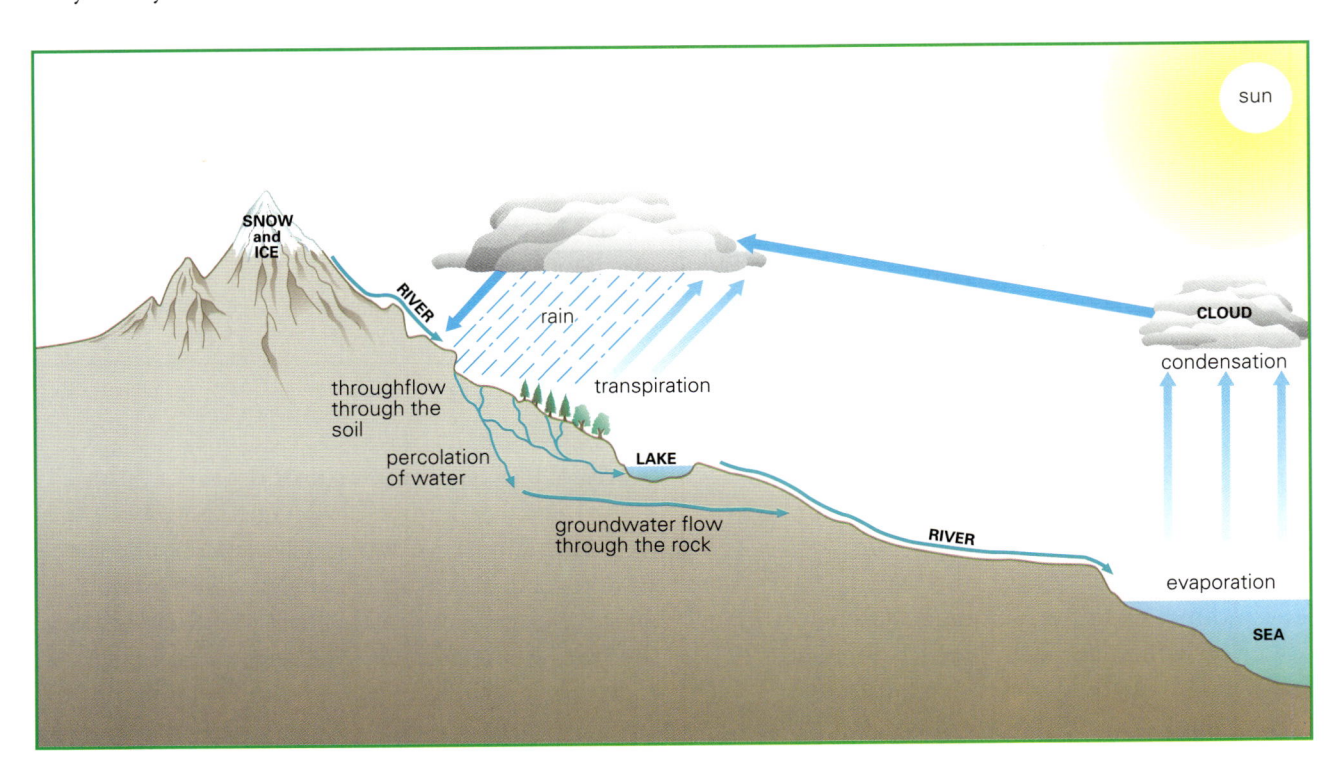

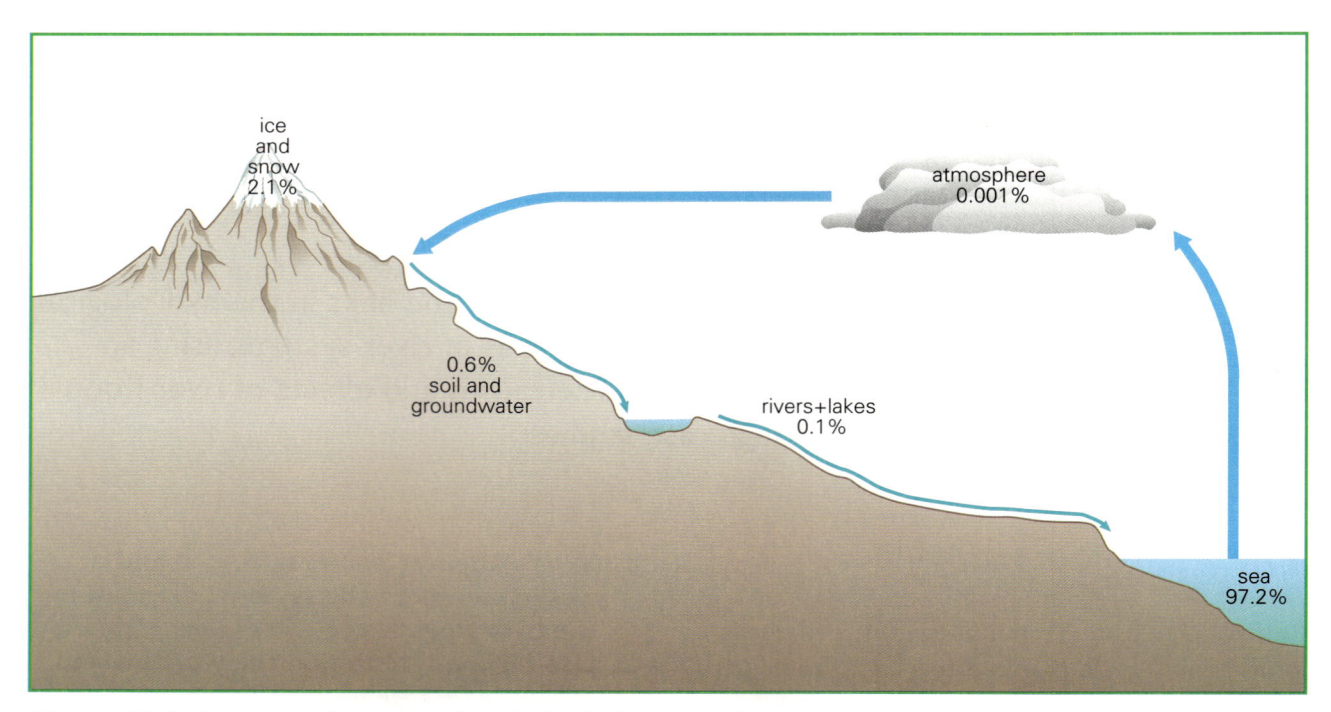

Figure 11.2 Amounts of water within the hydrological cycle

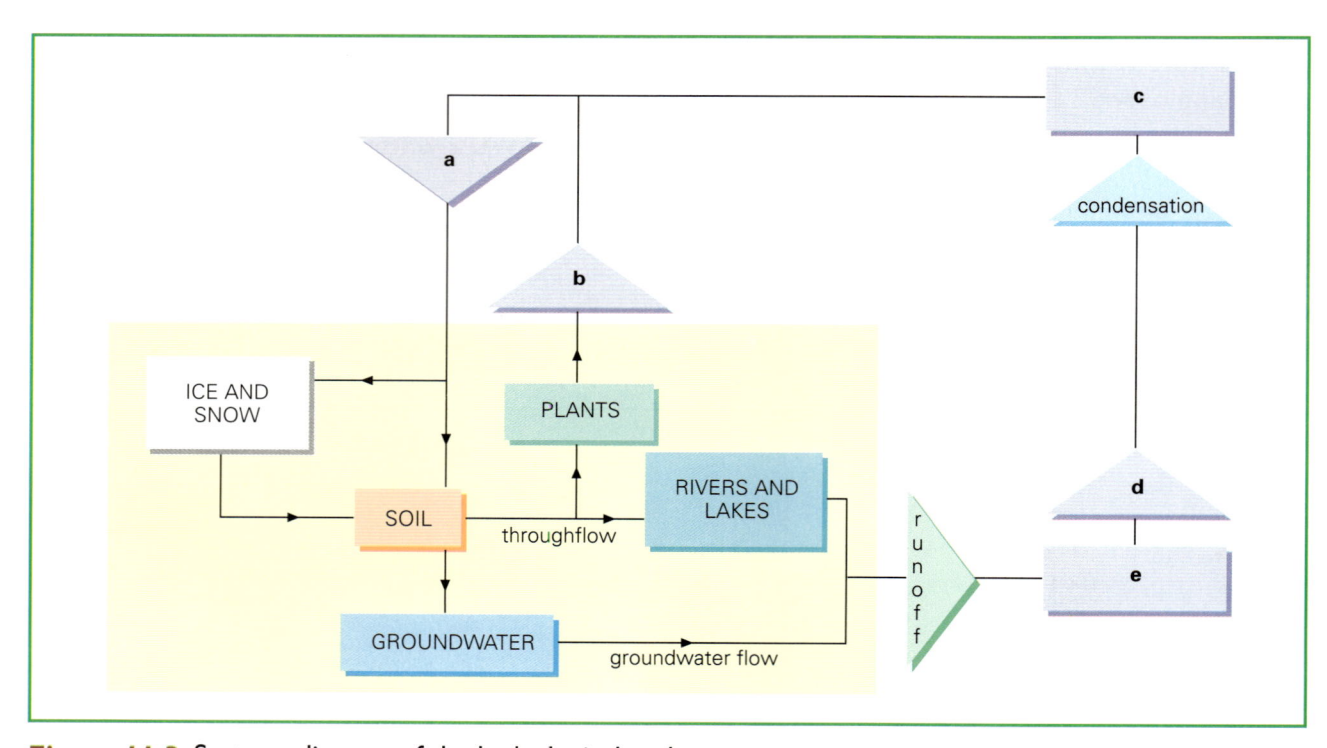

Figure 11.3 Systems diagram of the hydrological cycle

Rivers

The upper section

The mountains of Snowdon and Glyder Fawr tower over the narrow pass of Llanberis in Snowdonia, north Wales. At an altitude of nearly 400 m lies the source of the river Afon Nant Peris (see Figure 11.4). The channel of the river first appears in the marshy land beside the A4086 road, fed from numerous **rills** running down the steep mountainsides on either side of the pass. An average of 2500 mm of rain falls each year on these mountains and 80 per cent of

70 Change in the Physical Environment

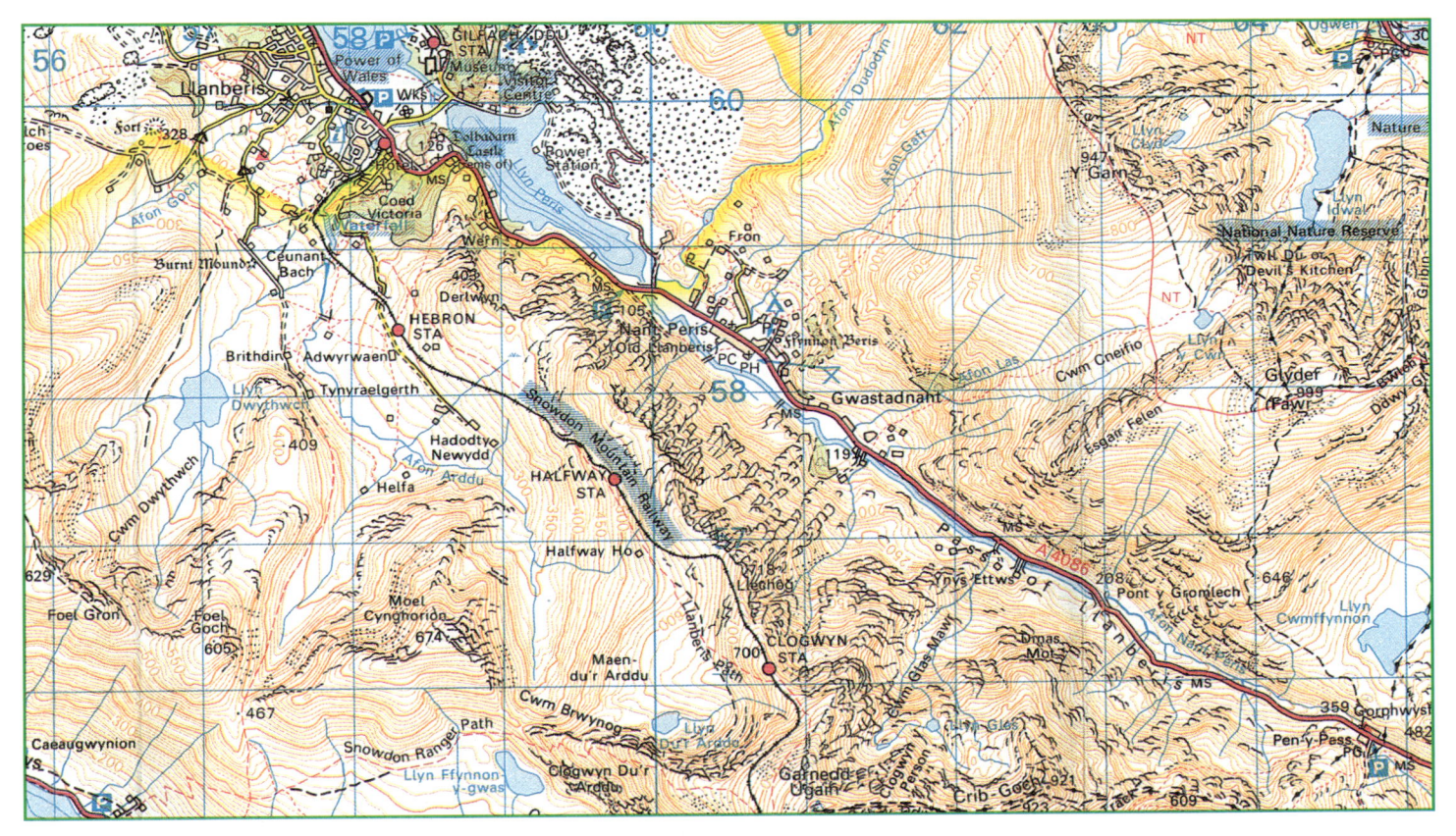

Figure 11.4 Ordnance Survey 1:50 000 map extract

it flows out along the river. This is a high percentage. In eastern England the percentage may be as low as 20 per cent.

Figure 11.5 shows the course of the Afon Nant Peris from its source to its mouth at Caernarvon on the Menai Strait. This is the longitudinal, or long, profile. As with most rivers the Afon Nant Peris has an uneven long profile. In some places it is steep, in others much less so.

The valley was glaciated during the Ice Age and two lakes occupy part of the valley. The labels in blue on Figure 11.5 show typical features of a river's long profile. We can use Afon Nant Peris as a model to compare with the long profiles of other rivers.

Figures 11.7–11.11 on pages 72–3 plot the statistics about the Afon Nant Peris from Figure 11.6.

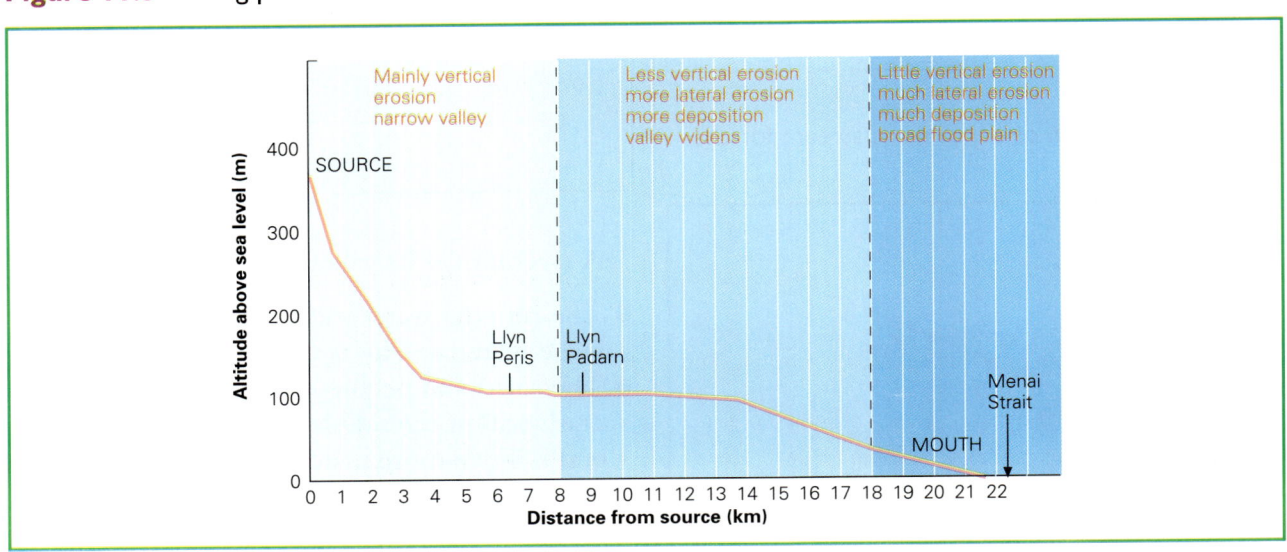

Figure 11.5 A long profile of the Afon Nant Peris

Rivers 71

Figure 11.6 Statistics for the Afon Nant Peris

Site	Width (m)	Depth (m)	Velocity (m/s)	Discharge (cumecs)	Angle (°)
1	2.7	0.33	0.174	0.155	5
2	3.12	0.13	0.137	0.056	4
3	6.8	0.21	0.41	0.59	3
4	7.1	0.25	0.743	1.32	3
5	8.1	0.36	0.833	2.43	2.5
6	8.3	0.44	0.865	3.16	2.0

As it flows down the pass, the channel of the Afon Nant Peris widens and deepens. The river erodes the rocks of its valley floor, transporting the debris and later depositing it elsewhere. The amount of erosion depends upon the speed of water flow, the amount of material carried and the type of rock over which the river flows. Soft rocks are eroded much more quickly than strong and resistant rocks.

Figure 11.7 Graph of downstream width of Afon Nant Peris

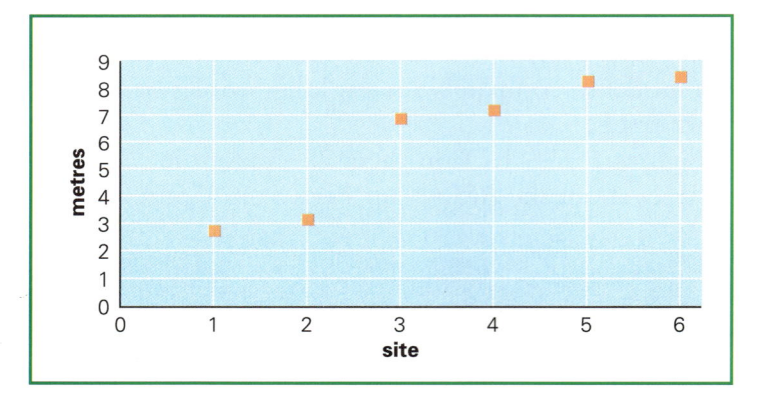

Figure 11.8 Graph of depth downstream for the Afon Nant Peris

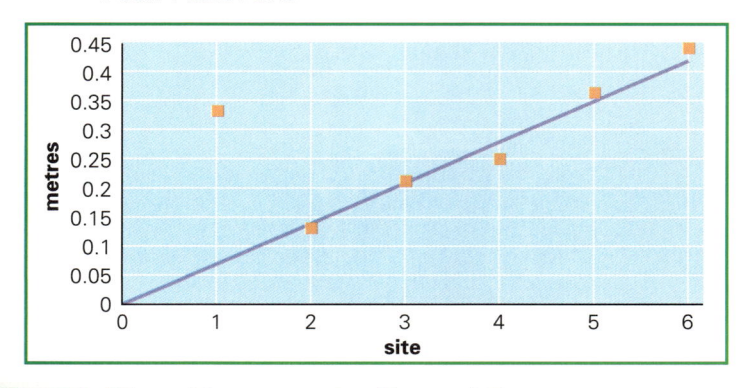

Figure 11.9 Graph of velocity downstream for the Afon Nant Peris

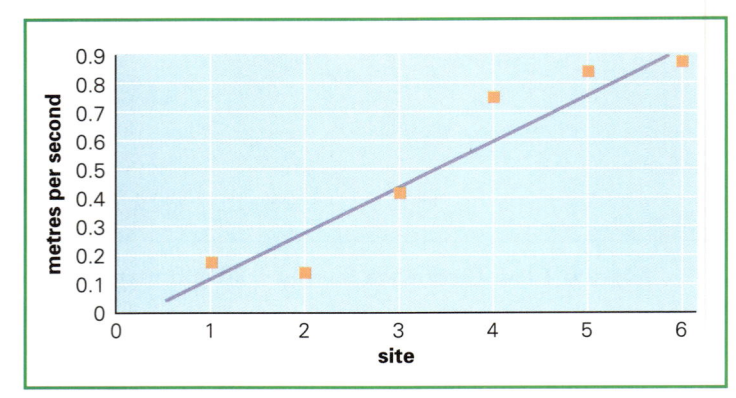

Figure 11.10 Graph of discharge downstream for the Afon Nant Peris

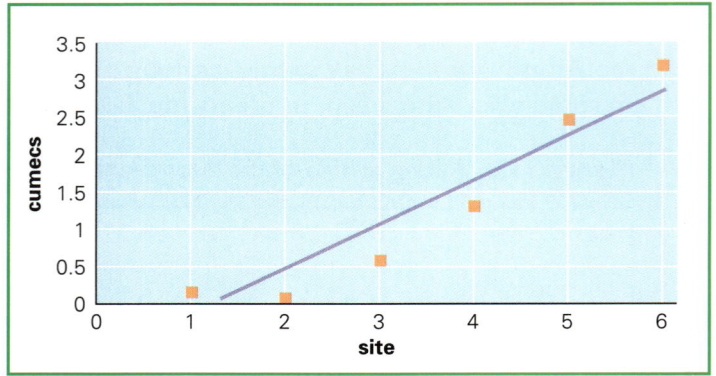

A river erodes its valley in several ways.

- The running water itself may carry away the loose material. This is called hydraulic action.
- The rocks and pebbles carried by the river crash against the sides and bed of the channel and remove more material. This is called corrasion.

Change in the Physical Environment

Figure 11.11 The Afon Nant Peris river, Snowdonia, in its upper stage

- The rocks and pebbles carried by the river crash into each other and break up into smaller fragments. This is called attrition.
- The water can dissolve the minerals in some rocks, for example the calcium carbonate in chalk and limestone. This is called solution.

Most of the time, little erosion actually occurs. It is during times of flood that most erosion happens. The increased input of water means that the river has much more energy. The discharge will greatly increase and the river will be able to carry much more material. Even large boulders can be swept along, crashing against the bed and banks of the channel. As the river loses energy, the flood subsides and much material is deposited by the river (deposition).

Figure 11.11 shows the Afon Nant Peris in its upper or torrent stage. The valley sides are very steep and the river's course is not straight. It flows around interlocking spurs of higher land, eroding rapidly downwards and transporting large amounts of material down river.

> 4. (a) What percentage of the rainfall in:
> (i) Snowdonia; and (ii) eastern England, runs off in the rivers?
> (b) Why do these two values differ so greatly?

The valley section

Figure 11.12 shows the Afon Nant Peris flowing across a broad area of flat land called the flood plain. The river's course is marked by a series of curves called meanders. Figure 11.13 shows how the main force of the river's flow is concentrated on the outside of the meander. Erosion is therefore greatest on the outside of the meander. On the inside of the meander the water is shallower and slower moving, so some deposition takes place.

Figure 11.12 The Afon Nant Peris river, Snowdonia, in its middle (valley) section

Figure 11.13 How meanders develop

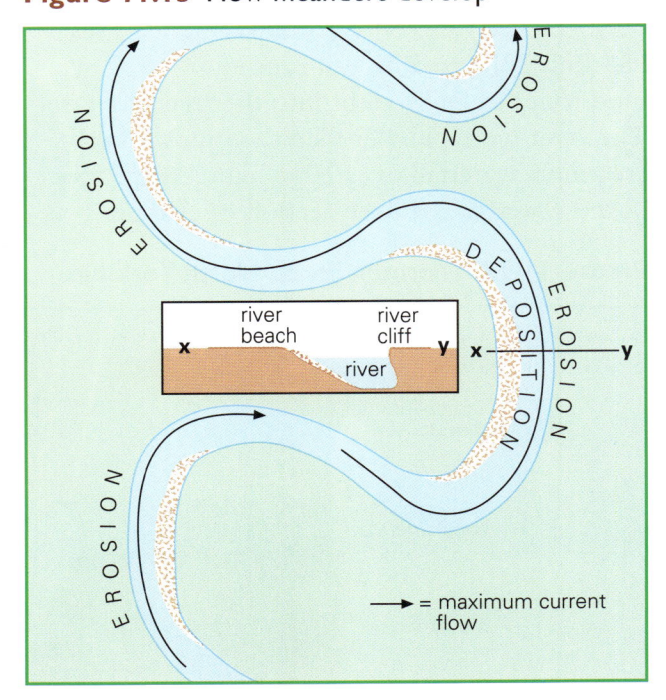

Rivers 73

In its valley stage, the river is in a state of balance. The input of water and sediment equals the output of water and sediment. There is deposition as well as erosion in this section, but the deposition is only temporary. Sooner or later the sediment will be eroded and transported further down river. Although the gradient of the river is much less in the valley section than in the upper section, the river's velocity is greater because the increased depth of the river creates less friction between the water and the channel's bed. The river's discharge also increases greatly (see Figures 11.6 and 11.10).

The Afon Nant Peris flows through two lakes in its middle section. The valley has a very shallow gradient here because of the over-deepening caused by the glacier which filled the valley during the Ice Age.

A series of tributary streams flow down the valley sides to join the Afon Nant Peris. The steep valley sides are the result of glacial erosion which has left several hanging valleys high above the main valley floor. The streams cascade down to the Afon Nant Peris in a series of small waterfalls. Some rivers have much more dramatic waterfalls along their length. Figure 11.14 shows Thornton Force, a waterfall on the River Greta in North Yorkshire. This waterfall has been caused by faulting, where the rock has been cracked by great earth movements. This has shifted the rock layers, causing softer mudstones to be brought into the river's course. The river has rapidly eroded the mudstones, creating a waterfall over 10 m high. At the foot of the waterfall is a deep section of channel

Figure 11.14 Thornton Force waterfall in North Yorkshire

called the plunge pool. The waterfall has an overhang at the top (see Figure 11.15) caused by water splashing back on to the softer mudstones and eroding them. The mudstones have been

Figure 11.15 Thornton Force, North Yorkshire

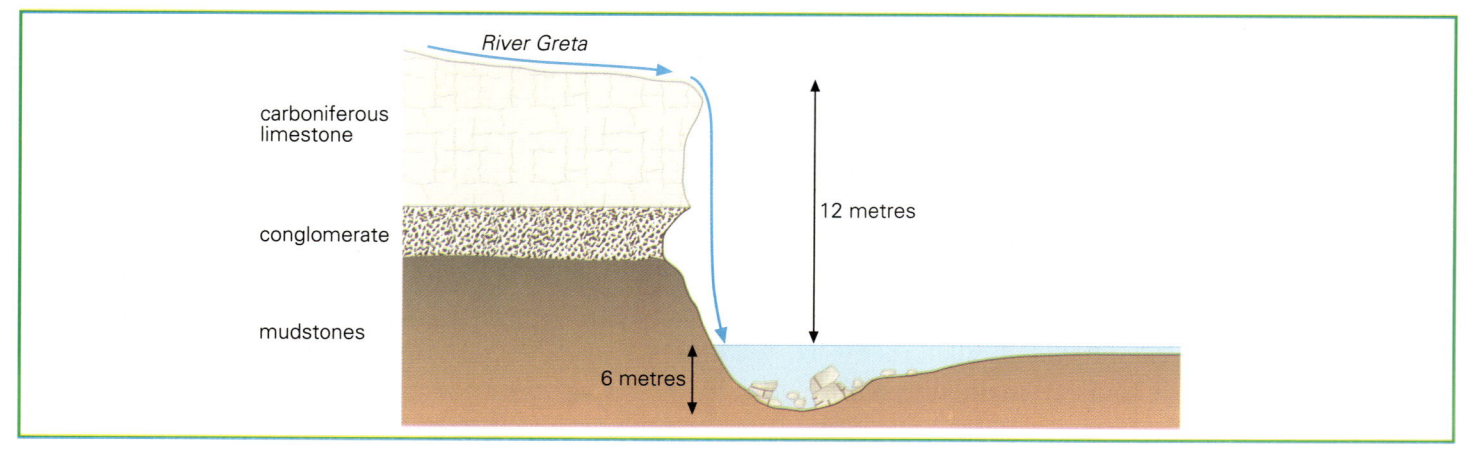

74 Change in the Physical Environment

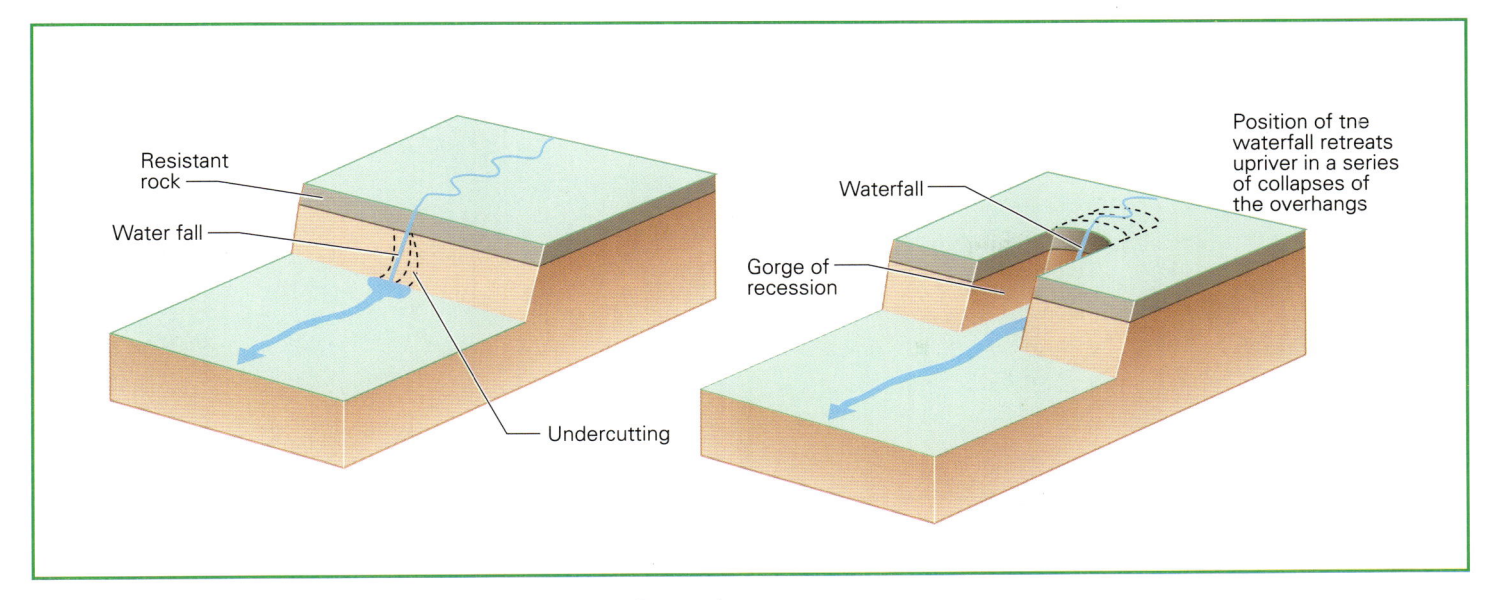

Figure 11.16 How a gorge of recession is formed

eroded back so far that it is possible to walk behind the waterfall and look at the curtain of falling water. Eventually this overhanging rock will collapse into the plunge pool. The undercutting will then start again. A series of such collapses causes the position of the waterfall to move slowly upstream. A narrow, steep-sided gorge of recession is left (see Figure 11.16).

5. **Study the Ordnance Survey 1:50 000 map extract (Figure 11.4, page 71).**
   (a) Give the six figure grid reference for the source of the Afon Nant Peris.
   (b) What building is close to the source?
   (c) Name the tributary which joins the Afon Nant Peris at GR 613577.
   (d) What boundary does the Afon Nant Peris cross at GR 599587?
   (e) How long is the course of the river from its source until it enters Llyn Peris?
   (f) How deep is Llyn Padarn?
6. **Which of the following descriptions apply to: (a) a meander; (b) a flood plain; (c) a plunge pool; (d) an overhang; (e) a gorge of recession?**
   (i) A deep section of channel at the foot of a waterfall.
   (ii) Water splashing back has eroded the softer rocks and left the stronger rock above.
   (iii) A bend in a river's course.
   (iv) A narrow, deep, steep-sided section of the valley formed by the retreat of the site of the waterfall.
   (v) A broad area of flat land on either side of a river, formed by the river's lateral erosion and deposition.

The lower section

Below Brynrefail the valley long profile steepens again in a second concave section. Now known as the Afon Selant, the river meanders across a broad flood plain east of Caernarfon before entering the sea of the Menai Strait. In its final kilometres the river is so close to sea level that the process of vertical erosion has almost stopped. Velocity and discharge are now at their maximum (see Figures 11.6, 11.9 and 11.10).

Over hundreds of years rivers in their lower section may change course as meanders are cut off to form ox-bow lakes (Figure 11.17, page 76). The ox-bow lakes will eventually fill with sediment and dry up.

The mouth of the Afon Selant is quite narrow, but many British rivers enter the sea through broad tidal inlets called *estuaries*. Estuaries have large areas of mudflats which are exposed at low tide. The lower reaches of some rivers have been drowned by a rise in sea level. A drowned river valley is called a *ria*, an

Rivers 75

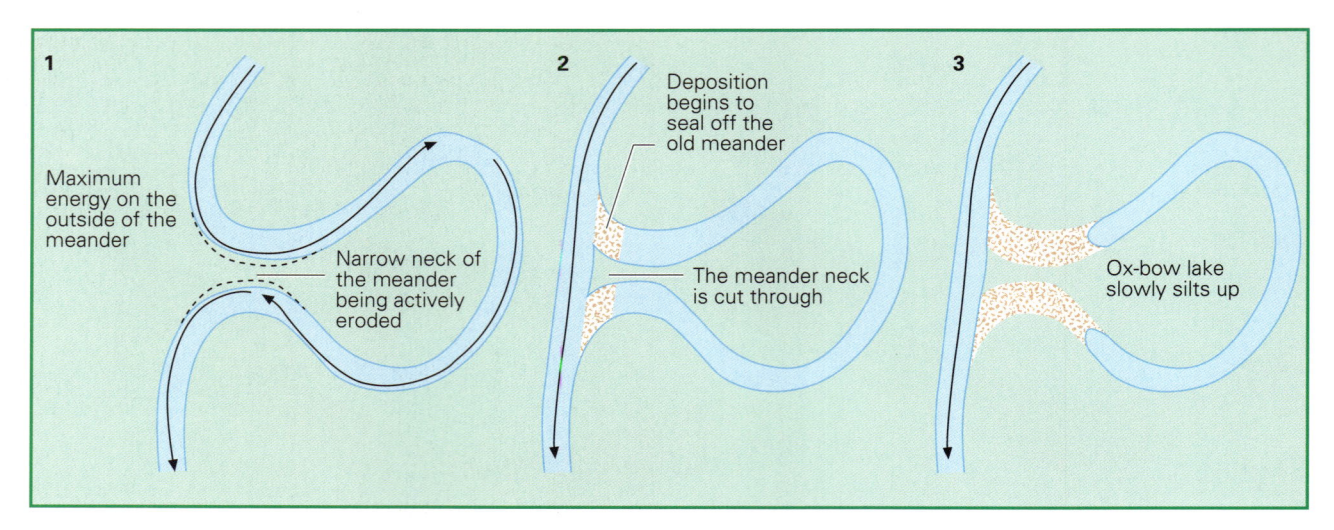

Figure 11.17 How ox-bow lakes form

Figure 11.18 The Lynmouth disaster

example of which is the River Tamar at Plymouth. The sea runs inland along the former river valley, forming a narrow, deep sea inlet. In south east England such drowned river valleys are called creeks.

> 7. Study Figure 11.5 on page 71. How far does the river descend: (a) over its first 4 km; (b) over its last 4 km? How do you explain the difference?

Floods

The Lynmouth flood

Sometimes the circulation of water within the hydrological system increases locally. Heavy rain may cause rivers to burst their banks and flood. On 16 August 1952 the village of Lynmouth in North Devon was the scene of Britain's worst river flood disaster this century. Figure 11.18 tells the story.

The flood killed 34 people and caused £150 million damage. Why did such a disaster happen? The answer lies in a combination of the landscape of the area and the weather. As Figure 11.19 shows, the East and West Lyn are short rivers which flow north from Exmoor to the Bristol Channel. They flow in steep, narrow valleys called gorges and they join at Lynmouth. The period before the flood had been wet. It had rained for 12 out of the previous 14 days. The ground was waterlogged. No more rain could infiltrate into the thin soils which cover

> Down these gorges on that terrible night pounded millions of tonnes of flood water. At times, a solid wall of water nearly 15 metres high raced down to the sea at 30 kilometres per hour. The water gouged out huge rocks and boulders – some weighing 15 tonnes – and carried them to the shore. Telegraph poles and motor cars followed. Trees were swept into the sea. The next morning, over half a kilometre out to sea, hundreds of trees, presumably weighted down by rocks and soil entangled in their enormous roots, had their upper branches showing above the waves – a fantastic sea forest of stunted trees.
>
> The flood waters dug deep into the earth. Road surfaces were scoured away. The Lynmouth sewerage system and water mains were wrecked.
>
> When dawn broke the scene on the shore was fantastic. It was littered with the debris of scores of wrecked homes and buildings; smashed cars; telegraph poles; tree trunks, branches and complete trees; some 200 000 cubic metres of silt, mud, gravel and stones, in some places massed over 8 metres high; some 40 000 tonnes of rocks and boulders; iron girders and bridges; broken masonry; and the bodies of animals, birds, fish – and people.

Change in the Physical Environment

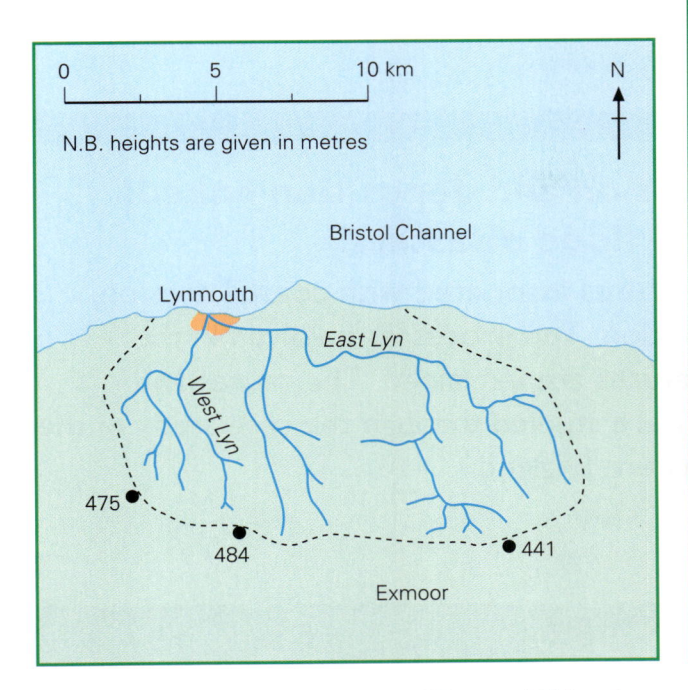

Figure 11.19 Drainage basin of East and West Lyn Rivers

Figure 11.20 Damage following the flood in Lynmouth, North Devon, August 1952

the hard, impermeable sandstone and slate rocks of Exmoor. On the day of the flood, it rained extraordinarily hard. Normal steady rain for 24 hours measures about 25 mm in a range gauge. At Lynmouth, 230 mm of rain fell on 15 August 1952, although higher rain fall figures have been recorded in Britain in the past 100 years.

Whilst the Lynmouth flood was a tragic event, it was small-scale compared to some flood disasters. For example, during the twentieth century over 300 000 people have been drowned by the flood waters of the Yangtze river in China.

12. (a) Where is Lynmouth?
    (b) When did the flood disaster occur?
13. (a) Approximately how long are the East and West Lyn rivers?
    (b) How did (i) the landscape of the area; and (ii) the weather contribute to the flood disaster?
14. You are a newspaper reporter visiting Lynmouth a few hours after the flood. Write an article to describe and explain the flood for your readers; include eyewitness accounts and your own observations.
15. Use a library to help you discover the techniques which have been developed to prevent river flooding. The use of embankments and channel straightening are examples of channel modifications; afforestation is an example of flood abatement; floodproofing of buildings is an example of flood adjustment; find out the meanings of these terms and provide other examples.

Summary

- Water is transferred between the sea, air and land in a system called the hydrological cycle.
- Conditions can sometimes cause rivers to flood with disastrous consequences for people and their property.

Rivers

Chapter 12 Coasts

How are coastal erosion and deposition linked? What causes coastal flood disasters?

This unit examines the features associated with coastal erosion, transportation and deposition. The processes involved in the development of these features are explained. The causes and effects of coastal flooding are studied through the case study of the 1953 flood disaster in Eastern England.

Coastal erosion

The Atlantic waves shown in Figure 12.1 are crashing against the Cornish coast with a pressure of up to 30 tonnes per square metre. Loose or weakened rock is washed away from the cliffs. The waves can also compress air into cracks and joints in the cliff face. The compressed air is released with explosive energy as the water retreats, loosening even the strongest rocks. This process of erosion is called hydraulic action.

The sea erodes the land in three other ways:

- corrasion, in which the waves throw rocks and pebbles against the cliffs, wearing them away;
- attrition, which occurs as the rocks and pebbles crash against each other under water, wearing each other away;
- solution, the process by which the sea water, which is slightly acidic, dissolves some minerals within rocks, such as calcium carbonate in limestone.

Coastal erosion produces a number of features. Figure 12.2 shows the Foreland, a chalk headland near Swanage in Dorset. At one time the two islands, Handfast Point and Old Harry, were joined to the mainland. Erosion has created a series of landforms: caves, arches, stacks and wave-cut platforms. Figure 12.3 shows how they are formed. The rate of erosion largely

Figure 12.1 Cliffs in Cornwall under wave attack in a high wind

78 Change in the Physical Environment

Figure 12.2 The Pinnacles at Studland Bay, Dorset

depends upon the type of rock forming the coast. The Foreland's chalk is moderately resistant to erosion. The rocks forming the Cornish coast shown in Figure 12.1 are formed of much stronger granite. By contrast, the Holderness coast of East Yorkshire is composed of weak boulder clay which is easily eroded at a rate of over 2 m per year.

Coastal erosion threatens people's homes and property. Expensive coastal protection schemes attempt to halt the advance of the waves. Concrete sea walls line long stretches of our coasts. One of the oddest schemes for coastal protection is the proposal to build an artificial barrier reef made of 100 million old tyres off the coast of Holderness. The reef, 50 km long, 100 m wide and 5 m high, will reduce erosion and also help dispose of every old tyre in the north east of England, thus solving another environmental problem. If the scheme is a success it offers a cheap means of protecting vulnerable coasts throughout the world.

1. It has been stated that the rate of erosion largely depends upon the type of rock forming the coast. What other factors do you think may affect the rate of coastal erosion?
2. Study Figure 12.2.
   (a) What is the evidence that some parts of the rock are more resistant to erosion than other parts?
   (b) What evidence is there that the sea is actively eroding the headland?
   (c) Was the photograph taken at high or low tide? How can you tell?
   (d) Name all the features you can see in Figure 12.2. How has each of them been formed?

Figure 12.3 A cave, arch, stack and wave-cut platform

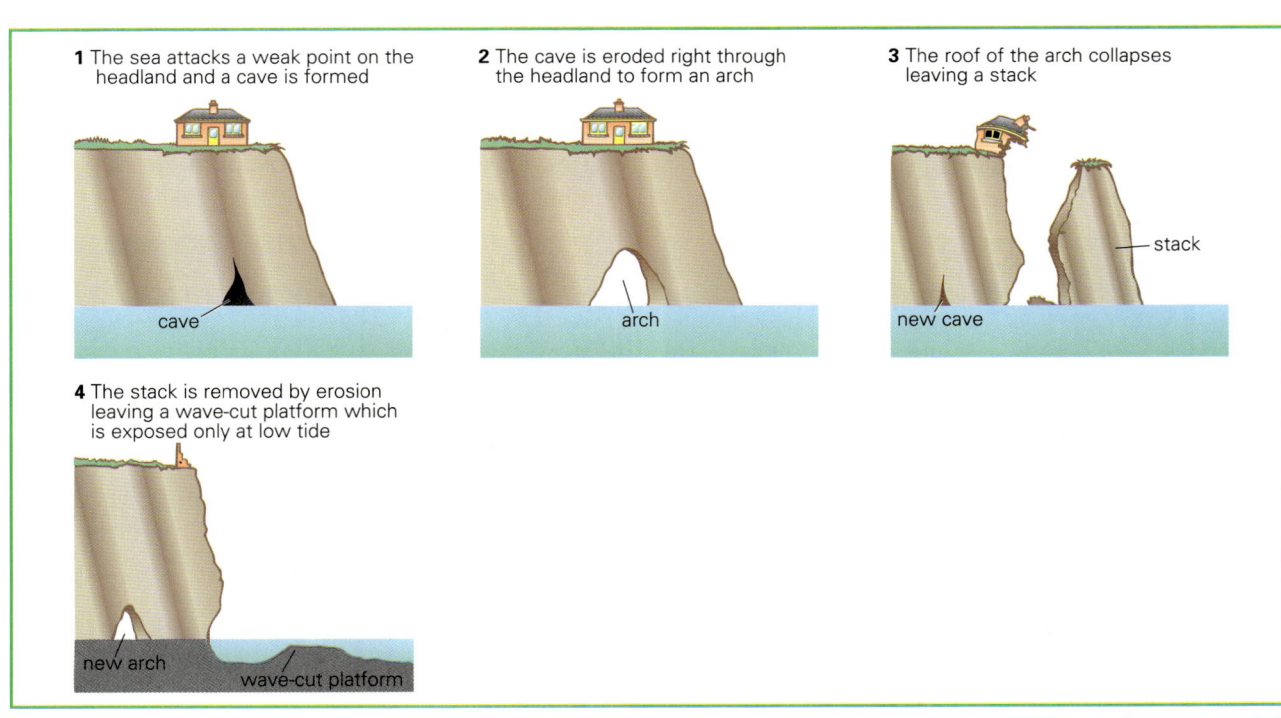

1 The sea attacks a weak point on the headland and a cave is formed — cave

2 The cave is eroded right through the headland to form an arch — arch

3 The roof of the arch collapses leaving a stack — new cave, stack

4 The stack is removed by erosion leaving a wave-cut platform which is exposed only at low tide — new arch, wave-cut platform

Coasts 79

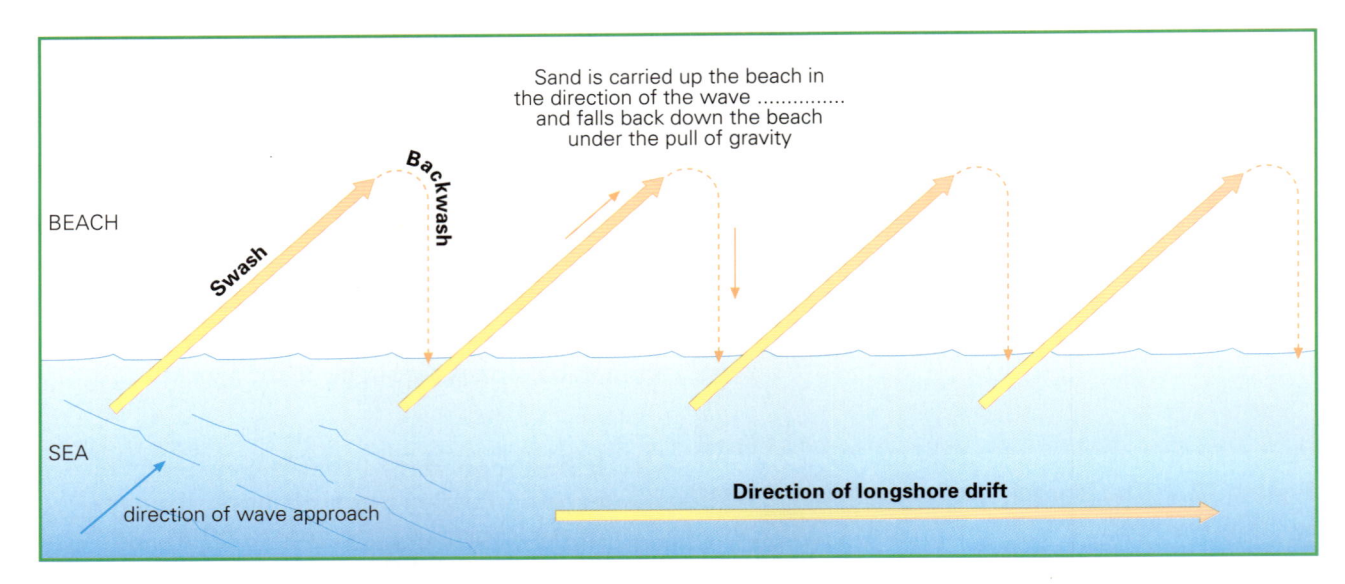

Figure 12.4 Longshore drift

Longshore drift

The rock eroded from the coast is moved along the shore by the action of waves in a process known as longshore drift (see Figure 12.4). Figure 12.5 shows a breakwater, or groyne, built across a beach at Mappleton on the East Yorkshire coast. It is clear that there is a large build-up of sand on one side of the groyne, and little on the other. At high tide there is no beach at all on the other side of the groyne. This is the result of longshore drift.

Longshore drift provides the link between erosion and deposition along the coast. Material eroded from one place is transported along the coast and deposited elsewhere.

Figure 12.5 A breakwater or groyne at Mappleton, East Yorkshire

Coastal deposition

Figure 12.6 shows an aerial view of Spurn Head. This 6 km ridge of sand and shingle extends nearly half way across the mouth of the Humber Estuary. Spurn Head is an example of a feature called a spit. The spit forms a sweeping curve which continues the line of the coast. The sand and shingle have been transported by the action of longshore drift from the north.

In some places, a spit may grow right across a bay to form a bar. An example is Slapton Sands in Devon, formed of flint shingle (see Figures 12.7 and 12.8). The stretch of water dammed up behind the bar is called a lagoon. The lagoon is

Figure 12.6 An aerial view of Spurn Head, Humberside

80   Change in the Physical Environment

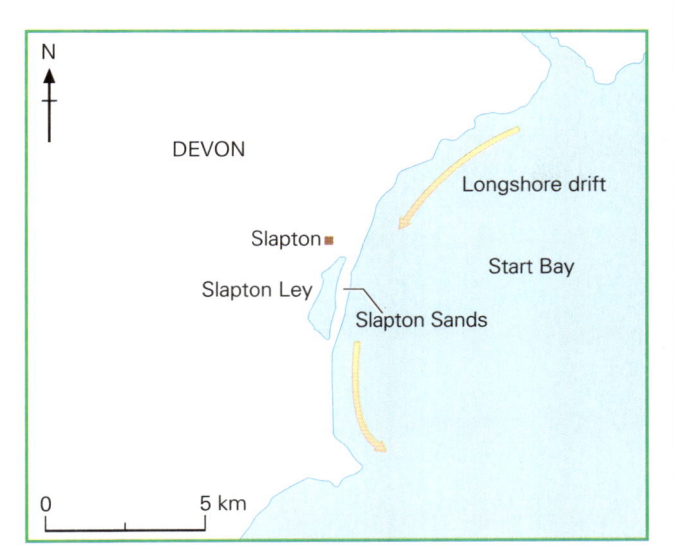

Figure 12.7 Slapton Sands, South Devon

Figure 12.8 Slapton Sands, South Devon and Slapton Ley

only a temporary feature in geological terms. In thousands of years it will be filled in by material deposited there by waves breaking over the bar or by rivers flowing into the lagoon. Sometimes a spit may grow out into the sea until it meets an island. In this case the landform is called a tombolo. Chesil Beach, which joins the south Dorset coast to the Isle of Purbeck, is an example of a tombolo (see Figures 12.9 and 12.10).

3. Describe the scene in Figure 12.5 and explain the appearance of the beach on either side of the groyne.
4. Copy and complete the table below listing some landforms of coastal erosion and deposition:

Landform	Description	Example and Location
Arch	A natural archway through a headland	Handfast Point, Dorset
Stack		
Spit		
Bar		
Tombolo		

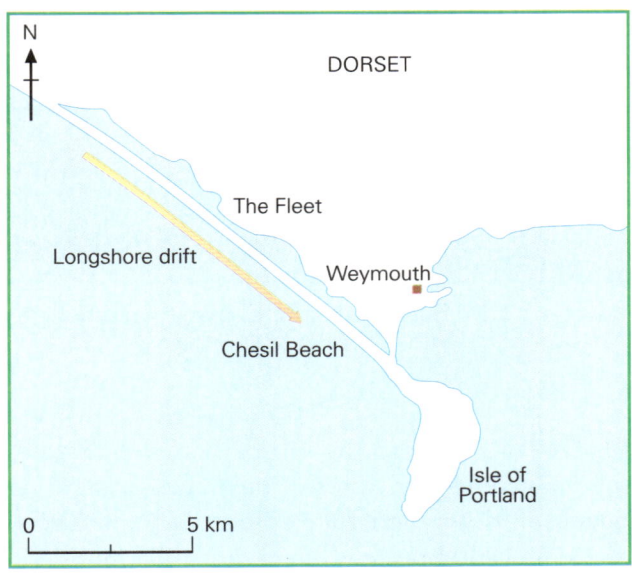

Figure 12.9 Chesil Beach, Dorset

Figure 12.10 Chesil Beach, Dorset

Coasts 81

Figure 12.11 Sunken Marsh, Canvey Island during the coastal floods of 31 January 1953

Coastal flooding

On 31 January 1953 the North Sea swept across the sea defences of eastern England flooding dozens of towns and villages from Lincolnshire to Kent. 1200 breaches of the sea wall were recorded. Three hundred and seven people were killed in England in the worst peace-time disaster in living memory (see Figure 12.11). On the opposite shore of the North Sea, over 1800 people were drowned in the Netherlands and Belgium. Hundreds more died at sea, including 132 drowned when the Stranraer to Larne ferry sank.

The cause of this disaster was a **storm surge** (see Figure 12.12). Hurricane-force north-westerly winds reaching 180 km per hour pushed more water from the Atlantic Ocean into the North Sea. The very low atmospheric pressure caused the sea to rise 60 cm higher than normal and the storm surge happened at the same time as high spring tides.

The sea level rose the most in the confined areas of estuaries. At Felixstowe and Harwich on the Orwell Estuary, over 50 people died. An estate of pre-fabricated houses at Felixstowe was swept away. In the Thames Estuary 130 were drowned, 58 of them at Canvey Island, which

Figure 12.12 How a storm surge produces coastal floods

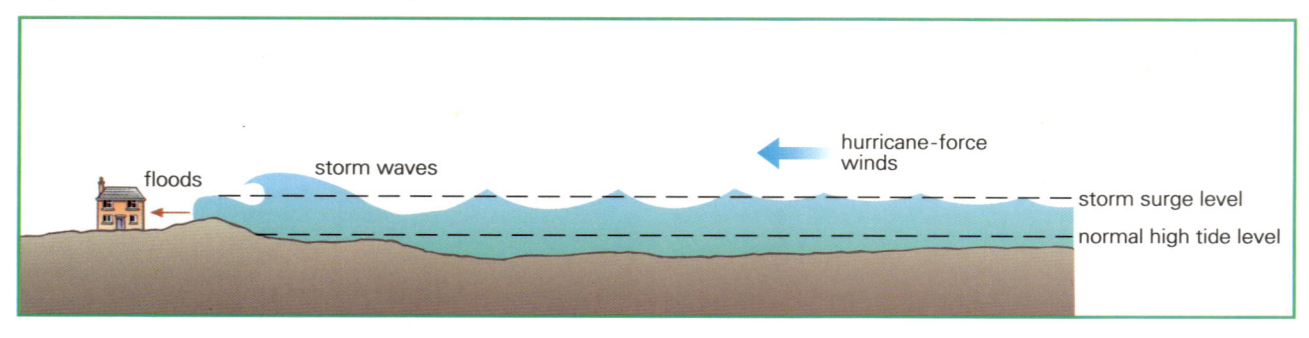

82 Change in the Physical Environment

was submerged. Houses were submerged under 4 m of water.

Each year, £120 million is spent throughout Britain on sea defences. Forty-two million of this is spent in eastern England. Seven hundred and fifty thousand people live below high tide level, protected by sea walls. Advanced computer modelling and better weather forecasting allow the National Rivers Authority (NRA) to operate a 24-hour flood warning system all year round from Peterborough. The police can be given 12 hours' warning of a red alert when the flood defences are threatened, and evacuation plans can be put into operation. On the River Thames the flood barrier can be raised.

The flood defences were raised along much of the coast after the 1953 disaster, but by the mid-1990s they were in need of replacement. However, the expensive concrete wall methods of the 1950s have given way to softer but more effective barriers. The importance of beaches and salt marshes in absorbing wave energy and preventing flooding is now recognised. Beaches are artificially heightened by dumping sand and shingle and sand traps are built offshore to build up the lower beach. For the first time, the Government has accepted a policy of strategic retreat from the coast – where the cost of defending land cannot be justified, it is abandoned to the sea.

5. **Using Figure 12.12 to help you, describe the causes and effects of a storm surge.**
6. **What were the effects of the 1953 flood disaster?**
7. **Discuss the possible measures which can be taken to prevent coastal flooding. Why has the approach changed since the 1950s?**

Summary

- Coastal erosion and deposition create many distinctive landforms. Longshore drift provides the links between erosion and deposition along the coast. Storm surges can bring disaster to coastal areas and threaten peoples' lives and property.

Coasts

13 Highland glaciation

How have glaciers affected the scenery of highland areas?

This unit discusses the Ice Age and examines the landscape features resulting from the glaciation of highland areas.

Ice sheets

Figure 13.1 shows a view of Earth from space. The view is dominated by Antarctica, a continent of ice. In places, the Antarctic **ice sheet** is over 4 km thick. Only a few mountain peaks rise above the icy wastes (see Figure 13.2).

Antarctica contains 90 per cent of the world's ice. Another 7 per cent is the Greenland ice sheet. Yet, in the earth's recent past, ice sheets spread across much of Europe, North America and northern Asia (see Figure 13.3), during a period called the **Ice Age**. It began about 3 million years ago and there have been over 20 advances and retreats of the ice sheets since then.

Figure 13.1 Satellite view of the earth from space, showing the southern polar area

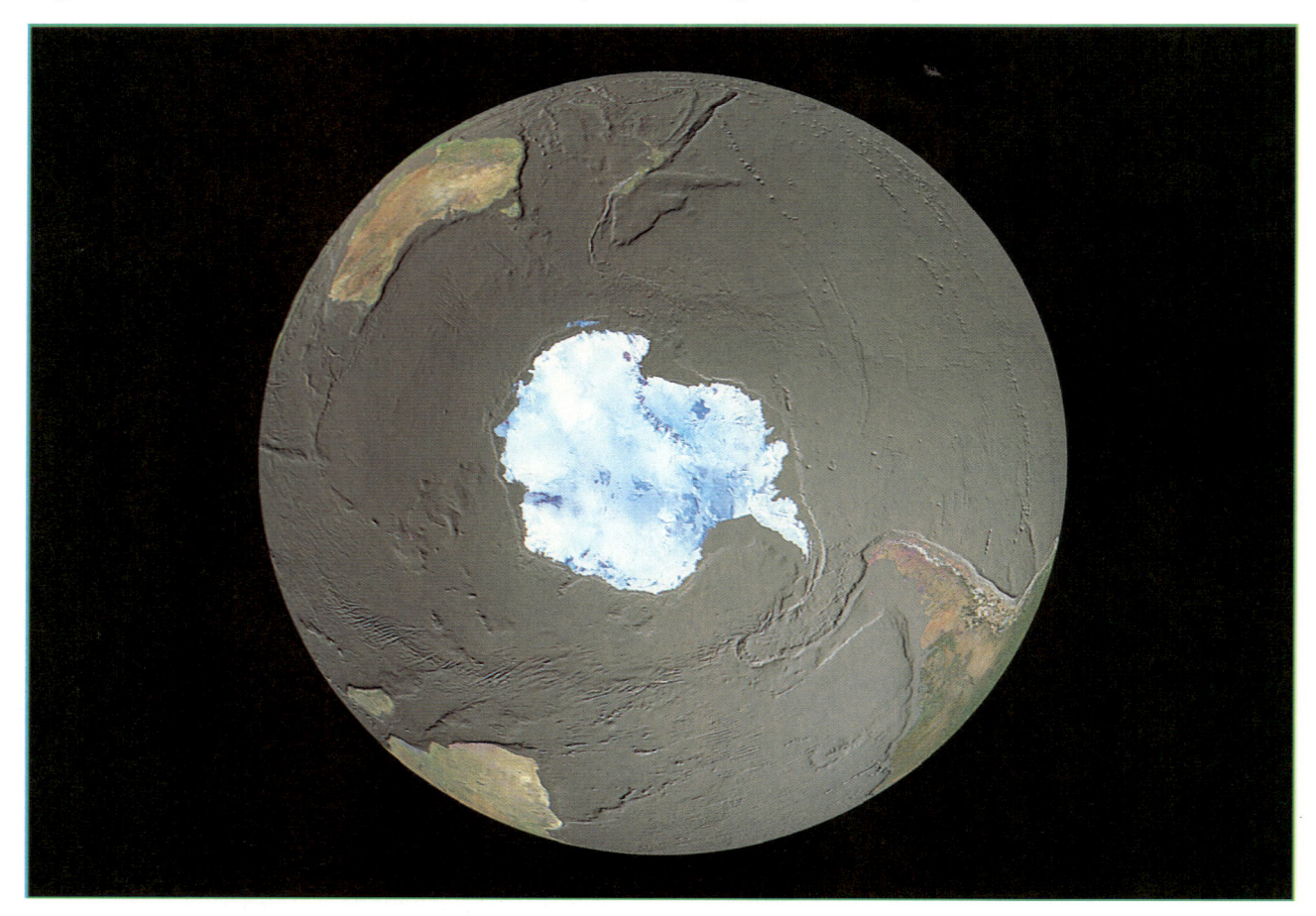

84 Change in the Physical Environment

Figure 13.2 Mountain peaks rising above the Antarctic ice sheet

Figure 13.3 The world's ice sheets

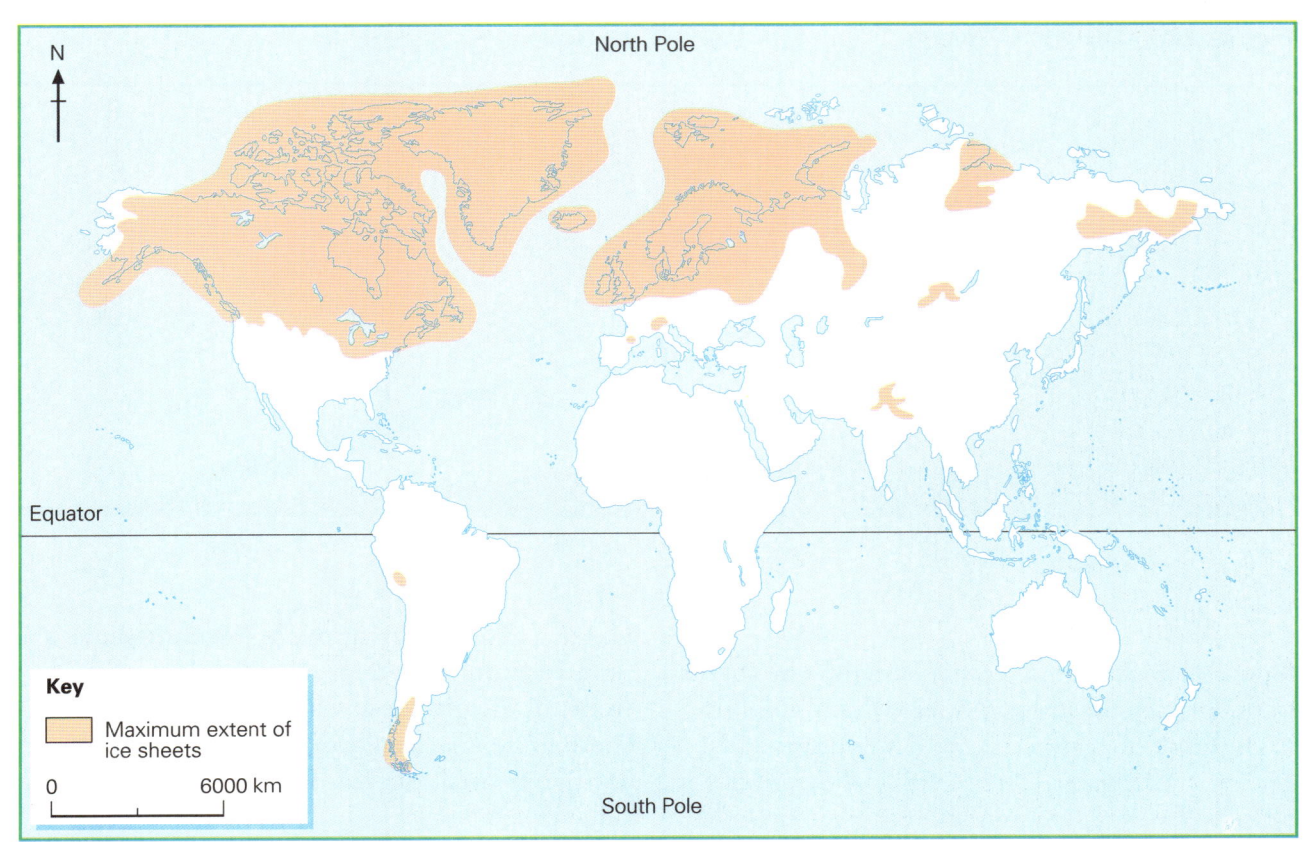

Key: Maximum extent of ice sheets

Highland glaciation 85

The Ice Age

The last glaciers melted in Britain about 10 000 years ago but the Ice Age has not ended, because ice sheets exist on the earth today. For most of the earth's history there have been no ice sheets at all and we know of only a few earlier ice ages, the most recent of which ended over 250 million years ago.

During the Ice Age, there have been many periods, called **interglacials**, when the ice retreated and the climate became warmer. Many scientists think that we are currently in an interglacial period. In previous interglacials, the temperature was higher and there was less ice around – 100 000 years ago hippopotamus and elephant lived as far north as Leeds! The earth is still a planet gripped by the Ice Age and one day the ice sheets may return to Britain.

Figure 13.4 shows a map of the Ice Age in Britain. Glaciers flowed out from ice centres in the mountains and joined to form ice sheets which, at their furthest extent, covered almost all of the British Isles.

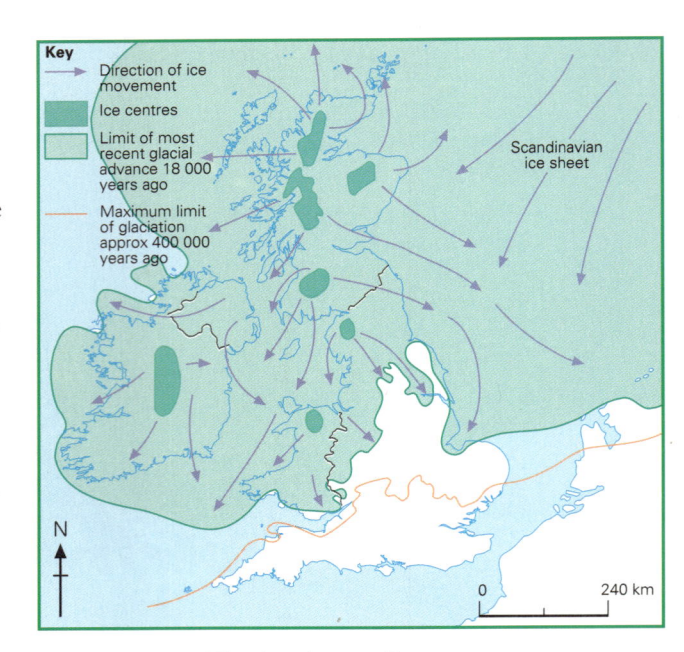

Figure 13.4 The Ice Age in Britain

1. Study Figure 13.4. With the aid of an atlas, name five ice centres in Ice Age Britain.
2. It is possible that, in the future, part or all of the Antarctic ice sheet could melt. What effects might this have on:
(a) Antarctica; (b) the world as a whole?

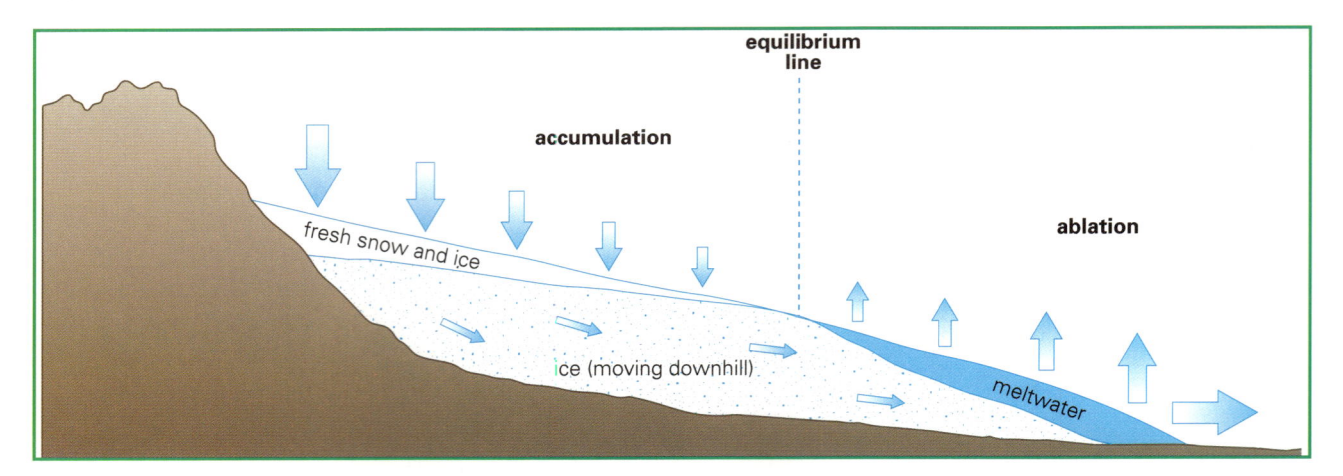

Figure 13.5 The glacier system

The glacier system

Figure 13.5 shows the glacier system. The inputs to the glacier are snow and ice, which build up in the zone of accumulation. The output of the glacier is meltwater. The melting of the glacier is called **ablation**. Accumulation is greatest in the winter when temperatures are lower. If there is more accumulation than ablation, the snout (front) of the glacier will advance, and vice versa. The Rhône Glacier, shown in Figure 13.6, has clearly retreated, since it occupied more of the valley in the past.

86 Change in the Physical Environment

Figure 13.6 The Rhône Glacier, Switzerland

Glacial erosion

The Rhône Glacier has carved out a deep valley, over 1 km wide. The glacial ice acts like a giant sheet of sandpaper as fragments of rock frozen into the ice scratch and polish the rock over which the glacier passes. This process is called abrasion. A glacier can also erode by the process of plucking, which occurs when the ice freezes on to rock which has been weakened by freeze–thaw action. As the glacier moves, it pulls away the rock.

Features of glacial erosion

Like most glaciers, the Rhône glacier's source is a large, circular hollow high on a mountainside, called a corrie, cwm or cirque (see Figure 13.7). Corries begin as much smaller hollows which fill with snow. The snow builds up, year by year, and the lower layers are compressed by the weight of the snow above. Air is forced out of the snow and it slowly turns to ice. Freeze–thaw

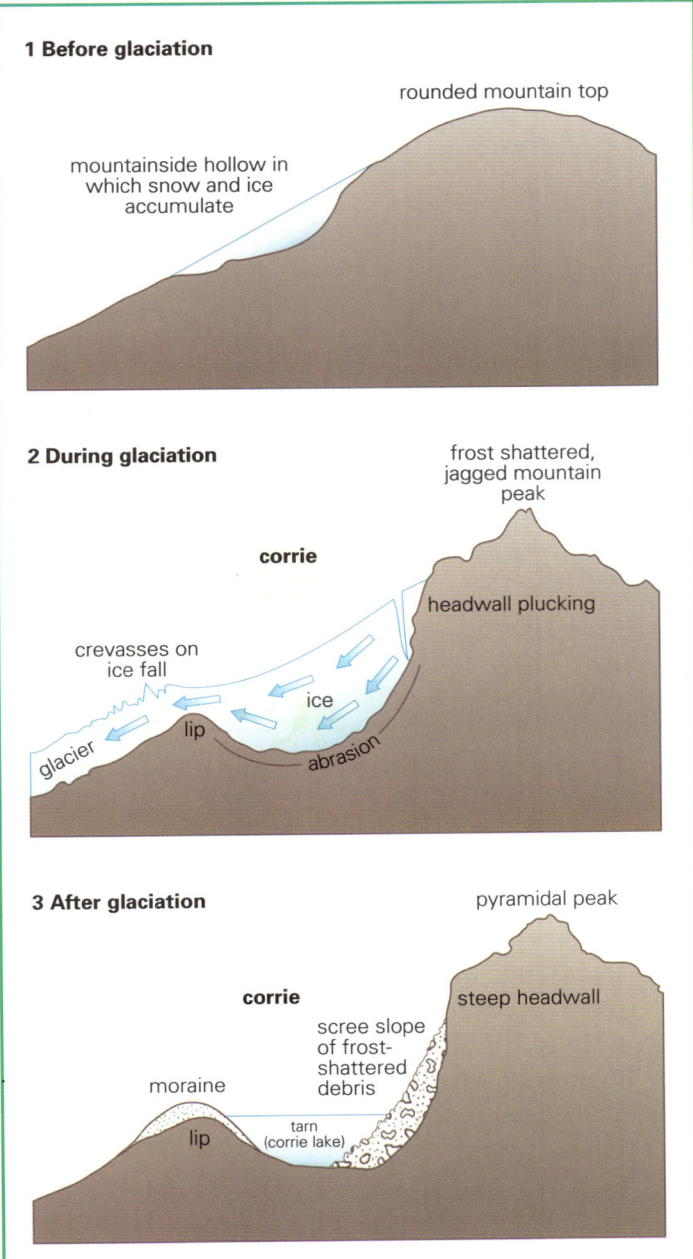

Figure 13.7 The formation of a corrie

action increases the size of the hollow and as the ice increases in depth, it begins to slip, gouging out the hollow and creating a corrie by the processes of abrasion and plucking.

Corries grow by erosion of the base and sides. They have steep headwalls and a lip (Figure 13.7). Nethermost Cove is a corrie on the easter side of Helvellyn in the Lake District (Figure 13.8, page 88). It is over 300 m deep and has a narrow outlet to the east, through which the glacier flowed down a steep ice fall into the

Highland glaciation 87

Figure 13.8 Corrie on east side of Helvellyn containing Red Tarn

valley of Grisedale. After the glacier melted, lakes called tarns formed in many corries.

An arête is a very narrow ridge of land separating two corries. Nethermost Cove is separated from another corrie, Red Tarn, by an arête called Striding Edge. In places, Striding Edge is less than 1 m wide, with steep slopes falling away more than 300 m on either side (see Figure 13.9).

When several corries have eroded into a mountain from all sides, only a shattered remnant of the original mountain top remains. This is called a pyramidal peak. The Matterhorn, in Switzerland, is a famous example (see Figure 13.10).

Glaciers have great erosive power. Flowing downhill along river valleys, glaciers are able to widen and deepen the valleys. The V-shaped cross-section of the river valley is replaced with an open U-shaped cross-section, as the glacier erodes deep into the rock (see Figure 13.11). At the same time, the winding river valleys are replaced by straighter, deeper glacial valleys known as glacial troughs. The interlocking spurs are removed, leaving the upper sections as truncated spurs.

Figure 13.9 Striding Edge, Lake District

Figure 13.10 The Matterhorn, Switzerland

88 Change in the Physical Environment

Figure 13.11 The formation of a U-shaped valley

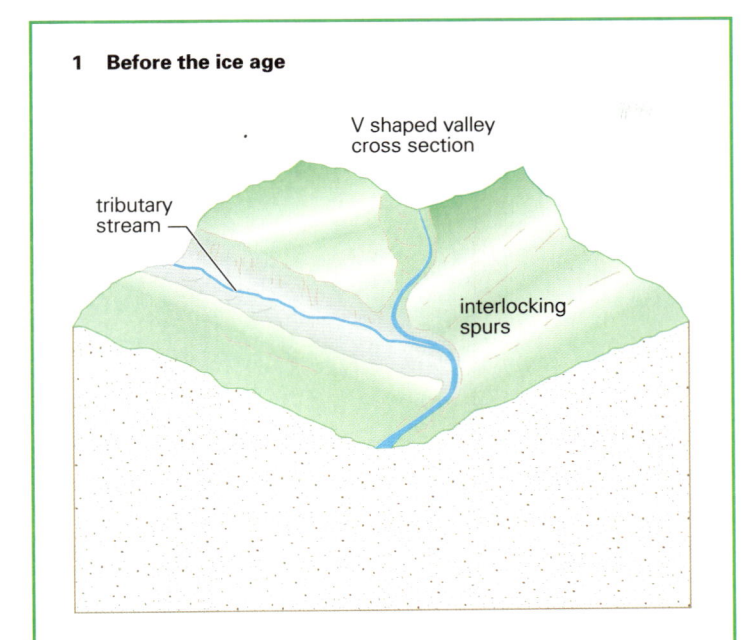

1 Before the ice age

2 During the ice age

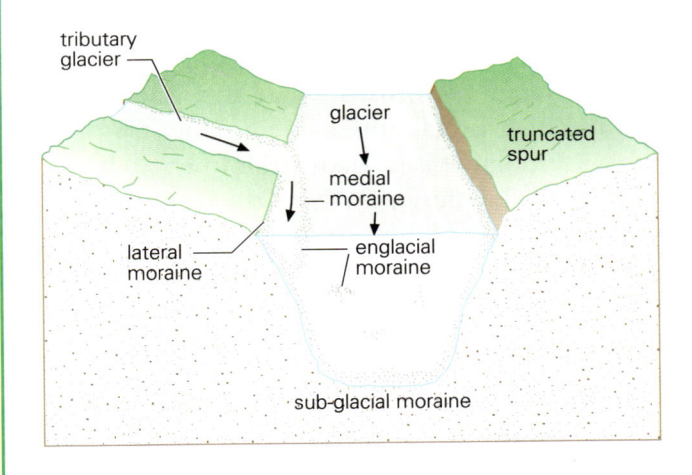

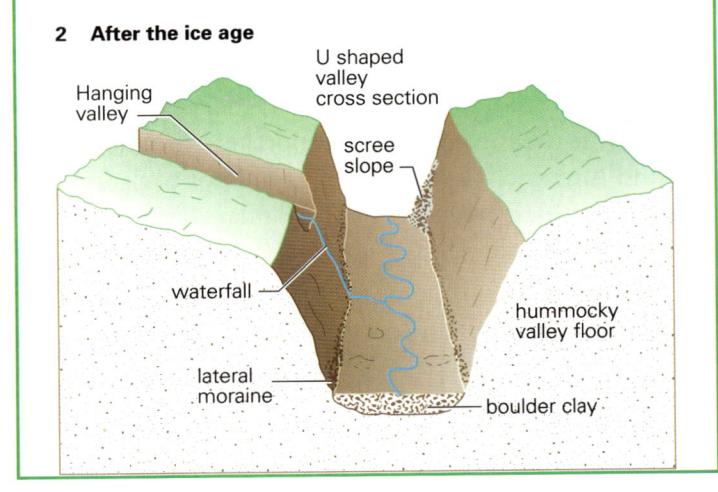

2 After the ice age

Hanging valleys (see Figure 13.11) are formed as a result of the different amount of erosion between the main valley glacier and its tributary glaciers. The tributary valley is lowered much more slowly than the main valley because the main valley glacier has much greater erosive power and so a hanging valley forms.

Some glacial troughs, such as the fjords of Norway, may be up to 3000 m deep. A fjord is a glacial trough which has been drowned by a rise in sea level. Glacial troughs do not have a smooth profile (see Figure 13.12). Deeper sections are called rock basins. After the ice has retreated, the rock basins may be occupied by long narrow lakes called ribbon lakes, an example of which is Lake Windermere.

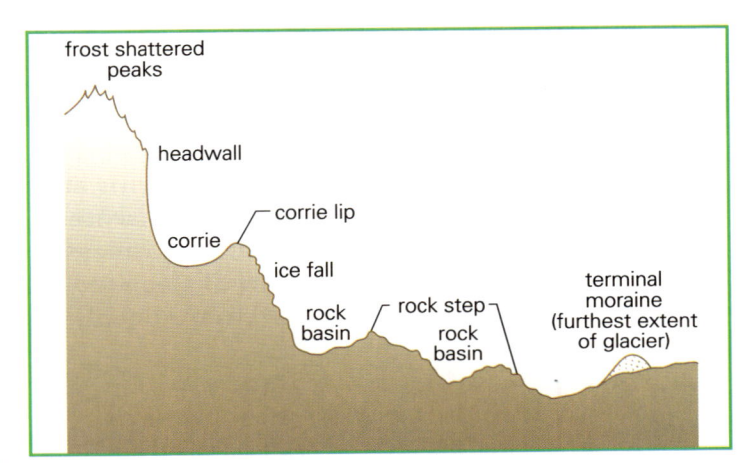

Figure 13.12 Long view of a glacial trough

Edinburgh Castle is built on a crag of very resistant basalt rock, once the plug of a volcano, which withstood the passage of a glacier. In the lee of the crag, a tail of weaker sedimentary rock has survived, protected from the glacier's erosion (see Figure 13.13).

Figure 13.13 A crag and tail

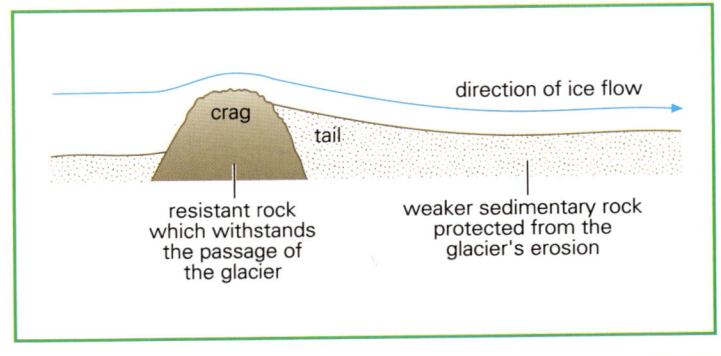

Highland glaciation

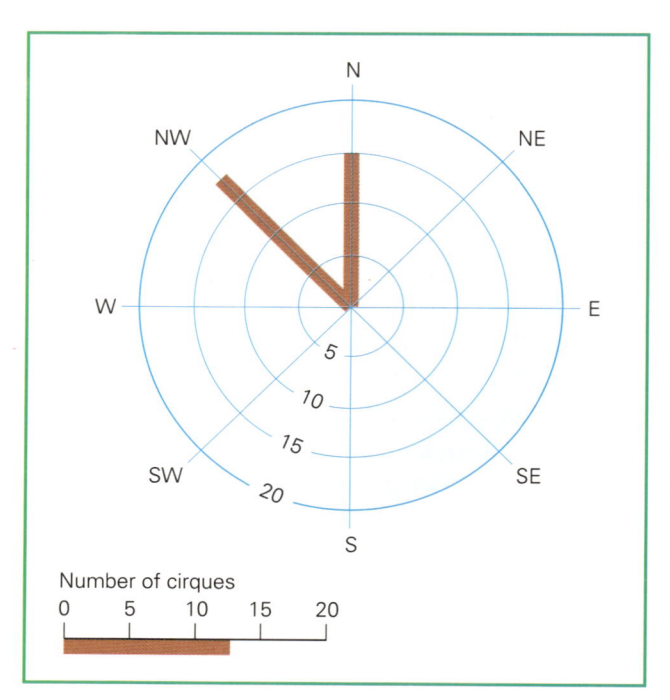

Figure 13.14 A vector diagram of corrie orientation

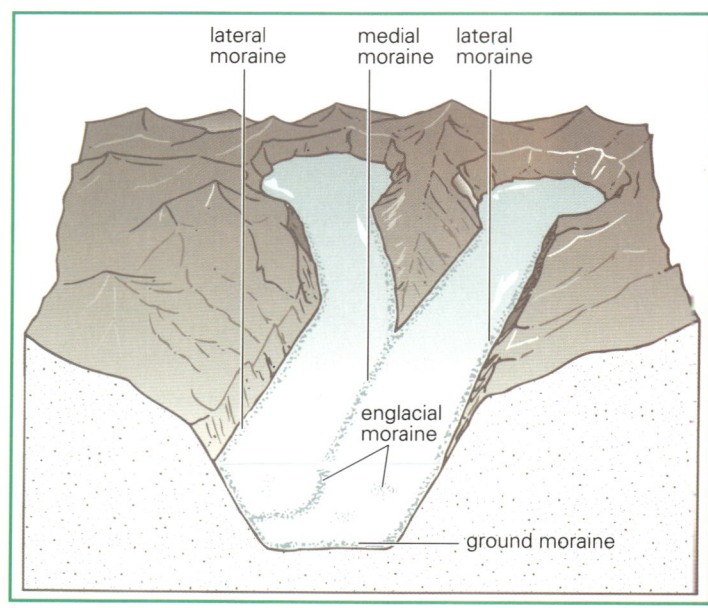

Figure 13.15 A cross-section of a glacier, showing moraines

3. Explain how the following landforms are formed: (a) pyramidal peaks and arêtes; (b) truncated spurs; (c) hanging valleys.
4. Why might some sections of glaciated valleys have been eroded more deeply than others?
5. Figure 13.14 is a vector (or star) diagram. It is used to show patterns involving directions such as wind directions. In this case, the graph shows the direction which corries face, known as orientation. Only two of the sectors have been drawn on.
   (a) Complete the vector diagram by drawing on the bars for the other sectors.
   (b) What patterns are revealed by the diagram?
   (c) What factors might explain these patterns of corrie orientation? Think about the direction from which the sun shines.

Glacial transport

Glaciers can carry large amounts of eroded rock. The scattered debris of rock fragments is called *moraine*. Some of the fragments fall onto the glacier from the rocky slopes above, broken off by frost shattering. Moraine can be transported by a glacier in several ways.

- Lateral moraine is carried along the sides of the glacier (see Figure 13.15).
- Medial moraine is formed where two glaciers join and their lateral moraines combine.
- Englacial moraine is carried within the ice. It may have fallen down cracks in the ice called crevasses.
- Ground moraine is dragged along the bottom of the glacier.

Glacial deposition

The load of a glacier will be dropped where the ice melts. This is mainly at the snout of the glacier, but it can also happen underneath or at the sides of the glacier. The deposited material is called ground moraine, *boulder clay* or *till*. It covers large areas of central and northern Britain. Ground moraine is an unsorted jumble of rock fragments which are jagged and angular. It is unstratified (not layered).

Features of glacial deposition

At the snout of a glacier, much of the debris cannot be carried any further. As the ice melts,

Change in the Physical Environment

the debris piles up to form a ridge called a terminal moraine. Many glaciated valleys have terminal moraines stretching across them, often reduced to a series of hummocks. A good example is found in Kingsdale, North Yorkshire. The terminal moraines of ice sheets are much larger features. The Cromer Ridge in Norfolk (see Figure 13.16) marks the limit of an ice sheet moving southwards across the North Sea which is over 100 m high in places. The Cromer Ridge includes boulders and stones from the nearby chalklands, as might be expected, but more surprising are the rocks from the north of England, Scotland and even Norway which can be found. Such rocks, which have been carried so far away from their place of origin are called erratics.

The retreat of a glacier or ice sheet was rarely smooth or rapid. Usually the ice retreated in stages, sometimes with small advances as well. If the ice halted for long enough during its retreat, another terminal moraine might be formed. Such a moraine is called a recessional moraine and there may be several points along its line of retreat, marking where the ice halted (see Figure 13.17). When the ice melted, the lateral moraine subsided to form a bench along the valley side (Figure 13.16).

Figure 13.16 The Cromer Ridge, a terminal moraine in Norfolk

A drumlin is a low, rounded hillock (see Figure 13.18, page 92), lying parallel to the direction of ice flow with its steeper (stoss) end facing up-glacier. There are many drumlins in the Vale of Eden, east of the Lake District. They are 10–50 m high and 50–500 m long. Most drumlins consist of boulder clay. Nobody is sure how drumlins are formed; they may have been

Figure 13.17 Moraines after glaciation

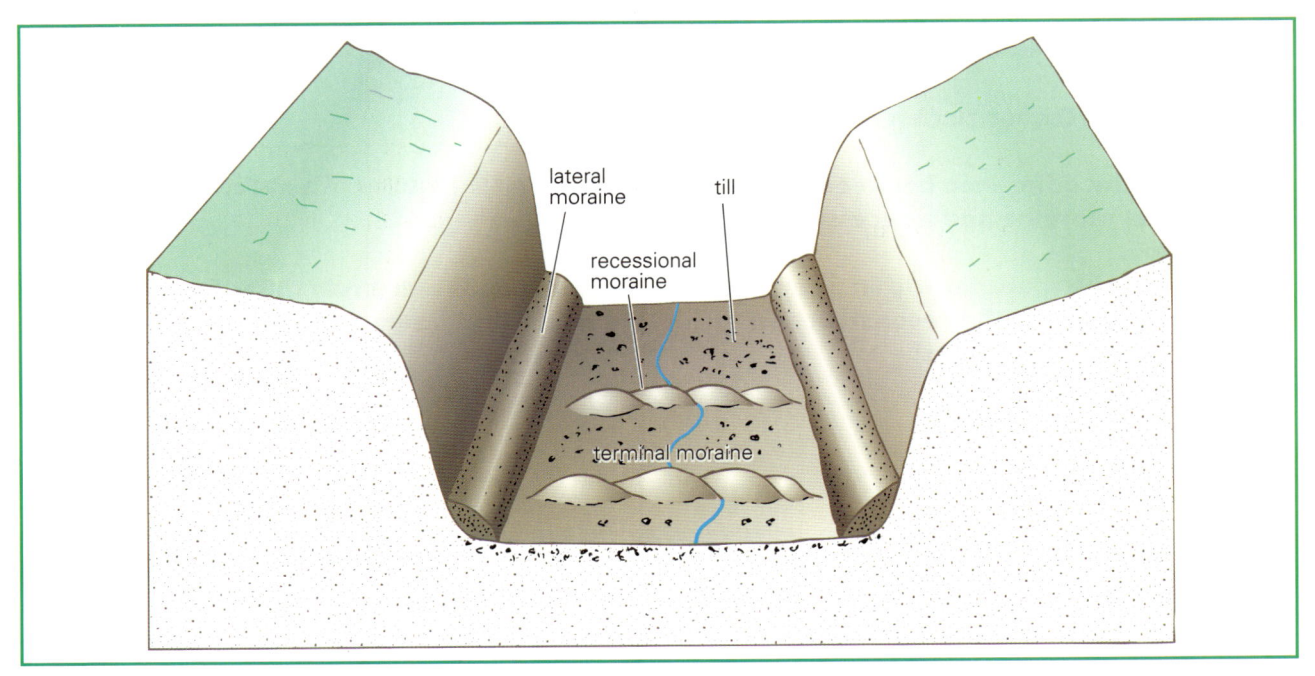

Highland glaciation

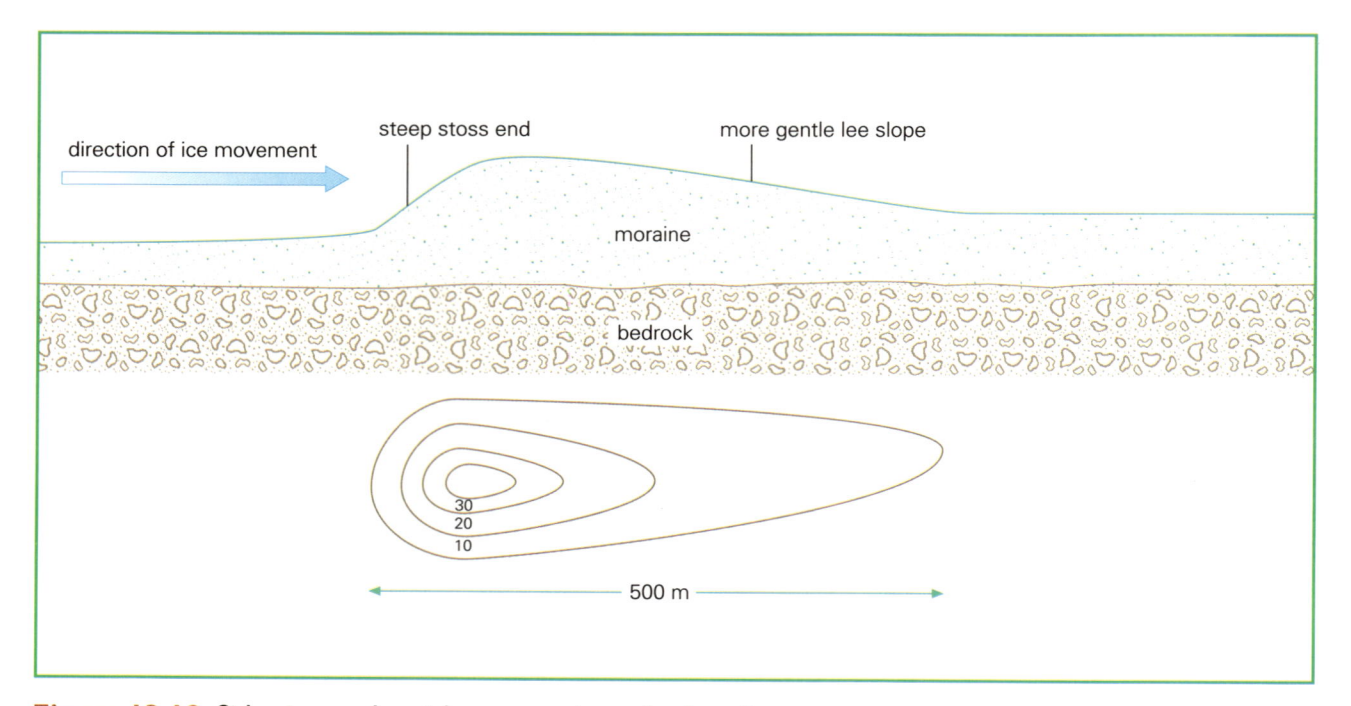

Figure 13.18 Side view and aerial contour view of a drumlin

deposited when the glacier became overloaded with material and dumped masses of ground moraine. It is thought that the ground moraine could have been shaped into drumlins by later ice flowing over it. The streamlined shape of drumlins reflects the wave-like movement of the ice.

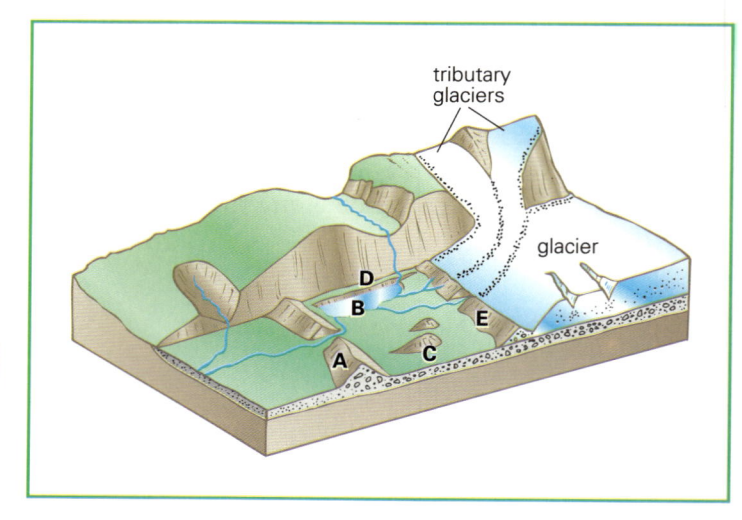

Figure 13.19 Features of a glaciated landscape

6. Look at Figure 13.19.
   (a) Name the landforms labelled **A** to **E**.
   (b) Explain the formation of landform **D**.
7. Explain the difference between a terminal moraine and a recessional moraine.
8. How can the material within a terminal moraine assist in the reconstruction of past glacial movements?
9. How does a drumlin differ from a crag and tail? Illustrate your answer with diagrams.

Summary

- Glaciated highland areas have many distinctive landform features which are the result of the actions of glacial erosion and deposition.

92 Change in the Physical Environment

Chapter 14 Weather and climate

How does the weather in Britain vary throughout the year?

How do people affect weather and climate?

In this unit the causes of rainfall are explained. Differences in the mean seasonal distribution of temperatures and rainfall over the British Isles are explained. The role of air masses, depressions and anticyclones is discussed. The world pattern of climate and the effects of human actions on climate are explained.

What is weather?

Weather is the daily changes in local conditions of the atmosphere. In the British Isles, the weather conditions can change quickly. Weather conditions for an area over a number of years are referred to as the climate. Climate can be said to be 'average weather'. The climate of the British Isles is described on an atlas map of world climates as 'a warm temperate rain climate with rain at all seasons'. However, the climate in different parts of the British Isles varies considerably, as Figures 14.1–14.4 indicate.

Figure 14.1 Average monthly temperature and rainfall for Bournemouth

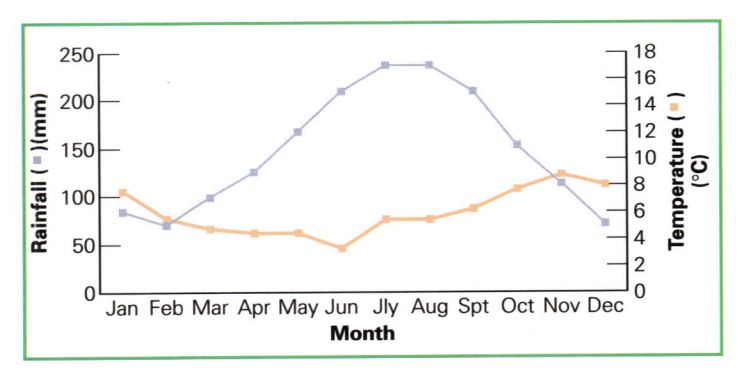

Figure 14.2 Average monthly temperature and rainfall for Norwich

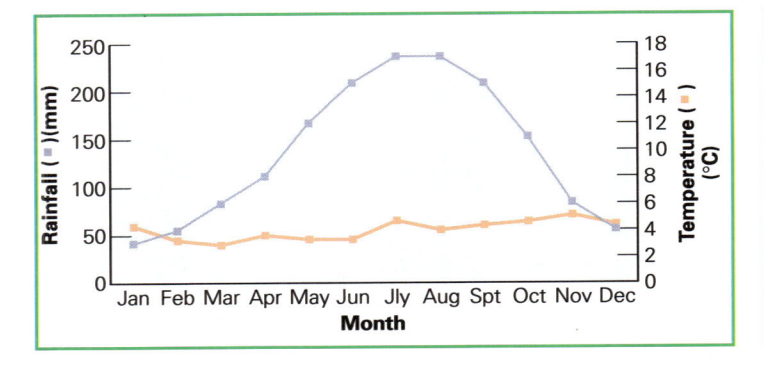

Figure 14.3 Average monthly temperature and rainfall for Keswick

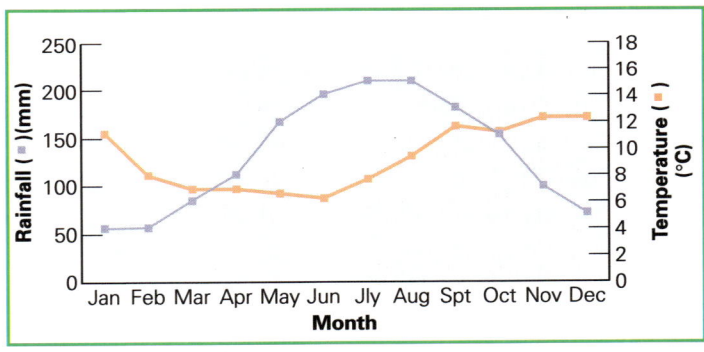

Figure 14.4 Average monthly temperature and rainfall for Fort William

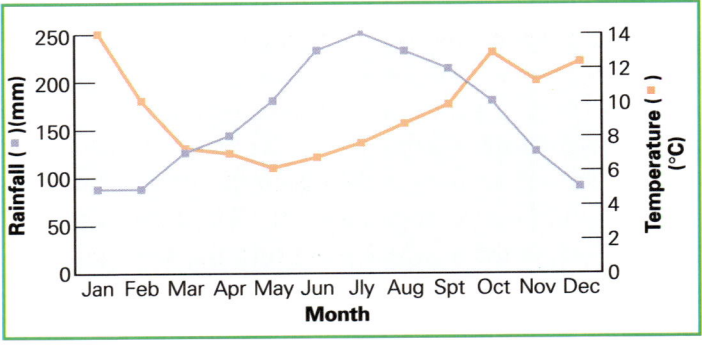

Weather and climate 93

1. **Study Figure 14.2. Copy and complete the table below:**

Place:	Bournemouth	Norwich	Keswick	Fort William
Average January temperature				
Average July temperature				
Average annual temperature				
Average annual temperature range				
Average January rainfall				
Average July rainfall				
Average annual rainfall				
Total annual rainfall				

2. **Use an atlas or computer database to obtain climate statistics for a place on the western coast of the Irish Republic. Draw graphs similar to those in Figures 14.1–14.4 and add the figures to the table you produced for Question 1.**

Figures 14.5–14.8 show the seasonal patterns of climate across the British Isles. These seasonal patterns are caused by various factors.

- Latitude – the further north the place, the cooler the summers.
- Land and sea – these can affect the rainfall and the temperature. Coastal places have milder winters and cooler summers than places well inland. This is because the sea warms up more slowly than the land, but retains the warmth for longer. Coastal areas also have more rainfall than areas inland.
- Relief – highland areas have more rainfall than lowland areas because air is forced to rise over high land. As the air rises, it cools and the water vapour condenses to form cloud and rain.
- Prevailing winds (prevailing means that which happens most often) – over most of the British Isles the prevailing wind is from the west. Westerly winds have blown across the Atlantic Ocean so they have a high moisture content and bring clouds and rain. When the wind blows from other directions, the weather can be quite different (see page 96).

Figure 14.5 January isotherms for the British Isles

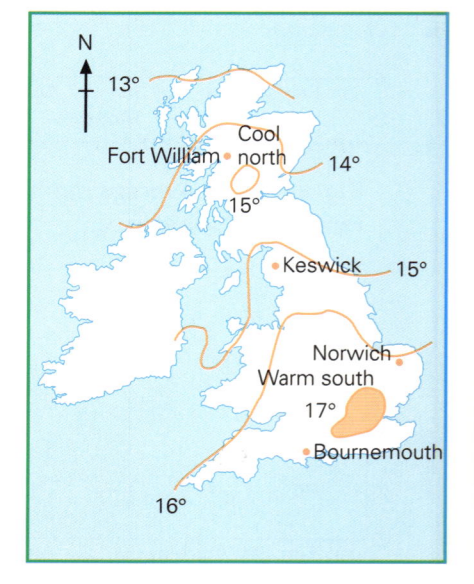

Figure 14.6 July isotherms for the British Isles

94 Change in the Physical Environment

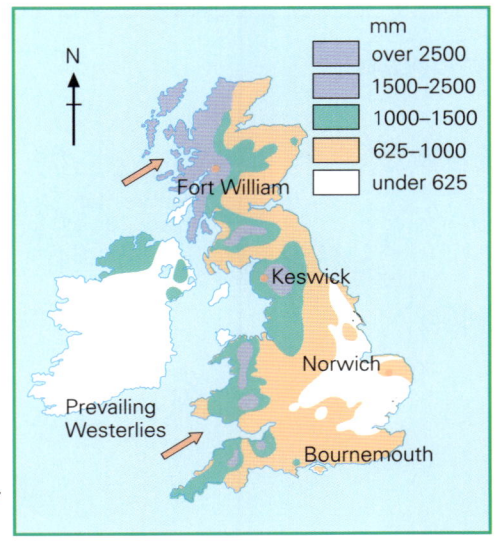

Figure 14.7 Annual rainfall for the British Isles

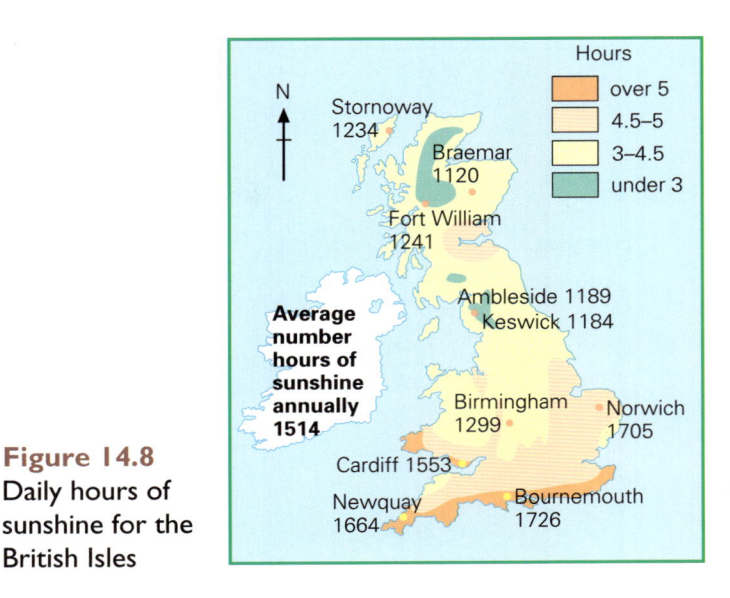

Figure 14.8 Daily hours of sunshine for the British Isles

Precipitation (rain, snow, sleet and hail)

Why does it rain? Air can hold only a limited amount of water vapour. The amount depends on the temperature of the air: warm air holds more water vapour than cold air. As air rises its temperature falls. As it cools so the water vapour contained in the air *condenses* into tiny droplets of water which form a cloud.

Often, the sky is cloudy but no rain falls. Rain will only fall if the tiny cloud droplets become too heavy to remain in the cloud. The droplets grow bigger and heavier by joining together. In larger clouds there is more chance of this happening.

Figure 14.9 shows three ways in which rainfall is caused by air rising and cooling.

Air masses

Air is mainly heated by contact with the earth's surface. When a mass of air remains over a region for several days it will take on the temperature and moisture conditions of the region. Air above a cold, dry region will become colder and drier compared with that over a warm and moist region. If the region is very similar over a large area then a body of air called an air mass will develop, with similar temperature and moisture content over the whole of its area. Examples of such regions are deserts, plains and oceans. Air masses are given labels according to their latitude and whether they have formed over land or sea, for example, Polar maritime (Pm) or Tropical continental (Tc).

Figure 14.9 Three ways in which rainfall is caused by air rising and cooling

1 Relief rising
Moist air forced to rise over mountains. The air cools and water vapour condenses to form cloud. It rains.

2 Convectional rising
Warm air rises and cools. Clouds form and it rains.

3 Frontal rising
Warm air rises over colder air. Clouds form and it rains.

Weather and climate 95

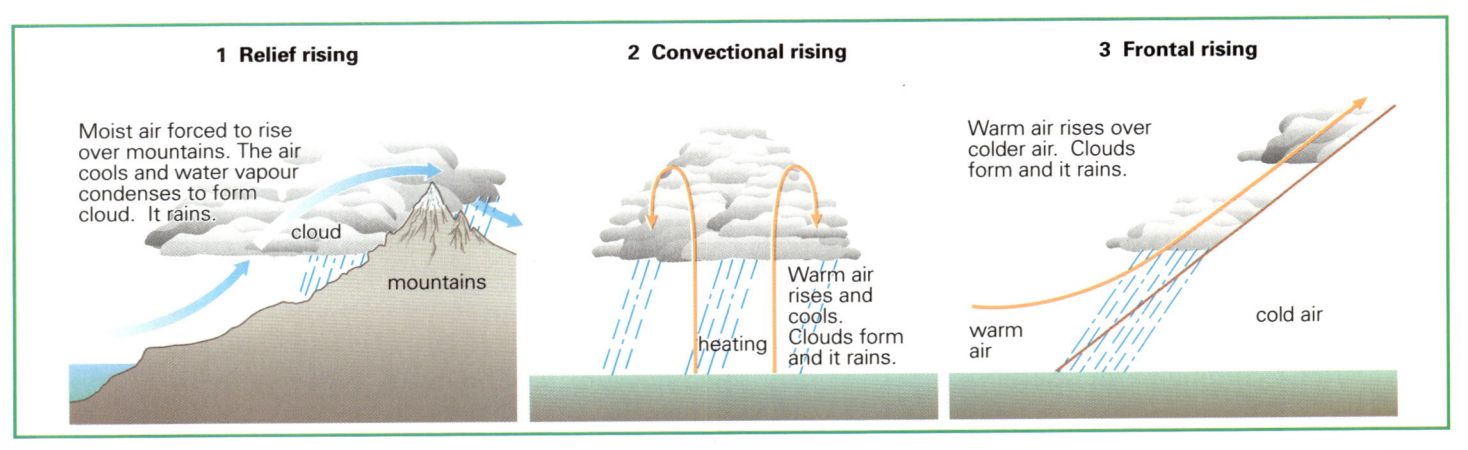

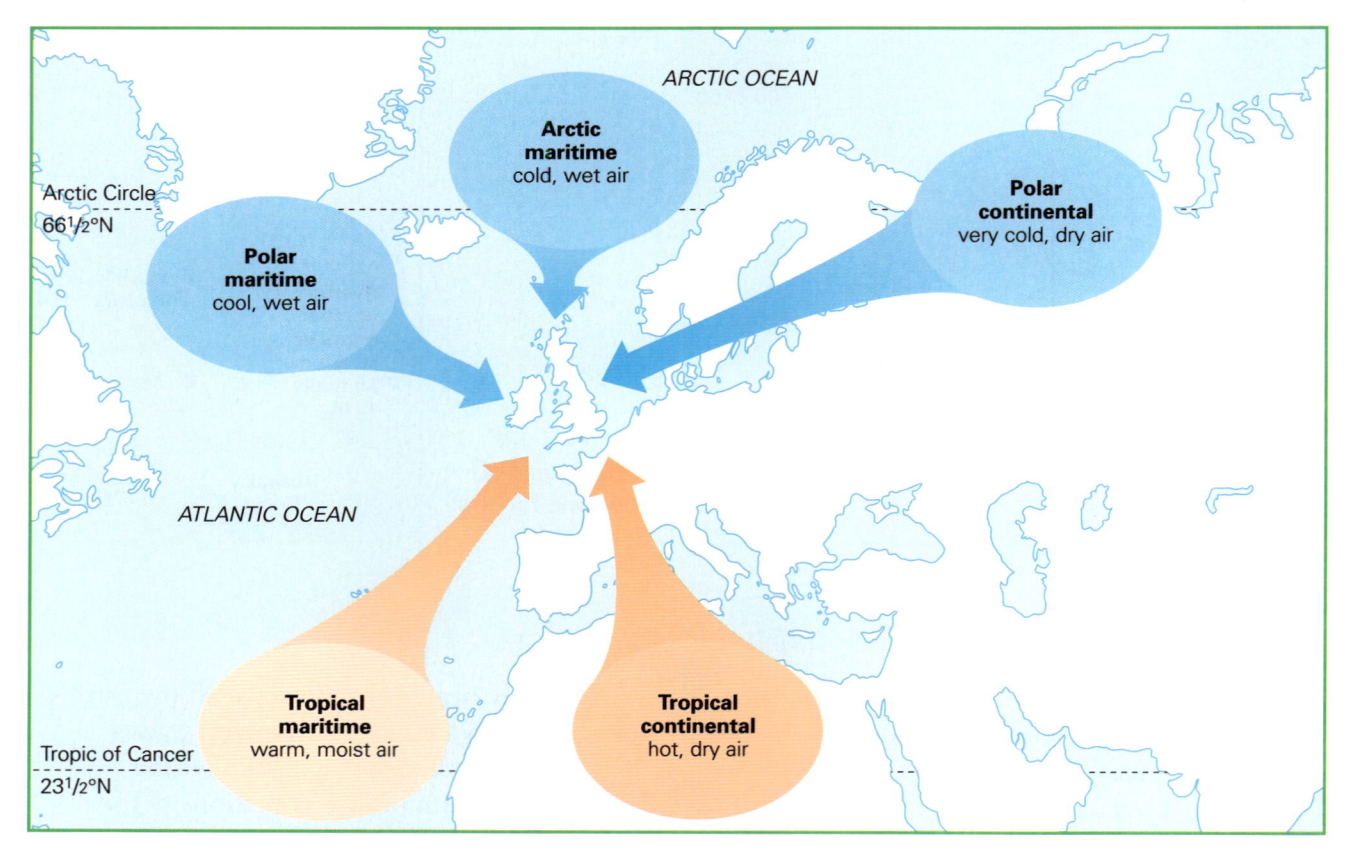

Figure 14.10 Air masses affecting the British Isles

When an air mass begins to move it will take many days for the temperature and moisture conditions of the air to change. The British Isles may be affected by many of the five air masses as shown in Figure 14.10. The weather resulting from these air masses varies considerably. Air from the tropical maritime air mass brings mild, moist air to the British Isles and north west Europe. By contrast, north east America receives Tropical continental air from the heart of the continent, bringing hot summers and cold winters.

Linked with the air mass affecting Britain is the type of pressure system that is experienced, whether it be high pressure – an anticyclone – or low pressure – a depression.

High pressure – the anticyclone

Winds blow outwards from the centre of an anticyclone in a clockwise direction. The weather in the British Isles in an anticyclone varies according to the season.

- In the summer, anticyclones bring dry, sunny weather. Skies are clear and it can be hot, especially if the winds blow from the south. Southerly winds will occur if the anticyclone is centred to the east of Britain.
- In winter, however, the weather can be much less pleasant. Since there are few clouds in an anticyclone, the earth's heat escapes quickly at night. It becomes cold and there will be frost. Winter anticyclones often bring fog. The cold ground causes water vapour in the lower air to condense into droplets. These hang in the air until the heat of the sun raises the temperature. The fog may linger all day because of the weak winter sun.

Low pressure – the depression

Low pressure areas, or depressions, bring periods of unsettled weather. As Figure 14.11 shows, depressions have a sector of warm air and a larger sector of cold air. The warm and cold air do not mix. The boundary between the two

Change in the Physical Environment

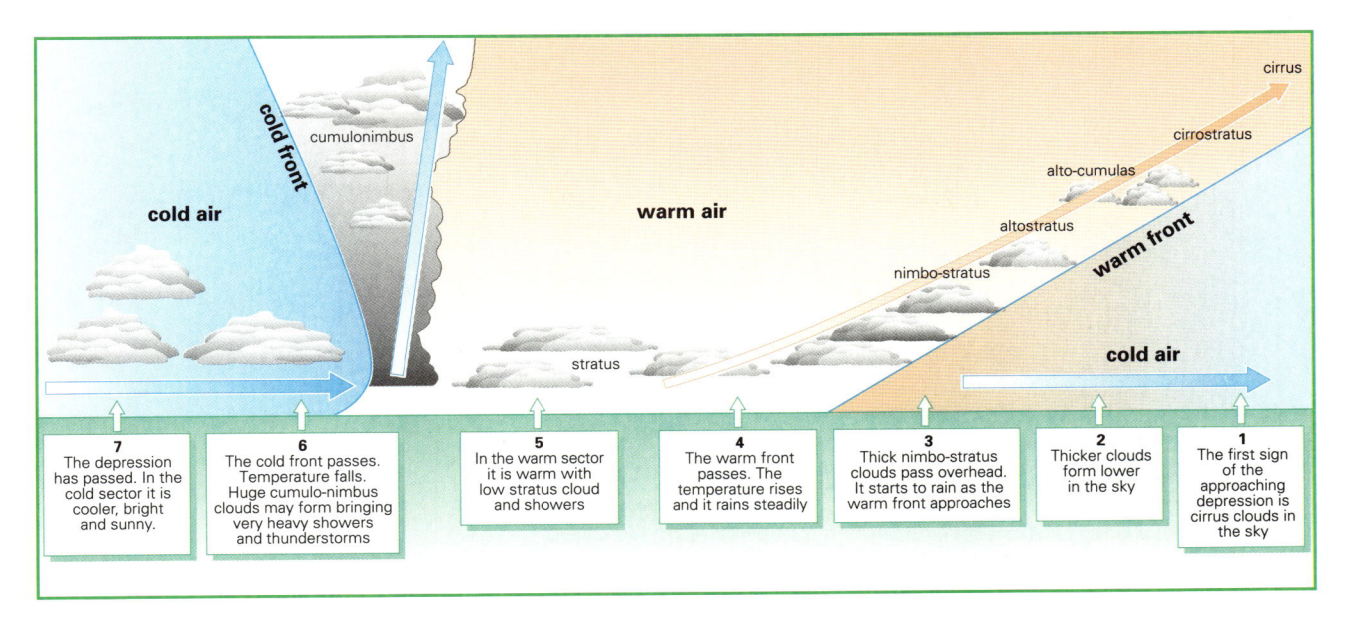

Figure 14.11 A cross-section through a depression

types of air is called a **front**. The depression has a warm front and a cold front which mark the division between the warm and cold air. Lighter warm air rises over the colder air to form a warm front; heavier cold air moves underneath the warm air from behind to form a cold front (see Figure 14.11). Both fronts bring cloud and rain.

Figure 14.12 An aerial view of a cross-section through a depression

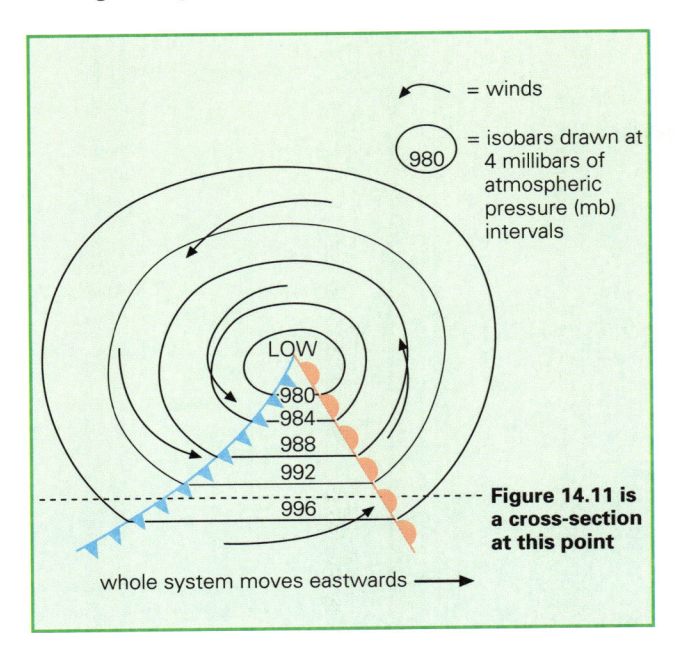

The depression is a large system, hundreds of kilometres across. Depressions develop where warm air meets cold air and, as a result, many form over the Atlantic Ocean. Depressions usually move eastwards or north eastwards. As a depression passes overhead, the area below will experience a sequence of weather, mostly wet and windy. Eventually the warm air rises completely above the ground and the depression fades away, or 'fills'. Figure 14.12 is an aerial view of a cross-section of a depression.

Satellite photos and synoptic charts

Figure 14.13 (page 98) is a satellite image. It shows a depression across the British Isles. This is not a photograph but an infra-red image showing the heat emitted – the coldest areas are white, the warmest black. Figure 14.14 (page 98) is a weather map, known as a synoptic chart, drawn at the same time as the satellite image was produced. Figure 14.15 (page 98) provides a key to the symbols used on the synoptic chart.

The synoptic chart provides the following useful information.

- The clouds clearly show the position of the fronts. The warm front runs down the North Sea while the cold front crosses Scotland and Ireland.

Weather and climate

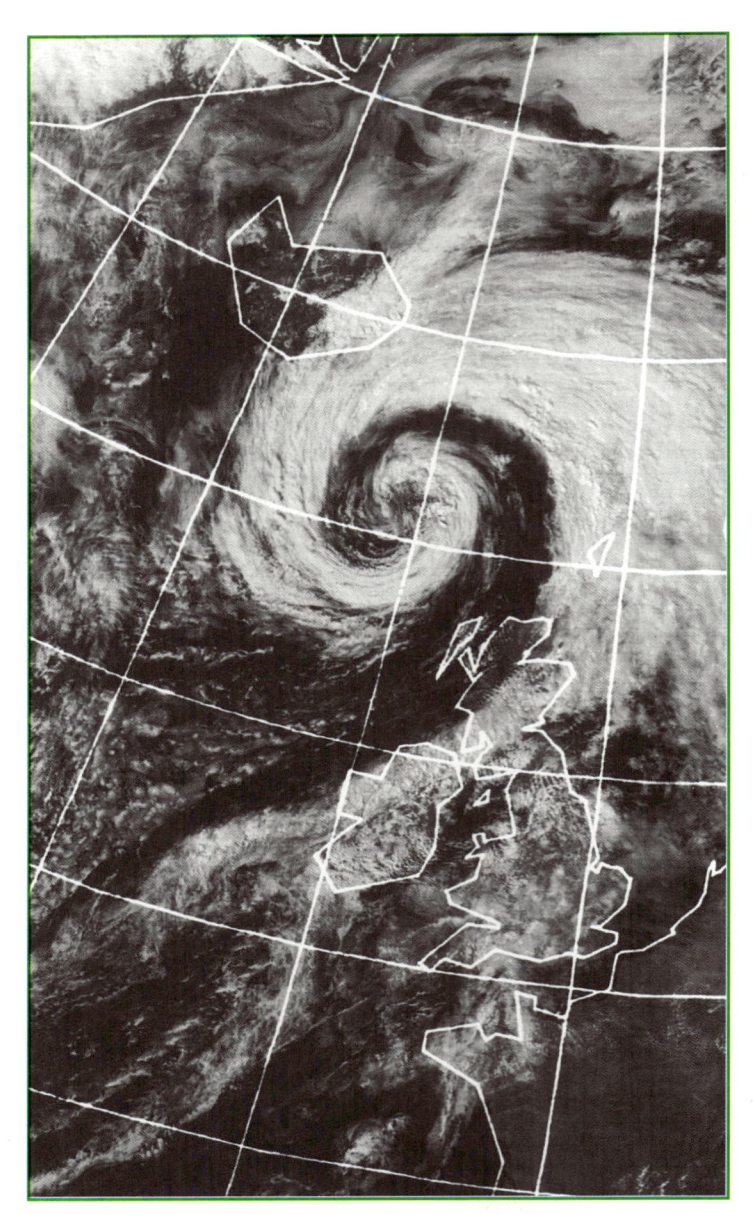

Figure 14.13 Satellite image of a depression over the North Atlantic

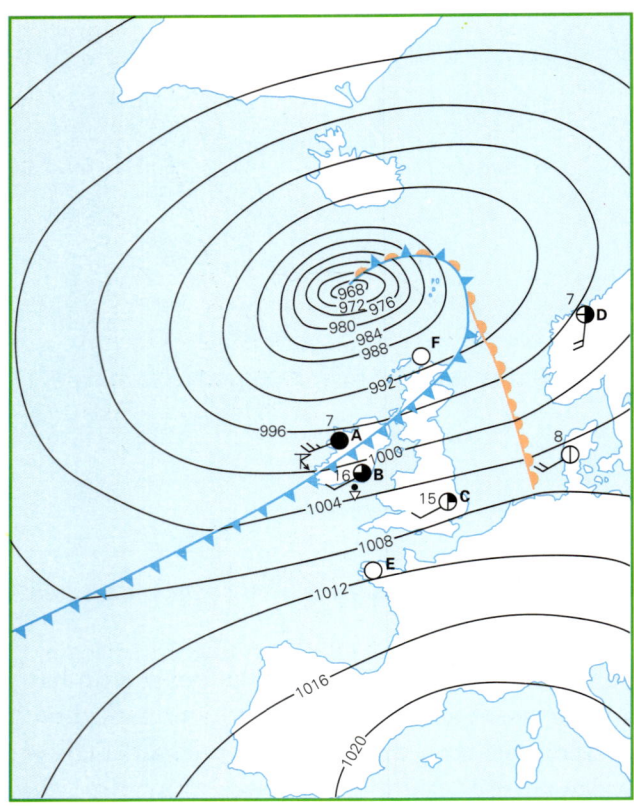

Figure 14.14 Synoptic chart of the North Atlantic

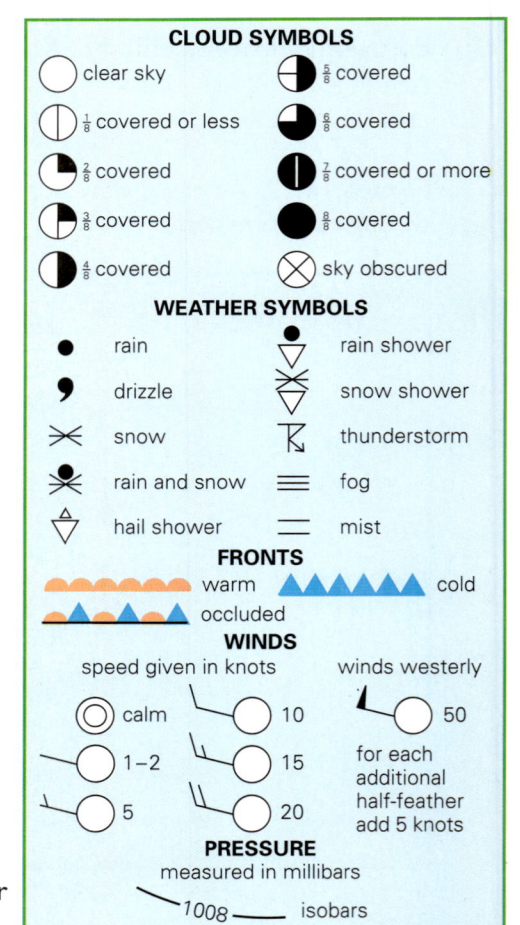

Figure 14.15 Synoptic weather symbols

- The swirl of cloud spiralling in to a vortex between Scotland and Ireland marks the centre of the depression. This is the point of lowest atmospheric pressure within the depression. Winds are blowing in an anti-clockwise direction in to the centre.
- England and Wales are in the warm sector of the depression, with low cloud and showers over much of the area.

3. Copy and complete the table on page 99 for points A, B, C and D, marked on Figure 14.14.

98 Change in the Physical Environment

Place	Temperature	Cloud cover	Wind direction	Wind speed	Weather
A	7		WSW		
B		6 oktas		10 knots	
C	15		SW		
D					

4. Explain the difference in temperature between places **A** and **B**.
5. Draw the symbols for the probable weather conditions at places **E** and **F**.

Global patterns of climate

There are many climates on earth. Figure 14.16 shows a simple classification of the world's climates into five major types.

The hot deserts are the driest places on earth. However, many other places have unreliable rainfall (see Figure 14.17, page 100) and most of these areas have low average rainfall totals. This is mainly due to the prevailing winds which move across from the dry land out to the sea and are usually very dry since they pick up little moisture.

The general atmospheric circulation

The global distribution of areas with unreliable rainfall is closely related to the general atmospheric circulation governing the prevailing winds (see Figure 14.18). Air in the equatorial regions is intensely heated. It rises, causing low pressure at the surface of the earth beneath. The rising air moves north and south towards the Poles. The air which moves northwards is diverted to the right by the rotation of the earth and it cools and sinks at about 30° N. Cool air then moves towards the Equator, completing a circulation known as a convection cell. The surface winds, blowing from the north east, are called the trade winds. The air moving south from the Equator is diverted to the left. The

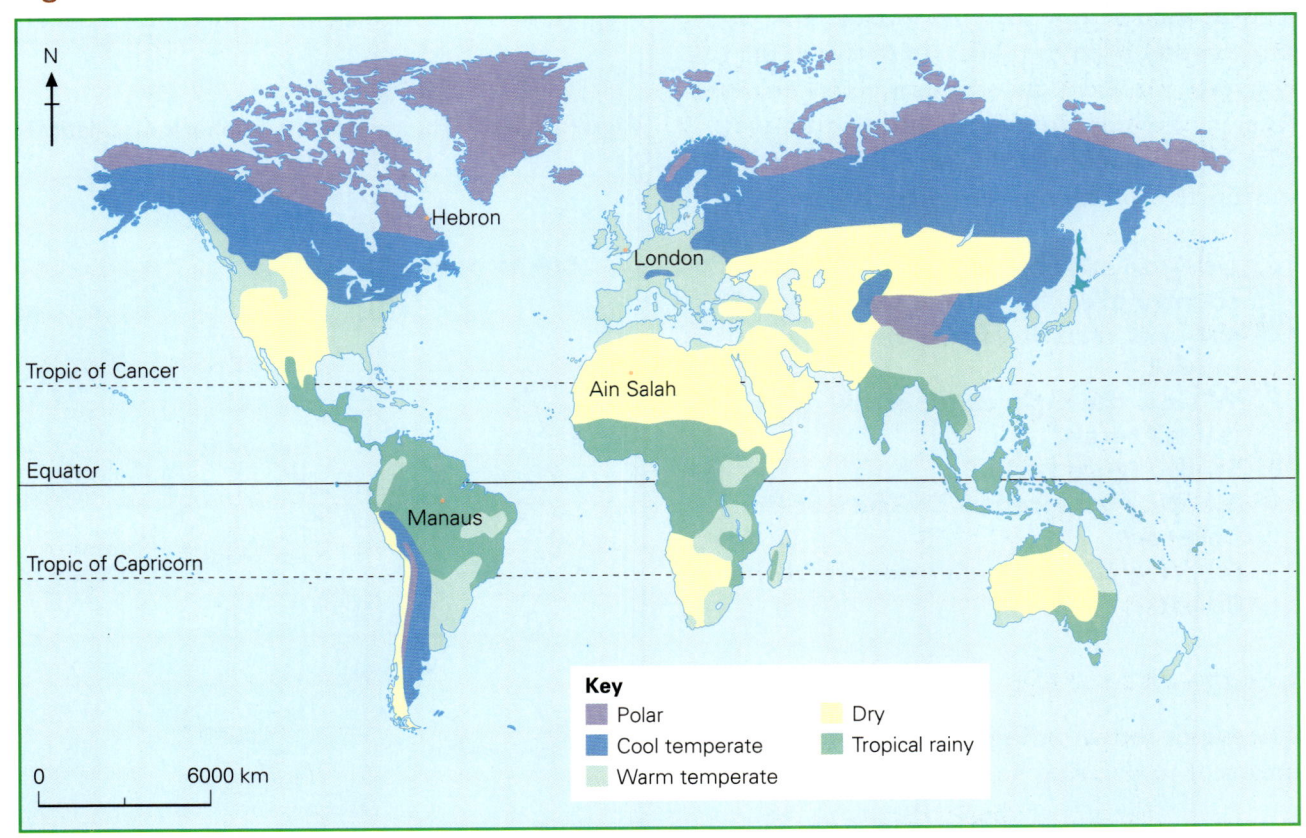

Figure 14.16 The world's climates

Weather and climate 99

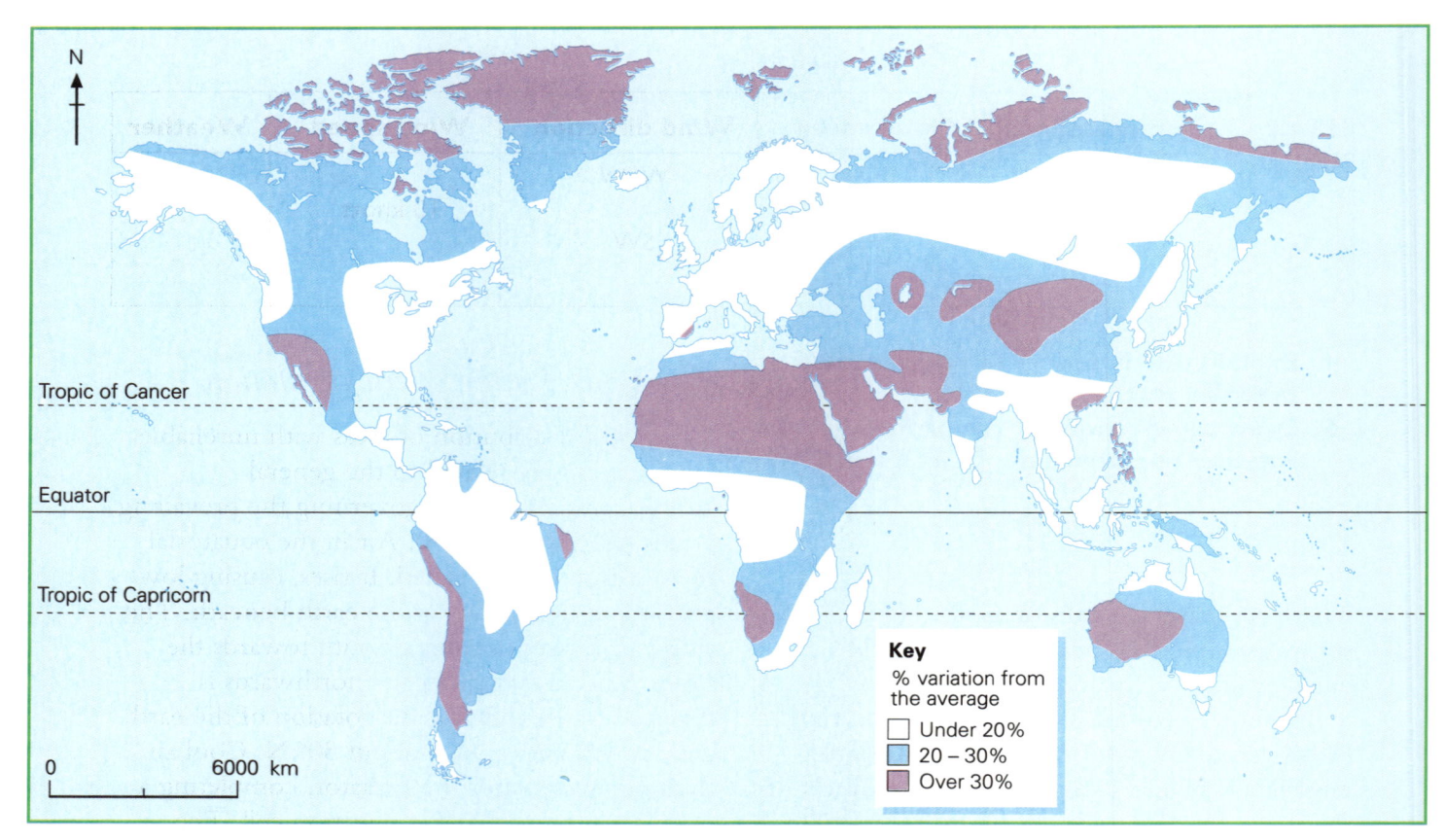

Figure 14.17 Reliability of rainfall

surface winds blowing northwards from 30°S are the south east trade winds.

There is another convection cell at the Poles. The air is cooled by the cold surface, sinks and moves away from the Poles. In between the two convection cells in the northern hemisphere is an area of winds blowing from the south west. The circulation in the southern hemisphere mirrors that of the northern hemisphere.

> 6. Using an atlas to help you, name a country in each continent with over 30 per cent variation from the average rainfall.
> 7. What is the main cause of low average rainfall totals?
> 8. Study Figure 14.18.
>   (a) Why is there low pressure at the Equator?
>   (b) Why is there high pressure at the Poles?

Ocean currents

The winds shown in Figure 14.18 are the major means of transferring heat from the equatorial and tropical regions to the temperate and polar regions of earth. Another important means of heat transfer is provided by the ocean currents (Figure 14.19). These are movements of surface

Figure 14.18 The general atmospheric circulation

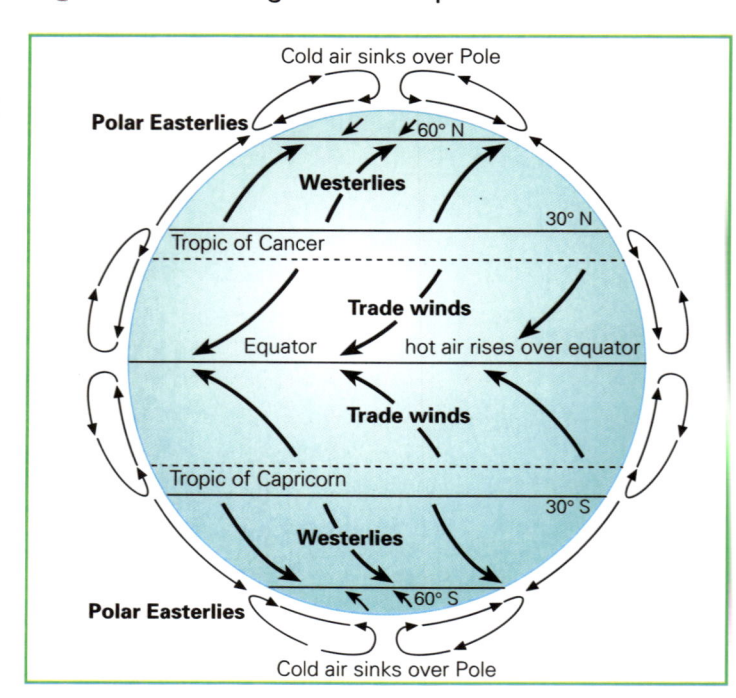

100 Change in the Physical Environment

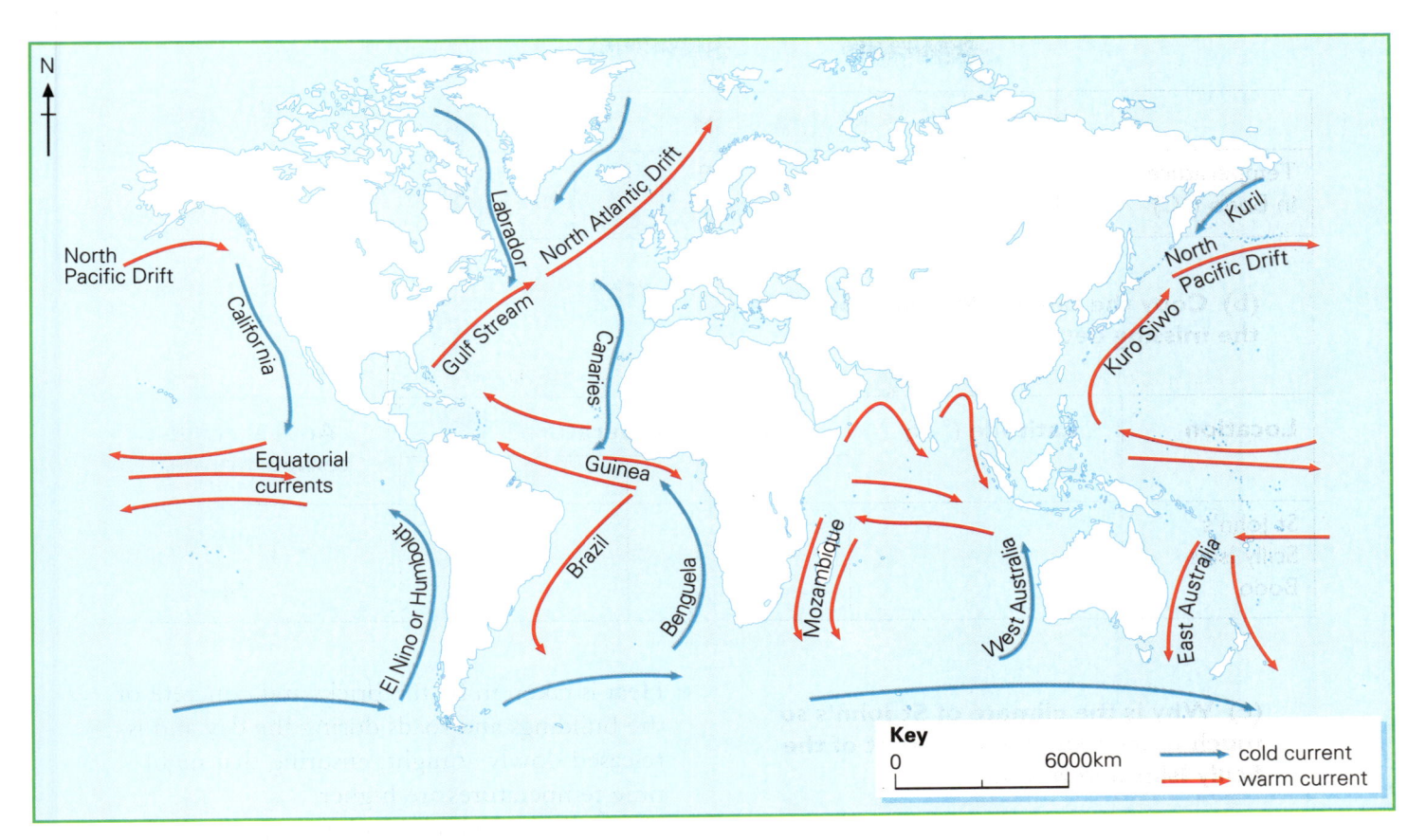

Figure 14.19 Ocean currents

water, rarely affecting more than the top 150 m of the ocean, which can reach speeds of up to 3 km per hour. There is a clear circulation pattern in each half of the major oceans, clockwise in the northern hemisphere and anti-clockwise in the south.

The main cause of ocean currents is the wind. The surface water is dragged along because of friction between the air and the water. Currents which transport warm water to colder parts of the oceans are called warm currents. The Gulf Stream is an example. Currents flowing in the opposite direction carry cold water into warmer areas; they are called cold currents and the Canaries current is an example.

Ocean currents have a major influence on the climates of the coastal areas. Figure 14.20 shows the importance of their role, and that of the prevailing winds. In winter, the temperature difference between the western and eastern coasts of the north Atlantic is most marked. Sea ice extends along the coast of Newfoundland, further south than the latitude of the English Channel and even the coast of northern Norway is ice-free. This is due to the warm ocean current called the North Atlantic Drift and the prevailing south-westerly winds.

Figure 14.20 Average monthly temperatures for St John's, Newfoundland (Canada), and the Scilly Isles (UK)

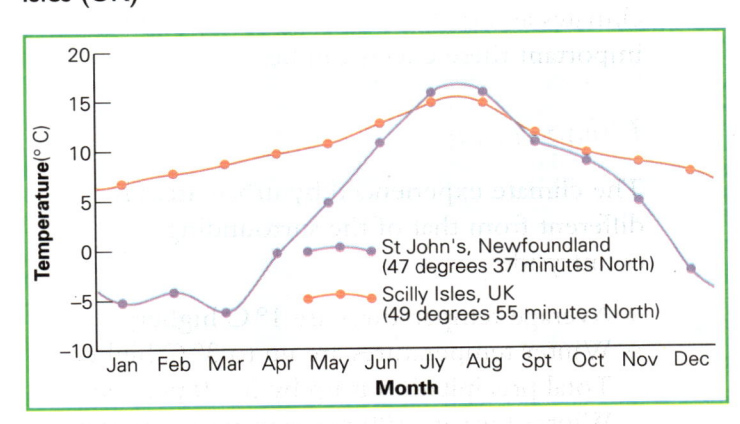

9. Look at Figure 14.20.
(a) Draw a similar graph to show the average monthly temperature of Bodo in northern Norway, using the statistics on page 102. Bodo is 67° 21" North.

Weather and climate   101

	J	F	M	A	M	J	J	A	S	O	N	D
Temperature in Bodo (°C)	−1	1	3	6	9	11	13	13	10	8	4	2

(b) Copy the table below and complete the missing details:

Location	Latitude (° N)	Average temperature (° C) January	Average temperature (° C) July	Annual range of temperature (° C)
St John's		−5		
Scilly Isles			15	
Bodo				14

(c) Why is the climate of St John's so much more extreme than that of the Scilly Isles and Bodo?

Human effects on climate

Humans can affect climate on a variety of levels, from local to global. Two examples – urban climates and global warming – show how important these effects can be.

Urban climates

The climate experienced by urban areas is different from that of the surrounding countryside:

- Average temperatures are 1° C higher;
- Winter temperatures are up to 3° C higher;
- Total precipitation is up by 5–10 per cent;
- Winter fogs are 100 per cent more frequent;
- Summer fogs are 30 per cent more frequent;
- Cloud cover is 5–10 per cent greater.

There are three reasons for these differences.

- Heat is released by the heating systems of homes, offices and factories. This warms the air and is particularly important during the winter when the sun's heat input is much reduced.
- Heat is taken in by the bricks and concrete of the buildings and roads during the day and is released slowly at night, ensuring that night time temperatures are higher.
- The pollution which blankets cities raises the temperature by preventing the escape of heat. There are ten times more dust particles found in the atmosphere over cities. These particles provide the condensation nuclei needed for cloud formation and help to account for the increase in cloud, fog and precipitation over cities.

Global warming

Average global temperatures have increased by 0.5° C during the twentieth century and the 1980s was the warmest decade world-wide since the 1850s, when reliable records began. Computer models developed in the USA and the UK predict a warming of several degrees during the next century. Opinions differ on the causes of global warming. Many climatologists claim that it is caused by an intensification of the greenhouse effect through human actions, especially the release of gases into the atmosphere through the burning of fossil fuels. The amount of carbon dioxide in the atmosphere has increased by 25 per cent during the twentieth century and is predicted to double by the year 2050 (see Figure 14.21).

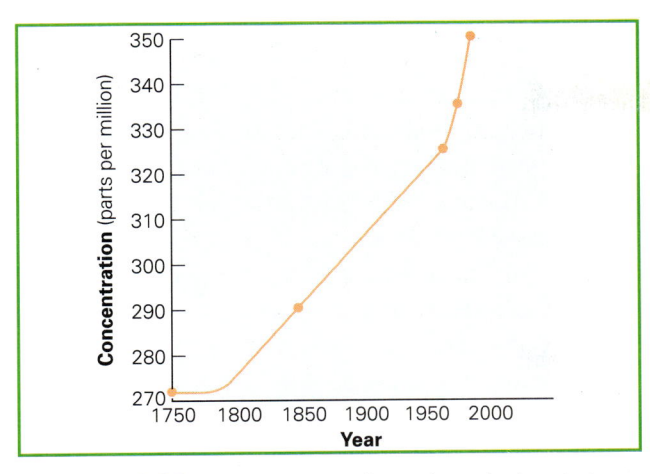

Figure 14.21 Increasing carbon dioxide levels in the atmosphere

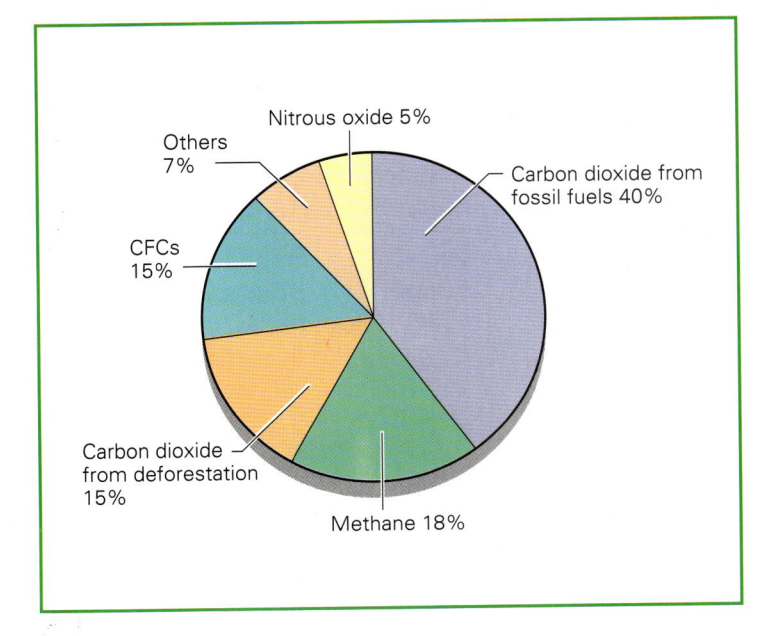

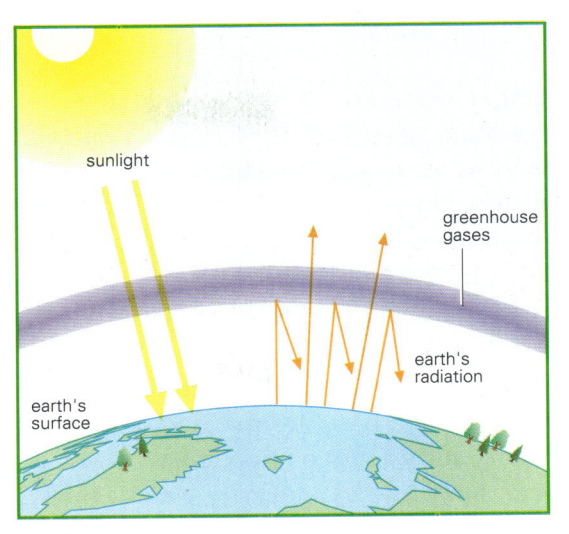

Figure 14.22 The greenhouse effect

The greenhouse effect

The greenhouse effect is a natural process. Without it, the average temperature of the earth would be approximately 25° C lower than the present 15° C, making it very difficult for humans to survive. The glass of a greenhouse allows the heat from the sun to pass in, but prevents the warm air within from escaping. In a similar way, the earth's atmosphere allows the sun's radiation to reach the surface of the planet but prevents it from escaping into space (Figure 14.22). Sunlight (solar radiation) is shortwave, the earth's radiation is longwave. The greenhouse gases in the earth's atmosphere (see Figure 14.23) let shortwave radiation pass through them to the planet's surface, but absorb much of the longwave radiation. These greenhouse gases in the atmosphere, especially carbon dioxide, are the cause of the greenhouse effect. The gases occur naturally, but their levels are being increased by human actions in several ways.

- Carbon dioxide is released when fossil fuels (coal, oil and gas) and wood are burned to provide energy (e.g. for fuel). Coal releases more carbon dioxide than oil which, in turn, releases more than gas. Carbon dioxide emissions increased at an annual rate of 0.5 per cent during the 1980s.
- Carbon dioxide is released through the burning of forests. The rate of deforestation has been increasing rapidly during the twentieth century. Tropical rainforests are disappearing at the rate of 11 million ha per year.
- Chlorofluorocarbons (CFCs) are released from coolants in refrigerators, aerosols, solvents and during the manufacture of plastic foams. CFC emissions increased at a rate of 6 per cent during the 1980s. Their effect on the ozone layer is described later. Production of CFCs is to be banned from the year 2000.
- Methane is released by the bacterial breakdown of organic matter. Humans have increased the emissions of methane by increasing herds of cattle, waste dumps and sewage treatment, each of which emit

Figure 14.23 The gases that cause the greenhouse effect

Carbon dioxide from fossil fuels 40%
Methane 18%
Carbon dioxide from deforestation 15%
CFCs 15%
Others 7%
Nitrous oxide 5%

Weather and climate

methane. During the 1980s, world methane emissions increased by 10 per cent. Methane levels in the atmosphere doubled between 1850 and 1990.

- Nitrous oxide is released from fertilisers, the burning of fossil fuels and from vehicle exhausts. Many climatologists predict an increase in average global temperatures of between 1.5 and 7°C by the year 2050. Such an increase could have several adverse effects.
- Low-lying areas could be flooded as rising temperatures cause the polar ice caps to melt and some small island nations such as the Maldives could disappear completely. Densely-populated river deltas, such as the Ganges and Nile, would be threatened. The homes of hundreds of millions of people would be swamped by the rising waters, as sea levels are predicted to rise by 0.2–1.6 m. Figure 14.24 shows the effect this would have on the British coastline.
- The world's agriculture could be severely disrupted by extremes of weather, resulting in droughts, storms, floods and frosts. The great plains of the USA might become too dry for the growth of wheat and rice and soya bean yields in South East Asia could decrease as a result of higher temperatures.
- Higher temperatures could cause the world's desert areas to increase substantially as the rising temperatures cause drier conditions. The same cause could greatly reduce the area of coniferous forest.

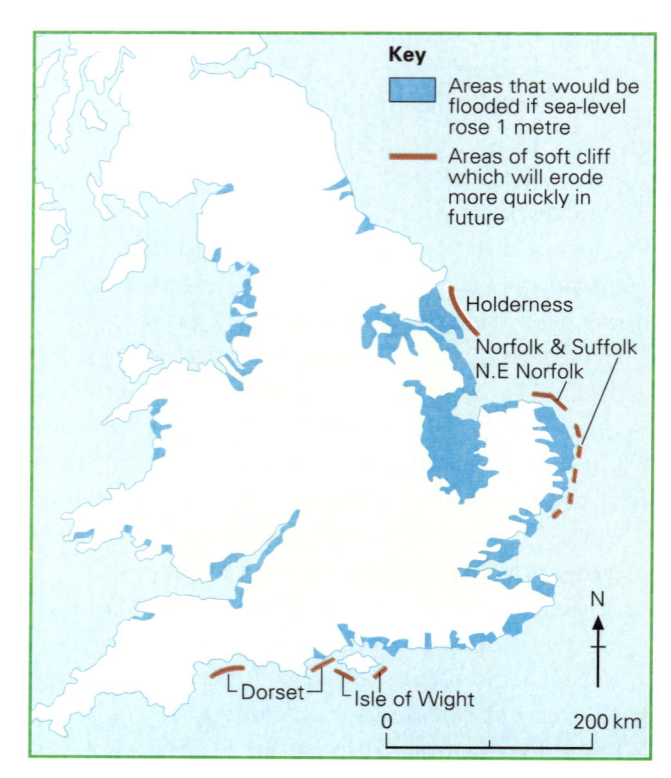

Figure 14.24 The possible state of the coastlines of England and Wales in 2050, following global warming

10. (a) What do you understand by the 'greenhouse effect'?
    (b) What effect are human actions having on the greenhouse effect?
11. Study Figure 14.23.
    (a) What percentage of the greenhouse effect is caused by carbon dioxide?
    (b) What are the two main sources of carbon dioxide emissions resulting from human activities?
12. The table below shows the sources of carbon dioxide emissions in the UK.

Source	Amount (million tonnes)
Power stations	52
Other industry	37
Road vehicles	28
Domestic	24
Commercial	9
Other	9
Total	159

(a) Draw a pie graph or divided bar graph to show this data.
(b) Name another greenhouse gas emitted from vehicle exhausts.

13. Copy and complete the table below.

Gas	Sources	Rate of increase during 1980s	Per cent of the effect caused by this
Carbon dioxide			
CFCs			
Methane			
Nitrous oxide			

104 Change in the Physical Environment

It is difficult to be certain about the effects of global warming. The ocean currents would certainly be disrupted by the increased temperatures, but this could mean that some areas would actually become cooler, including the British Isles and western Europe, if the Gulf Stream ocean current was affected.

Opinions about the greenhouse effect are divided and other climatologists claim that the recent increase in global temperatures is simply a natural fluctuation. They say that there is no need for concern over increased levels of carbon dioxide since the oceans will simply absorb the increase.

Governments and international organisations have shown great concern about the greenhouse effect. There are no easy solutions, but there are various possible options.

- Cutting carbon dioxide emissions – the EU has agreed that emission levels will be restricted to 1990 levels by the year 2000.
- Introducing energy conservation measures to reduce fossil fuel consumption – for example, improving the insulation in buildings.
- Increasing efficiency in the burning of fuel to reduce overall consumption – for example, 'lean burn' vehicle engines, the increased use of diesel engines, and more efficient power stations (currently only 37 per cent of the energy in coal is converted into electricity).
- Introducing a 'carbon tax' to make fossil fuels more expensive to use.
- Replacing coal- and oil-fired power stations with gas.
- Encouraging the use of renewable forms of energy such as wind, wave and solar power.
- Reducing rates of deforestation and planting new forests.

14. Study Figure 14.26, which shows carbon dioxide emissions for 12 countries.
    (a) What type of countries have the highest emission rates of carbon dioxide?
    (b) Why do you think Brazil and Indonesia feature among the highest emitters?
15. Suggest how individuals in Britain might limit their personal contribution to the intensification of the greenhouse effect. Give reasons.
16. What practical measures could governments take to limit global warming? Why might some measures be unpopular?

Figure 14.25 Levels of CO_2 emissions in selected countries, 1994

Country	Emissions per head of population (tonnes)
USA	5.8
Russia	3.4
Germany	3.2
Belgium	3.1
UK	3.1
Netherlands	3.0
Japan	2.8
Brazil	2.6
Italy	2.6
France	2.6
Indonesia	1.5
Spain	1.4

The ozone layer

Ozone is a form of oxygen that occurs throughout the atmosphere but is most concentrated in a layer 20–30 km above the earth's surface, in the **stratosphere**. The ozone layer shields the earth's surface from the sun's ultraviolet rays (see Figure 14.26, page 106).

Human actions are causing a thinning of the ozone layer, largely due to CFC emissions. Ultraviolet light causes chlorine to break away from the CFC, and chlorine destroys ozone. CFCs can survive in the atmosphere for 110 years and a single chlorine molecule can destroy 100 000 ozone molecules.

In 1984, British scientists discovered a hole in the ozone layer over Antarctica. This was seen to occur each spring as sunshine returned to the area after the long dark winter. Ozone levels slowly build up during the rest of the year, but

Weather and climate

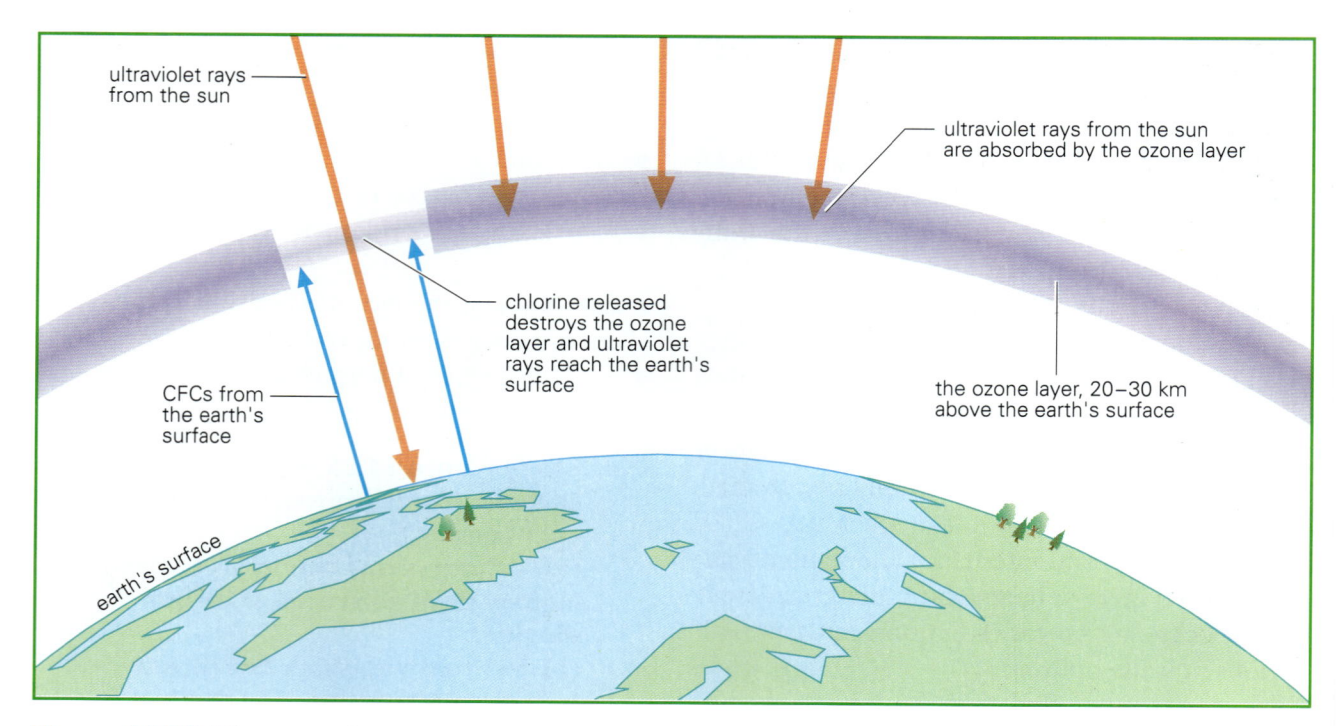

Figure 14.26 The ozone layer in selected countries

are reduced the following spring. This discovery was supported by US satellite observations.

Ultraviolet radiation can be lethal. All forms of life, including humans, are at risk from increased ultraviolet levels, which can cause melanoma and other skin cancers, eye cataracts which can lead to blindness, and an increase in infectious diseases due to the effect on immune systems. It has been estimated that a 1 per cent decrease in the ozone layer will cause a 2–3 per cent increase in human skin cancers. Crop yields would be reduced by increased ultraviolet levels since photosynthesis would be disrupted; fish and plankton would also be affected.

In the late 1980s, ozone depletion was discovered over North America and northern Europe. In the spring of 1991, the level of ozone over Antarctica had fallen to 50 per cent of the normal level. The ozone hole had spread to cover the southern tip of South America. There were reports of skin burns and blindness affecting sheep, cattle and rabbits in southern Chile.

By spring 1992, the level of ozone over Belgium had fallen by 18 per cent. This led to health warnings, advising people to avoid sunbathing, especially in the early summer. There were calls to re-schedule outdoor sports events to avoid the noon sun, and sales of sun protection creams soared.

In 1985 the Vienna Convention for the Protection of the Ozone Layer was adopted by 21 states. This pledged that governments would work towards reducing CFC production, with the target of eliminating CFCs completely. In 1987 the Montreal Protocol on Substances that Deplete the Ozone Layer was signed. Revised in 1990, the Protocol has a deadline of the year 2000 for the complete phasing-out of CFC production. It has been signed by over 70 states. The EU has since agreed on an earlier deadline of 1997 for ending CFC production. This is the first occasion on which environmental reasons have forced the ending of production of a group of chemicals.

The greenhouse effect and the depletion of the ozone layer are global challenges requiring international co-operation. This will not be easy, because different governments have different priorities, particularly those of LEDCs. Some poorer nations suspect that richer nations are cynically using environmental arguments to prevent the poorer countries from developing their own industries. In 1990 the International Institute for Environment and Development stated: 'Third World citizens find it difficult to share western concerns regarding global warming. Questions of survival 20 years or more into the future are of little interest to those concerned with survival today.'

Summary

- Rain is caused by air rising and cooling, condensing into clouds.
- The uplift of air may be caused by relief, convection and fronts.
- The world pattern of climates is affected by the circulation of the atmosphere and the ocean currents.

Change in the Countryside

15 Agricultural change in more economically developed countries

How has farming changed in developed countries? What have been the effects of the changes in farming?

This unit examines the ways in which farming has changed in more economically developed countries and how this has affected the environment. It also looks at different types of farm systems.

The changing farm

Farming in the UK has changed considerably in the last 40 years. These changes can be seen in one typical British farm in the Vale of York (see Figures 15.1 and 15.2). Treblesykes Farm is at Helperby, near York and covers 178 ha. In Figure 15.3, Mr Sowray, the farmer, describes how the farm has changed since he took over in 1970. Figure 15.4 shows land use changes at Treblesykes Farm since 1970.

Figure 15.1 The Vale of York and Treblesykes Farm

Figure 15.2 Treblesykes Farm

108 Change in the Countryside

Figure 15.3 The changes at Treblesykes Farm since 1970

'When I took over the farm in 1970 we concentrated on rearing beef cattle and so most of the fields were permanent or temporary grassland. We did grow some turnips and barley to feed to the animals, whose manure we used to improve the quality of the grass. Fields were smaller in those days with more hedgerows and fences. We employed four full-time workers to look after the cattle and help around the farm. Some jobs, like maintaining hedgerows, were done by hand, but we had two horses for some of the heavier work.

Things changed in the 1970s and 1980s, when the Government wanted farmers to grow more food. We went over to wheat and barley, together with some potatoes and peas. We had to buy big new tractors and combine harvesters and we bought machines for spreading fertilisers and for spraying pesticides and herbicides. The machines saved a lot of time, and, by 1986, we only needed two full-time labourers plus some part-timers for the potato harvest. The machines needed large fields to work efficiently, so we took out 1 km of hedgerow to create bigger fields.

In the 1980s the Government guaranteed good prices for wheat and barley, so this encouraged us to expand. We bought more new equipment, and put drains in many fields. We used 200 tonnes of artificial fertilisers each year to get high yields, especially on the cereals, and we sprayed fungicides and herbicides to protect the crops. As a result, crop yields increased by 60 per cent between 1970 and 1986. The chemicals got more and more expensive.

But things changed after 1986. There was a national surplus of wheat and barley so we had to cut our production. Instead we have gone in for more oil-seed rape, together with more peas and potatoes. Half the potatoes go for crisps and half for frozen chips. The peas go to a local freezing factory. We still use some artificial fertilisers as well as herbicides and pesticides but we have cut back a lot. We have also planted half a hectare of trees along the line of an abandoned railway. We take water from the River Swale to **irrigate** the crops. Each day we measure the rainfall. Then we telephone the local centre which measures **evapo-transpiration** rates and they advise us by computer on how much water to put on the fields. Farming is much more hi-tech now.'

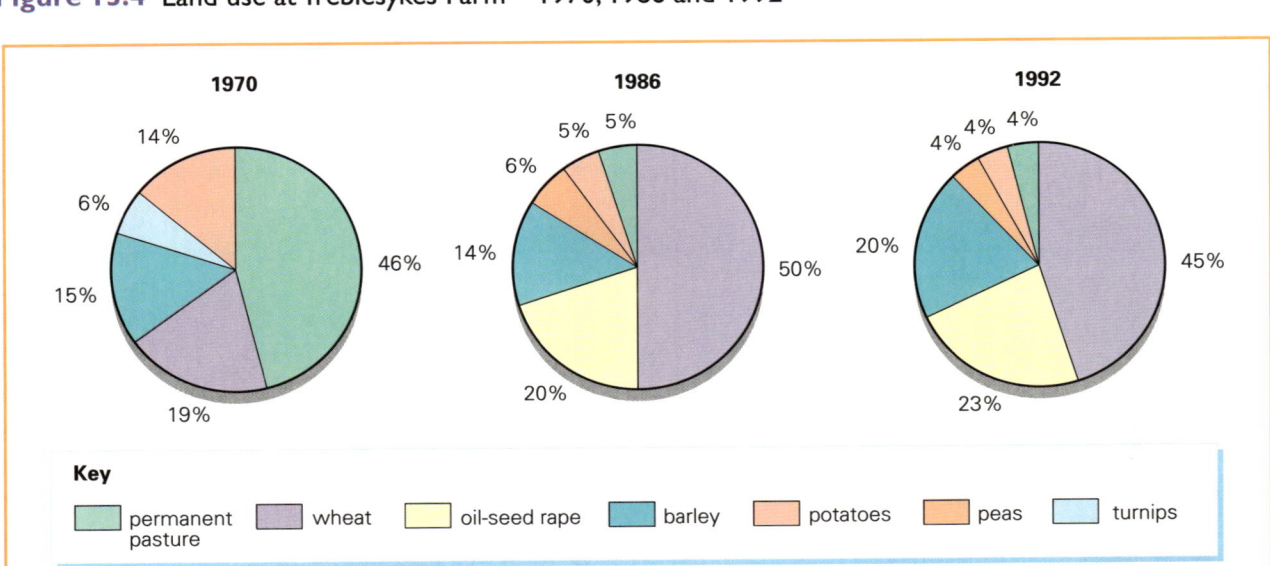

Figure 15.4 Land use at Treblesykes Farm – 1970, 1986 and 1992

1970
- permanent pasture: 46%
- wheat: 19%
- barley: 15%
- turnips: 6%
- potatoes: 14%

1986
- wheat: 50%
- oil-seed rape: 20%
- barley: 14%
- potatoes: 6%
- peas: 5%
- permanent pasture: 5%

1992
- wheat: 45%
- oil-seed rape: 23%
- barley: 20%
- potatoes: 4%
- peas: 4%
- permanent pasture: 4%

Key: permanent pasture, wheat, oil-seed rape, barley, potatoes, peas, turnips

Agricultural change in more economically developed countries

1. Treblesykes Farm is typical of many other British farms. Use the information in Figures 15.3 and 15.4 to write: (a) a summary of the main changes between 1970 and 1986, using the headings: crops; animals; hedgerows and field size; equipment; labour force; use of chemicals; crop yields; buildings; land use; (b) another summary of the main changes on the farm between 1986 and the present.

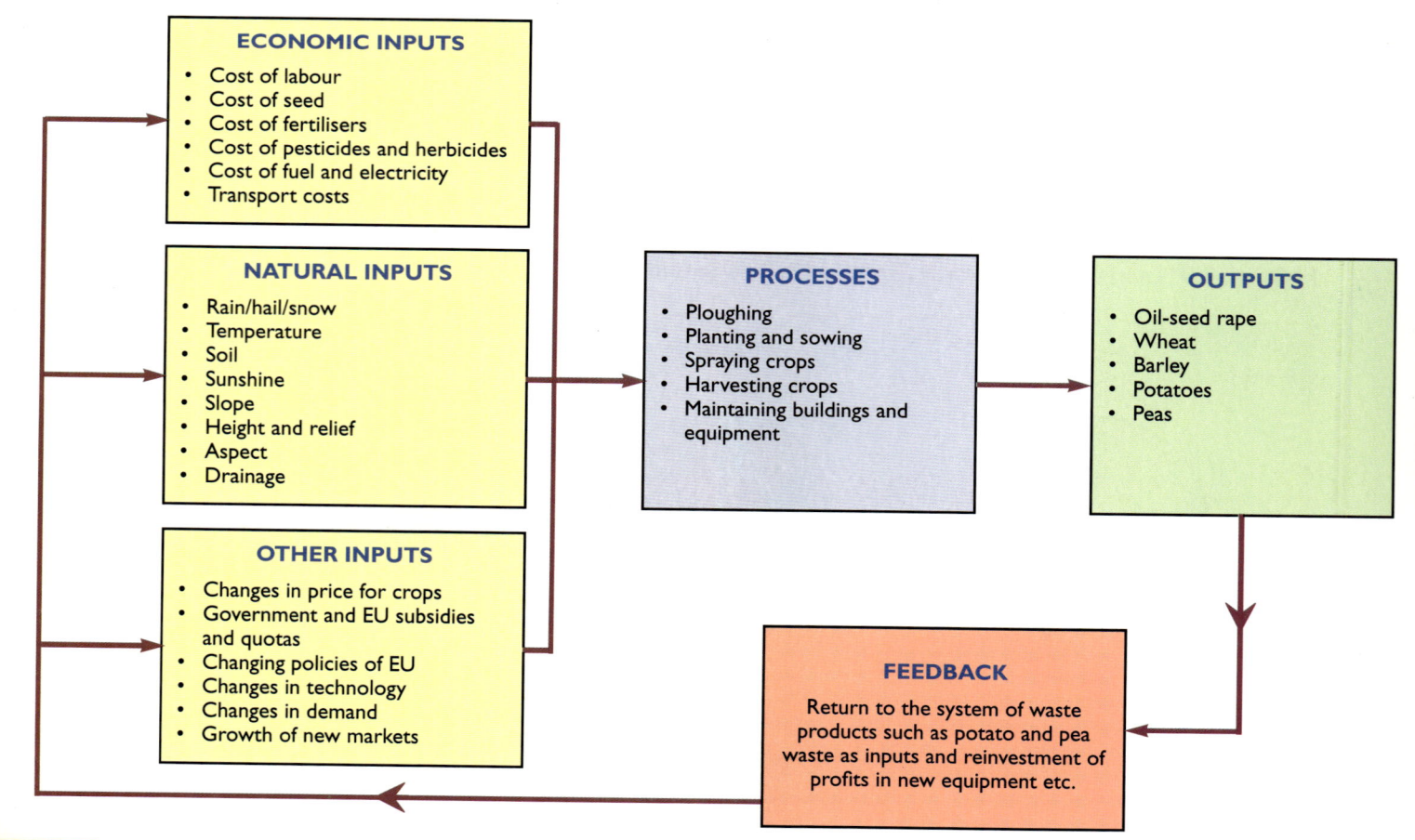

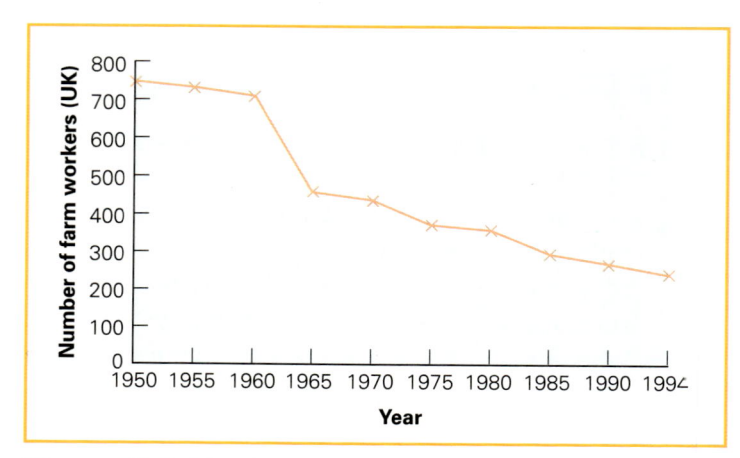

Figure 15.6 Numbers of UK farm workers, 1950–1994

The farm system

Like all farms, Treblesykes Farm is a system, that is it consists of a series of inputs (such as rainfall, seeds, money and fertilisers), processes (such as ploughing and harvesting) and outputs (such as oil-seed rape, potatoes and wheat and barley). Figure 15.5 shows this system in detail.

2. Look at Figure 15.5.
   (a) Which inputs is Mr Sowray unable to control?
   (b) What natural hazards might affect Treblesykes Farm? Think about hazards to crops from weather, insects, the river.
3. Draw a system diagram for Treblesykes Farm in 1970 to show inputs, processes, outputs and feedback at that date.

Figure 15.5 The Treblesykes Farm system

ECONOMIC INPUTS
- Cost of labour
- Cost of seed
- Cost of fertilisers
- Cost of pesticides and herbicides
- Cost of fuel and electricity
- Transport costs

NATURAL INPUTS
- Rain/hail/snow
- Temperature
- Soil
- Sunshine
- Slope
- Height and relief
- Aspect
- Drainage

OTHER INPUTS
- Changes in price for crops
- Government and EU subsidies and quotas
- Changing policies of EU
- Changes in technology
- Changes in demand
- Growth of new markets

PROCESSES
- Ploughing
- Planting and sowing
- Spraying crops
- Harvesting crops
- Maintaining buildings and equipment

OUTPUTS
- Oil-seed rape
- Wheat
- Barley
- Potatoes
- Peas

FEEDBACK
Return to the system of waste products such as potato and pea waste as inputs and reinvestment of profits in new equipment etc.

Change in the Countryside

1970

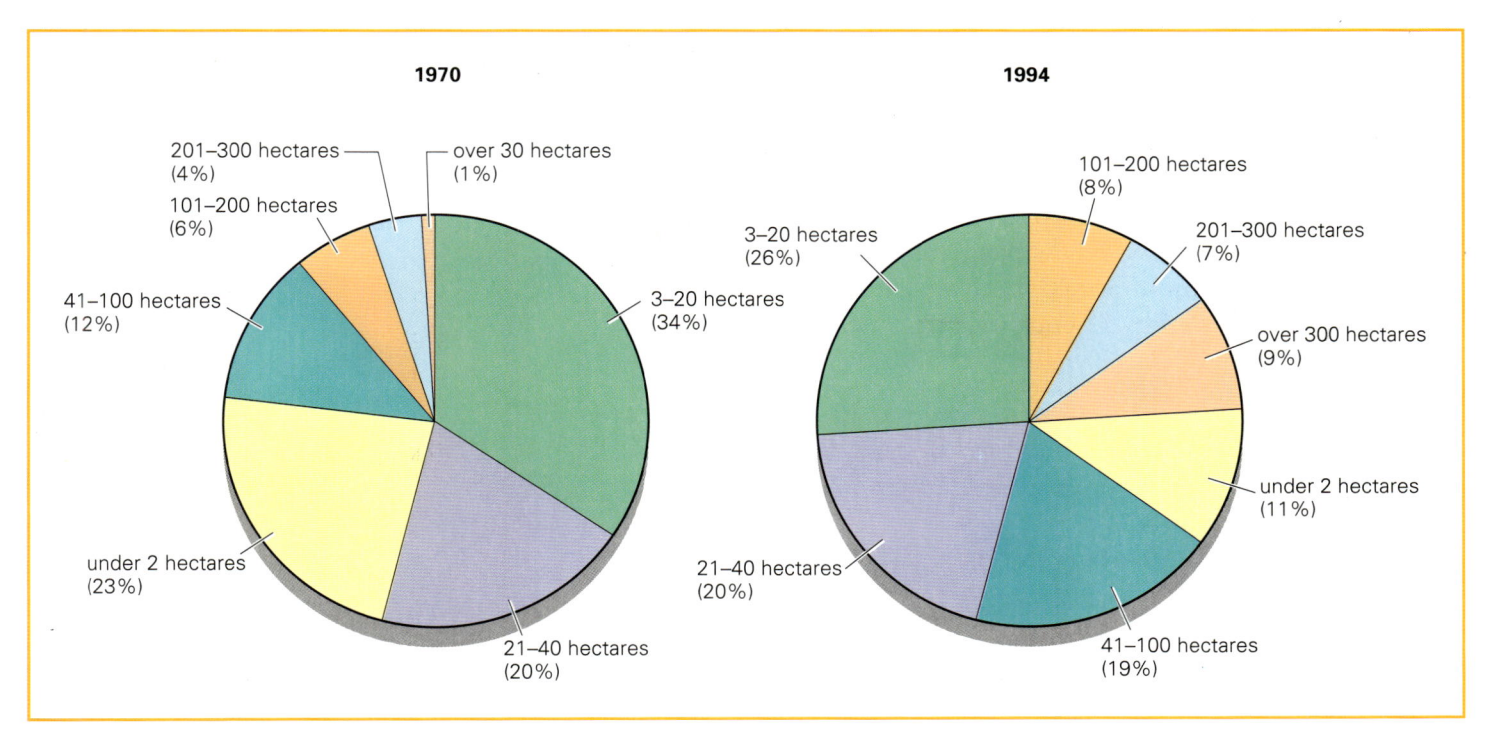

- 201–300 hectares (4%)
- over 30 hectares (1%)
- 101–200 hectares (6%)
- 41–100 hectares (12%)
- 3–20 hectares (34%)
- under 2 hectares (23%)
- 21–40 hectares (20%)

1994

- 101–200 hectares (8%)
- 201–300 hectares (7%)
- 3–20 hectares (26%)
- over 300 hectares (9%)
- under 2 hectares (11%)
- 21–40 hectares (20%)
- 41–100 hectares (19%)

Figure 15.7 UK farm sizes, 1970 and 1994

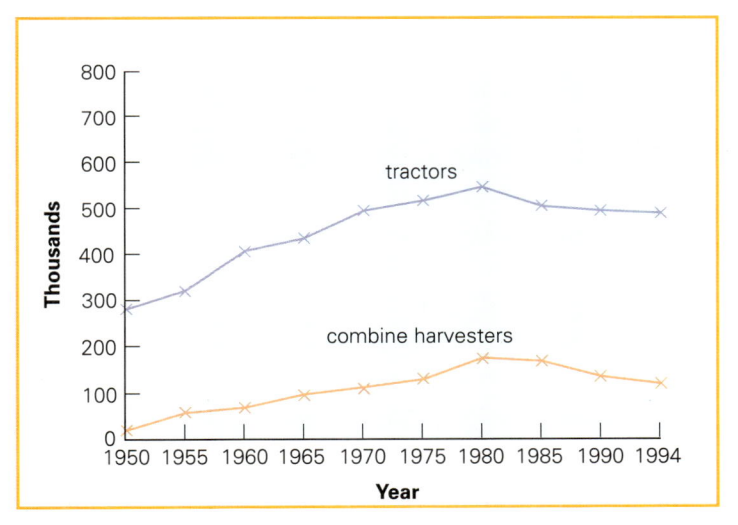

Figure 15.8 Tractors and combine harvester ownership in the UK, 1950–1994

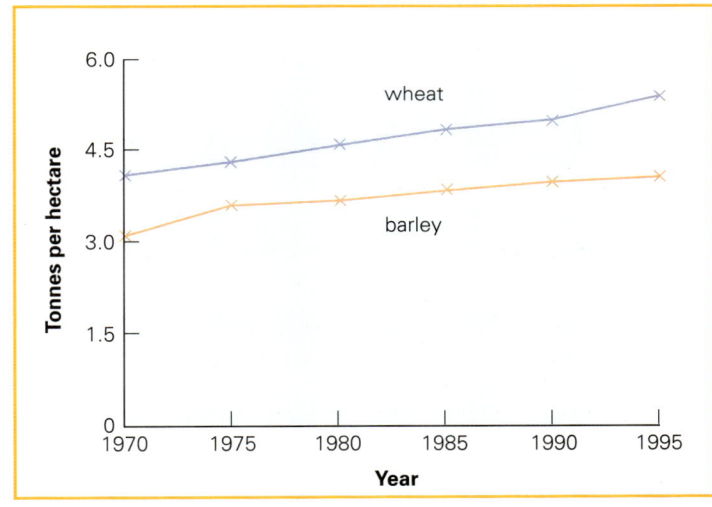

Figure 15.9 Yields of wheat and barley in the UK, 1970–1994

---

4. Look at Figures 15.6–15.9 and refer back to Figure 15.4.
   (a) How many British farm workers were there in 1950, 1970 and 1994?
   (b) What happened to the number of small farms (below 2 ha) between 1970 and 1994? What happened to the number of very big farms (over 200 ha) in the same period? Can you suggest reasons for these changes?
   (c) Describe the changes in the numbers of tractors and combine harvesters between 1970 and 1994. Can you suggest reasons for the changes?
   (d) Why do so many farms use a lot of chemicals and machines?
   (e) By how much did the annual yields of wheat and barley increase between 1970 and 1994?

Agricultural change in more economically developed countries

Farming and government policy

Before the Second World War (1939–45) Britain had to import 60 per cent of its food. Shortages during the war showed how dangerous it was to rely so heavily on imported food. So, after 1945 the British Government encouraged farmers to grow more food by:

- giving subsidies to help farmers to buy new machines, put up new buildings or drain land;
- advertising to encourage people to purchase more British produce;
- regulations to control pollution and so protect the environment.

The Common Agricultural Policy

In 1973 Britain joined the European Union (EU) and so had to follow the EUs Common Agricultural Policy (CAP). The CAP is intended to:

- give all farmers a fair standard of living;
- ensure a reliable supply of food;
- ensure reasonable prices for consumers.

The policy works by setting a minimum price for produce, from beef, lamb and milk to wheat and oil-seed rape. Farmers are guaranteed this price so they know that they will be able to sell their produce and make a profit. For example, in

Figure 15.10 Grain in an intervention store

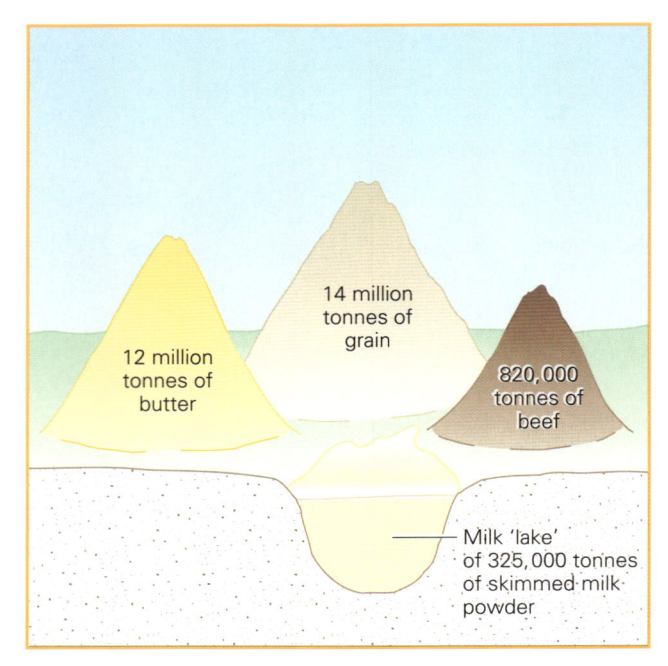

Figure 15.11 EU surpluses in 1988

the early 1980s, the EU encouraged farmers to grow grain, like wheat and barley. If farmers produced more than was needed, the surplus was stored in warehouses (see Figure 15.10) or freezers (for milk and meat). Farmers were very successful and produced much more food than Europe needed, so big surpluses, called 'mountains' of grain and meat and 'lakes' of milk had built up by 1987. Some of these surpluses are shown in Figure 15.11. Storing all this surplus food is very expensive, costing over £8000 per minute, but the food is available if there is a harvest disaster in Europe.

Reducing surpluses

In the 1980s the EU and the British Government agreed that surpluses had to be reduced. In the short term, some beef, butter and cheese were given away to pensioners, but in the longer term three methods have been used:

- reducing guaranteed prices for crops like wheat and barley where there was over-production;
- establishing an agreed maximum amount, called a quota for each product that a farmer was allowed to produce. By reducing milk and

112 Change in the Countryside

grain quotas, surpluses had been reduced by the 1990s;
- paying farmers not to cultivate 15 per cent of their land. This policy is called **set aside**. Farmers leave 15 per cent of their land fallow each year. This policy also achieved reductions in surpluses in the 1990s.

Effects on people and the environment

The CAP changes described above have affected many farmers. Unfortunately, some of the changes came too late to save large parts of the British countryside from the adverse effects of modern farming. Figure 15.12 shows how the countryside has changed since 1945.

In the early 1980s, when wheat and barley prices were high, many farmers drained marshes and ponds, took out hedgerows and woodland and used chemicals to increase production. Soon, parts of Britain in summer looked like the prairies of the USA with huge rolling wheat fields. In the process, Britain lost valuable wildlife habitats such as ponds, heathland, chalk grassland, lowland bog, ancient woodland and hedgerows.

Larger fields and fewer hedgerows have led to increased soil erosion, especially in eastern England. Dust storms have blown away precious topsoil and rain storms have added to the problem. Ponds, bogs, hedgerows and heathland all provided habitats for insects, birds and small animals. As the habitats were destroyed, so the wildlife died out.

Chemicals such as fertilisers and pesticides have been washed from the fields into streams and eventually into drinking water supplies. These chemicals can cause illnesses, such as stomach cancer, especially in young children or old people. The chemical sprays also killed many beneficial insects such as bees and butterflies. Even the common frog has disappeared from some parts of Britain. Over 300 plants and wildflowers are now listed as endangered.

Figure 15.12 Loss of the natural countryside in the UK since 1945

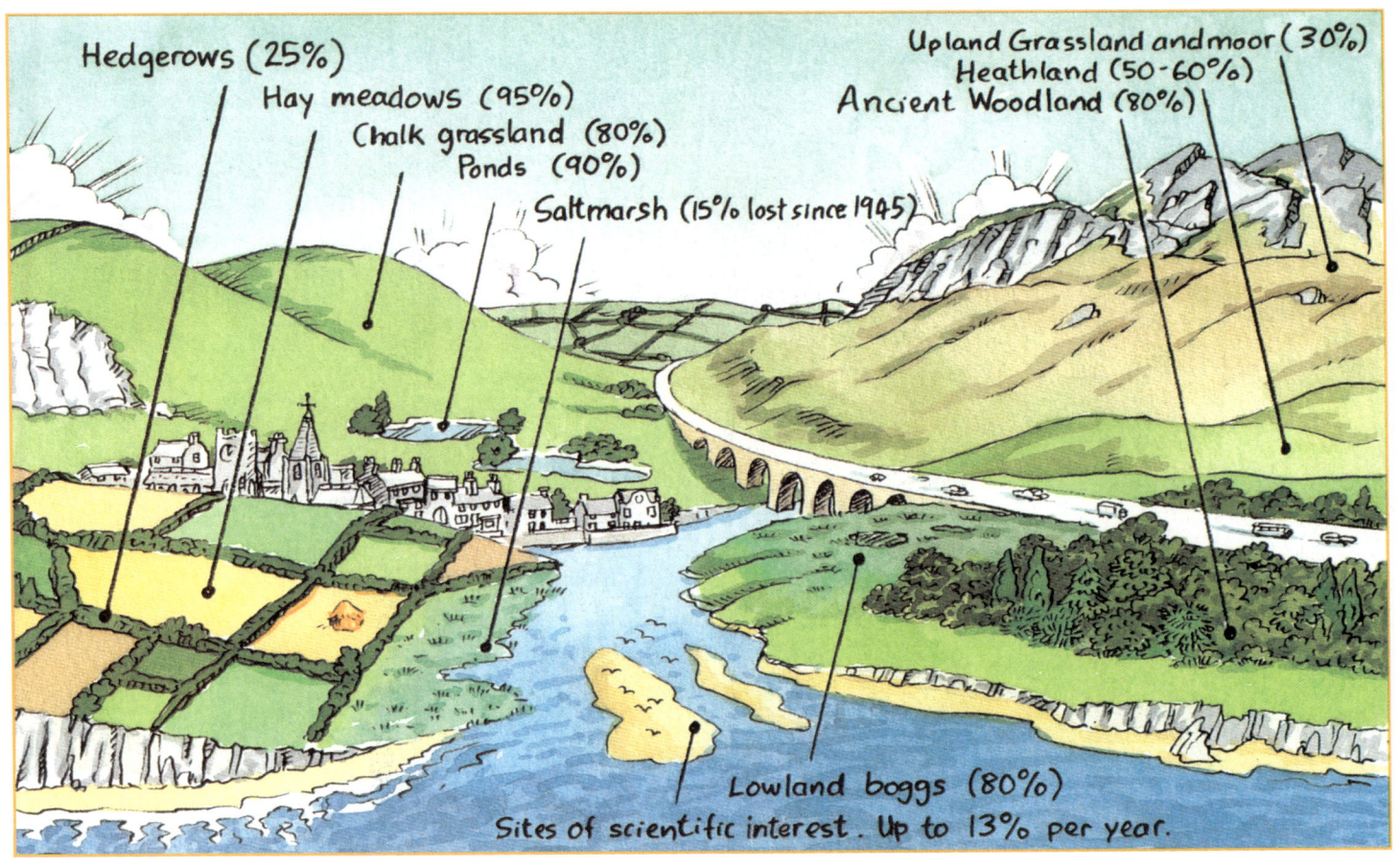

- Hedgerows (25%)
- Hay meadows (95%)
- Chalk grassland (80%)
- Ponds (90%)
- Saltmarsh (15% lost since 1945)
- Upland Grassland and moor (30%)
- Heathland (50-60%)
- Ancient Woodland (80%)
- Lowland boggs (80%)
- Sites of scientific interest. Up to 13% per year.

Agricultural change in more economically developed countries

Factory farming

The 1980s also saw the use of factory farming methods in rearing animals such as sheep, cattle and chickens. The animals were housed in cages (see Figure 15.13) in specially built rearing units where food, water, light and temperature were all controlled. Due to this close environmental control it was cheaper to produce eggs, meat and milk. However, by the 1990s many people felt that these systems were cruel to the animals and sometimes produced diseased food. For example there was public concern about an increase in the salmonella virus in both eggs and chickens as a result of these intensive methods. Now more shops and supermarkets are selling free range products (about 20% of all eggs) from farms where the animals are allowed to wander more freely outdoors. Sales of free range products are growing by 5 per cent per year despite being more expensive.

UK farming in the future

> **5. For each of the main agricultural changes in Britain from 1960–1990, give: (a) the reason for the change; (b) its effect on production; (c) its effect on people and the environment; (d) your own view of whether the change has been positive or negative; (e) a suggested alternative.**

Figure 15.13 Interior of a battery hen unit

By the 1990s, some of the worst problems of earlier methods in UK farming had become apparent. New trends in farming are now taking place.

- Organic farming is becoming increasingly significant. Farmers are not using artificial chemicals any more but instead are raising crops like carrots in a more traditional, chemical-free way. As people have become aware of the possible harmful side effects of chemically treated food, the demand for organic produce in supermarkets has grown.
- As EU quotas and prices have changed, many farmers have switched from milk, wheat and meat to farming alternative crops. Many now grow oil-seed rape (for oil) or evening primrose (for oil).
- Set aside has shown that there may be 3–5 million ha of surplus farmland in the UK. Alternative land uses include: creating golf courses (see Figure 15.14), planting forests, building factories or houses and using less intensive farming methods.

Water wars in Spain

Like Britain, Spain's agriculture has changed dramatically in the last 30 years. In the 1970s,

114   Change in the Countryside

Figure 15.14 Pycombe golf course built on farm land

40 per cent of all Spaniards worked in agriculture. Farms were often not very productive because they had few modern machines, soils were poor and thin, and many farmers did not have the capital to buy better seed, new machinery and fertiliser. Many farms were fragmented, due to inheritance laws, others were very big estates with absentee landlords.

Climate provided two major problems.

- A very uneven distribution of rainfall. Almera in the south east has the lowest rainfall in Europe. But while the south east is very dry, the north western part of the country is drenched by 1200 mm of rain each year.
- Unreliable rainfall. The years between 1970 and 1995 were extremely dry, but the unreliability of the rainfall was a more serious problem than the quantity. Most farmers grew wheat, vines and olives – crops which can tolerate drought – and reared sheep and goats.

The only exceptions to this pattern of farming in the 1970s occurred in the irrigated areas of the south and east. Here, fruits, rice and vegetables were intensively grown using fertilisers and modern equipment such as mechanical harvesters.

Spanish farming in the 1990s

Farming began to change in the 1970s and 1980s, when the government, using money from the EU, started to make reforms. The main changes have been:

- land reform to break up some of the large estates and sell the land cheaply to small farmers;
- government help to amalgamate scattered small farms into compact holdings;
- government help to persuade some people to find an alternative livelihood; by 1992 only 12 per cent of the Spanish population were farmers;
- grants and loans for farmers to buy new machinery, better seed and fertilisers;
- programmes to educate farmers about modern methods;
- extending the irrigated area to 3.2 million ha in 1990 (21 per cent of all farmland). The irrigated land is very productive, and is used for cotton, tobacco, citrus fruits, vines, almonds, vegetables and rice (see Figures 15.15 and 15.16 on page 116).

The effect of all these changes has been to make Spanish agriculture more efficient and

Agricultural change in more economically developed countries

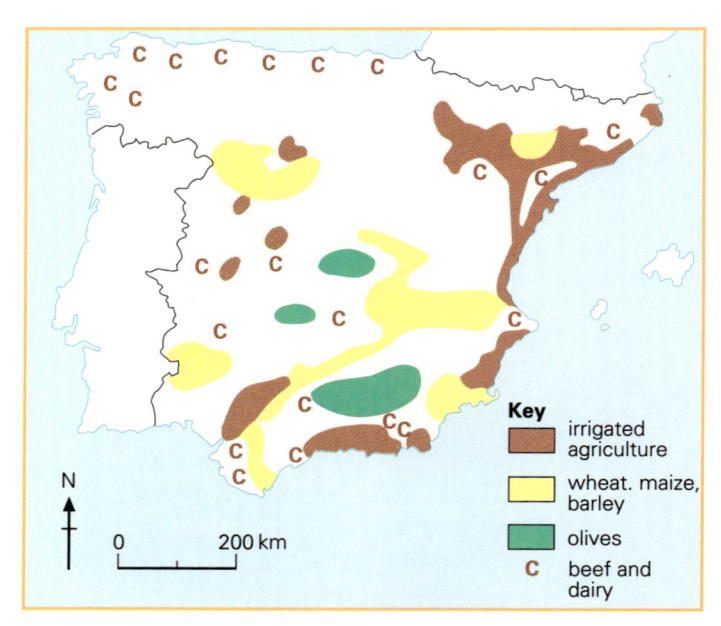

Figure 15.15 The distribution of agriculture in Spain

Figure 15.16 Irrigated farming in Malaga, Spain

profitable but very water-reliant. Farmers have moved away from drought-resistant crops like vines, olives and figs to crops like strawberries and rice that need a lot of water. This has made Spain the world's fourth largest water user after the USA, Canada and Russia. It has also led to disputes between Spain's regions over water rights. For example, the diversion of water from the River Tagus to the River Segura has led to conflict between the two regions of Valencia and Castille as to who will control this scarce resource.

Spanish farming in the future

The Spanish Government is worried that the problems of drought and the uneven distribution of rainfall will halt Spain's progress in the next century. As a result, they have come up with the National Hydrological Plan which is shown in Figure 15.17. The aim of the plan is to transfer water from the wet north and west of the country to the dry south and east. This would involve building 272 dams and hundreds of kilometres of aqueducts and canals to distribute the water. The water would be used to irrigate an extra 600 000 ha of land and so boost Spain's agricultural production. Some of the main advantages and disadvantages of the plan are shown in Figure 15.18, together with some alternatives to the plan.

Figure 15.17 Spain's National Hydrological Plan

116   Change in the Countryside

6. Look at Figure 15.18.
  (a) What will be the main economic benefits of the plan?
  (b) What will be the environmental and political drawbacks of the plan?
  (c) Assess the three main alternatives to the National Hydrological Plan.
  (d) Do you think the plan should be implemented? Give your reasons.

Figure 15.18 Views on Spain's National Hydrological Plan

Farming decisions

The pattern of fields, ponds, woodland and hedges in all countries of the world is partly the result of decisions taken by thousands of farmers. These decisions are about:

- what to produce;
- how much to produce;
- where to produce;
- the method of production.

There is an increasing number of factors which influence farmers' decisions.

Physical factors

- Height of the land – higher land may be cooler and harder to farm.
- Slope of the land – steep slopes make farming difficult.
- Aspect – south-facing slopes are warmer than those facing north.

Agricultural change in more economically developed countries 117

- Drainage – poor drainage makes farming difficult.
- Soil type and depth – thin, infertile soils are harder to farm than deep, fertile soils.
- Weather and climate – local conditions such as winds or frost pockets can have a major influence on farming.

Economic factors

- Profit – farmers need to earn profit to invest in the farm.
- Labour – cost, availability and skill of labour.
- Markets – some are high risk, like fruit, while others, like vegetables, are more secure. Some markets have higher prices than others.
- Capital – many farmers need to borrow money from banks to finance improvements or obtain grants and subsidies from government.
- Costs – such as seed or livestock, fuel, chemicals, transport, electricity.
- Demand – changes in the demand for different products.

Personal factors

- Risk – some farmers are prepared to take higher risks than others.
- Efficiency and work – some farmers are better managers and work harder than others.
- Choices – some farmers have a wide choice of what to produce, others do not.
- Personal preference – some farmers prefer to produce some products.
- Technology – farmers' attitudes to new technology and its costs vary.

Government policy

Government or other (e.g. European Union) policy may be to encourage the production of goods in short supply (e.g. oil-seed rape) and discourage production of others (e.g. wheat, milk, beef). Government policies also affect product prices.

Social factors

- Land ownership – farmers who own their own land may work harder than those who do not.
- Information – farmers need advice and information from computers, radio, television and magazines.

Environmental factors

- Conservation – in areas of special environmental importance the government may encourage conservation at the expense of farming.

Case study – Roberto and Maria

Roberto and Maria Mendoza own a small irrigated farm near Valencia in south eastern Spain. They concentrate on producing oranges which are mostly sold to Britain and other EU countries. Their orange trees are now ten years old and are not yielding as much fruit. Oranges need 600–800 mm of water each year and the water must be supplied relatively cheaply if the Mendoza's are to make a profit. The growing season extends from November until the end of May.

The Mendoza's have options. They could replant with new orange trees, which would take six years to grow before they gave fruit. Recently, South African, Israeli and Californian oranges have started to compete with the Spanish product. Alternatively, they could convert to growing strawberries, peppers, aubergines and calibrese, which could go by air to markets in northern Europe. A third option would be to revert to growing more traditional drought-resistant crops like vines and olives, with a small crop of wheat. This would reduce their demand for water, which is becoming very expensive.

> 7. (a) Give your view on each of the three alternative options for Roberto and Maria.
> (b) What other factors might be relevant to their decision?
> (c) Choose the solution you think is the best and give reasons for your choice.

Change in the Countryside

Case study – Ken and Joan

Ken and Joan Touse are tenant farmers in the Yorkshire Dales, where they rent 50 ha of land. The land is only suitable for dairy cattle. Since the EU set quotas on milk production the Touse family have had to cut back production, so reducing their income. They do not own the land so cannot sell up and use the money to go into another business. At 52, Ken feels he is too old to get another job although Joan could probably find work. Their local MP and MEP (Member of the European Parliament) have told them that they can do nothing to help.

Ken wants to take a small EU grant to give up dairy farming and retire early to York. Joan wants to stay on, try and sell their milk quota to another farmer, and raise beef cattle whilst offering bed and breakfasts to tourists.

8. What do you think Ken and Joan should do? Give reasons.

Case study – Jeff and Pat

Jeff and Pat Blackburn farm 200 ha close to the southern outskirts of Coventry. They grow wheat, barley, oil-seed rape and potatoes. However, the Blackburns have had an offer from a developer to turn their land into a golf course. There is a huge local demand for new golf courses, especially close to large towns, and EU quotas on wheat and barley mean that their income has fallen in recent years. The developer needs all their land, including the farmhouse, so the Blackburns would have to move. Jeff has been a farmer all his life and, at 42, does not really want to start a new career. Pat has always worked on the farm with Jeff and feels the same. However, they could make a lot of money by selling the land.

9. Do you think the Blackburns should sell their farm to the developer? Explain your answer.

Summary

- Farming in more economically developed countries has become more intensive in the last 20 years.
- Farms are systems with inputs, processes and outputs.
- The Common Agricultural Policy (CAP) of the EU has a big effect on farming patterns in the member countries.
- The policies of the CAP have sometimes led to environmental damage.
- Recent alternative approaches to farming in the UK include organic farming and the growth of set aside.
- Farming in Spain depends heavily on irrigation.
- The rapid growth in the demand for irrigation water in Spain has led to conflict between regions and the development of the controversial National Hydrological Plan.
- Farming is about making decisions, which are affected by many factors.
- Decisions about farming can have a major impact on the environment.

Chapter 16 Agricultural change in less economically developed countries

How have poorer countries succeeded in feeding their booming populations?

This unit describes the Green Revolution and uses the example of Thailand to illustrate how less economically developed countries have successfully increased agricultural production in order to keep pace with their rapid population growth.

Increasing production

The population of many of the world's poorer countries has been growing rapidly in recent decades (see Figure 16.1). With all these extra mouths to feed, it has been essential for food production to increase rapidly. This has been achieved in two ways:

- extension of the margins of cultivation by farming new sites such as areas of poorer soil, steeper slopes and forested areas;
- intensification of production by increasing yields from the existing cultivated areas through increased use of machinery and of agro-chemicals, including fertiliser, soil conditioner and pesticide.

The 'Green Revolution'

The 'Green Revolution' is the term given to the introduction of modern intensive farming methods to LEDCs and especially the development of new hybrid varieties of cereals from the late 1960s. New higher yielding varieties (HYVs) of rice seeds were developed at the International Rice Research Institute in the Philippines. The IR-8 seed became known as 'miracle rice' because it increased yields six-fold at its first harvest.

The Green Revolution resulted in a dramatic increase in yields, which doubled within a decade. However, the Green Revolution was heavily criticised at first because the hybrid plants required expensive fertiliser and pesticides. Only richer farmers could afford to buy and grow the new seeds. There was little benefit for poorer farmers. There were also environmental concerns – heavy applications of fertiliser, pesticide and other agro-chemicals were easily washed off the fields and into water sources, harming wildlife and polluting the water supply.

Figure 16.1 Population growth

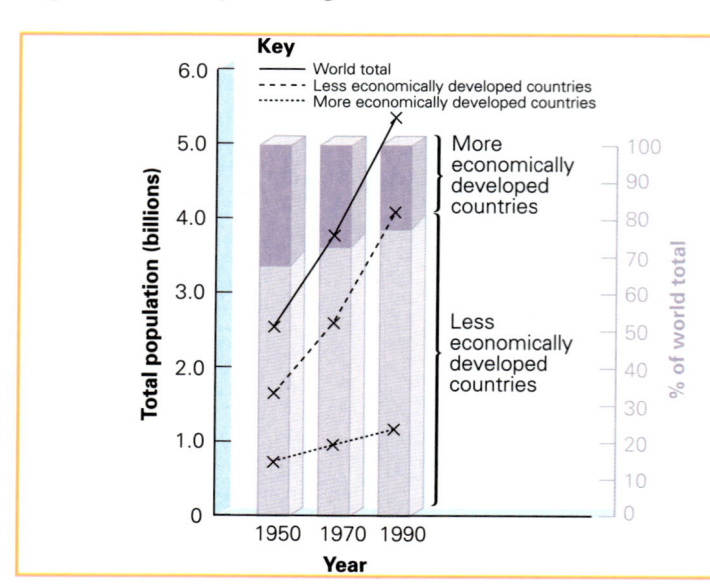

120 Change in the Countryside

These early criticisms of the Green Revolution were widely publicised. Less widely publicised have been the results of more recent research, which suggests that the benefits of the new hybrid seeds are now spreading to a wider range of farmers. More recently developed hybrids require less fertiliser and chemicals and are more resistant to disease than IR-8 was. Without the Green Revolution it is difficult to see how widespread famine could have been averted in many poorer countries. It is worth noting that all the terrible famines that have occurred since the 1960s have been caused primarily by war and disruption of food distribution rather than by food shortages.

Figure 16.2 India: agricultural statistics

Year	Average rice yield (kg per ha)	Total rice production (tonnes)	Fertiliser use (kg per ha)
1960	10	50 million	1.5
1970	11	63 million	12.2
1980	13	75 million	29
1990	17	113 million	64
1995	20	128 million	72.2

1. Explain the difference between extending the margins of cultivation and intensifying production.
2. Figure 16.2 shows statistics for India.
   (a) Draw a line graph and plot the total rice production statistics from Figure 16.2.
   (b) Draw a line graph and plot the statistics for rice yields and fertiliser use.
   (c) What conclusions can you draw about the relative success or failure of the Green Revolution from your graphs from 2(a) and (b)?

Agricultural change in Thailand

Over two-thirds of Thailand's labour force is employed in the agricultural sector, and agriculture directly supports over 60 per cent of the country's population. Thailand's population has been growing very rapidly, from 36 million in 1970 to 60 million in 1995. During the 1960s the population grew at an annual rate of 3.6 per cent. The growth rate had fallen to 3.1 per cent during the 1970s and 2.2 per cent during the 1980s, reflecting a successful family planning policy and rising standards of living. During the 1990s the population growth rate has fallen below 1 per cent per year. Even at this lower rate, there are still over half a million extra mouths to feed each year.

Extending the margins of cultivation

Most of Thai agriculture still uses traditional, unintensive methods. Until recently, production increases had been mainly achieved by extending the margins of cultivation. Between 1950 and 1975 the cultivated area increased at an average annual rate of 2.7 per cent. Since the late 1970s the rate of expansion has slowed to under 1.2 per cent per year so that by the mid-1990s there was little marginal land available other than forested areas. Much recent forest clearance has been illegal – in 1990 it was estimated that some 3.7 million people had illegally encroached on over 9 million ha of forest. The area of Thailand covered by forest has plummeted from 55 per cent in 1965 to 25 per cent in 1995. There are now serious problems of soil erosion in steep areas cleared of vegetation for cultivation.

Intensification of production

By extending the margins of cultivation, less productive soils have been brought into use. This resulted in a decline in average yields. During the 1970s, for example, yields of rice, by far Thailand's most important crop, declined by

Agricultural change in less economically developed countries 121

2.4 per cent per year. Only during the 1980s did large-scale intensification of production begin. Intensification took various forms:

- Increased use of machinery, especially powered rice cultivators. The number of tractors in use in Thailand increased from 73 000 in 1980 to 160 000 by 1995.
- Increased use of fertiliser. In 1980 average fertiliser use amounted to 16 kg per ha; this had increased to 51 kg per ha by 1995 (see Figure 16.3).
- Increased use of irrigation. The irrigated rice area doubled between 1985 and 1995 from 10 per cent to 20 per cent of total area.
- Farmers in the central plain of Thailand have introduced double cropping.
- Higher yielding strains were introduced, but not on the scale of many other rice producing countries. The Thai farmers are proud of their high quality, traditional varieties of rice and are wary of introducing the new strains which have a blander taste.

The overall result of the intensification has been an increase in rice yields of 2.9 per cent per annum since 1980. In 1980 total rice production was 17.4 million tonnes and, by 1994, it was 21.3 million tonnes.

Intensification has also occurred in Thailand's other major crops. Sugar cane has been especially successful – average yields have increased by 4.2 per cent per annum since 1980, compared with an average annual decrease of 1.9 per cent during the 1970s.

There has been a marked diversification of production since 1980. Maize, cassava, soya beans, pineapples and rubber have become important products (see Figure 16.4). The percentage of arable land planted with rice fell from 88 per cent in 1950 to 55 per cent in 1995. Poultry production has also increased, with

Figure 16.3 Applying fertiliser to a Thai field

Figure 16.4 Pineapple field in Thailand

exports of frozen chickens rising from 65 000 tonnes in 1986 to 114 000 tonnes in 1995, principally to Japan and the Middle East.

The growth of Western-style supermarkets and the rise of a fairly wealthy middle class in Bangkok and Chiang Mai have led to the development of packaging and grading of a wide range of produce. The supermarkets are increasingly supplied by contract farming as big business moves into Thai agriculture.

3. Why is it important for Thailand to increase food production?
4. (a) How did Thailand achieve food production increases until recently?
   (b) What effects did this have?
5. How has intensification of production occurred in Thailand?
6. Why do you think big business has started to take an interest in Thai agriculture?

Summary

- The use of intensive methods of production and higher yielding strains of crops have allowed less economically developed countries to increase agricultural production rapidly.

17 Leisure and tourism

What are popular tourist sites?

This unit explores the conflicting demands on areas of great scenic attraction using a number of case studies. Particular attention is given to the harm which some leisure activities can do to these areas. The development of theme parks is studied through the example of EuroDisney, and Thailand provides a case study of the benefits and disadvantages which tourism can bring to a developing country.

Case study – Stonehenge

Stonehenge, on Salisbury Plain in Wiltshire, is one of the most important ancient sites in the world. The great circle of sarsen stones was erected over 4000 years ago for a purpose that is not definitely known. This mysterious site has intrigued visitors for centuries. The first written record of Stonehenge dates from the twelfth century. Today, the monument attracts three-quarters of a million visitors each year, making it one of Britain's most important tourist attractions. Such a popular tourist site is sometimes known as a 'honeypot'; honeypots have many problems.

Figure 17.1 shows Stonehenge in the 1970s, when visitors could walk freely among the stones. Figure 17.2 shows Stonehenge in 1995. It has been fenced off and visitors can no longer walk among the stones. This change is partly due to the ever increasing number of visitors.

The visitors to Stonehenge have harmed the monument. The grass has been heavily eroded by the trampling of millions of feet. Vandals have attacked the stones and sprayed them with graffiti. Extensive facilities have been constructed to cope with the numbers of vehicles coming to the site. A shop, exhibition room and large car park were built across the road from Stonehenge and a concrete subway was built under the road to give access to the site. Steel mesh paths have been laid and there are notices warning people to keep to these paths.

Figure 17.1 Stonehenge in the 1970s

Figure 17.2 Stonehenge in 1995

124   Change in the Countryside

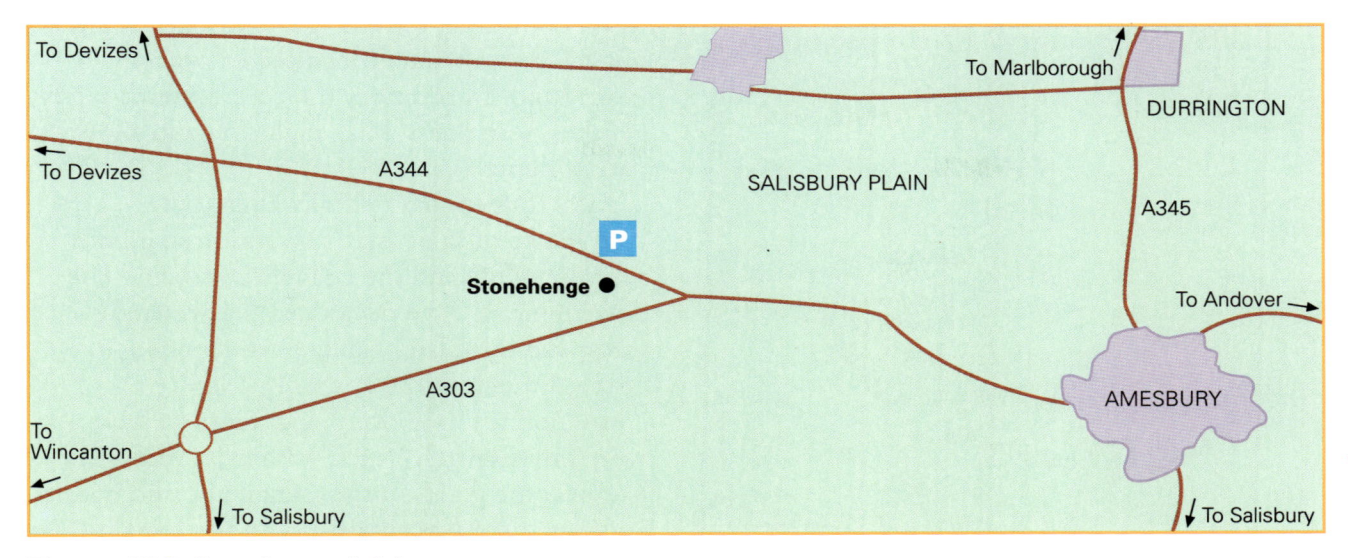

Figure 17.3 Stonehenge, Salisbury

There is no doubt that the facilities provided for the tourists have changed the character of Stonehenge. Many people protest about the intrusive paths, notices and fences. The busy A344 and A303 roads pass close to the site (see Figure 17.3) and the traffic causes noise and pollution, destroying the mysterious atmosphere of the place. Yet it is also clear that Stonehenge must be protected so that visitors can continue to enjoy it. Several proposals have been made, including a scheme to build a replica of Stonehenge on a nearby site in order to protect the original!

After many years of planning, a £15 million visitors' centre was planned at Larkhill, 1 km north of Stonehenge. In 1993 the scheme was scrapped and it was announced that the A344 past Stonehenge was to be closed.

Figure 17.4 Visitors to Stonehenge

Year	Number
1955	202 000
1960	310 000
1965	399 000
1970	598 000
1975	711 000
1980	586 000
1985	597 000
1990	703 000
1995	754 000

1. (a) Describe the location of Stonehenge.
   (b) Why is Stonehenge an important tourist attraction?
2. (a) Draw a graph to illustrate the statistics in Figure 17.4.
   (b) Why do you think the number of visitors increased so much between 1957 and 1995?
   (c) What may have caused the decline of visitors between 1975 and 1980?
   (d) What are the effects of the increasing number of visitors to Stonehenge?
3. Describe the scenes in Figures 17.1 and 17.2. What has caused the changes?
4. (a) What are the drawbacks of tourism on Stonehenge?
   (b) What can be done to protect Stonehenge, yet still allow tourists to visit the monument?
5. (a) What is meant by a tourist 'honeypot'?
   (b) Name a 'honeypot' close to where you live. Why is it so attractive to tourists? How does it cope with large numbers of visitors?

Leisure and tourism

Figure 17.5 The Spanish costas

Case study – the Costas of Spain

Europe's most popular coastal tourist centres are the *costas* (coasts) of southern Spain (see Figure 17.5). Fifty-two million tourists visited Spain in 1994 and 90 per cent of them went to the costas. Tourism is very important to Spain, providing nearly 10 per cent of the total GNP and employing over 1 million people.

The development of the costas dates from the 1960s when Spain became a destination for the inclusive tour (package holiday) industry. The introduction of jet airliners during this decade allowed a fast shuttle service between airports in northern Europe and the Mediterranean coast of Spain. The tourists were attracted by the hot, dry summers (see Figure 17.6), offering what the travel companies termed 'guaranteed sunshine' but the warm winters encouraged tourism all year round. In addition, the costas offered sandy beaches, warm seas, busy night-life and a low cost of living.

Mass tourism has radically altered the appearance of the costas, revolutionising both the way of life and the coastal ecosystem. The developments have devastated the wetland, forest and shrubland habitats which once covered much of the costas. In 1960 Torremolinos, Benidorm and Tossa de Mar were tiny fishing villages; within 15 years they had become giant tourist complexes, and within 25 years there was almost no undeveloped or unspoilt coastline left along the costas (see Figure 17.7). Thousands of high-rise hotels, villa complexes, discos, restaurants, marinas, dual carriageways and promenades have covered the coastline in concrete. Benidorm alone has accommodation for over 400 000 tourists.

The coastal developments have led to greatly increased pollution. Some hotels and camping sites dump their litter and raw sewage straight into the sea. There have been outbreaks of typhoid among holidaymakers on the Costa Brava, due to lack of planning as rapid urban growth outpaced the provision of services. Steps to resolve some of the problems were only taken during the 1980s after 20 years of almost unrestricted growth. Benidorm spent £315 million on improving its water supply, sewage system and general infrastructure during the late 1980s.

Figure 17.6 Alicante's climate

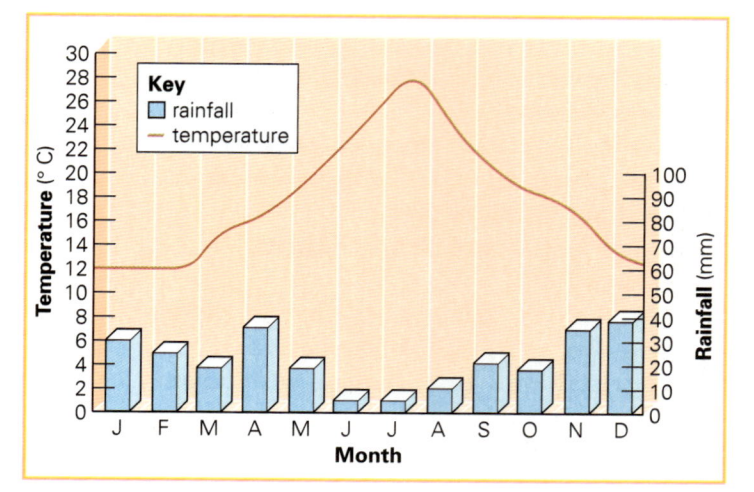

Figure 17.7 Benidorm

126 Change in the Countryside

It is easy to criticise the ugly developments on the costas, but it should be remembered that the creation of resorts such as Benidorm and Torremolinos has concentrated tourist development into purpose-built complexes able to handle millions of visitors each year. Inland, the Spanish countryside has been little affected by the tourist boom, thus preserving the environment.

The mistakes made in the tourist development of the Spanish costas have been repeated in other Mediterranean countries, notably Greece, Turkey and Cyprus. The United Nations (UN) estimates that, by the year 2025, there will be 760 million tourists to Mediterranean countries, more than seven times the present total. Ninety-five per cent of the Mediterranean coastline could be urbanised.

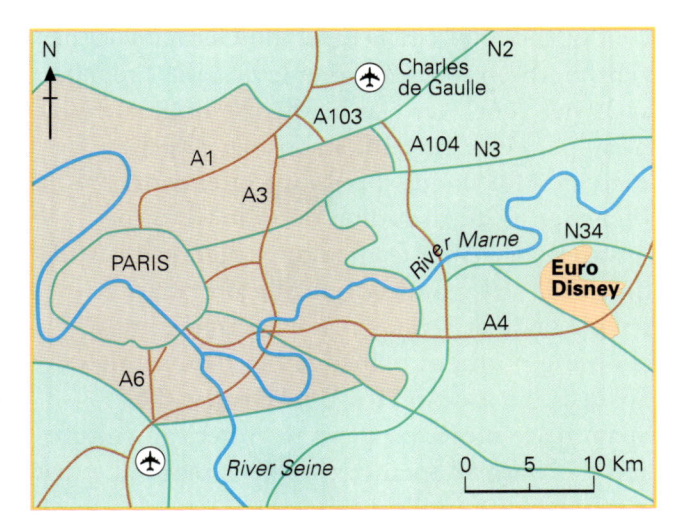

Figure 17.8 EuroDisney's location

> 6. (a) Study Figure 17.5 and name the costas of Spain.
>   (b) What are the attractions of a holiday on the costas?
> 7. Study Figure 17.6.
>   (a) Use an atlas to discover the July and January temperatures for London. How do they compare to those of Alicante?
>   (b) What is the total annual rainfall in Alicante? How does this compare with the total rainfall for London?
> 8. Write the dialogue of a conversation that might take place between two Spaniards living in Benidorm, one of whom is opposed to tourism and development, the other who is in favour of it. Include as many arguments for and against as possible.

Case study – Disneyland, Paris

Theme parks first began in 1955, when the US film-maker Walt Disney opened Disneyland in California. Since then, hundreds of theme parks have been built around the world, including Alton Towers and the Chessington World of Adventure in the UK. Disney opened two more theme parks – Disneyworld at Orlando, Florida in 1971 and Disneyland in Tokyo, Japan in 1983. In the 1980s the Walt Disney Corporation looked for a site for a fourth theme park, this time in western Europe.

Disney rapidly reduced the choice of location to two countries – Spain and France. The final decision was to locate at Marne-la-Vallée, a new town 30 km east of central Paris (see Figure 17.8). This site was chosen for the following reasons:

- it was easily accessible from many urban centres in north west Europe, the wealthiest part of the continent, by motorway, rail and air;
- Paris was already a major tourist centre;
- there was a large expanse of relatively cheap, flat land available, with scope for future development.

Disneyland, Paris opened in April 1992. It covers 600 ha of a 2000 ha site. There are rides, shops, restaurants and a golf course, plus six hotels, all with an American theme – Frontierland, Adventureland, Fantasyland, Main Street USA and Discoveryland. Visitors can roller-coaster down Big Thunder Mountain or through the Phantom House.

Unfortunately, Disneyland, Paris has not been as successful as its owners had expected. In its first year Disneyland, Paris had planned to attract 11 million visitors but less than 10 million visited the theme park and it made losses of over £100 million. While the British represented 20 per cent of the total visitors and the Germans 15 per cent, both up to their target levels, the French, at 29 per cent, were far below the original target of 50 per cent. Several reasons have been suggested for the disappointing attendance by French visitors, including opposition to the 'invasion' by American culture, high prices and the mild, wet winters of northern France. Some people say that Disney made a mistake in choosing northern France rather than southern Spain as the location for EuroDisney. The Spanish are more receptive to American culture and the warmer Spanish climate is more like that of California and Florida.

Case study – tourism in Thailand

Following the rapid growth of mass tourism in the Mediterranean countries, a demand developed for holidays in more exotic locations. Tourism first spread in to LEDCs in the 1970s as tourists from the wealthy nations of the MEDCs were lured by a range of attractions (Figure 17.9).

Tourism brings many benefits to Thailand.

- Tourism is Thailand's most important source of foreign revenue.
- Over 1.5 million Thais have jobs in the tourist sector. Thousands more earn a living through selling craft goods to tourists.
- Tourism has provided the stimulus for major projects such as the construction of new international airports at Bangkok and Chiang Mai, and of new highways and sewerage systems.
- Tourism gives Thailand international prestige.

Outside Bangkok, the main tourist centres are the beach resorts of Pattaya, Hua Hin and Phuket and the northern city of Chiang Mai. Chiang Mai was developed as a resort during the

> 9. (a) Why was Marne-la-Vallée chosen as the site for Disneyland, Paris?
> (b) Why do you think that Disney did not choose to build EuroDisney in the UK, despite the shared language and culture?

Figure 17.9 (a) Thailand's tourist attractions

Figure 17.9 (b) Thailand's tourist attractions

Figure 17.9 (c) Thailand's tourist attractions

1980s in a deliberate attempt to relieve the increasing pressure of tourism on Bangkok and to spread the benefits of tourism more widely throughout Thailand.

It is dangerous for a country to become too heavily dependent on tourism for income and employment. Thailand has little control over the most important influences on tourist numbers. The holiday decisions of tourists are largely based on personal interests, social pressures, cost and safety. They can be heavily influenced by bad publicity. For example, a military coup in Thailand in 1991 was followed by a massacre in May 1992 when 50 students were shot dead by troops attempting to break up an anti-government demonstration in Bangkok. The result of this political instability and violence was a 4 per cent drop in the number of tourists visiting Thailand.

As well as jobs, money and prestige, tourism has also brought problems for Thailand. A vast sex industry has developed in association with tourism. Bangkok and Pattaya have two of the world's most notorious red light districts where prostitutes and sex shows operate. In Bangkok alone there are an estimated 250 000 female prostitutes, many of them migrants from the poverty-stricken farming areas of the north. There has been a rapid growth in HIV infection and in the risk of AIDS. Child prostitution is also a major problem, with rich tourists from countries like Germany travelling to Thailand for this purpose.

Tourism has had some negative environmental effects. In some coastal areas of Thailand hotel construction has denied access to the beach to local people. Wildlife habitats have been affected and natural vegetation destroyed.

Leisure and tourism

Figure 17.10 Tourism in Thailand

Year	1986	1987	1988	1989	1990	1991	1992	1993
Tourists ('000s)	2800	3472	4121	4810	5300	5088	5137	5959
Income ($million)	1600	2001	2944	3855	4023	4600	4840	5614

The construction of golf courses has created great demand for water which has been diverted from sources used by local people.

In recent years there has been a growth in 'green tourism' in Thailand. Tour companies offering trekking holidays through the northern highlands and a taste of traditional rural Thai life have attracted more tourists. Such tourism is on a smaller scale and poses less environmental and social threat than mass tourism.

10. Tourists visiting Thailand come from the following countries:

Malaysia	15%	Germany	5%
Japan	13%	UK	5%
Taiwan	11%	France	4%
Singapore	7%	Italy	2%
USA	6%	Canada	1.5%
Australia	5%	Others	25.5%

   (a) Draw a pie graph to illustrate these statistics.
   (b) From what type of country do most tourists to Thailand come?

11. Figure 17.10 shows the number of tourists visiting Thailand between 1986 and 1993, and the income they generated.
   (a) Draw a line graph to illustrate these statistics.
   (b) Why did the number of tourists visiting Thailand fall between 1990 and 1992?
   (c) Why is it dangerous for a country to become heavily dependent upon tourism?

Summary

- Tourists visit a wide range of attractions.
- Large numbers of tourists can harm the areas which they visit.
- There is increasing pressure to protect the most vulnerable areas.
- 'Green tourism' attempts to reduce the impact on the environment.
- There are economic and other advantages to local people in tourist areas but tourism can also bring disadvantages.

18 Migration to the countryside

Why has the population of rural areas increased rapidly in recent years?

Counterurbanisation is the movement of people from urban to rural areas. It has brought both advantages and disadvantages to the rural areas involved.

What is counterurbanisation?

Since the 1950s there has been an increasing trend for people in Britain to move out of urban areas into rural areas. This movement into rural areas has been termed **counterurbanisation**. In fact, it is an extension of the process of **suburbanisation** which had been occurring for several decades before 1950.

Why has counterurbanisation happened?

Several factors help to account for the growth of counterurbanisation. There has been a rejection of city living and a desire to live in rural areas beyond the suburbs. Rising standards of living have meant that more people have been able to realise this desire.

One of the most important factors in counterurbanisation is the growth of car ownership (see Figure 18.1). In 1980, 60 per cent of all households in Britain had cars (see Figure 18.2) and, by 1995, 70 per cent of all households had cars. The car freed people from the limitations imposed by restricted public transport routes. It became possible to commute daily over longer distances. This led to the growth of **commuter villages** where new housing estates developed for the car-owning commuter.

The most accessible villages have grown most rapidly. In 1960 the village of Holmes Chapel in

Figure 18.1 Number of motor cars in Britain, 1950–1995

Year	Number of cars (millions)
1950	1.8
1955	3.5
1960	5.5
1965	8.9
1970	11.5
1975	13.7
1980	14.9
1985	16.5
1990	19.7
1995	21.1

Figure 18.2 Number of households owning a car in Britain, 1970–1995

Year	Percentage having one or more cars	Percentage having two or more cars
1970	51.6	7.0
1975	57.0	10.6
1980	60.3	15.3
1985	62.8	17.5
1990	66.8	22.9
1995	69.8	27.8

Figure 18.3 More new homes at Holmes Chapel, Cheshire

1. Define the term counterurbanisation.
2. (a) Draw a graph to illustrate the statistics in Figure 18.1.
   (b) How do your graph and Figure 18.2 help to explain the growth of counterurbanisation?
   (c) What other factors also help to explain the growth of counterurbanisation?

Cheshire had a population of 1143. During the 1960s the M6 motorway was completed and Junction 18 was sited 2 km outside Holmes Chapel. The M6 provided a fast link from the village to the cities of Manchester (40 km north) and Stoke-on-Trent (22 km south). There was an immediate demand for housing in Holmes Chapel. Property developers moved in and, over the next 20 years, Holmes Chapel was ringed with housing estates. The population increased to 5520 by 1981. Neighbouring villages further from the motorway have not grown to the same extent, partly because of planning controls which have sought to preserve the character of selected villages.

Commuters are not the only counterurbanites.

- An increasing flow of people retiring to rural areas has taken place. The retired seek peace and quiet and an attractive environment. Coastal locations are especially favoured. The mild, sunny climate of south west England has proved particularly attractive to retired migrants.
- There has been a rapid growth in second home ownership, especially in National Parks such as the Lake District, Peak District and Snowdonia and other areas of scenic beauty such as the Cotswolds and mid-Wales. Second home owners are usually wealthy people whose first home is close to the urban area in which they work. They visit their second homes at weekends and during holiday periods.

What are the effects of counterurbanisation?

Counterurbanisation has involved the movement of people with urban attitudes into rural societies which may not share these attitudes. There have been conflicts over such issues as bloodsports and factory farming. The influx of wealthy newcomers has resulted in house prices increasing out of the reach of local people. This has meant that many young adults have had to move away from their villages in order to find cheaper accommodation elsewhere. The conspicuous wealth of some of the newcomers can create tensions with poorer local people.

The positive aspects of counterurbanisation are that it brings wealth into villages, some of which will be spent in local shops and on local services, helping to maintain employment. The children of incomers attend small local schools, perhaps allowing them to remain open.

Teleworking

Some counterurbanites have become **telecommuters** (see Figure 18.4, page 133). This means that they work at home, linked by telecommunications to their offices in the city. Modems allow electronic data transfer between computers, and fax machines allow transfer of documents and photographs. It is even possible to 'attend' meetings via video-conferencing equipment.

It is likely that professional people will increasingly work from home, telecommuting

Change in the Countryside

Figure 18.4 A 'tele-commuter' working at home

across the world via the Internet information superhighway. Such people are likely to move out of the cities to more attractive rural environments. This opens up the possibility of moving work from high-wage developed countries to low-wage developing countries (see Figure 18.5).

A special instance of teleworking is the telecottage, a concept developed in Scandinavia and now introduced in Britain. It involves the conversion of a barn or farmhouse into offices by installing computer and telecommunications facilities. The village of Kington in Herefordshire has one of the first British telecottages.

> 3. Draw up a table showing the positive and negative effects of counterurbanisation on rural areas.
> 4. (a) Use the information in the text and in Figure 18.5 to define teleworking and give examples of jobs suited to teleworking.
> (b) How could teleworking affect rural areas in the long term?

Figure 18.5 Teleworking

After tending the 250 sheep on his Orkneys farm [Scotland], John Ruscoe returns to his house to spend seven hours working as a software designer for ICL, the UK-based computer company.

John Ruscoe gave up three hours a day of commuting to and from ICL's office in Manchester and moved to his 200 acre farm in the Orkneys. It is over two years since he has had to travel on ICL business.

"I make a local call using the BT [British Telecom] network which gets me through to my office in Manchester. Once I have got into one of our mainframes, I can send electronic mail to colleagues in Australia, Hong Kong or anywhere. I can get to all the information I need. I do not see why what I am doing cannot be done from anywhere."

The concept of the global office, where work is not concentrated in specific geographic locations, has been most eagerly adopted by the industries whose products make it possible – the computer and telecommunication companies.

The Guardian,
15 October 1994

Summary

- Counterurbanisation is the movement of people from urban areas to rural areas. This movement has brought both positive and negative effects to the rural areas.

Migration to the countryside 133

Changing Resources

Chapter 19 What are resources?

What are resources?
How can we classify resources?
Why are resources so important?

This unit looks at different types of resources and their use and availability around the world.

What are resources?

There are many definitions of resources, but they can most simply be defined as any material or product that people find useful. For example, stone becomes a resource when people use it to build houses and grass is a resource when cows eat it, and produce meat and milk.

People's ideas about resources change over time. For example, in the past oil was regarded as a nuisance by people in Middle Eastern countries like Saudi Arabia. The black, tarry pools of oil contaminated sand and water holes and often caught fire. It was only after the 1920s, with the development of oil refining technology and the growth of the car industry in the USA and Europe, that people saw the value of oil, now a very valuable resource.

Classifying resources

Resources can be classified in different ways. One method of classification (shown in Figure 19.1) is to divide resources into **renewable** and **non-renewable**. Non-renewable resources are those like coal and oil which, once they have been used, are gone forever. Renewable resources are those like **solar** and water power which can be used continuously without running out, or timber which can be replanted.

1. Look at Figure 19.1. Explain the meaning of the four sub-categories of resources shown in the diagram. Give two new examples of each.
2. Why are some resources, for example, uranium, not recycled?

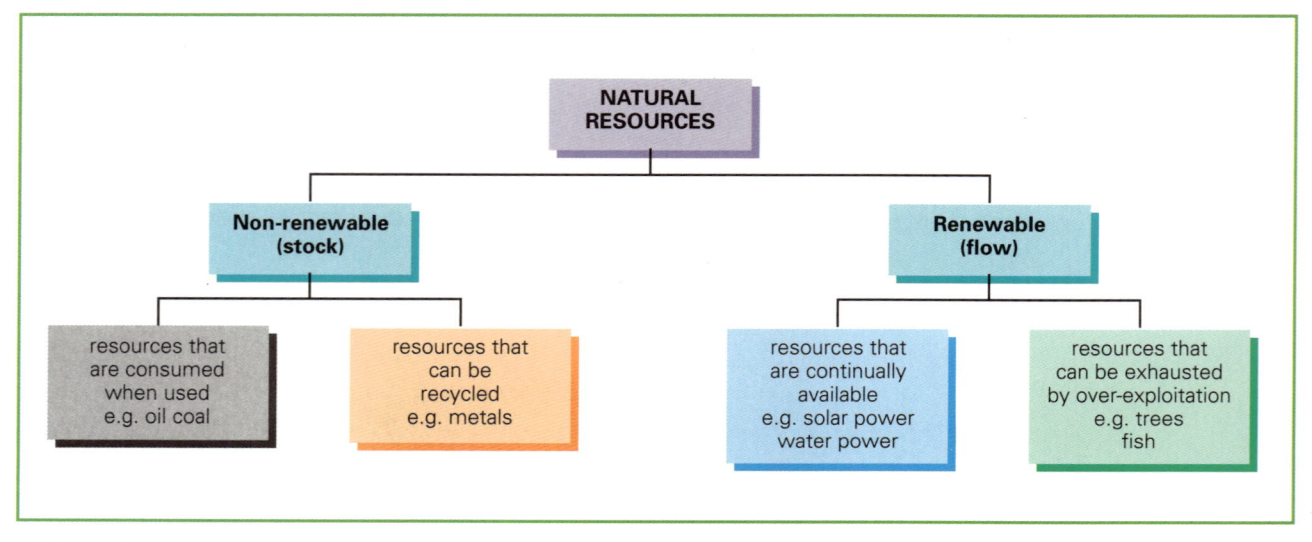

Figure 19.1 A classification of natural resources

```
                    NATURAL
                    RESOURCES
                   /          \
          Non-renewable      Renewable
            (stock)           (flow)
           /       \         /        \
   resources   resources  resources   resources
   that are    that can   that are    that can be
   consumed    be         continually exhausted
   when used   recycled   available   by over-exploitation
   e.g. oil    e.g.       e.g. solar  e.g. trees
   coal        metals     power       fish
                          water power
```

134   Changing Resources

3. Classify the following resources:
   wave energy; limestone;
   bauxite; tin;
   sand; gold;
   diamonds; a tropical forest;
   a lake; wind energy.
4. Explain how human activities can damage renewable resources like fish stocks or forests.

Some important points about resources

Resources are not distributed evenly around the world. Some areas are rich in resources – for example, areas with coalfields or oilfields – other areas have few resources. As a result, some countries like Saudi Arabia are resource rich in relation to others like Iceland.

Many resources are in limited supply, such as coal, oil and natural gas and despite new discoveries and new methods of extraction these resources will eventually run out. Because resources are limited there is competition from many different potential users. Figure 19.2 illustrates this, showing a site on the edge of a city. In turn, competition makes it important to manage resources effectively, making the best use of each resource without destroying it. Many resources, especially those connected with scenery and the countryside are very fragile. They can easily be damaged or destroyed by thoughtless or careless use as Figures 19.3 and 19.4 show. Many LEDCs have begun to exploit their resources, such as iron ore, bauxite, coal or oil in order to generate income from exports.

Once a resource is used, this starts a process which will benefit some people and not others.

Figure 19.2 Some key groups competing for resources

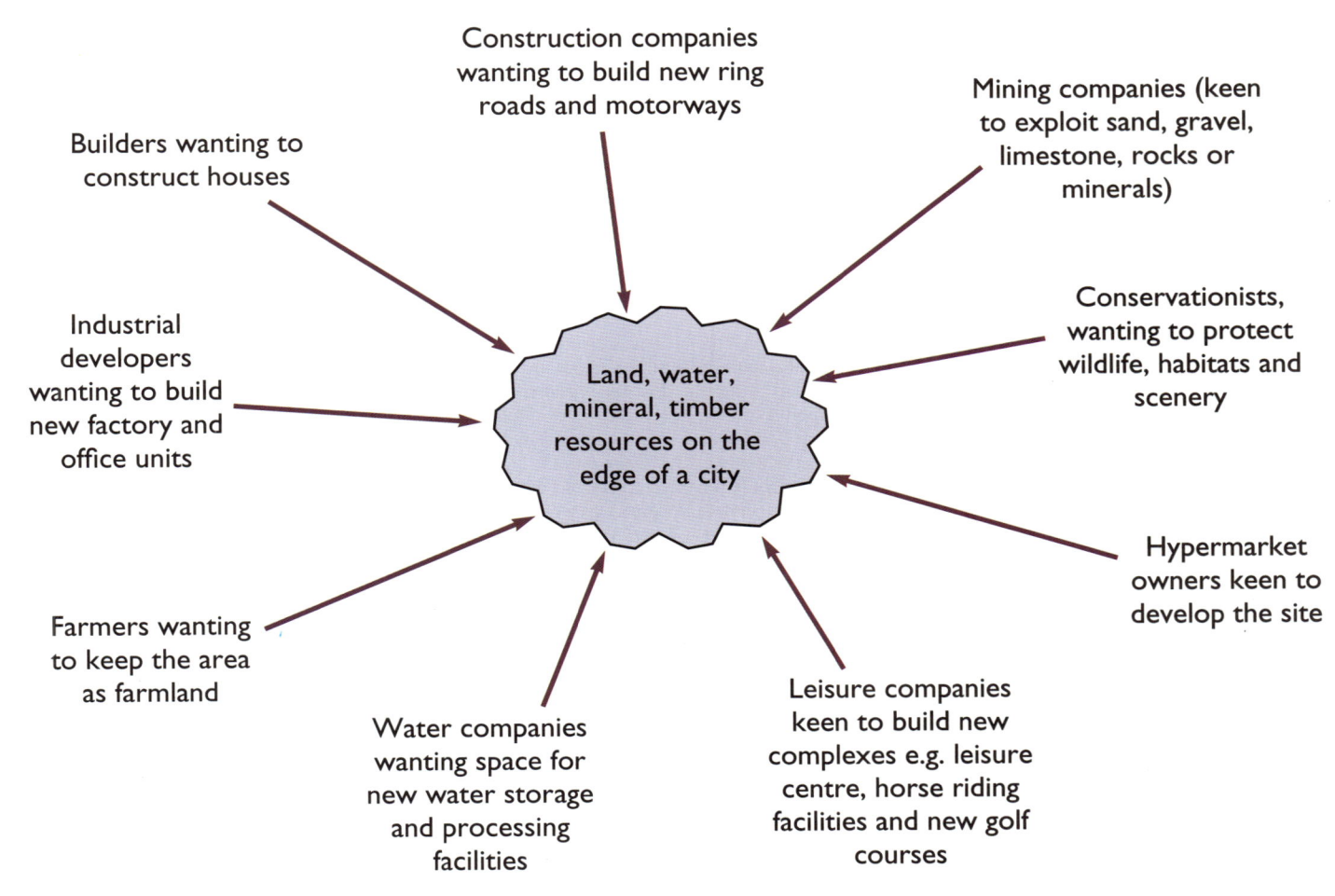

- Builders wanting to construct houses
- Construction companies wanting to build new ring roads and motorways
- Mining companies (keen to exploit sand, gravel, limestone, rocks or minerals)
- Industrial developers wanting to build new factory and office units
- Conservationists, wanting to protect wildlife, habitats and scenery
- Farmers wanting to keep the area as farmland
- Water companies wanting space for new water storage and processing facilities
- Leisure companies keen to build new complexes e.g. leisure centre, horse riding facilities and new golf courses
- Hypermarket owners keen to develop the site

Central: Land, water, mineral, timber resources on the edge of a city

What are resources?

Figure 19.3 Destruction of the environment created by mining

For example, the development of Topley Pike limestone quarry in the Peak District National Park provides many jobs, but local people complain about noise and dust from the quarry as well as the danger and damage of heavy lorries on country roads.

> 5. What is resource management? Why is it necessary? Why is it so difficult?
> 6. Look at Figure 19.4. What could local authorities do to reduce or stop further damage to the coral reef?

Figure 19.4 Coral reef damage

At a depth of 30 feet, where the coral suddenly rose in a ledge from the sandy ocean floor, it seemed that the entire reef had been wrapped in plastic string.

This was fishing line, dozens of fishing lines, cast off by impatient anglers when their hooks caught in what they thought was the ocean floor.

The results are devastating. Delicate sea fans tangled in line were pulled from the reef. Finger, branching, and staghorn coral is wrenched off by the tuggings from above.

Then there were the plastic bags looped over the brain coral, and starving them of nutrients. Finally were the great gouges in the reef where anchors had been dropped to moor the boats.

"Right now, the reefs are dying at a rate of about five per cent a year," says Dr Brian Lapointe, who has just completed a reef pollution survey for the Florida Land Trust.

"We have a water quality problem which is really a people problem. People pollute. The sharp increase in population and in tourism in Florida, and particularly in the Keys, has overloaded our waste disposal systems. The septic tanks are leaking into the sea, producing nutrients which are force-feeding algae, which overgrow and kill the coral."

After an energetic local campaign by Reef Relief, the local government of Monroe voted for a ban on the sale of phosphates in detergents, soaps and fertilisers.

There are four main threats to the reefs. The first is direct damage, from anchors and moorings and divers. A human touch can remove the protective slime and expose the reef to bacteria.

The second threat is phosphates. The third is marine debris. "Seals being slowly throttled by plastic nets, fish trapped in a loop of plastic rings that used to hold a six-pack of beer, or throttled by a cigarette filter – we see them all," says DeeVon.

The fourth, and potentially the most lethal, is oil drilling. About 25 miles off the reef, nine oil companies hold some 73 leases. In each of the last three years, Congress had stopped the drilling by refusing to fund that section of the Department of the Interior legally required to monitor the leases.

The Guardian, 6 March 1990

136 Changing Resources

Putting a value on resources

Countryside is one of the most important resources all over the world. In order to decide how best to use areas of countryside, planners and others have to find ways of measuring the quality of different landscapes. Only in this way can it be decided which areas of countryside must be preserved and on which areas development can be allowed. Figure 19.6 illustrates a possible way of assessing the quality of the countryside. For an area of countryside under assessment, points are awarded or deducted for each feature in Figure 19.6.

Figure 19.6 Scoring system for assessing landscapes

Land use	Score
Wild landscape (e.g. heather, marshland)	+10
Varied landscape (e.g. fields, woods, hedges)	+7
Farmland with trees	+2
Farmland with no trees	+1
Blocks of coniferous trees	−2
Urban or industrial area	−8
Landforms	
Mountains	+10
Hills	+8
Undulating land with low hills	+6
Lowland	0
Other scores	
There is water in the distance	+2
There is water in the foreground	+4
It is a coastal area	+8

Figure 19.5 The Needles, Hampshire

Figure 19.7 Malhamdale, Yorkshire Dales

7. Apply the scores in Figure 19.6 to the landscapes shown in Figures 19.5 and 19.7. Which seems to be the 'most valuable' landscape?
8. Can you develop a better scoring system than that in Figure 19.6? What other features would you take in to consideration? Try both scoring systems on different photographs in this book.

What are resources?   137

Summary

- Resources are things people find useful.
- Resources are in limited supply.
- There is competition between different users for the same resources.
- Resources are often fragile and easily damaged.
- Resources have to be managed to ensure their continued use.
- The development of resources benefits some people but not others.

Chapter 20 Mineral resources

Why are mineral resources important?
What are the effects of mineral extraction?

This unit considers some of the different minerals that are dug out of the earth. It examines the importance of different types of minerals and the effects of mining on people and the environment.

The importance of minerals

Every time you get into a car, make a telephone call, switch on a sound system or take an aspirin you are using some of the earth's mineral resources. Most minerals in use today are either minerals in their 'raw' form or are the result of *refining* or a manufacturing process that involves minerals. There are four main groups of minerals:

- metals – e.g. iron, gold, copper;
- building materials – e.g. sand, gravel, limestone;
- industrial minerals – e.g. lime, soda ash;
- energy minerals – e.g. coal, oil, natural gas.

Figure 20.1 Limestone quarry near Kirkby Stephen, Cumbria

Figure 20.2 Kennecott copper mine, USA. The deepest open-cast mine in the world

Minerals and the environment

Extracting minerals has an environmental cost. Most minerals are extracted from the earth in one of four ways:

- quarrying on or close to the surface, as with limestone, sand and gravel;
- open-cast mining, which removes a shallow surface layer of rock to expose minerals such as coal;
- underground mining, as with salt, coal, diamonds, gold and copper;
- dredging rivers, lakes and streams to extract minerals like tin and gold.

Each of these methods of mining leads to significant environmental changes such as the alteration of the landscape shown in Figures 20.1 (page 139) and 20.2.

In order to obtain minerals, the land surface has to be moved and re-shaped. Mining and quarrying remove more material from the earth than all the processes of erosion carried out by wind, water and ice put together. For example, one open-cast coal mine at Kansk-Achinsk in Siberia involved the removal of 3000 million tonnes of material from an area of 8 km², to a depth of 500 m. This created a huge hole and a mountain of waste. Such features can be found all over the world from Britain to Zambia. When a mine has been exhausted, the holes fill with water and can become dangerous as well as being unattractive. The spoil heaps of waste rock can become unstable, especially after heavy rain, with results such as those shown in Figure 20.3.

Surface collapse is one result of underground mining. When old underground workings collapse the layers of surface rock subside and can damage houses, roads and factories.

140 Changing Resources

Village in fear after clay tip collapses

A china clay tip which collapsed and swept through a Cornish farm, depositing hundreds of tons of mud and boulders has renewed local arguments for greater safety measures.

There are hundreds of tips of the sandy material left over from china clay mining in the St Austell area, some at the very heart of villages. The tips tower over the villages, and every week get higher and higher. Some villagers even have tips in their gardens.

The collapse of the 15 metre Little John tip, near the village of Roche, was caused by heavy rain. The built-in drainage system could not cope and a cascade of water, sand and rocks poured 100 metres down a country lane. 'It happened incredibly quickly,' said Mr Peter Rawlings, whose year's supply of silage at Coldwreath Mill Farm was destroyed by the landslide. 'If I'd been in the way of it, I'd have been killed.'

The Guardian 15 March 1992

Pollution of rivers, lakes and streams is a serious problem connected with some mines. In the 1980s and early 1990s in Brazil, thousands of prospectors used mercury to extract gold from river deposits. This poisoned all fish and plant life for many kilometres along the Amazon River.

> 1. What could be done to prevent disasters like the one described in Figure 20.3?
> 2. Look at Figure 20.4.
>   (a) What do you think were the causes of the changes in output of the three minerals between 1955 and 1970?
>   (b) Explain the changes in output of the three minerals since 1980.

Figure 20.3 Cornish slip

Damage to wildlife habitats can be another effect of mining and quarrying. In the Philippines, coral reefs are being destroyed as the coral is mined for use as a building material and for sale to tourists. As a result, over 50 per cent of the coral reef habitats have been severely damaged.

Figure 20.4 UK mining

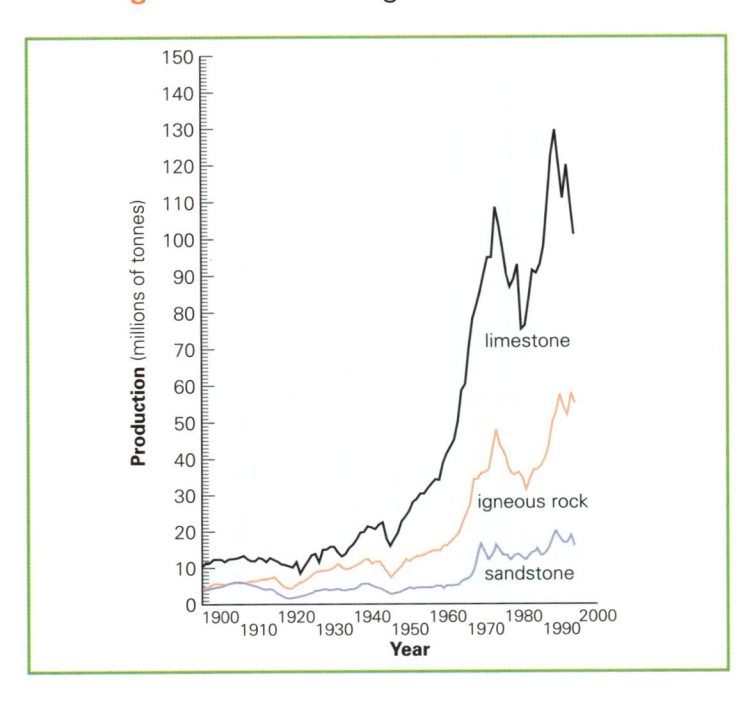

Quarrying limestone in the Yorkshire Dales

Figure 20.4 shows how the UK is extracting minerals from the countryside to meet the rising demand for rocks, sand and cement to build motorways, superstores and houses. All such construction schemes need concrete, which is made of cement (made from limestone or chalk) and aggregate (crushed rock such as sandstone, granite, limestone, sand or gravel).

The Yorkshire Dales hold one of the UK's most important resources – carboniferous limestone, which is currently being extracted by eight quarries (see Figure 20.5, page 142) at a rate of 4.6 million tonnes a year. Quarrying in the Dales is big business. It employs 7 per cent of the working population and annually earns £6 million for the local economy.

The Yorkshire Dales is a National Park and an area of outstanding scenic quality and there is a conflict between the economic benefits of mineral extraction and the environmental impact of such quarrying (see Figure 20.6, page 142).

The limestone of the Dales is very pure – 95 per cent calcium carbonate. This is in demand in the steel, glass, paper and sugar refining industries. However, only 20 per cent of the limestone quarried in the Dales goes to these

Mineral resources

Figure 20.5 Quarries in the Yorkshire Dales

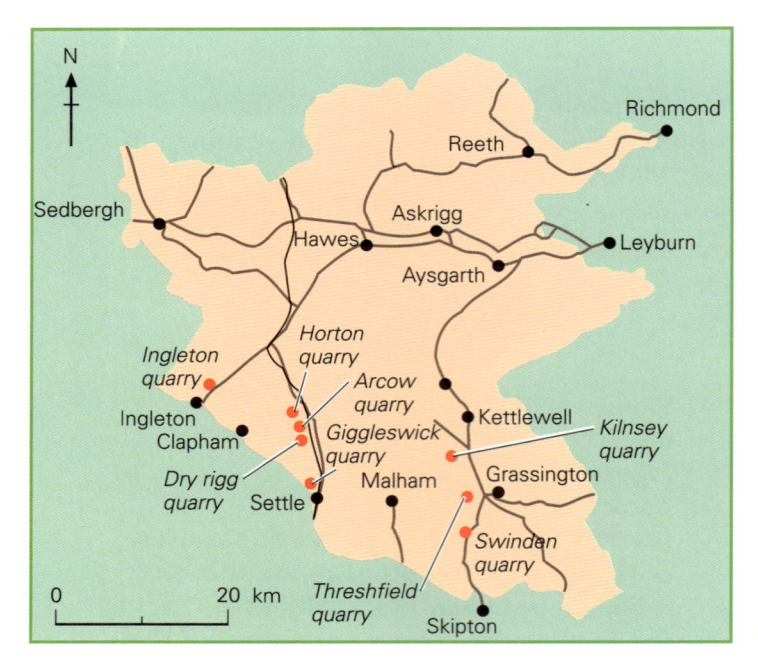

industries. The remaining 80 per cent is broken up for aggregate and used to build motorways and hypermarkets. But there are many alternative materials which could be used as aggregate instead of limestone, such as broken sandstone, gritstone, igneous rock and even artificial materials. This would prevent what many people regard as a waste of such pure limestone.

Ninety per cent of the limestone is taken out of the area by road. Quiet country lanes are damaged and later have to be upgraded. Operators are reluctant to switch to rail transport

Part of the economy

The Yorkshire Dales National Park has great natural beauty, its beauty fashioned by the underlying limestones and gritstones. Equally important, it is a living community. Quarrying has been a part of its economy for centuries and today employs 7 per cent of the working population of the Dales, contributing more than £6 million a year to the local economy.

Nevertheless, calls are heard from pressure groups for quarrying to cease, though seldom are they echoed by the communities whose well-being depends on the industry.

Quarries in the Dales supply essentially local markets, normally within 80 kilometres of the quarry. If local quarries are closed, the monetary, social and environmental costs of construction activity will increase dramatically. Escalating haulage costs, increasing road congestion and lorry pollution will be the consequence of hauling aggregates from further afield.

To deliberately destroy jobs in the Dales would be a folly of gigantic proportion.

Of course, the industry recognises its responsibilities to the environment. Great strides have been made in both landscaping and housekeeping, but we are not complacent. My own company, ARC, recently opened a new aggregate processing plant at Ingleton costing £7 million.

Over £1 million was spent on environmental improvements, including landscaping, dust prevention and a programme to plant 37,000, mainly broad-leaved, trees.

Good transport facilities are a basic aspiration. Providing the raw materials from local sources is good for the local economy and a good environmental solution too.

Dales '94, 1994

Despoiling our heritage

For both residents and visitors it is a wrench to watch the heartland of the Yorkshire Dales – crushed lumps of its incomparable limestone landscape – loaded daily on numberless wagons to feed unfeeling maws somewhere beyond Settle and Skipton.

The quarries gash or even remove the hills. Earlier this century, while production was small, the workings were tolerably in scale with their surroundings. Now they are savagely disproportionate.

They ravage the landscape and destroy the smaller gems of beauty and interest.

The stone loads themselves, most of them on the roads and not the railway, can form a torrent of noise, nuisance and danger.

Besides, much of this is chemical grade limestone, a non-renewable resource, the bulk of it going as roadstone and aggregate.

Where will it end? Demand for stone will never cease, and as the planing consents begin to run out there will be pleas to extend them. Today we hold the Dales in trust. Generations to come will loathe and despise us for despoiling their heritage. We do not have to let these things happen.

Company profits are beside the point, even if these pure limestones are cheaper than the mixed strata elsewhere. Existing jobs are not an issue. No-one is proposing to buy out the planning consents for these big quarries and close them down.

When the operators want to extend their workings, that is when public opinion must give firm backing to the national park committee in showing responsible trusteeship.

Dales '94, 1994

Figure 20.6 Data file on the Yorkshire Dales

142 Changing Resources

because it is so expensive to install the new lines and sidings required. The industry prefers the flexibility of road transport, but large lorries can be a threat to the environment and a danger to other road users.

Other disadvantages of the quarries include the fact that they are very visually intrusive in an area of high scenic quality. Attempts have been made to build earth mounds and to plant trees to screen the workings. The quarries also generate some noise, dust and air pollution but operators are working to reduce these problems.

---

3. Study all the data about limestone mining in the Dales. Analyse the extent to which you agree or disagree with each of the arguments in Figure 20.6 by using the ADIF technique. To do this, first divide each statement of each argument into short phrases. The first ones have been done for you below. Then evaluate each phrase by deciding whether: you agree (A); disagree (D); if it is irrelevant (I), or if it is a statement of fact (F). Give all the statements in both arguments a letter (A, D, I or F). Add up the As, Ds, Is and Fs and give reasons to support your evaluations.

The argument against mining in the Dales

The Yorkshire Dales National Park has a great natural beauty	A
Its beauty is fashioned by underlying limestones and gritstones	F
Equally important, it is a living community	A
Quarrying has been part of its economy for centuries	F

Minerals and less economically developed countries

Many less economically developed countries are rich in minerals. For example, Jamaica has large reserves of bauxite, Zambia of copper, Morocco of phosphates and Malaysia of tin. In theory, the development of mineral extraction should bring numerous benefits to these countries, such as:

- income from the export earnings on the sale of minerals to other countries;
- income from royalties and taxes on the large transnational corporations (TNCs) which often extract minerals;
- 'development' of more remote areas by the accompanying spread of infrastructure, especially the railways, electricity and water supply necessary for mining operations;
- the introduction of new industrial skills to the local population and the nation as a whole;
- employment for local people in areas which frequently have few alternatives to agriculture;
- increased state income from higher taxes on local people, who in turn should receive higher incomes from work in the mining industry.

Countries that have become heavily dependent on the export of minerals include: Zambia, 95 per cent of whose export earnings come from copper; Zaire, 75 per cent of whose export earnings come from copper; and Chile and Peru both of whom derive 60 per cent of their export earnings from copper. However, the reality is that whilst mineral exports have produced some benefits these have usually not been sufficient to significantly affect the economy of the country. In effect, the mining industry has become a modernised enclave in countries like Zambia, Chile and Malaysia with few links to the rest of the economy. So benefits such as higher wages, export earnings and increased employment have been on a much smaller scale than originally anticipated. There are five main reasons for this.

Firstly, because mining is such an expensive operation, many poorer countries had to rely on TNCs to provide the huge investment involved. This means that some of the profits from mining go to the shareholders of the transnational rather than to the host country. Because transnationals are so rich and powerful, they exercise close control over exploration, production and marketing and it is difficult for governments of poorer countries to change this relationship and increase their own input.

Secondly, the more profitable, later stages of mineral production are located in the richer countries such as Japan, the USA and the UK, so the greater profits derived from refining and producing finished goods do not go to the host country.

Thirdly, the value of mineral exports has declined over the last 20 years. This is because world mineral prices are decided by the richer consuming countries rather than the poorer producing nations. The result is that, for example, the number of tonnes of copper, bauxite or tin which have to be sold to purchase manufactured goods such as trucks increased by an average of 25 per cent between 1984 and 1990. LEDCs are producing and exporting more and more minerals, but the purchasing power of these exports is declining.

Fourthly, mining activities are concentrated in a small part of each LEDC and so the benefits of employment or income that they generate go to only a small sector of the population. Rich, ruling, urban elites and the military are often the main beneficiaries of mineral development, thus widening the gap between rich and poor within the host country. Such elites often allow transnationals to pay low wages to the local workers, and to neglect their responsibilities regarding pollution and the environment. TNCs are able to override the rights of native peoples such as the Aborigines of Australia or the Indians of the Amazon rainforest, in their search for minerals. These peoples have often had their environment, livelihood and way of life destroyed in the pursuit of mineral deposits.

Lastly, mining is a capital-intensive industry which may generate few jobs for local people. Skilled personnel and equipment are often brought in to the host country from richer nations and few local workers are required.

The balance between these various costs and benefits is illustrated by the example of Chile.

Mining in Chile

Northern Chile is a desert. As such, it is a very inhospitable environment for mining or indeed any other human activity. The main climatic features are shown in Figure 20.7. Pipelines have had to be built to bring water from the Andes mountains to the towns and settlements of eastern and coastal Chile (see Figure 20.8). The settlement of northern Chile, including the establishment of cities and ports (see Figure 20.9) and the development of transport routes, is based entirely on mineral exploitation.

Nitrates, used for fertilisers were the first minerals mined in northern Chile. When Chile's nitrate industry declined the copper industry expanded, especially at Chuquicamata (see Figure 20.10), which became a huge open-cast site. A whole new town of 28 000 people grew up at Chuquicamata centred on the mine and its smelting, refining and power production industries. Copper is in demand to supply the world's electrical and plumbing industries.

Figure 20.7 Features of the climate in northern Chile

Temperature (°C)		Minimum	Maximum
Winter	Day	−4	20
	Night	−10	−4
Summer	Day	2	32
	Night	−4	2

Precipitation 33 mm per year on the coast
15 mm per year near Andes
Humidity Very low

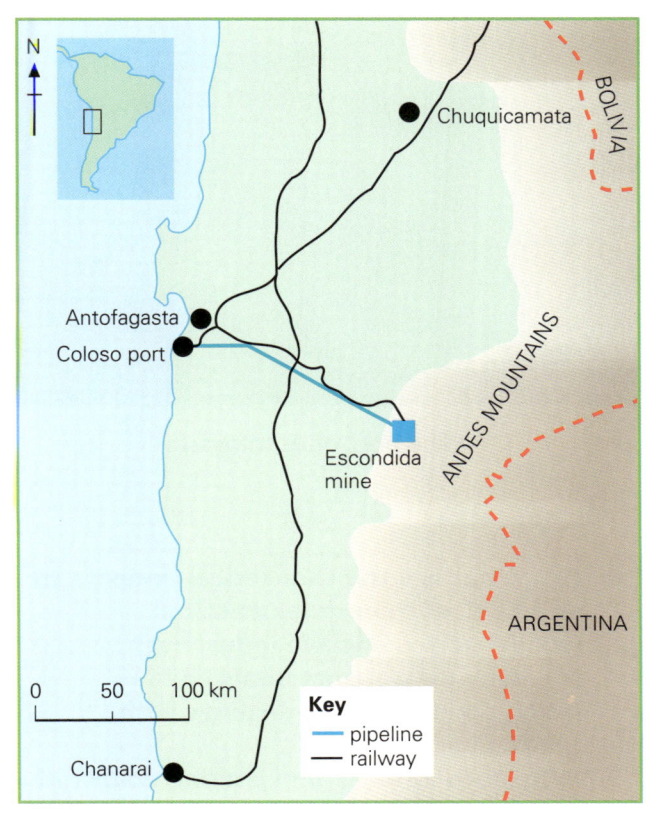

Figure 20.8 Northern Chile

Figure 20.9 Santiago, the capital of Chile

The latest development is La Escondida (the hidden one) a deposit of copper, first located in 1981 it lies 160 km south east of Antofagasta (see Figure 20.11). The deposits cover an area 4 km by 1.5 km, which contains 1.8 billion tonnes of low-grade (1.59 per cent) copper. Production at La Escondida, led by a consortium of transnational companies, did not start until 1990. Power to the mine has to come 200 km by transmission line, and water has to be pumped to the site from wells 25 km to the south. A 165 km pipeline has been built to transport the slurry (50 per cent water, 50 per cent copper ore) from the mine to the port of Coloso, from where it is exported to Japan, Germany, Finland and South Korea. The tailings (mixture of waste slurry and ore) are deposited in a natural hollow close to the mine. Water from the tailings is recycled for use in the plant.

The 850 employees at La Escondida are mostly local and travel to the mine from Antofagasta by bus. Because of the housing shortage in Antofagasta the company has built houses which employees can buy under a government subsidised scheme.

Mineral resources 145

Figure 20.10 Chuquicamata copper mine

Figure 20.11 The port of Antofogasta

The copper industry contributes relatively little to wider developments in Chile because it has given rise to few ancillary industries. Copper is an export orientated industry, whose exploitation has been largely controlled from outside Chile. Although important, the industry has failed to make any significant contribution to the development of northern Chile and few other industries are established there.

4. (a) What are the theoretical benefits to an LEDC of mineral extraction?
   (b) What are enclave industries?
   (c) Why do transnationals have so much power in their dealings with LEDCs?
5. Why does a mineral exporting country not always bring the planned economic benefits?

Summary

- Minerals are vital to modern industrial society.
- Extracting minerals has an environmental cost.
- People disagree on the costs and benefits of extracting minerals.
- Less economically developed countries often do not reap the benefits of extracting their own minerals.
- Mineral extraction often takes place in hostile environments like deserts.

Chapter 21

Forest resources

Why are forests such important resources? What are the causes and effects of the cutting of tropical rainforests?

This unit looks at forest ecosystems and their importance. It examines the reasons why rainforests are cut down, the use of the wood and the effects of cutting on the environment.

Why are forests so important?

Forests are one of the world's most important natural resources. They not only provide raw timber, fuelwood and charcoal, but also food, drugs and animal fodder. In addition, forests harness the sun's energy through the process of **photosynthesis** and contribute to the supply of soil humus through leaf fall and decay. Forests contain 85 per cent of the world's **biomass** and are a key element in the **cycle of nutrients** as well as being protectors of soils in watershed areas and home to millions of plants, insects, birds and larger animals.

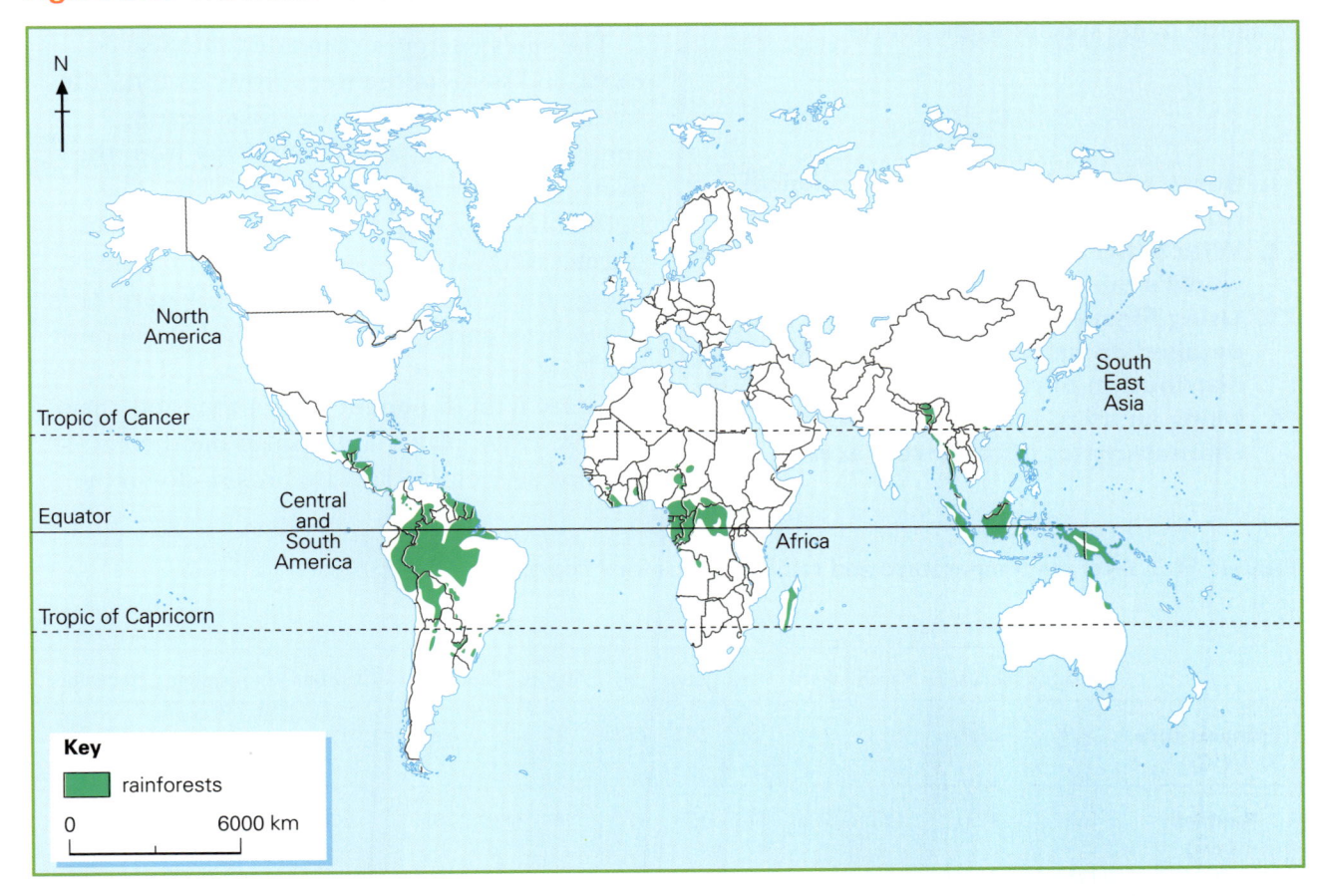

Figure 21.1 The location of the world's rainforests

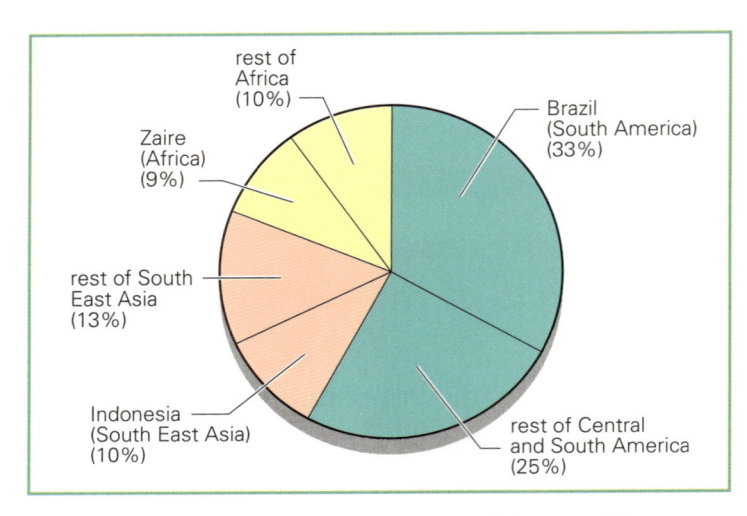

Figure 21.2 The distribution of the world's rainforests

- rest of Africa (10%)
- Zaire (Africa) (9%)
- rest of South East Asia (13%)
- Indonesia (South East Asia) (10%)
- Brazil (South America) (33%)
- rest of Central and South America (25%)

Tropical rainforests

The world's tropical rainforests are spread in a broad band around the Equator, as Figure 21.1 (page 148) shows. These tropical rainforests are a rich biological resource which have evolved into specialised, complex systems containing over half of all the living species in the world.

> 1. Between which latitudes are tropical rainforests located?
> 2. Which three countries have most of the world's rainforests?
> 3. Using Figures 21.1 and 21.2, give a detailed description of the location and distribution of rainforests.
> 4. Using an atlas, identify the climatic characteristics of rainforest areas.

> 5. Using Figure 21.7, how many million hectares of land were lost by: (a) Asia; (b) Africa; and (c) America (South and Central) between 1985 and 1992?

The rainforest food chain

Figure 21.3 shows the type of climate in which tropical rainforest develops, using Malaysia as an example. With continuously high temperatures and heavy rainfall, plant growth in these areas is rapid. Figure 21.4 shows the rich structure of the Malaysian tropical rainforest.

Within the rainforest the trees are the **primary producers** shown in Figure 21.5. They take in water, minerals and carbon dioxide and in the presence of sunlight make sugars by a process called photosynthesis. At the same time they give out oxygen. The sugars are used as a source of nutrient for the plant's growth and development. They are respired, in a process which produces the energy for growth and which releases carbon dioxide into the atmosphere.

The sun's energy is converted into leaves, roots, and stems as the trees grow. In turn, the trees are eaten by herbivores (plant-eating animals) so there is a flow of energy from the plants to the animals (see Figure 21.5). The herbivores may then be eaten by carnivorous (meat-eating) animals, again continuing the energy flow. The whole process in Figure 21.5 shows how energy flows through the rainforest **food chain**.

Decay is an important part of the food chain because when plants and animals die their remains decompose and are broken down by

Figure 21.3 Average temperature and rainfall figures for Malaysia

	January	February	March	April	May	June	July	August	September	October	November	December
Temperature (°C)	26.4	26.9	27.5	27.5	28	27.5	27.5	27	26.6	26	25.7	25.2
Rain fall (mm)	251	173	193	188	173	173	170	196	178	208	254	257

Changing Resources

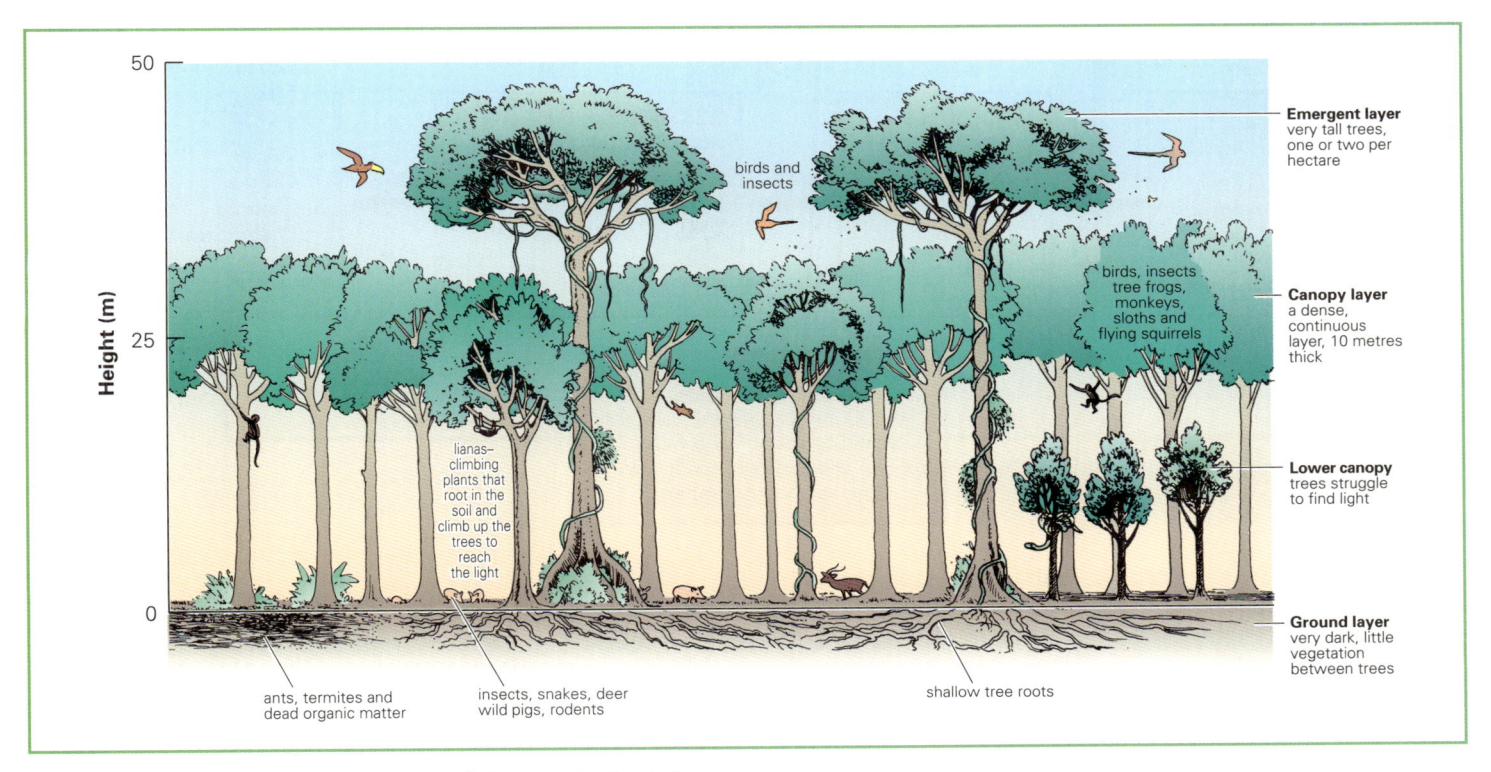

Figure 21.4 The structure of the tropical rainforest

bacteria and fungi. In this way, minerals are returned to the soil to be taken up again by plants, because the food chain is a continuous cycle.

Figure 21.5 The tropical rainforest food chain

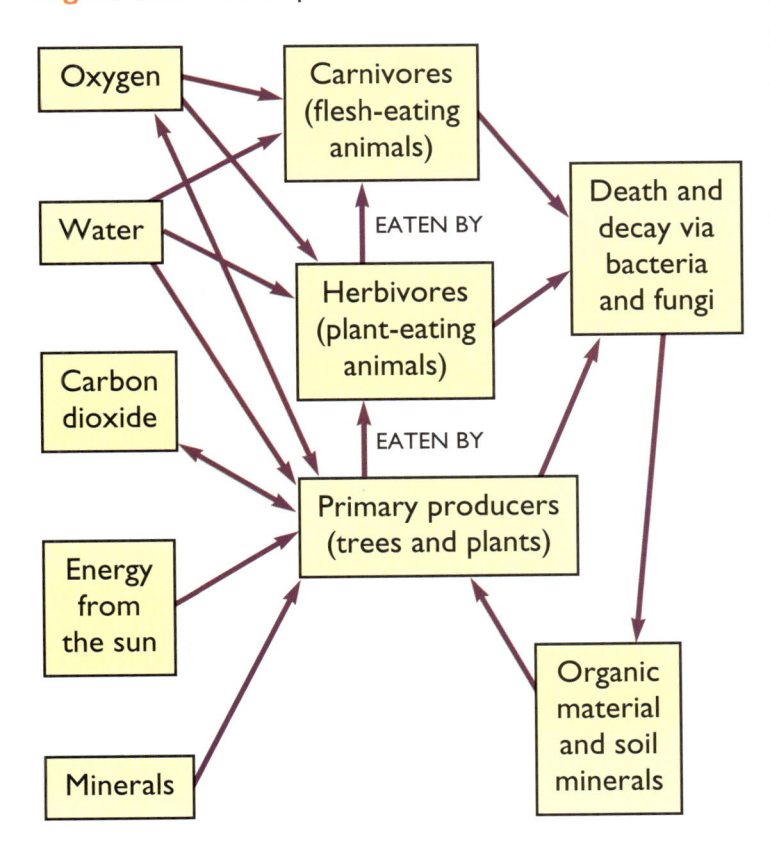

The rainforest ecosystem

The plants, insects, birds and animals living together in the rainforest depend on each other. For example, the insects, birds and animals depend on the plants for food, water and shelter. In turn, the plants depend on insects and birds to pollinate them and spread their seeds and on animals to provide nutrients in their manure. These organisms living together form a community. They also depend on the non-living things in the environment, such as water, soil and air. Together, the living and the non-living things make up an *ecosystem*. The rainforest is one of the world's most important and productive ecosystems, which has reached maturity in Malaysia.

Like all ecosystems the tropical rainforest ecosystem has inputs, processes, stores, and outputs. These are shown in Figure 21.6 on page 150. The feedback arrow on the diagram emphasises the continuous nature of the ecosystem. For example, when outputs such as organic material, water and carbon dioxide are returned to the environment, they become new inputs. The tropical rainforest ecosystem also has flows of energy, water and nutrients through the system.

Forest resources   149

INPUTS	PROCESSES	STORES OF ORGANIC MATERIAL	OUTPUTS
• Sunlight • Rainfall • Soil minerals • Organic material • Oxygen • Carbon dioxide	• Photosynthesis • Respiration • Feeding • Decomposition	• Trees – 11 100 kg per ha • Litter – 1540 kg per ha • Soil – 180 kg per ha	• Water • Oxygen • Minerals • Organic material • Carbon dioxide

FEEDBACK
Minerals and organic material are returned to the soil and water, oxygen and carbon dioxide are returned to the atmosphere.

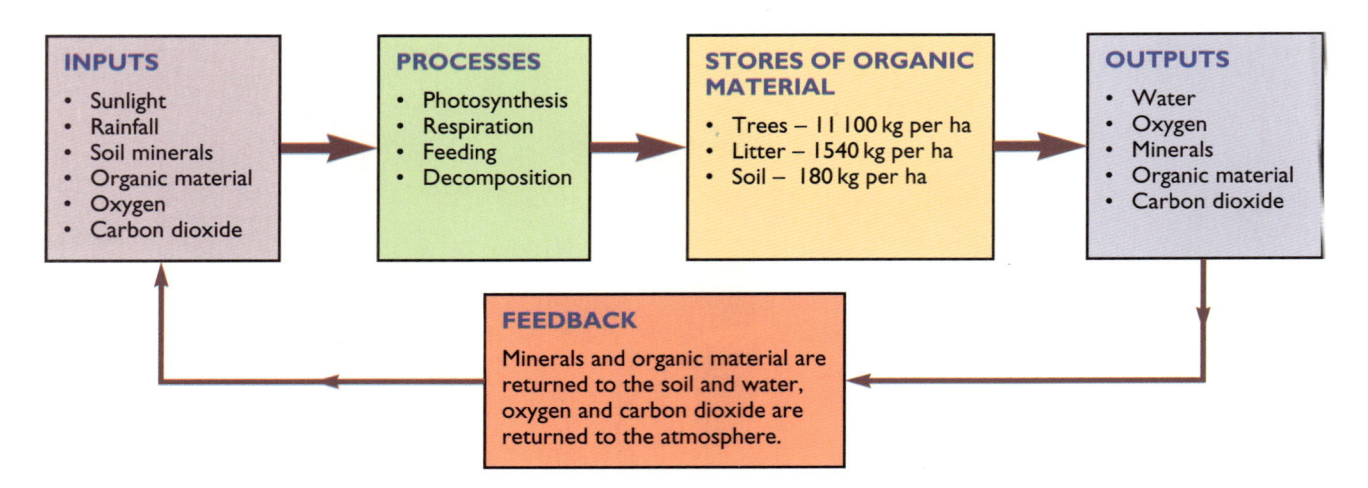

Figure 21.6 The tropical rainforest ecosystem

6. Use the data in Figure 21.3 to draw a climate graph for Malaysia.
7. Use the graph to write a detailed description of Malaysia's climate.
8. Use Figure 21.4 to describe the structure of the tropical rainforest. In your answer: (a) describe the main layers; (b) describe the animals, insects and birds found in the different layers; (c) explain how lianas are adapted to get light and water.
9. Describe and explain the flow of water and energy through the food chain in the tropical rainforest, using Figure 21.5 to help you.
10. Look at Figure 21.6. What percentage of the total organic matter in the tropical rainforest is stored in: (a) the trees; (b) the litter; (c) the soil?
11. The organic matter in a UK oak woodland is stored as follows: 4200 kg per ha in the trees (75 per cent of total); 400 kg per ha in the litter (8 per cent of total) and 1000 kg per ha in the soil (17 per cent of total).
    (a) Compare the total amount of organic matter in tropical rainforest with that of a UK oak woodland.
    (b) Compare the different distribution of the organic matter in the two ecosystems.
    (c) Explain the differences you have identified.

Why are tropical rainforests so important?

- Tropical rainforests are important in their ability to maintain environmental and climatic stability. The forests help to reduce soil erosion, as the tree roots hold the soil together. Trees also help to prevent flooding by absorbing rainfall and releasing it slowly into rivers and streams. Tropical rainforests influence both regional and global weather patterns through their control over the flow of moisture through the ecosystem.
- Tropical rainforests are an important economic resource, providing timber for construction and fuel, fodder for livestock, and oils, resins, nuts, latex and chemicals which form the basis of much of the pharmaceutical industry.
- Tropical rainforests are a source of huge genetic diversity in the plants, insects and animals they contain. For example, the Malaysian peninsula has 7900 recorded species

of flowering plant compared to the 1420 plant species found in Britain, which is over double the area. The tropical rainforests represent a huge biological resource which, if properly managed, could provide an almost endlessly renewable source of wealth. For example, the trees could be managed to achieve a sustainable harvest of timber and wood pulp. Scientists also believe that resins from rainforest trees may be vital to medicine in the future.

The destruction of the rainforests

Despite their importance, forests are being cut down at the rate of 40 ha every minute. The United Nations Food and Agriculture Organisation has calculated that half of the world's rainforests have been destroyed since 1950. However, this average figure conceals large variations between nations. For example, Central America has lost 67 per cent of its forest and South East Asia 45 per cent. If present trends continue, by the year 2010 the only remaining areas of tropical rainforest will be in western Brazil and Central Africa.

Rainforests are cut down for a number of reasons.

- Timber is an important crop of the rainforest, especially hardwoods like mahogany, which are particularly good for veneers on furniture. Only 6 per cent of the wood taken from forests is exported, but it is still worth over £10 000 million per year. Asian forests were the first to be cut down in the 1970s but more recently companies have turned to the forests of Latin America. Loggers only fell 1 per cent of trees per ha, but damage half the remaining trees in the process.
- Rainforests provide wood pulp which is used to make paper.
- Shifting cultivators are small groups of nomadic peoples living in the rainforests. They clear a patch of land, cultivate it for three years until the soil is exhausted, then move on. This gives time for the soil to regain its fertility and for the trees to grow again. However, as the population of these peoples grows they have to clear larger areas, and may be forced to return to previously cleared land before it has had time to recover.

Figure 21.8 Area of tropical rainforest in eastern Ecuador where deforestation and felling has taken place for an exploratory oil well

Figure 21.7 Rates of tropical rainforest destruction, by continent, 1985–1992

	Area of forest in 1992 (millions of hectares)	Percentage of total area lost each year 1985–1992
Asia	312	2
Africa	210	4
South and Central America	642	6

Forest resources

Figure 21.9 Clearance of rainforest land in the Amazon Basin

- Most of the cutting of rainforests is done in order to create farms for landless settlers. Huge parts of the Amazon basin in Brazil have been cleared in this way, as Figure 21.9 shows.
- Large-scale cattle ranches occupy 25 per cent of the cleared rainforest areas in the Amazon. These areas are planted with grasses which do not supply enough nutrients to the soil. As a result, many ranches have failed because the grass has died. Beef from the cattle is used to make burgers in Brazil and the USA.
- Mines and **hydro-electric** dams have led to the clearing of large tracts of rainforest.
- Plantations of pineapple, rubber and other trees have been introduced on areas of cleared tropical rainforest in Malaysia. By having one species of tree all together on a plantation, operations are rendered cheaper and more efficient.

What are the effects of deforestation?

When trees are cut down the tropical rainforest ecosystem is dramatically changed, as shown in Figure 21.10. The trees protect the soil from heavy rain and sun and the tree roots hold the soil together and this means that deforestation causes soil erosion. The soil is washed away and the top, most fertile layers of soil are the first to be eroded and the remaining soil is thin and less fertile. As a result of soil erosion, a hard crust called laterite forms as the soil dries out in the heat. Plants cannot grow in laterite. Eroded soil blocks the streams and they flood.

12. **Re-draw Figure 21.6 to show the effects of cutting down the forest on the systems inputs, processes and outputs.**

152 Changing Resources

What is the future of the tropical rainforests?

The world is becoming more aware of the importance of tropical rainforests and conservationists are campaigning to prevent further deforestation. Some key changes have included debt for nature deals. In these cases, LEDCs like Brazil and Malaysia agree to reduce the rate of rainforest clearance in exchange for a cancellation of part of their international debts to richer nations. In other cases, companies have ceased using rainforest products. For example, furnishing firms like Habitat advertise that they do not sell products from the rainforest and fast-food chains Burger King and Macdonalds have ceased to use meat reared on former Central American rainforest. Other changes include the development of agroforestry systems which combine agriculture with forestry. Under this system, farmers in Malaysia plant crops such as maize, rice or cassava between bushes such as coffee or tea, together with trees for fuelwood and fruit. In this way, the vegetation protects the soil from wind, sun and rain, provides organic matter and shade and stores water whilst the roots bind the soil together.

Figure 21.10 A soil-eroded area of tropical rainforest due to deforestation

Summary

- Forests are one of the world's most important resources.
- The tropical rainforest has a delicately balanced ecosystem.
- There are flows of energy, nutrients, water and gases through the rainforest ecosystem.
- Tropical rainforests are being cut down for economic gain.
- Once the tropical rainforest is removed the soils quickly become infertile.
- In future, systems of development such as agroforestry may help to conserve some of the rainforests.
- If the rainforests are to be saved, there must be recognition that biodiversity is as valuable a resource as monetary wealth.

Forest resources

Chapter 22 Energy resources

How have energy demands changed?
What issues arise from the use of energy resources?
What alternatives are there to the fossil fuels?

An increasing demand for energy depletes the world's reserves of fossil fuels, the hunt is on for economic alternative energy sources.

Energy consumption

Energy is used in all aspects of life, from the electric lights in our homes and offices powering computers, videos, televisions, photocopiers to the fuel used in transport and to prepare food. The average Briton uses an amount of energy equivalent to over five tonnes of coal each year!

In 1970, the average citizen of the USA used the equivalent of 10.82 tonnes of coal annually. By contrast, the average Thai used only 0.18 tonnes (see Figure 22.1). However, by 1995 the average American used slightly less energy, but the average Thai's consumption of energy had more than tripled to 0.64 tonnes. The rapid growth of energy consumption in the Newly Industrialising Countries (NICs) of South East

Figure 22.1 Energy use per person – 1970, 1983, 1990

Country	Tonnes of coal (equivalent) per person		
	1970	1983	1990
USA	10.82	9.30	10.13
UK	4.87	4.67	5.03
France	3.84	3.99	3.95
South Korea	0.67	1.45	2.20
Malaysia	0.56	0.89	1.38
Indonesia	0.12	0.24	0.27
Thailand	0.18	0.35	0.64
Argentina	1.58	1.69	1.94
Brazil	0.50	0.68	0.80
Ethiopia	0.06	0.02	0.02
Burkina Faso	0.01	0.03	0.03
World average	1.89	1.97	1.96
World total (millions of tonnes)	6995	8750	10611

Changing Resources

Asia is a noticeable development in a world energy picture where most countries have a stable or declining consumption per person and, world-wide, average consumption per person fell between 1983 and 1990. Sources of energy consumed have also changed (see Figure 22.2).

Figure 22.2 Energy sources of world consumption, 1960 and 1994

Source	% of world consumption	
	1960	1994
Coal	49	26
Oil	30	39
Gas	11	18
Hydro-electric power	2	4
Nuclear	1	5
Others	7	8

Energy sources

Figure 22.3 shows the sources of energy consumed in the world in 1994. The three fossil fuels – oil, coal and gas – account for 82 per cent of total consumption. The world stock of these fuels is diminishing since they are non-renewable resources. In the future, renewable resources such as solar, wind and **geothermal energy** will become more important.

The world's energy resources are unevenly distributed. Most of the world's fossil fuels are concentrated in the MEDCs. As Figure 22.1 shows, people in MEDCs use much more energy than people in LEDCs. In fact, MEDCs, with only 25 per cent of the world's population, consume 80 per cent of the world's energy resources. The average American consumes over 16 times as much energy as the average person living in Thailand, and over 500 times as much energy as the average Ethiopian.

Figure 22.3 World energy consumption in 1994

Source	Millions of tonnes of oil (equivalent)	% of total
Oil	3200	39
Coal	2100	26
Gas	1450	18
Nuclear	400	5
Hydro-electric power	290	4
Fuelwood	600	7
Other renewables	75	1
Total	8115	

1. (a) List five renewable and five non-renewable resources.
   (b) What is the difference between a renewable resource and a non-renewable resource?
   (c) How can the use of non-renewable resources be extended?
2. (a) What was the energy consumption per year in 1990 of the average person living in: (i) the USA; (ii) France; (iii) Thailand; (iv) Brazil; (v) Ethiopia?
   (b) Why do you think the average American used so much energy in comparison with the average Ethiopian?
3. (a) In order to find out whether there is a link between the wealth of a country and its energy consumption, draw a graph to show the statistics in Figure 22.4 (page 156). Use a vertical axis showing annual per capita income ($US per person) in increments of 1000 and a horizontal axis of energy consumption in tonnes of coal equivalent per year.
   (b) What is the relationship between annual per capita income and energy consumption?
   (c) Why do you think that: (i) Spain has a lower energy consumption than might be expected; (ii) Saudi Arabia a higher energy consumption than might be expected?

Energy resources

Figure 22.4 Energy consumption and annual per capita income for selected countries, 1993

Country	Annual per capita income ($)	Energy consumption (tonnes of coal equivalent per year)
Belgium	16 390	5.8
Canada	19 020	10.9
France	17 700	4.0
Greece	5 340	3.1
Indonesia	500	0.3
Ireland	8 400	3.7
Kuwait	16 380	8.3
Malaysia	22 000	1.4
New Zealand	11 800	5.1
Saudi Arabia	6 230	6.4
Spain	9 150	2.5
South Korea	4 600	2.5
Syria	1 020	1.0
Thailand	2 600	0.8
UK	14 400	5.0
USA	21 200	10.0

Coal

Coal was the fuel of the Industrial Revolution in Europe which marked the start of our modern industrial world. Coalfields became the sites of vast industrial areas during the nineteenth and early twentieth centuries and small villages grew into bustling cities.

In Britain, coal mining employed 1 million miners in 1913, producing 300 million tonnes of coal. However, a long, slow decline meant that, by 1980, only 235 000 miners remained, producing 122 million tonnes of coal (see Figures 22.5 and 22.6). Coal had suffered through competition from oil and gas, which were more convenient and less expensive than coal. Several important users of coal, such as the railways, moved to other fuels. Another factor in the decline of coal was the loss of important export markets for British coal as coal mining increased in other countries.

Since 1980 the British coal industry has endured a rapid decline, and when the industry was privatised in 1994, only 16 deep mines employing 9000 miners remained and annual coal production had fallen to just 50 million tonnes. The main reasons for the decline were: (i) the British Government's requirement that the coal industry should act commercially and close all *uneconomic* pits;

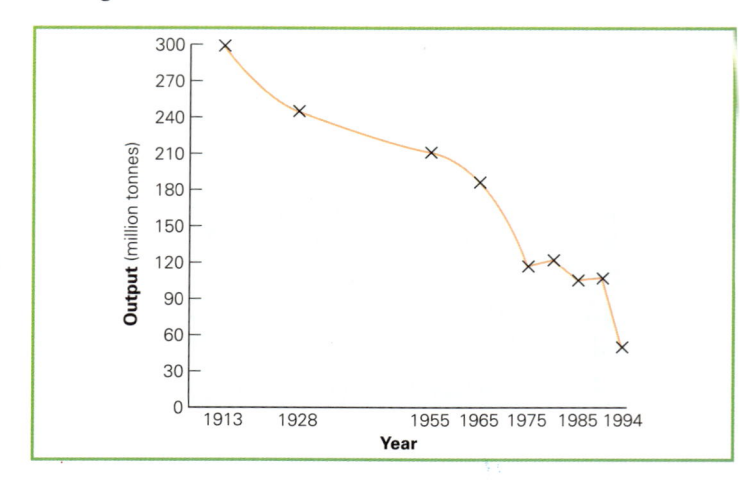

Figure 22.5 The declining output of British coal mining

156 Changing Resources

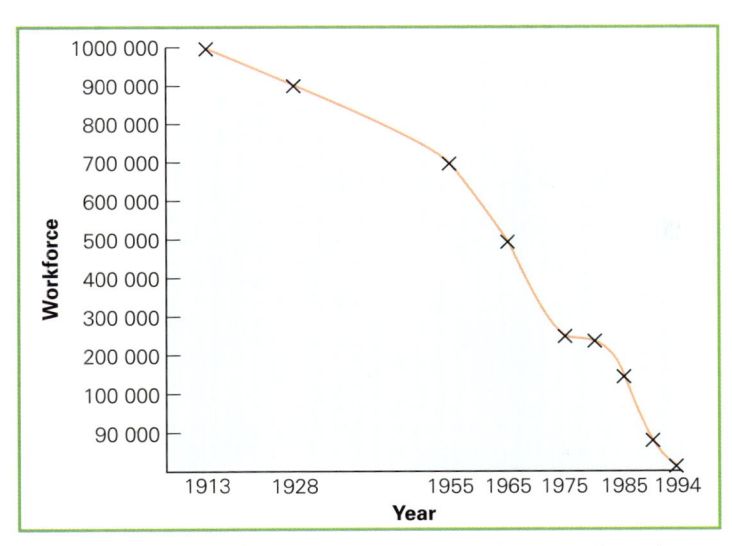

Figure 22.6 The declining workforce in British coal mining

- There was a rapid drop in service sector employment.
- Between 1981 and 1990 the number of men in full-time jobs fell by 39 per cent.
- Over the same period female full-time jobs increased by 20 per cent and part-time jobs by 13 per cent.
- Total employment in the district fell by 18.5 per cent from 32 500 in 1981 to 26 500 in 1990.
- The number of people in self-employment increased by 2000.
- The population of the district fell by 4 per cent from 101 000 in 1981 to 96 700 in 1991.
- Between 1984 and 1991 the direct and indirect effects of the job losses were estimated to have cost around £120 million.

(ii) the requirement that the electricity industry had to buy UK coal was relaxed, leading to rapid increase in the use of cheap imported coal and an overall switch to gas as a fuel.

The decline in coal mining was a serious social problem because there were very few alternative jobs for the miners in the coalfield regions. Many coalfield settlements have declined or even disappeared altogether and whole communities have lost their former way of life. Shops and services were also affected by their customers' loss of wages.

Money has been pumped into the coalfields in efforts to attract new employment and government grants and loans have been boosted by European Union Restructuring and Regional Development Funds. However, progress has been slow and most of the coalfields remain areas of high unemployment. Many of the jobs which have been attracted to the areas are in light industrial companies employing mainly female labour.

One area badly affected by **colliery** closures is Easington in County Durham, north east England. Ray Hudson, a geographer from Durham University, has studied the district's fortunes. In 1980 there were ten collieries operating in the Easington District; by 1994 there were none left and over 10 000 jobs had been lost. Hudson observed a number of social effects.

Open-cast coal mining

There are over 60 open-cast coal mines in Britain. These are quarry sites producing coal by stripping away the covering soil and rock (the 'overburden') to expose the coal seam. Open-cast mining is cheaper than deep-shaft mining and production has trebled in recent years (see Figure 22.7). A total of about 15 000 people are employed in open-cast mining – more than are employed in deep-shaft mines.

Since the average life of an open-cast mine in Britain is only five years, this means that 20 per cent of capacity has to be replaced every year merely to maintain a steady level of production. The rapid growth in recent years has resulted in

Figure 22.7 Open-cast coal production, 1970–1995

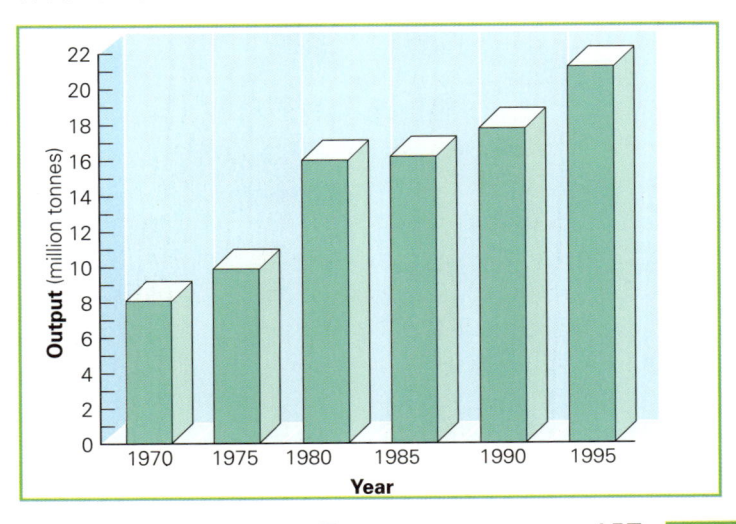

Energy resources

a large number of new sites being developed. Open-cast mines have been criticised on several environmental issues:

- loss of farmland;
- loss of hedges and other wildlife habitats;
- noise from heavy machinery such as vast dragging excavators and mechanical shovels;
- coal dust blowing from the site onto nearby land;
- increased traffic and associated danger and pollution on local roads.

Open-cast operators have taken several measures to reduce the environmental nuisance.

- Spoil material has been built up into **sound baffle mounds** encircling the sites.
- Water spraying helps to reduce the amount of windblown dust.
- The sites are restored to beneficial uses such as freshwater lakes, nature reserves, sports fields and golf courses after use.

An example of a restored site is the Rother Valley Country Park in South Yorkshire (see Figures 22.8 and 22.9). With four freshwater lakes, one stocked for anglers, and over 350 000 trees, the country park attracts more than 700 000 visitors per year. Over 163 species of bird have been recorded at the site and badgers are among the animals newly living in the park.

Figure 22.8 An open-cast coal mine in the Rother Valley

Figure 22.9 The same open-cast mine after restoration has been done

4. (a) Copy and complete the following table.

Coal in Great Britain: statistics for selected years

Year	1970	1980	1994
Number of coal mines	335		
Number of miners (thousands)	287		
Output (million tonnes)	135		

   (b) What caused the decline in the coal industry?
5. (a) What is open-cast mining?
   (b) Why has open-cast mine production increased in recent years?
   (c) What are the environmental issues involved with open-cast mining?
   (d) Describe methods of reducing the environmental effects.
6. You are a television reporter working for a current affairs programme. You have been instructed to visit the district of Easington. You have to prepare a five minute report on the effects of coal mine closures on the district. You can film a maximum of five scenes and interview four people.
   (a) Describe the scenes which you have chosen to film and explain why you chose these scenes.
   (b) Justify your choice of people to interview. List three questions for each person.
   (c) Write your script for the report, including the background information which you think necessary.

158   Changing Resources

Oil

Oil is a source of energy and a raw material for many industries. It is a mixture of hundreds of chemicals called hydrocarbons (because they contain hydrogen and carbon in varying amounts). The lightest hydrocarbons are gases, heavier ones are liquid (crude oil) and the heaviest are solid (tar).

Oil is produced by many countries. It is in greatest demand in MEDCs (see Figure 22.10). They do not produce enough oil to meet all their needs and so have to depend upon importing oil from LEDCs. A constant shuttle service of giant oil tankers operates from the oilfields of the Middle East, Africa, Asia and Latin America to the oil terminals of Europe, North America and Japan.

The only sure way to find oil is to drill for it. Only one well in ten actually finds sufficient oil to go into production. The search for oil has led companies into some of the most hostile places on earth – the Arctic wastes of Alaska, the deserts of North Africa and the Middle East, the rainforests of South America and the North Sea.

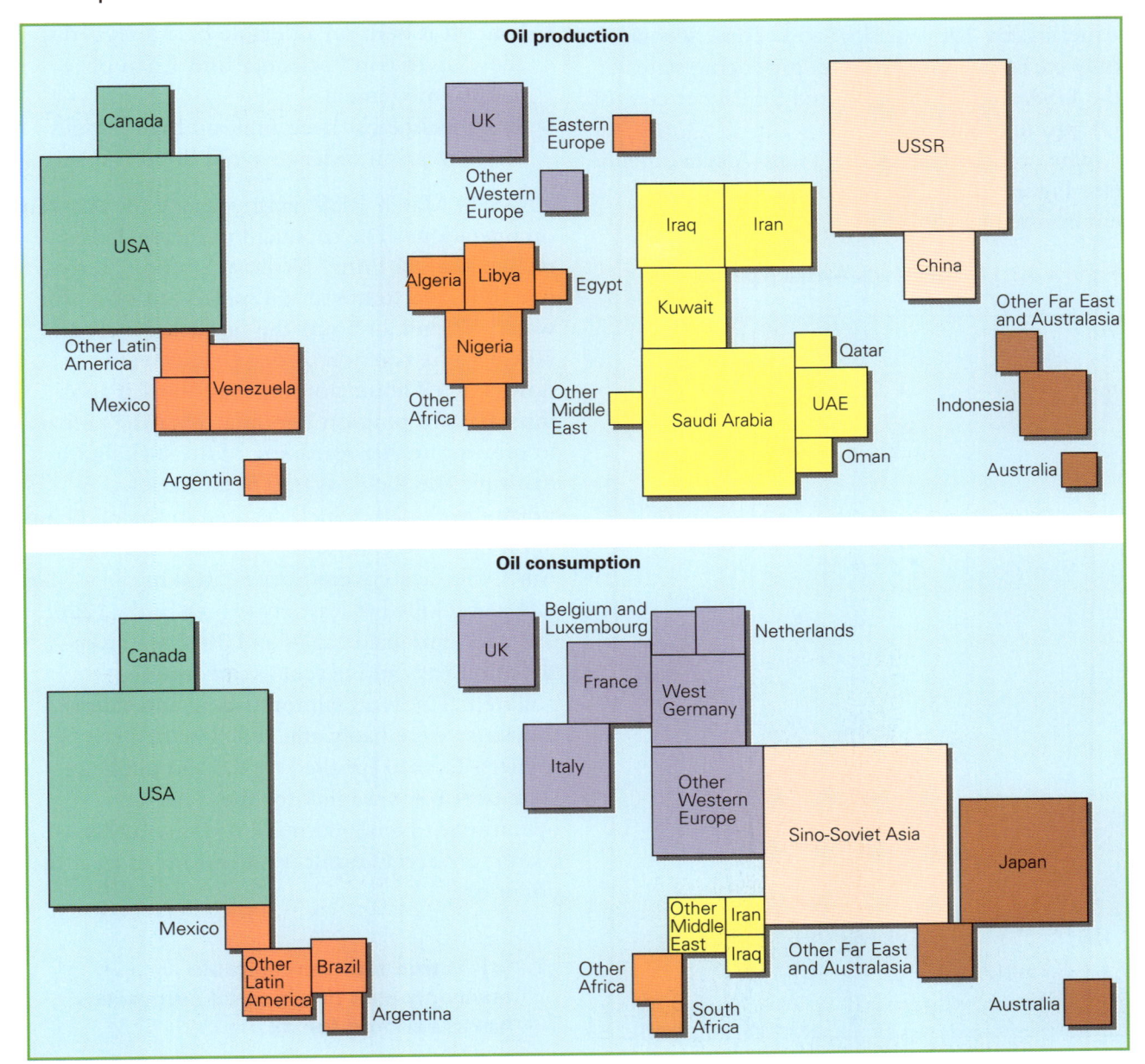

Figure 22.10 World oil production and consumption

Energy resources 159

Oil in Alaska

Oil was first discovered at Prudhoe Bay on the North Slope of Alaska in 1968. Proposals to produce the oil and pipe it south were strongly opposed by environmentalists who pointed out how fragile the *tundra* landscape and ecosystem was. Permission was finally granted in 1973 following the shock of the first oil crisis. It took four years and $8 billion to build a 1300 km pipeline from Prudhoe Bay to the ice-free port of Valdez on the southern coast of Alaska. Seventeen thousand tonnes of crude oil are pumped along the pipeline each day. The North Slope is the largest single oilfield in North America. By 1980 Alaska had become second only to Texas among the oil producing states of the USA and alone accounted for 25 per cent of US production.

The construction of the Trans-Alaska pipeline (see Figure 22.11) had encountered many environmental problems.

Figure 22.11 The Trans-Alaska pipeline

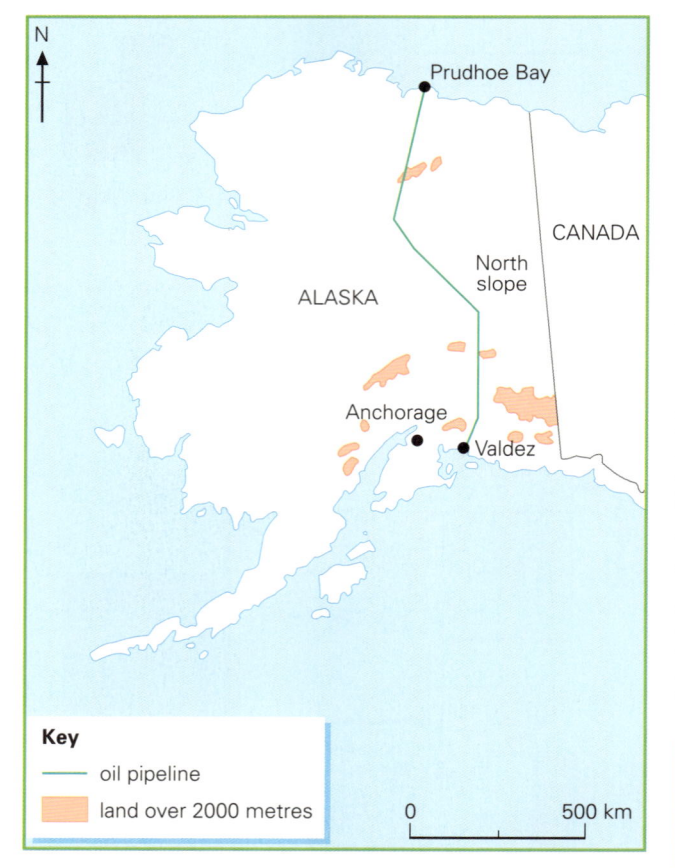

- *Permafrost* makes digging difficult and the surface melting could cause the pipeline to sag and break open.
- The oil has to be heated to 80° C in order to prevent it from freezing. Outside air temperatures can fall lower than −40° C.
- The pipeline has to be heavily insulated to prevent freezing on the stretches above ground and in order to prevent the permafrost from melting on the underground stretches.
- The pipeline crosses animal migration tracks. It has been built on stilts high enough to enable caribou to walk underneath.
- The pipeline crosses an active earthquake zone. It is built on a flexible base designed to allow up to 6 m horizontal and 1.5 m of vertical movement.
- The pipeline has been built on high bridges across rivers in order to avoid flood damage.

On 24 March 1989 disaster struck the Alaskan oil operations. The supertanker *Exxon Valdez* ran aground in Prince William Sound. Thirty-five thousand tonnes of oil spilled out on to the water. Within 24 hours the oil slick covered 70 km^2. The reaction to the disaster was very slow. For 12 hours nothing was done. It took three days to position booms around the tanker to prevent further spreading of the slick and by that time the slick covered over 200 km^2. A storm developed, which resulted in the oil being flung up on to beaches over a large area. By 2 April, the slick covered over 2500 km^2.

The oil killed at least 36 000 sea birds, 1200 seals, 156 rare bald eagles and 3000 sea otters. Beautiful bays and beaches were heavily polluted. The local salmon fishing and tourist industries were badly affected. The tanker's owners, Exxon, appalled by the bad publicity, took over responsibility for the clean-up operations. Over $600 million was spent by Exxon on largely unsuccessful efforts to treat the pollution.

> **7. (a)** Name four inhospitable environments in which oil companies have searched for oil.

160 Changing Resources

> **(b)** Why have the oil companies been forced to search in such areas?
> 8. List the environmental problems encountered by the Trans-Alaska pipeline into three categories, those caused by: (a) the intense cold; (b) animals; and (c) natural hazards.
> How have these problems been overcome?
> 9. **(a)** What were the results of the *Exxon Valdez* disaster?
> **(b)** What evidence is there that the authorities were not prepared for such a disaster?

Gas

The importance of natural gas as an energy source has increased rapidly in recent years. Until the 1960s much of the world's natural gas output was burned off as a waste product of oil production because there was no local demand for it. Gas produced from coal was used instead. However, in 1959 one of the world's largest natural gasfields was discovered in the Netherlands. The geological formation in which it was found continued under the North Sea. This led to an intensive search for gas under the North Sea.

In 1965 the first discovery was made, 65 km off the Humber Estuary at what is now known as the West Sole gasfield (see Figure 22.12). A larger field, the Leman Bank, was discovered off the coast of Norfolk. Several more gasfields were discovered in the southern North Sea. Attention then turned to the northern North Sea and in 1970 the Ekofisk oilfield was discovered in the Norwegian sector. Many more oilfields were discovered, and the Frigg, Troll and Cod gasfields gave Norway a valuable new export. In the British sector of the northern North Sea gasfields were also discovered, including Brae and Brent. Norway and Britain are now among the leading world producers of natural gas (see Figure 22.13, page 162).

Consumption of natural gas in the UK grew from zero in 1964 to 10 per cent of total consumption by 1974 and 25 per cent by 1984 (Figure 22.14, page 162). During the later 1980s natural gas consumption continued to grow. By 1990 gas met 32 per cent of the UK's total energy consumption. In the 1990s it grew very rapidly as gas became a popular fuel for use in electricity generation. From virtually nil in 1990,

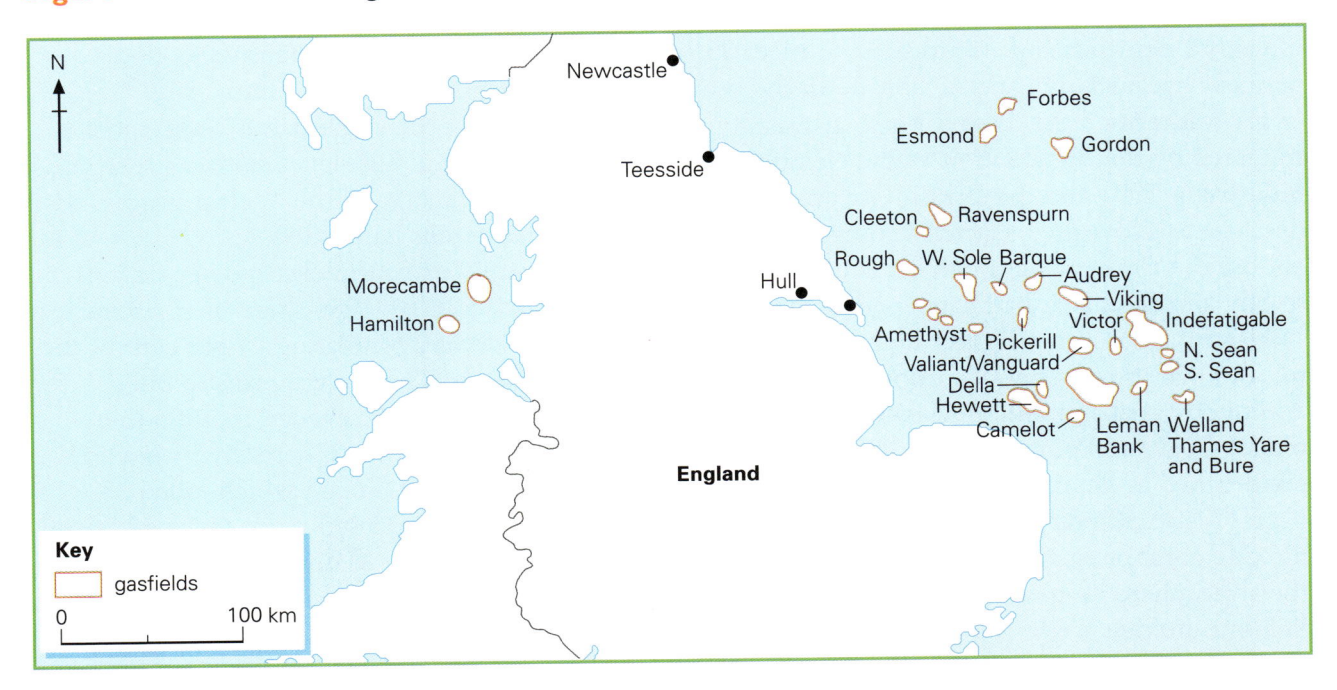

Figure 22.12 UK offshore gasfields

Energy resources 161

Figure 22.13 World production of natural gas

Country	Production (million tonnes coal equivalent)
Russia	941
USA	596
Canada	140
Netherlands	78
UK	63
Algeria	54
Indonesia	42
Romania	39
Norway	38
Saudi Arabia	36
Mexico	34
Venezuela	31

Figure 22.14 Natural gas consumption in the UK

Year	Consumption (million tonnes coal equivalent)
1973	44
1980	70
1985	82
1990	84
1995	98

by 1994 gas met 13 per cent of the electricity industry's demands and was forecast to meet 25 per cent by 1998. This rapid increase in the use of gas was termed the 'dash for gas'. It was triggered by the privatisation of the electricity industry in 1991 and the British Government's decision to allow the electricity companies to choose the cheapest fuels rather than force them to buy British coal as had happened in the past.

Natural gas is also a cleaner fuel than coal. It releases half the amount of carbon dioxide emitted by coal and only one-tenth of nitrous oxide. Coal-fired power stations have been condemned as the main source of 'acid rain' (see page 177). Acid rain is created by sulphur dioxide combining with water and oxygen in the atmosphere to create dilute sulphuric acid. Sulphur dioxide is released when coal is burned.

Power stations emit over 60 per cent of Europe's sulphur dioxide. Oil releases less sulphur dioxide than coal when burned, and natural gas releases very little.

> 10. Study Figure 22.14.
> (a) Why was no natural gas consumed in Britain before 1964?
> (b) Describe the pattern of growth since 1965.
> (c) Why did natural gas consumption increase rapidly between 1990 and 1994? What effect do you think this had on coal consumption?
> (d) What are the advantages of natural gas as a fuel?

Nuclear power

Today, around 5 per cent of the world's energy is produced by nuclear power stations. However, nuclear power is very controversial. It has both advantages and disadvantages. Nuclear power stations have the advantage that they use only small amounts of uranium as fuel, are cheap to operate and create no air pollution. In addition, they are less visually unattractive than fossil fuelled power stations because they do not need tall chimneys or cooling towers. Disadvantages of nuclear power are that nuclear power stations are very expensive to build. Once built, nuclear reactors are difficult and expensive to close down (decommission). In addition, it is expensive to process nuclear waste and there is no way of making high-level nuclear waste safe. Another disadvantage of the nuclear process is that uranium emits harmful radiation.

Britain build its first nuclear power stations during the 1950s. By 1986 there were 38 nuclear reactors in service, generating 19 per cent of the UK's electricity. There were plans to build several new stations. However, in 1986 there was a serious accident at Chernobyl, a nuclear power plant in the Ukraine which killed 35 people and forced 135 000 to be evacuated from the surrounding area. Many more people died in later years from diseases caused by the disaster. In 1995 the Ukraine Government announced that

Changing Resources

Figure 22.15 Sizewell B nuclear power station

Country	% of total	Country	% of total
Argentina	14	Mexico	3
Belgium	59	Netherlands	5
Bulgaria	37	Russia	13
China	1	Slovakia	54
Czech Republic	29	Slovenia	43
Finland	32	South Korea	40
France	78	Spain	36
Germany	30	Sweden	42
Hungary	43	Switzerland	38
Japan	31	UK	26
India	2	Ukraine	33
Lithuania	87	USA	21

Figure 22.16 The percentage of total electricity produced by nuclear power

over 100 000 people had died, or were seriously ill, as a result of the Chernobyl disaster. The effects were not limited to the Ukraine. A radioactive cloud drifted across Europe, reaching Britain. Rain washed the radioactivity in to the soil. Measures were taken for many years after the disaster to prevent the slaughter of sheep for food consumption which had grazed the contaminated grass in the mountains of Wales and the Lake District.

The Chernobyl disaster caused an increase in the already strong tide of public opposition against nuclear power. In the late 1980s the Government called a halt to any new nuclear power station construction in the UK. When the electricity industry was privatised in 1991 there were no buyers for the nuclear power stations and the Government was forced to keep them under state ownership for several more years.

Opposition to nuclear power has continued. Dangerously radioactive uranium fuel rods are removed from the reactor core after seven years' use and stored in cooling ponds until their radiation levels have fallen. They are then taken by rail to a reprocessing plant at Sellafield in Cumbria. Up to 2 tonnes of spent fuel elements are carried in massive steel flasks weighing 50 tonnes. The flasks are designed to survive rail accidents and fire, but their regular transport through built-up areas is strongly opposed by anti-nuclear groups.

11. How does a nuclear power station generate electricity?
12. What are the advantages and disadvantages of nuclear power?
13. What were the effects of the Chernobyl disaster?
14. Study Figure 22.16.
    (a) Draw divided bars to show the percentage of total electricity generated by nuclear power stations in the ten countries with the highest percentage.
    (b) On an outline map of Europe, draw small pie graphs to show the percentage of total electricity generated by nuclear power stations in each European country listed in the table.

Energy resources

Alternative energy sources

Figure 22.17 Main alternative sources of energy

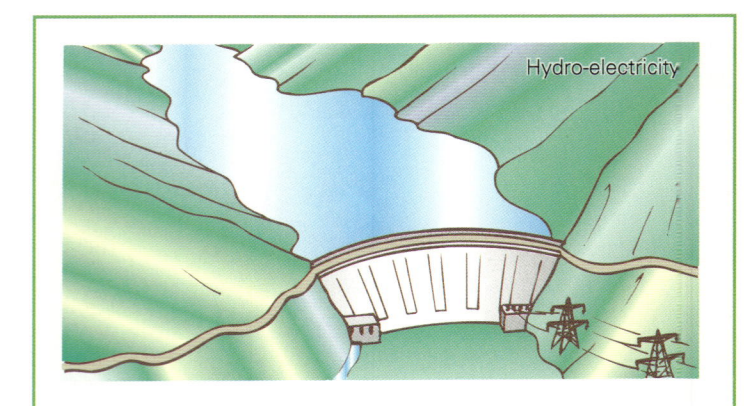

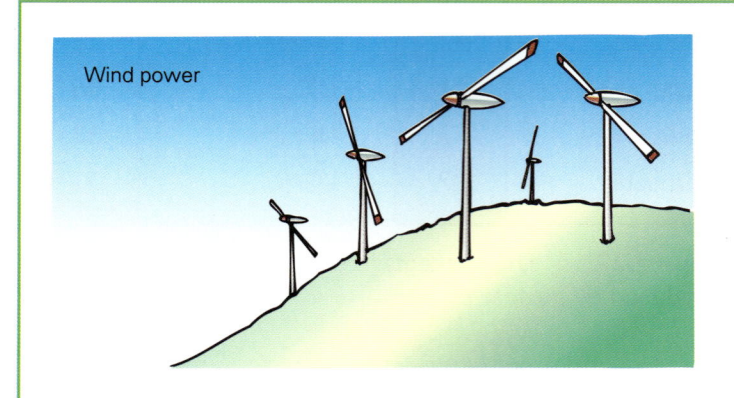

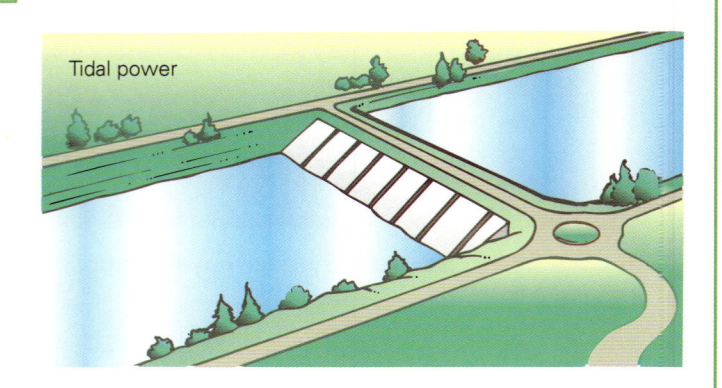

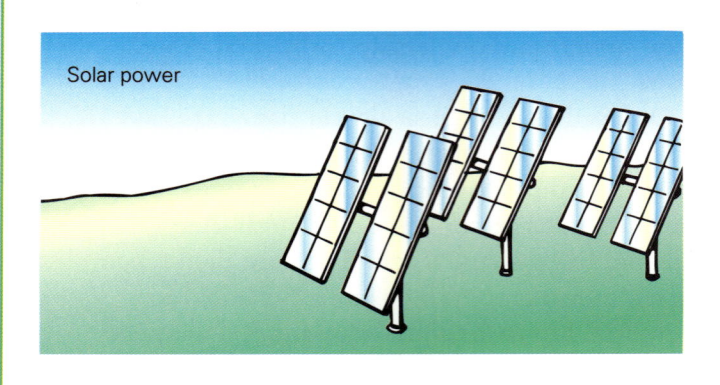

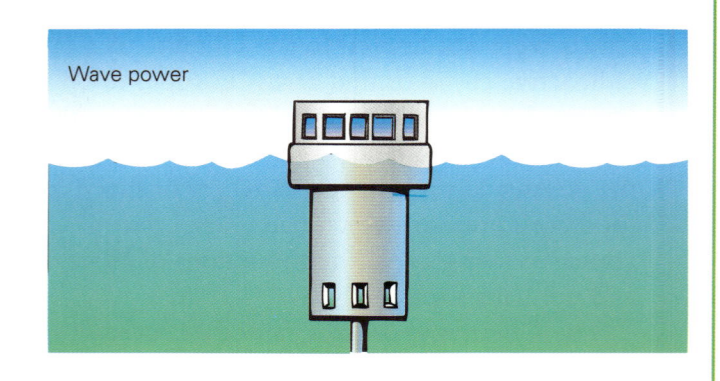

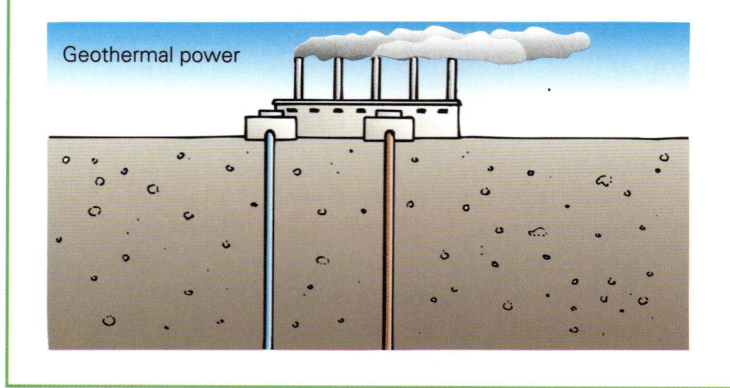

Figure 22.18 Lyn Peris and the entrance to the Dinorwic HEP station, Gwynnedd

Hydro-electricity

Hydro-electric power (HEP) is the most important of the renewable energy sources. It is cheap to produce and causes little pollution. However, HEP stations are expensive to build and there is a limited choice of suitable sites. Valleys may have to be flooded to create reservoirs, destroying farmland and disrupting local communities. However, such reservoirs can have a positive effect, as areas for recreation.

Inside the mountain shown in Figure 22.18 is a vast artificial cavern containing Europe's largest HEP station. This is Dinorwic in North Wales. The energy of falling water is used to spin turbines linked to alternators which generate electricity. Dinorwic can produce up to 1800 megawatts (mw).

Dinorwic is a pumped storage power station. The water falling over the turbines is retained within the lake in the photograph (Llyn Peris) and is later pumped back up the mountain to the upper reservoir of Marchlyn Mawr (Figure 22.19). Dinorwic generates electricity during the day when demand is high and pumps the water back up the mountain during the night. Dinorwic can reach full output from a standing start in just seven seconds and can therefore cope with unexpected surges in demand. No other type of power station can do this. Dinorwic has replaced a number of older, coal-fired power stations which were expensive to keep in operation purely to meet such demand surges.

Only 2 per cent of Britain's electricity is generated by HEP because of a lack of suitable sites. Most is generated in the highlands of Scotland, but conditions there are not ideal. Good sites for dams are rare because the valleys are usually wide. The major problem, however, is that the water catchment areas are too small to support large schemes and most British HEP stations produce less than 50 mw of electricity.

Wind power

The wind has been harnessed as a source of energy for thousands of years, through sailing ships and windmills. Recently wind energy has become an important alternative source of electricity generation.

Figure 22.20 shows a modern wind turbine at Burgar Hill in the Orkney Islands. The rotor is 60 m in diameter and its steel and glass fibre blades complete a revolution in under two seconds. The tips of the blades travel at nearly 400 km per hour. The capacity of the Burgar Hill turbine is 3 mw.

The Burgar Hill turbine stands alone, but increasingly wind turbines are being built together in clusters called wind farms. By 1995 there were over 400 turbines on 22 wind farms

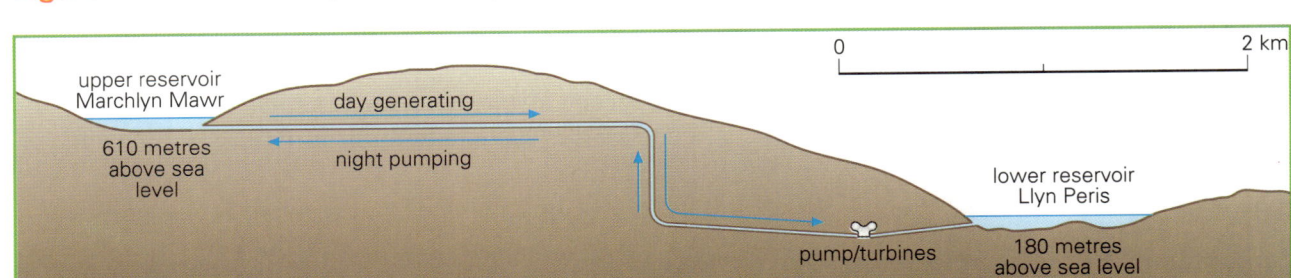

Figure 22.19 Dinorwic hydro-electric power station

Energy resources

Figure 22.20 Burgar Hill wind turbine, Orkney Islands

operating in Britain and plans for 60 more. The largest is at Llandinam in Mid-Wales. Here 103 30 m high turbines have a capacity of 31 mw. Opened in 1993, this is the largest wind farm in Europe (Figure 22.21). Total wind power capacity in 1995 was 120 mw, amounting to only 0.2 per cent of Britain's total electricity production. The most optimistic estimates suggest that wind power may produce 10 per cent of total electricity production by the year 2025.

Wind farms have been criticised by some people who live near them because of the noise and the visual impact of the wind turbines. However, environmentalists support wind farms because they cause no air pollution and thus do not contribute to acid rain or global warming. Another advantage is that wind power is 30 per cent cheaper than nuclear power and wind is an endlessly available resource.

> 15. (a) Which is the most important source of renewable energy?
> (b) What are its advantages and disadvantages?
> 16. (a) How does the Dinorwic power station generate electricity?
> (b) Dinorwic actually consumes more electricity in pumping than it generates. Why does this power station still make economic sense?
> 17. (a) What percentage of UK electricity is generated by hydro-electric power stations?
> (b) Why is it unlikely that this percentage will increase in the future?
> 18. What are the advantages and disadvantages of wind power?

Figure 22.21 Llandinam wind farm, Mid-Wales

Tidal power

Figure 22.22 shows a remarkable power station. Located on the River Rance in north west France, this is the world's first **tidal power** station. Opened in 1966 the tidal power station is a hollow dam over 700 m wide across the Rance estuary. Twenty-four turbines are housed in the dam. They are spun by the fast-flowing tidal current and generate 240 mw of electricity. The **tidal range** in the Rance estuary is the third highest in the world, producing a 12 m rise in the level (the 'head'). Other tidal power stations have been built in Russia, China and Canada.

Plans have been put forward for several tidal power stations in Britain. The Severn, Mersey and Humber Estuaries have all been studied as

166 Changing Resources

Figure 22.22 Rance tidal power station, Brittany

possible locations. The Severn Barrage could generate up to 7200 mw of electricity.

Tidal power stations do not create acid rain or release greenhouse gases, but they do have an environmental impact because they destroy tidal wetland habitats.

Tidal power stations have proved to be very expensive to build and maintain. Despite the technological success of the Rance scheme, there are no plans to build more tidal power stations in France.

Wave power

Anybody who has been on a ship on a windy day has experienced the great power of waves. Britain has a vast potential energy source from the waves crashing around its shores, especially on the western coast which is exposed to the Atlantic Ocean's breakers.

In 1991 a small wave-power plant was opened on the island of Islay in the Inner Hebrides. It uses an air-driven turbine to turn energy from waves entering a narrow rock gully into electricity. The waves compress air within a concrete water column. The compressed air is forced out through a tube at the back of the column, spinning the turbine. The Islay power station has a capacity of 2 mw, enough to supply the needs of 4000 people. The Isla plant is a *prototype* built for research purposes. In 1995 another wave-power station was towed in to position off the coast of Scotland, but it was destroyed by a storm within two weeks.

Wave power has great potential, but the technology to exploit it has not yet been perfected.

Solar power

You may have a calculator or watch powered by solar energy. The sun's rays fall onto solar cells made of silicon which convert the solar energy directly into electricity. Unfortunately, using solar energy on a large scale is very expensive. In order to create only half a watt of electricity a solar cell with a diameter of 75 cm is required. To supply a single British home with electricity would require 5000 cells! Nonetheless, small solar cell power stations have been built, including a 30 kw example near Southampton (now dismantled). The world's largest solar cell power station, in California, generates 10 mw.

Small solar power units using battery banks can provide energy for a wide range of uses including electric fences, pumps and navigation beacons. Solar energy can also be used to heat water directly. Many British homes have solar panels on their roofs. Water is fed through pipes across a black material which absorbs heat. The panel is covered by glass which prevents heat loss. During sunny summer days the solar panels can supply all the hot water needed.

Solar energy is not equally distributed across the earth's surface. Solar power devices are most efficient in direct sunlight. Britain's sunniest spot is Bournemouth with an average of 1730 hours of sunshine per year. Compare this with Saudi Arabia's average annual sunshine total – 3100 hours.

Solar power could have a promising future, but it is simply too expensive at present.

Geothermal power

The earth is an enormous nuclear reactor. Heat generated by radioactive decay in the molten core of the planet flows through the ground and out into space. Tapping a small fraction of this heat could supply all the human race's energy needs.

There are some areas where high temperature geothermal steam can be used to spin turbines to generate electricity. In the USA, 150 km north of San Francisco, is the Geysers, the site of a 500 mw geothermal power station. The Geysers

Energy resources

Figure 22.23 Larderello geothermal power station, Italy

taps over 100 **boreholes**. Figure 22.23 shows a 400 mw power station at Larderello in Italy.

Geothermal water is used in a number of countries. Almost all the buildings in Reykjavik, the capital of Iceland, are heated by geothermal water. Boreholes have been sunk 650 m underground to tap hot water which rises to the surface at a temperature of 86° C. In Britain, city centre buildings in Southampton are heated by geothermal water brought to the surface at 74° C from 1800 m underground.

The number of sites having naturally occurring geothermal steam or water are limited. We can only begin to realise the potential of geothermal energy when it can be used over a much wider area. The answer may lie in the 'hot, dry rock' method of generating electricity (see Figure 22.24). At Camborne in Cornwalll research has been conducted involving sinking two 2800 m deep boreholes down to a geothermally heated zone of granite. Cold water is pumped down one borehole and hot water at temperatures of 70–90° C returns up the second borehole. A turbo-generator at the surface generates 5 mw of electricity. The Camborne experiment still has some problems; sometimes, little of the water pumped down returns to the surface and at other times the water fails to reach a high temperature.

Figure 22.24 The hot, dry rock method of tapping geothermal energy

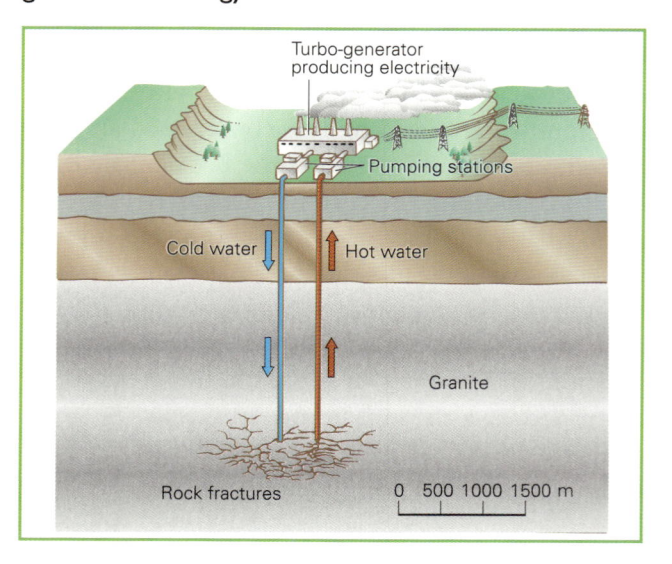

168 Changing Resources

Biomass

Biomass energy is obtained from burning wood, crops and animal waste. In Brazil alcohol from sugar cane is used as an additive to petrol in a 15 per cent:85 per cent mixture, thus reducing Brazil's high oil import bill. The EU has experimented with oil-seed rape as a source of alcohol. Another source of biomass energy is methane gas released at landfill waste sites as the rubbish decays. An example in the UK is the landfill gas electricity generation scheme at Daneshill Landfill site at Ranskill, Nottinghamshire. The scheme produces 0.4 mw of electricity.

There are plans for several biomass energy schemes within the UK, including the use of fast-growing willow plantations to provide wood for fuel.

> 19. (a) Describe the scene in Figure 22.22.
> (b) Where in the UK have tidal power stations been suggested?

> 20. 'Wave power and solar power have great potential, but are unlikely to make a significant contribution to the UK's energy needs in the foreseeable future.'
> (a) Why do these power sources have great potential?
> (b) Why are they unlikely to be important in the UK in the foreseeable future?
> 21. (a) What is geothermal heat? How is it created?
> (b) How do geothermal power stations generate electricity?
> (c) Why is Iceland an area of geothermal heat (see Unit 4).
> (d) How has Iceland used its geothermal resources?
> (e) Describe the developments in geothermal energy in the UK.
> 22. (a) What is biomass energy?
> (b) Describe some examples of the use of biomass as an energy source.

Summary

- The world's energy consumption is dominated by the fossil fuels coal, oil and gas. Slowly but surely alternative energy resources are growing in importance as the fossil fuel reserves become scarcer.

Energy resources

Chapter 23 Pollution

What is pollution?
What are the causes and effects of pollution?
What can be done to reduce and prevent pollution?

This unit looks at the ways in which people are damaging the earth's air, land and water. It also examines the effects of pollution and considers ways in which the damage caused by pollution can be reversed and further pollution reduced.

Water

Water makes the earth different from all other known planets. The earth could be called the 'water planet' because water covers two-thirds of its surface, making it look blue from Space, as Figure 23.1 shows. All life on earth depends on water and without it we would die.

Ninety-seven per cent of the earth's water is salt water. The sun's heat evaporates this water from the seas. Winds and clouds carry the water

Figure 23.1 Satellite image of the earth from space

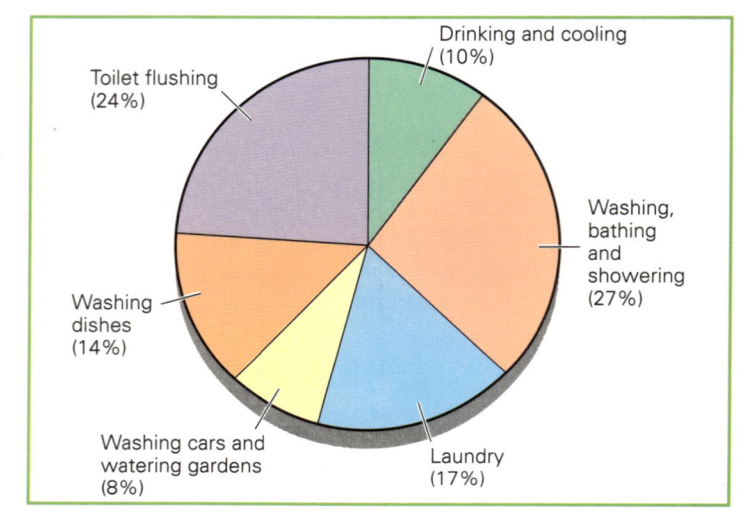

Figure 23.2 Domestic water use in Britain

- Drinking and cooling (10%)
- Toilet flushing (24%)
- Washing, bathing and showering (27%)
- Washing dishes (14%)
- Washing cars and watering gardens (8%)
- Laundry (17%)

vapour inland where some of it condenses as it is cooled and then falls to the ground as rain. The rain forms streams which unite to form rivers which return to the sea. Here it is mixed with salt again. This is known as the hydrological cycle (see Chapter 11).

People interrupt the hydrological cycle in order to make use of water, which is a vital resource used in farms, factories, offices and homes all over the world. It is also used to transport domestic and industrial waste back into the water. However, the amount of water being diverted from the natural cycle is increasing every year so less water is circulating in the hydrological cycle. As Figure 23.2 shows, people are using more and more water.

170 Changing Resources

> **1.** Look at Figure 23.2. Write a letter to a newspaper, pointing out how much water people use and suggesting ways in which they could cut down on the water they use. Try to include a suggestion for each type of domestic use. Include at least one suggestion on how the water companies might act to reduce waste of water (e.g. higher charges).

Polluting water in the countryside and in towns

Once rain falls it almost immediately starts to become polluted, whether it is in the countryside or in towns and cities (see Figures 23.3 and 23.4).

In MEDCs, like the UK, water is taken from rivers, filtered, and then chemically treated to remove impurities, before it is distributed to homes and factories. Filtering and purifying are very expensive processes but the water is soon polluted again through human use.

Most UK homes use between 150 and 500 litres of water each day. Of this only 100 litres needs to be very pure for drinking and cooking. The rest, such as water to flush the toilet, to wash the car or to water the garden, does not need to be so pure. Thus some scientists have suggested that homes could have a dual water system, with one set of thin pipes supplying pure drinking water, and another set of larger pipes bringing less pure water for other uses.

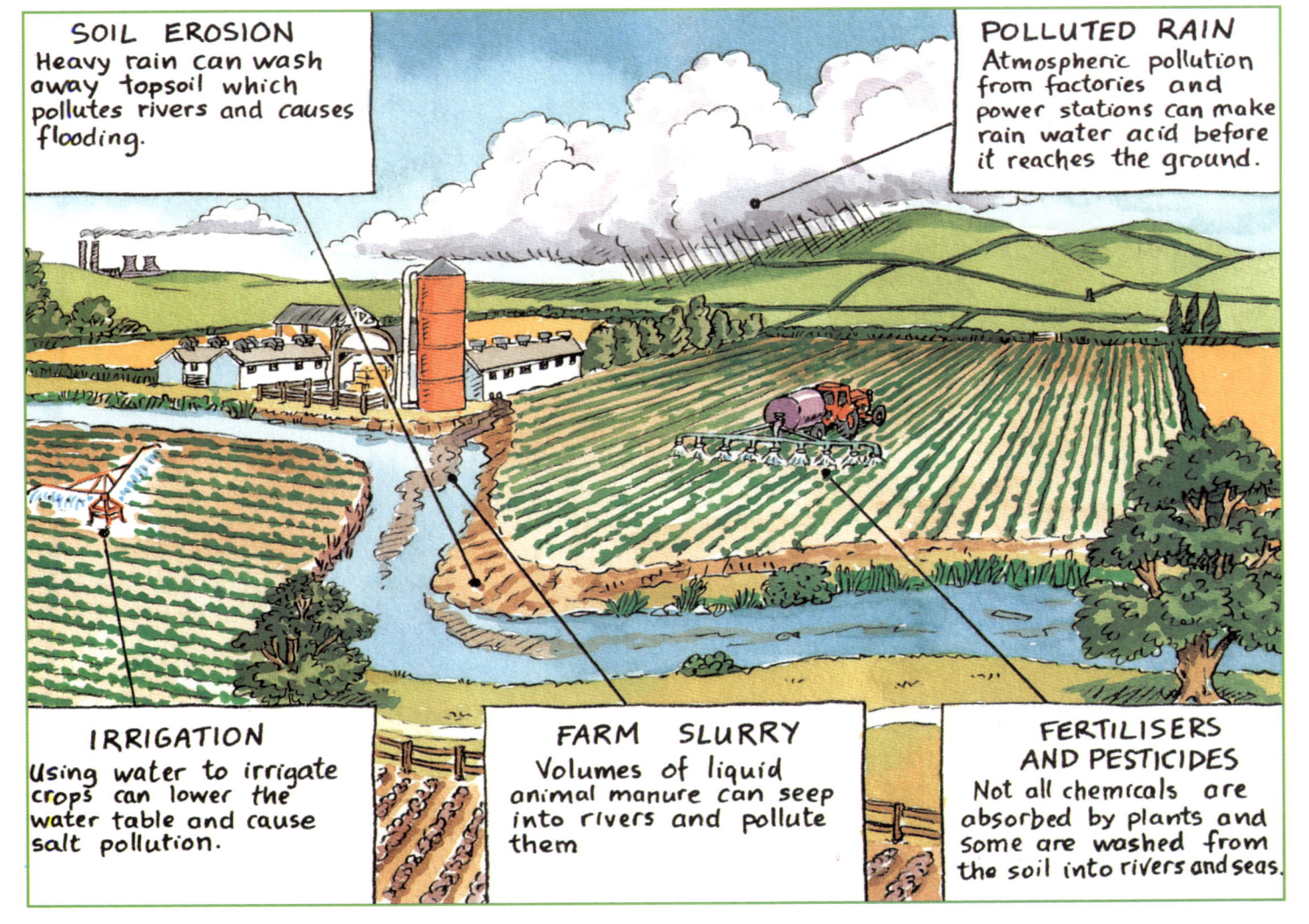

Figure 23.3 Water pollution in the countryside

SOIL EROSION Heavy rain can wash away topsoil which pollutes rivers and causes flooding.

POLLUTED RAIN Atmospheric pollution from factories and power stations can make rain water acid before it reaches the ground.

IRRIGATION Using water to irrigate crops can lower the water table and cause salt pollution.

FARM SLURRY Volumes of liquid animal manure can seep into rivers and pollute them

FERTILISERS AND PESTICIDES Not all chemicals are absorbed by plants and some are washed from the soil into rivers and seas.

Pollution 171

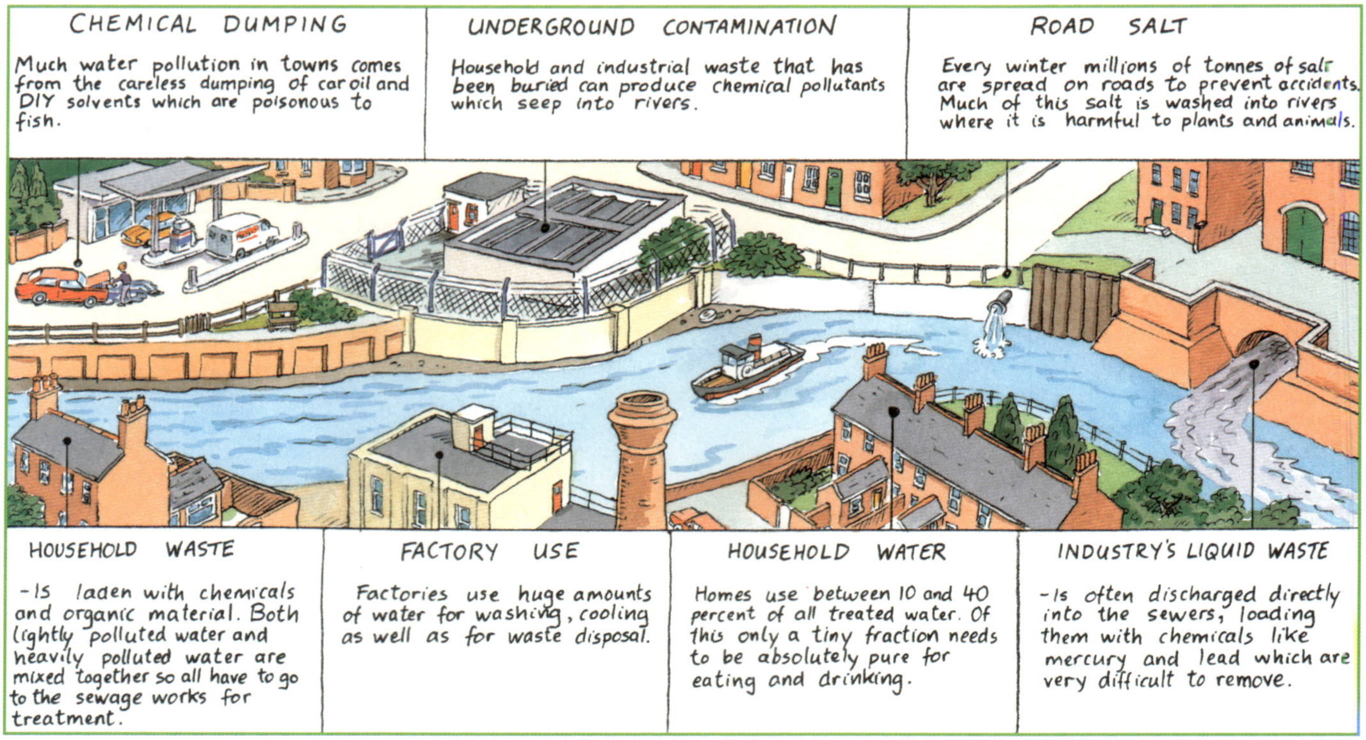

CHEMICAL DUMPING
Much water pollution in towns comes from the careless dumping of car oil and DIY solvents which are poisonous to fish.

UNDERGROUND CONTAMINATION
Household and industrial waste that has been buried can produce chemical pollutants which seep into rivers.

ROAD SALT
Every winter millions of tonnes of salt are spread on roads to prevent accidents. Much of this salt is washed into rivers where it is harmful to plants and animals.

HOUSEHOLD WASTE
- Is laden with chemicals and organic material. Both lightly polluted water and heavily polluted water are mixed together so all have to go to the sewage works for treatment.

FACTORY USE
Factories use huge amounts of water for washing, cooling as well as for waste disposal.

HOUSEHOLD WATER
Homes use between 10 and 40 percent of all treated water. Of this only a tiny fraction needs to be absolutely pure for eating and drinking.

INDUSTRY'S LIQUID WASTE
- Is often discharged directly into the sewers, loading them with chemicals like mercury and lead which are very difficult to remove.

Figure 23.4 Water pollution in urban areas

2. Use Figure 23.3 to describe how water becomes polluted in the countryside.
3. Now list all the changes that would be necessary to reduce such water pollution.
4. For each major cause of water pollution in Figure 23.4 suggest what could be done to reduce the problem.
5. Prepare a report for a television programme which tries to set out the advantages and disadvantages of the dual water system. Emphasise the costs and effects for both people and countries, and conclude with whether or not you support the idea.

Pollution in the Baltic Sea

The Baltic is an example of one of the world's seas whose pollution problems are only just coming to light. The Baltic Sea stretches from 50° N to 65° N and is surrounded by nine different countries, most of which are major industrial nations. The Baltic has three main arms: the Gulf of Bothnia to the north which is the coldest part of the sea and the first to freeze, the Gulf of Finland to the east and the smaller Gulf of Riga to the south east.

The Baltic Sea has a very narrow entrance and exit and because of this the water is only slowly replaced by fresher water from the North Sea. Once polluted, water tends to linger for as much as 20 years within the Baltic.

The main current within the Baltic flows from the Danish islands of Funen and Zealand in the west in an easterly direction along the south coast, as Figure 23.5 shows. In the process, sediments deposited by the Rivers Oder and Vistula are swept eastwards by the current, creating the distinctive long, thin sand spits of the south Baltic. Behind these sand spits are shallow lagoons with further sand dunes inland.

The Baltic is a shallow sea, mostly below 200 m in depth. This, combined with the winter freezing (from November to April, but longer in the north and east) and generally slow water

Changing Resources

Figure 23.5 The Baltic Sea and its currents

circulation, mean that pollution is very slow to disperse. High levels of pollution are found along the south and east shore of the sea, especially close to the mouths of the Rivers Oder and Vistula which bring so much inland pollution to the sea. The countries at the eastern end of the sea such as Finland, Russia and Estonia complain that they suffer from extra pollution, washed eastwards by the currents in the sea.

The Baltic countries

Recent changes in the countries around the Baltic have contributed to the problems of pollution.

- Political changes within Poland as it moves to becoming a non-communist country, have not halted the massive pollution from sewage and industrial waste transmitted from Warsaw and Cracow via the River Vistula.
- Despite the reunification of Germany in 1990 the River Oder still carries industrial, agricultural and domestic pollution from the eastern regions of Germany into the Baltic.
- There has been a decline of communism in the former Soviet Union and a subsequent emergence of Latvia, Lithuania, Estonia and Russia as separate independent countries. However the problems of pollution of the Baltic from mining, power generation and other heavy industry are still very severe. Environmental pollution has a low priority.
- Despite the entry of Sweden and Finland into the European Union, the timber and metal industries of these countries continue to add to pollution in the Baltic.
- The growth of tourism in Denmark, Germany, Poland and Russia has increased the pollution of beaches in the western and southern parts of the Baltic.

Until recently, pollution problems of the North Sea or the Mediterranean tended to dominate discussions in Europe. But the rapid growth of industry and population around the Baltic has highlighted existing pollution problems and the need for rapid action. Figure 23.6 (page 174) summarises some of the main causes, types and effects of pollution in the Baltic.

International clean up?

The Baltic nations agree on the need to reduce pollution in the Baltic Sea but international co-operation is required to achieve this. Some countries, like Poland, Estonia and Russia, cannot afford to pay to clean up pollution. Political disputes between some of the countries also make co-operation very difficult. For example, Latvia, Lithuania and Estonia are unwilling to work closely with Russia which until recently controlled these nations. There are disputes between countries over claims to areas of the sea bed which might yield minerals or oil and gas in the future. Again, this holds up any settlement regarding issues of pollution. In addition countries at the eastern end of the Baltic want extra help to clean up pollution in the sea because they suffer so much pollution from other countries.

1 **Nitrogen** – from farming in Germany and Denmark and from sewage in Russia, Poland, Latvia, Lithuania and Estonia. *Effects*: encourages growth of algae, which reduces the oxygen content of the water and kills fish.

2 **Sediments** – such as mud, sand and silt from mining in Sweden, Estonia, Latvia and Lithuania and forestry and farming in Sweden, Finland, Poland and Denmark. *Effects*: clogs gills of fish and carries toxic chemicals.

3 **Pathogens** – dangerous, from sewage and livestock waste from Russia, Poland, Latvia, Lithuania and Estonia. *Effects*: contaminates coastal swimming areas (e.g, Germany, Poland) and seafood such as Prawns.

4 **Toxic chemicals** – such as cadmium and arsenic from industries in Poland, Germany, Russia and Sweden. *Effects*: contaminates seafood (fish, lobsters, prawn) and poisons marine life.

5 **Oil** – from oil tankers and other shipping operating in the Baltic. *Effects*: low-level contamination can cause disease in fish. Oil slicks kill marine life.

6 **Plastics** – from fishing nets, beach litter and wastes from the plastics industry in Germany, Poland, Russia, Sweden and Finland. *Effects*: kills marine and bird life, pollutes beaches (e.g. Germany).

7 **Radioactivity** – from nuclear reactors in Russia, Latvia, Lithuania and Estonia. *Effects*: causes 'hots spots' of radioactivity which can contaminate fish (e.g. Poland, Latvia, Russia, Lithuania and Estonia).

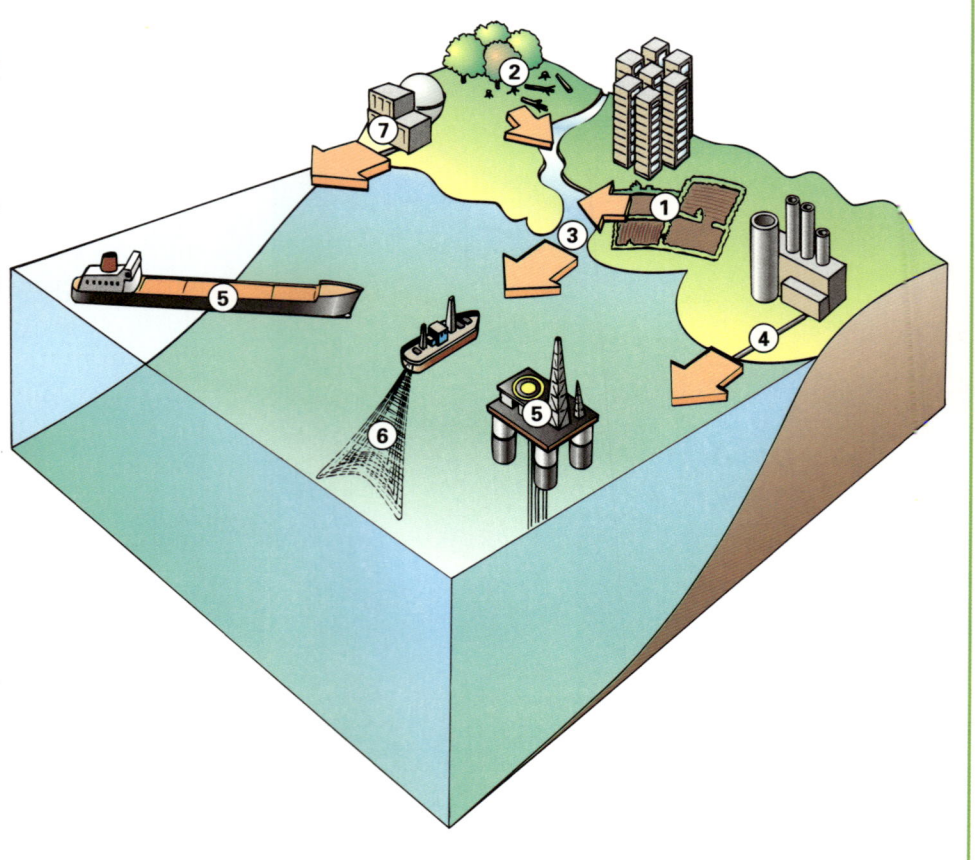

Figure 23.6 Pollution in the Baltic Sea

> **6. Write a report about pollution in the Baltic for an environmental organisation like Greenpeace. Refer to Figures 23.5 and 23.6 and mention: (a) the main causes and types of pollution; (b) how pollution is affected by ocean currents; (c) the effects of different types of pollution; (d) why international agreement to reduce pollution is so difficult; (e) your own conclusions and recommendations for cleaning up the sea.**

The chlorine sunrise along the River Danube

Pollution of major rivers like the Danube is a serious problem. The Danube is one of the world's great rivers, flowing from Switzerland and Germany through Serbia, the Slovak Republic, Hungary, Romania and Bulgaria to the Black Sea (Figure 23.7). Along its 2850 km course, the river is used by agriculture, industry and tourism, is also a source of drinking water to over 30 million people and is home to millions of fish and birds like the pelican and the white egret.

However an 'industrial revolution' has taken place along the banks of the river, the focus of which are the former communist countries of Serbia, Slovakia, Romania and Bulgaria. During the period from 1950 to 1989 the communist governments of these countries struggled to establish as many industries as possible in order to catch up with western Europe. The overriding aim was production, and the communist governments largely ignored environmental protection, allowing factories to take as much water as they needed and to pump as much waste back into the Danube as was necessary. The result of such rapid industrialisation is a mass of oil refineries, chemical works and heavy industries along the Danube, producing a tide of dangerous pollution which is destroying the river.

Changing Resources

Figure 23.7 The course of the River Danube

The Danube after 1989

The overthrow of the communist governments after 1989 has done little to improve conditions along the river. The new democratic governments have no money to clean up the river or to stop further pollution. They still need rapid industrial growth in order to raise living standards, and they cannot agree about how best to use the river.

There is currently a range of problems with the Danube.

- The Danube contains nearly every known **contaminant** that is dangerous to human life, from heavy metals like mercury and cadmium to oil, nuclear waste and sewage sludge.
- There are few controls on factories using the Danube, so they are within the law to continue with their pollution. For example, the caustic soda factory at Copsa Mica in Romania (Figure 23.8, page 176) pours out chlorine. People in the town block their doors and windows to keep out the gas and sleep with damp towels over their faces to avoid inhaling the gas. The pollution burns holes in plastic bags and has led to deformities in new born babies. All this pollution seeps into the Danube, and colours the sunrise red with all the chlorine.
- Farmers in the former communist countries are poor and are forced to use cheaper but dangerous chemicals like DDT which have been banned in other countries. A recent survey found levels of DDT in the Danube at ten times higher than the accepted danger level. Such chemicals are killing the fish that used to be plentiful in the river, and this affects other wildlife in the river's ecosystem.
- Many towns and cities, like Belgrade, Ruse and Giurgiu, discharge raw sewage into the Danube.
- The Danube is an important highway for barges carrying oil (Figure 23.9, page 177). Fuel discharge pollutes the river, as do the oil refineries along the banks.
- Romania has recently developed and

Pollution

Figure 23.8 Copsa Mica in Romania

improved procedures in its nuclear power programme but still disposes of some of its nuclear waste in to the Danube.
- Romania has taken water from the Danube to generate hydro-electricity so the river has shrunk, wetlands have dried out and wildlife and fish have died.
- Hungary and the Slovak Republic disagree over the building of two giant hydro-electric stations along the river which forms the border between the two countries. The Slovak HEP station is build (see Figure 23.10) and the Danube has been diverted to provide it with water. This has left Hungary short of water and with rapidly disappearing wetlands. The Hungarians have withdrawn from building the second HEP station and now want the river returned to its original course.

Figure 23.9 An oil barge on the River Danube

> **7. What are the main sources of pollution along the Danube?**

Figure 23.10 The Gabcikovo Dam in the Slovak Republic

> 8. What have been the effects of pollution on the Danube?
> 9. Why is it so difficult to get agreements between the countries to clean up the Danube and stop further pollution?

Acid rain

Acid rain was first reported in the 1960s when scientists in Scandinavia noticed that large number of fish were dying in lakes and rivers. They discovered that the water in the lakes and rivers had become very acid. This acid is carried by rain and so they called the problem acid rain. The acid comes from power stations which burn coal or lignite (brown coal). The power stations produce sulphur dioxide and nitrogen oxide from burning the coal and lignite. Nitrogen oxide from car exhausts also adds to the problem. The chemicals are carried up into the atmosphere and then are spread over wide areas by the prevailing winds as Figures 23.11 and 23.12 (page 178) show. The rest of this section looks at acid rain in the USA and Canada where the problems are particularly severe.

Dry deposition, wet deposition

Some of the chemicals fall back to the ground within a day (up to 300 km from the power station). This is called **dry deposition**. But more of the chemical combine with water vapour in the air to form dilute acids. When this acid rain falls it is called **wet deposition**.

There are several effects of acid rain.

- Acid rain not only kills fish, it also kills trees, especially conifers like pine, fir and spruce. At first, the tops of the trees turn yellow, then growth slows down and the bark may split before the tree finally dies.

Pollution 177

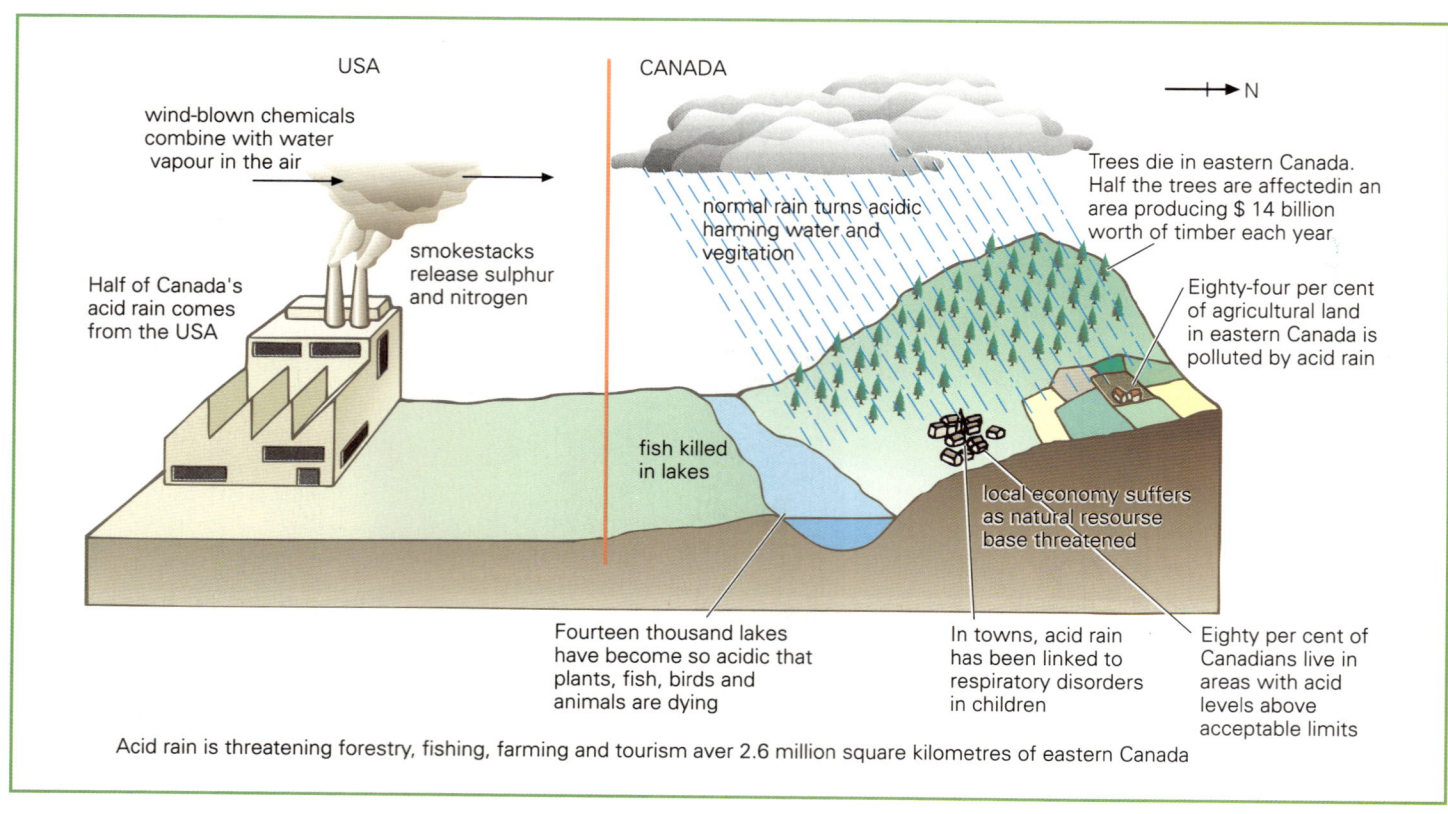

Figure 23.11 Some effects of acid rain in Canada

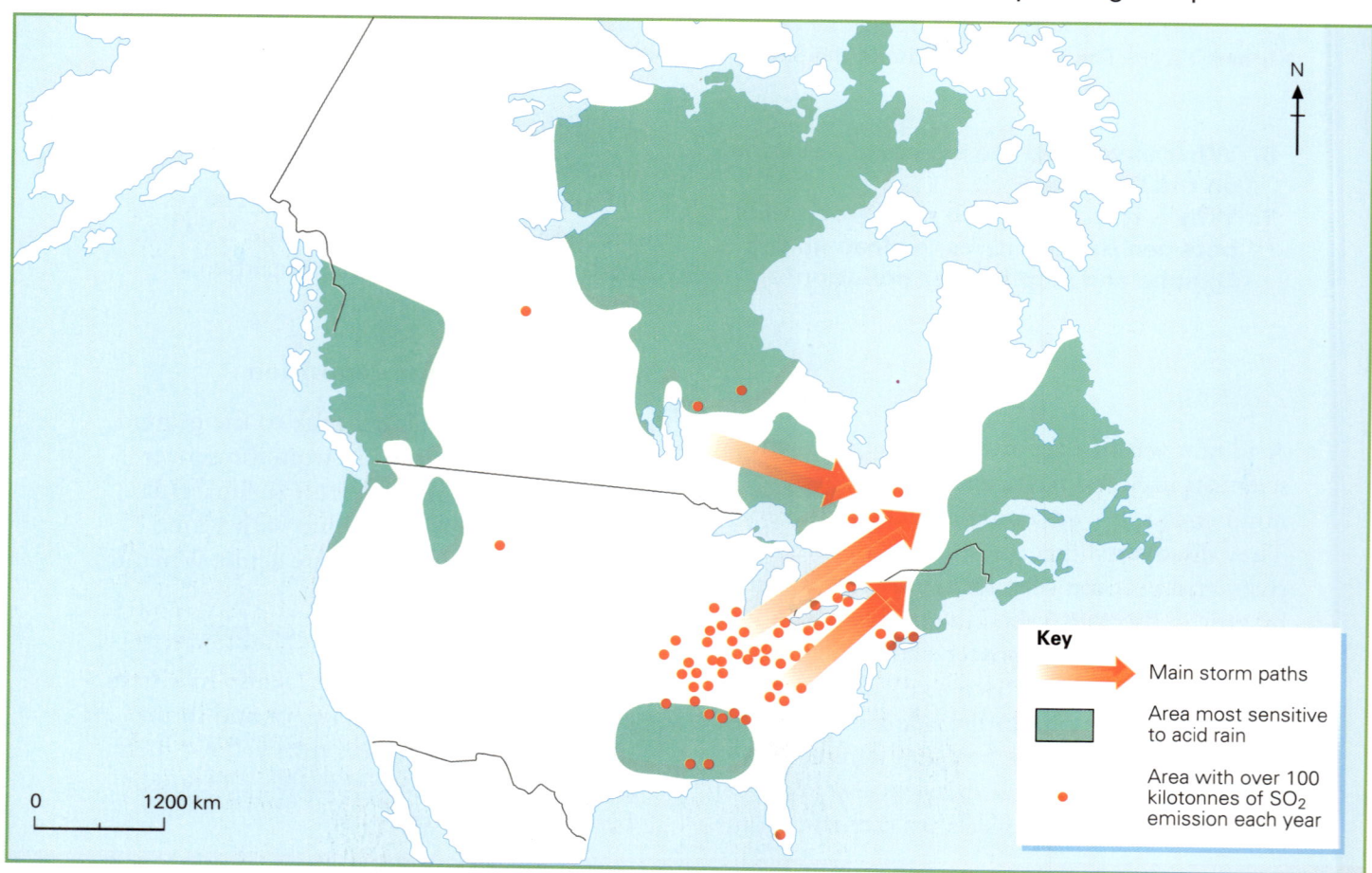

- wind-blown chemicals combine with water vapour in the air
- Half of Canada's acid rain comes from the USA
- smokestacks release sulphur and nitrogen
- normal rain turns acidic harming water and vegetation
- Trees die in eastern Canada. Half the trees are affected in an area producing $14 billion worth of timber each year
- Eighty-four per cent of agricultural land in eastern Canada is polluted by acid rain
- fish killed in lakes
- local economy suffers as natural resource base threatened
- Fourteen thousand lakes have become so acidic that plants, fish, birds and animals are dying
- In towns, acid rain has been linked to respiratory disorders in children
- Eighty per cent of Canadians live in areas with acid levels above acceptable limits

Acid rain is threatening forestry, fishing, farming and tourism over 2.6 million square kilometres of eastern Canada

Figure 23.12 Major sources of sulphur dioxide emissions in North America and prevailing wind patterns

Key:
- Main storm paths
- Area most sensitive to acid rain
- Area with over 100 kilotonnes of SO_2 emission each year

178 Changing Resources

Figure 23.13 Canada's sulphur dioxide emissions

	Sulphur dioxide emissions in 1980 (tonnes)	Sulphur dioxide emissions in 1994 (tonnes)
Manitoba	738 000	550 000
Ontario	2 194 000	885 000
Quebec	1 085 000	600 000
New Brunswick	215 000	185 000
Prince Edward Island	6 000	5 000
Nova Scotia	219 000	204 000
Newfoundland	59 000	45 000

- Acid rain water seeps into underground water supplies. This may pose a hazard to health as well as corroding the water pipes.
- Buildings are crumbling under the attack of acid rain. Marble, granite and limestone are the most easily eroded rocks and buildings in Canada are losing 4 per cent of their weight each year.
- Crop yields fall in areas affected by acid rain.

What can be done to solve the problem?

The Canadian and US Governments have tried different ways of solving the problem of acid rain.

- In some areas trees are sprayed with water to wash off the acid. This is expensive and not very effective.
- Lime has been added to lakes, rivers and soils to neutralise the acid. This, too, is expensive as well as time consuming.
- Some power companies have been forced to fit equipment to remove sulphur dioxide and nitrogen dioxide from their emissions. This is very expensive but effective. Figure 23.13 shows how sulphur dioxide emissions in Canada were reduced between 1980 and 1994.
- Canada now has a policy of building gas-fired power stations to replace the coal burning ones.
- Raising public awareness of the nature and extent of the acid rain problem is another important factor.

---

10. Use an atlas and Figure 23.12 to name the states of the USA which produce over 100 kilotonnes of sulphur dioxide each year.
11. Using Figure 23.13, calculate the percentage decrease in sulphur dioxide emissions for each Canadian province between 1980 and 1994. Which two provinces had the largest percentage decrease?
12. Imagine you work for Environment Canada, a group of people concerned about the effects of acid rain. You have been given a two minute slot on a US radio programme to publicise your campaign against the effects of acid rain. Decide on the key points you wish to make and then write a script.
13. Design your own poster to highlight the damage acid rain can cause to people and the environment.

Pollution

Summary

- Pollution damages the earth's environment, especially the water and air.
- Water pollution comes from towns, factories, offices and farms.
- Pollution of major seas like the Baltic needs an international effort to clear it up.
- Major rivers like the Danube suffer serious pollution which will take many years to clean up.
- Sulphur and nitrogen oxides pollute the air and create acid rain, an international problem.

Industrial Change

24 Types of industry

What is industry?
This unit considers the nature of primary, secondary and tertiary industry.

What is industry?

Industry is often taken to mean only making things, but this is more correctly called manufacturing and is only a part of industry. Industry means any form of employment which involves using or producing goods and services. It includes manufacturing, trade, commerce, transport, agriculture, mining, education, entertainment and many other activities.

It is clear that industry is a very broad term covering a wide range of activities. It is usual to divide industry into three sectors:

- *primary industry* means those industries which produce or exploit raw materials and includes farming, fishing, forestry and mining;
- *secondary industry* means those industries which make things from raw materials, often called manufacturing industries;
- *tertiary industry* means those industries which provide a service to other industry and to people and includes transport, retailing, administration, financial, professional and public services. Tertiary industries are often called service industries.

Sometimes a fourth sector, called quaternary industry, is identified. Quaternary industry means high-technology industry, research and development activities and information services.

The sectors of industry are closely related, as can be illustrated through the production of a book like this one.

- The raw materials for the book come from the forests of Scandinavia. The growing and felling of trees is a primary industry.

Figure 24.1 Setting plough shears on a farm

Figure 24.2 A canning factory

Figure 24.3 A supermarket assistant

- The wood is processed into pulp in Scandinavia then shipped to the UK where it is turned into paper in a paper mill. This is a secondary industry. China clay, quarried in Cornwall, is added to the paper.
- Tertiary industries then take over. The authors type the manuscript into word processors. Reviewers and the editor suggest amendments. Photographs are taken or obtained. Artists draw final versions of the authors' rough maps and diagrams. The manuscript is typeset using desktop publishing software.
- Secondary industry then becomes involved again as the book is printed.
- Lorries distribute the book to warehouses and shops.
- Financial staff monitor the sales and distribute the income.
- At each stage of the process, people in offices update computer spreadsheets, print hard copies, fill in forms and sign papers concerning the book.

The publication of this book involved hundreds of people in dozens of different jobs in primary, secondary and tertiary industry. This is typical of most of the goods which we buy.

---

1. Define industry.
2. Study the list of industries and jobs below and list them as primary, secondary or tertiary.

Plumber	Car assembly
Forester	Coal miner
Insurance broker	Nursing
Bus driver	Steelworker
Professional cricketer	Musician
Farmer	Fishing
Actor	Teacher
Engineer	Paper manufacture
Journalist	Shop assistant
Car assembly	Oil refining
Quarrying	Electronics
Bank clerk	Lawyer
Furniture maker	

3. Study Figure 24.4 which shows the number of people employed in Britain, broken down within each sector of industry.
   (a) Draw a pie graph showing the total percentages employed in the three sectors.
   (b) (i) Draw a bar graph to show the ten largest sub-sectors by percentage of total employees. Use different colours to indicate whether the type of industry is primary, secondary or tertiary.
   (b) (ii) How many of the five largest sub-sectors are in the tertiary sector?

182   Industrial Change

Figure 24.4 The industrial employment structure in Britain

Type of industry	Total employees ('000s)	Percentage of total
Agriculture	265	1.2
Forestry	18	0.1
Fishing	20	0.1
Mining and quarrying	332	1.5
Total primary	**674**	**3.0**
Food, drink and tobacco	563	2.5
Chemicals	316	1.4
Metal manufacture	337	1.5
Engineering	1 891	8.3
Cars	223	1.0
Aerospace	195	0.9
Textiles and clothing	446	2.0
Construction	962	4.3
Other manufacturing	1 261	5.6
Total manufacturing	**6 224**	**27.5**
Gas, electricity and water	320	1.4
Transport and communications	1 349	6.0
Distribution	3 123	13.8
Financial and professional services	4 635	20.5
Public administration and the armed services	1 634	7.2
Hotels and catering	1 251	5.6
Education	1 799	7.9
Medical and other health services	1 514	6.7
Total tertiary	**15 754**	**69.5**

4. (a) Draw a flow diagram to show the different industries involved in the publication of this book. Use a different colour for primary, secondary and tertiary industries.

(b) Draw a similar flow diagram to show the different industries involved in the production of an item of furniture.

Summary

- Industry can be divided into the three sectors of primary, secondary and tertiary. These sectors are often closely related.

Chapter 25 Industrial growth and development

How does industrial growth happen?
How do levels of industrial development vary across the world?
What are the causes and consequences of rapid industrial growth?

This unit studies the process of industrial growth and the models which have been developed to help explain the process. Thailand provides a case study illustrating the causes and effects of industrial growth.

Industrial growth

Great Britain became the world's first industrial nation during the early nineteenth century in what is known as the Industrial Revolution. Factories burned coal to power steam engines which were used to manufacture textiles, forge iron and roll steel. Small towns grew into vast sprawling industrial cities. In 1801, 80 per cent of Britain's population lived in the countryside and worked on the land. However, by the end of the century 70 per cent lived in towns and worked in industry. The population had exploded from 10 million to 38 million and average living standards had started to rise.

Where Britain led, others followed. Germany, Belgium, the USA and then much of the rest of western and central Europe developed industrial economies. Japan led the way to industrialisation in Asia during the early twentieth century, to be joined by countries like South Korea, Taiwan, Singapore, Thailand and Indonesia during the century's final quarter.

Rostow's growth model

Figure 25.1 shows how levels of industrial development today vary across the world. In 1960 the US economist Rostow said that MEDCs had passed through a series of stages of development. At each stage the wealth of the country increased as factories and, later, service industries replaced agriculture and craft industries (see Figure 25.2).

Figure 25.3 shows when several MEDCs entered the different stages of the growth model. Rostow claimed that the LEDCs could follow the same course of development. In recent years, this idea has been heavily criticised because the model is based solely on the development of the western industrial nations. It is unlikely that many LEDCs could follow this course because:

- today's MEDCs were able to exploit the resources of the whole world, much of it through their empires. They built up power and wealth on such a scale that it was impossible for LEDCs to compete.
- MEDCs ensure that there can be no large-scale development of manufacturing in poorer countries by charging tariffs on imports of manufactured goods.

Those who still support Rostow point to the success of some developing countries, such as South Korea, Taiwan and Thailand, the so-called Newly Industrialised Countries (NICs).

184 Industrial Change

Figure 25.1 Varying levels of industrial development across the world

Country	Agriculture	Manufacturing	Other industry	Services
Bangladesh	44	7	7	42
Bolivia	24	13	17	46
Ethiopia	42	11	5	42
Kenya	31	12	8	49
Saudi Arabia	8	8	37	47
Malaysia	23	22	20	35
South Korea	10	26	18	46
Taiwan	6	38	8	48
Thailand	17	21	17	45
France	4	21	8	67
Japan	3	30	11	56
Spain	6	18	9	67
UK	2	20	17	61
USA	2	17	12	69

Figure 25.2 Rostow's industrial growth model

Stage 1 Traditional society

Stage 2 Beginnings of Industry
- Transport improvements
- Agricultural improvements

Stage 3 Economic take-off
- Manufacturing industry develops
- Urbanization

Stage 4 Drive to maturity
- Rapid increase of industry

Stage 5 High mass consumption
- High production of consumer goods
- Many service industries
- High living standards

Stage 6 Post-industrial
- Slow or zero growth
- Decline of manufacturing
- High-technology increased leisure

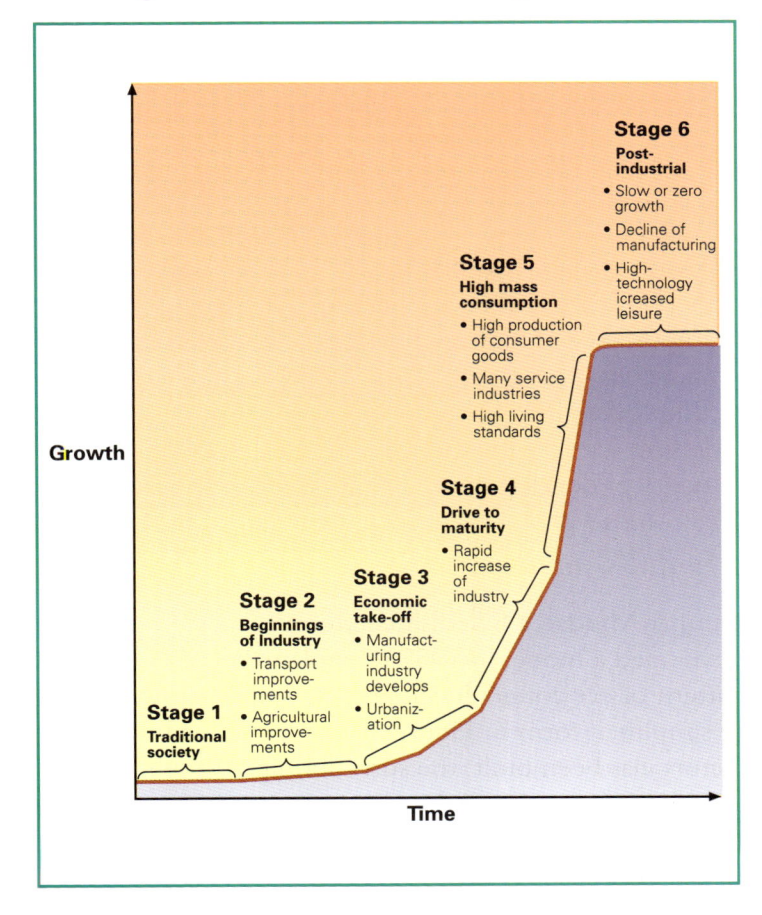

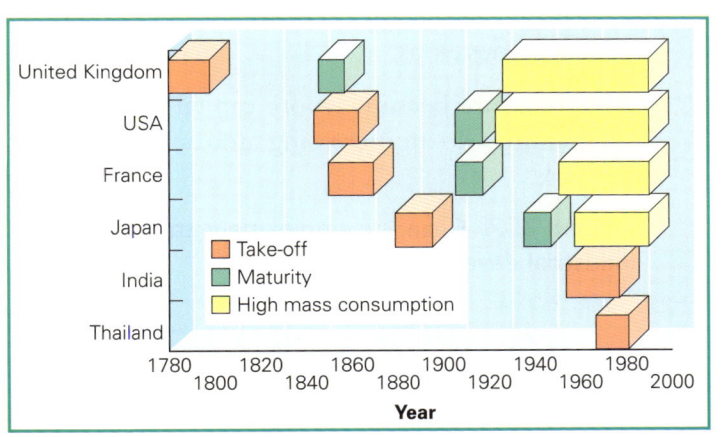

Figure 25.3 Times at which selected countries entered the different stages of Rostow's growth model

They claim that the NICs have passed through stage three and on into stage four of the model. South Korea is fast approaching stage five.

A sixth stage has been added to Rostow's model which takes account of the decline of manufacturing industry in several MEDCs, such as the UK, and the growth in leisure time.

Industrial growth and development

1. (a) By how much did the percentage of the British population living in urban areas increase between 1801 and 1900?
   (b) What was the main cause of the increase?
2. Study Figure 25.3.
   (a) When did the UK enter: (i) stage three; (ii) stage four; (iii) stage five of the growth model?
   (b) Which of the countries shown in Figure 25.3 reached stage five first?
   (c) Which of the countries passed through stage four most rapidly?
   (d) Why is it unlikely that all developing countries will pass through all the stages of Rostow's growth model?
   (e) How do you think the following countries fit into Rostow's growth model: (i) NICs such as South Korea; (ii) oil-rich countries such as Saudi Arabia?

Case study – the USA

As industrial development takes place, the percentages of the workforce employed in the different industrial sectors changes (Figure 25.4). Figure 25.5 shows how the structure of employment in the USA changed between 1880 and 1990. By 1990 only 18 per cent of the US workforce was employed in manufacturing while about 80 per cent worked in service occupations.

Within each sector there are changes as the economy develops.

- Agriculture becomes more capital intensive. Machines do an increasing amount of the work.

Figure 25.4 Changing employment structure as industrial development takes place

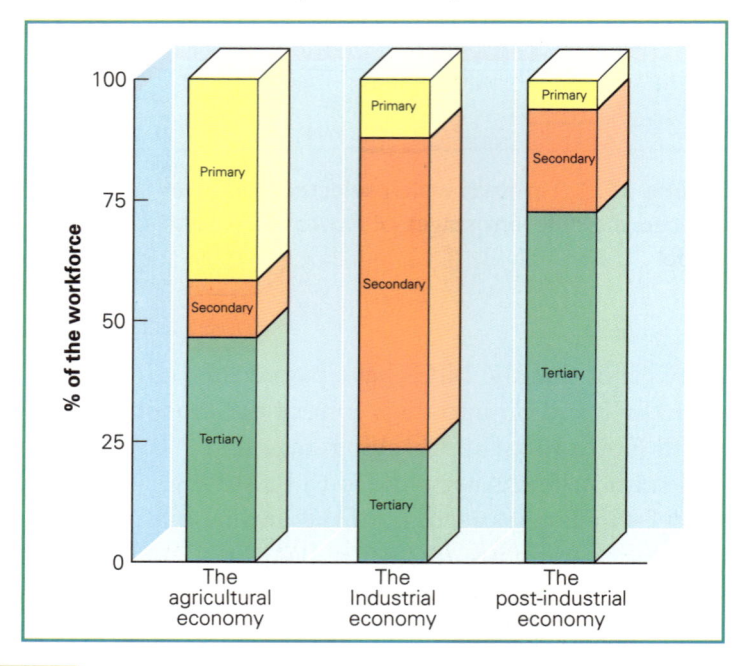

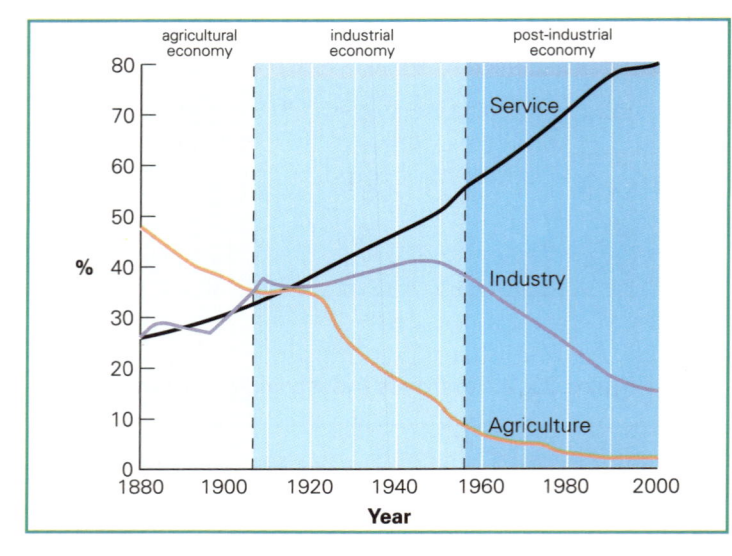

Figure 25.5 The changing structure of employment in the USA, 1880–2000

- Heavy manufacturing industry such as steel, shipbuilding and engineering declines in importance as high-technology manufacturing increases.
- Employment in financial, information and leisure services increases rapidly in the later stages of development.

Myrdal's model

Gunnar Myrdal, a Swedish economist, developed a model in 1957 to explain the pattern of economic development. This is shown in simplified form in Figure 25.6. Once a new factory has been built, the surrounding area will attract money, other industries and people. An industrial region will develop. This 'snowballing' of growth is called the **multiplier effect**

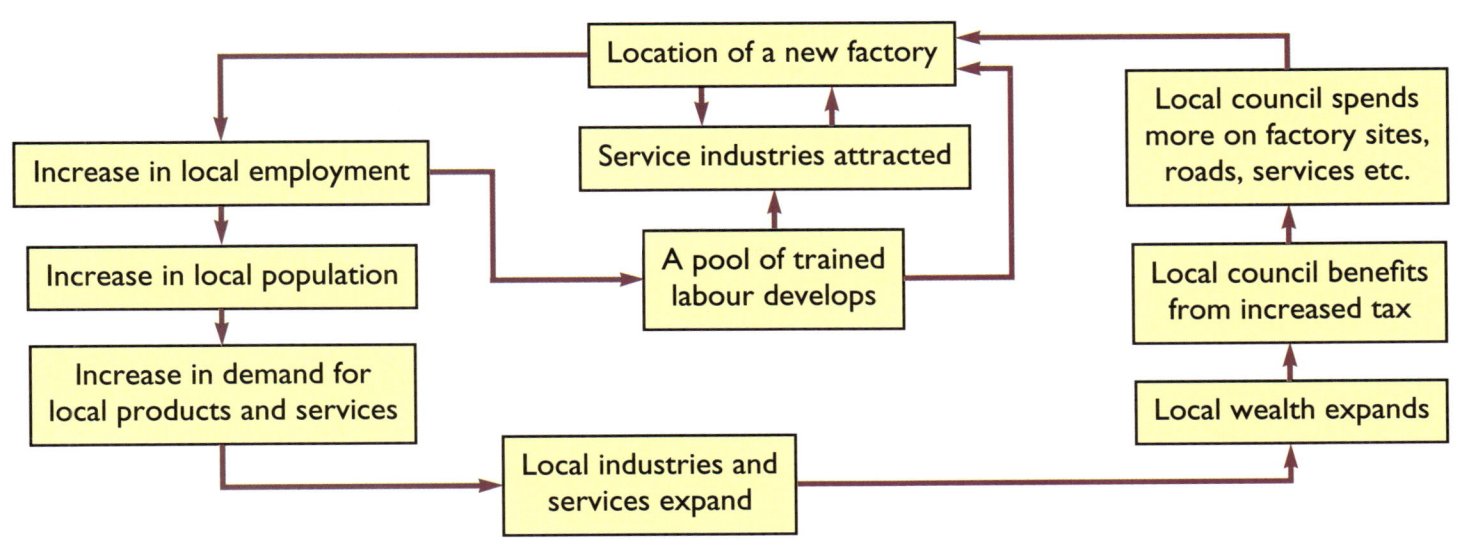

Figure 25.6 Myrdal's model – the 'multiplier effect'

Myrdal realised that a region developed at the expense of other regions. On a large scale, Myrdal's model can be applied to western Europe growing at the expense of the developing world. Myrdal said that there would eventually be a spread of development outside the region because of the effects of congestion.

The multiplier effect can also work in reverse. If several factories are closed, an industrial region can decline almost as quickly as it developed, unless it has reached a large enough size (or critical mass) to survive.

Friedmann's core-periphery model

In 1966 Milton Friedmann of the USA looked at the geographical differences in development which Myrdal had mentioned (Figure 25.7). His model consists of three concentric circles which he identified as a core, an upward transition and a downward transition region. The core grows at the expense of the periphery.

Thailand can be seen to fit this model as it has a clear core and periphery (see Figure 25.8). The central region is an area of fertile lowland, the broad flood plain of the Chao Phraya River. It is the most important agricultural area and, in Greater Bangkok, has the capital city and major industrial area. Containing 11 per cent of Thailand's total population, Bangkok is the focus of the country's transport network, has 78 per cent of the country's manufacturing and accounts for half of the country's total GDP. The central region is surrounded by mountains, leaving the other regions of Thailand as the periphery.

Figure 25.7 Friedmann's core-periphery model

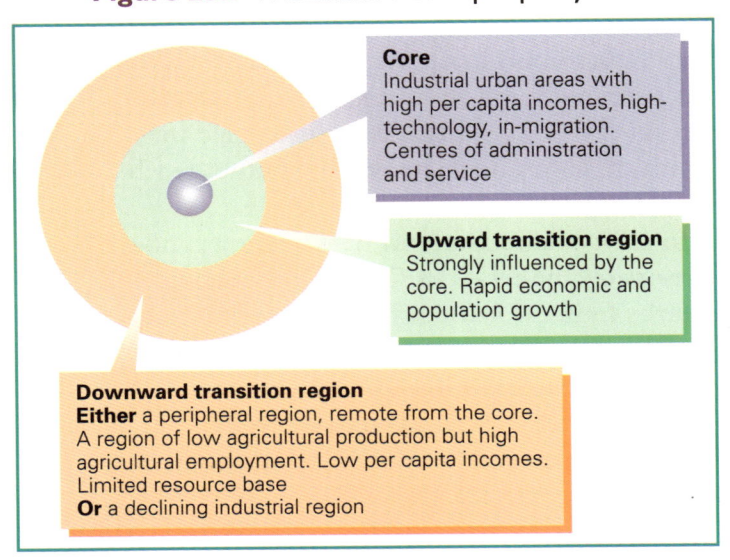

Core
Industrial urban areas with high per capita incomes, high-technology, in-migration. Centres of administration and service

Upward transition region
Strongly influenced by the core. Rapid economic and population growth

Downward transition region
Either a peripheral region, remote from the core. A region of low agricultural production but high agricultural employment. Low per capita incomes. Limited resource base
Or a declining industrial region

Figure 25.8 Regions of Thailand

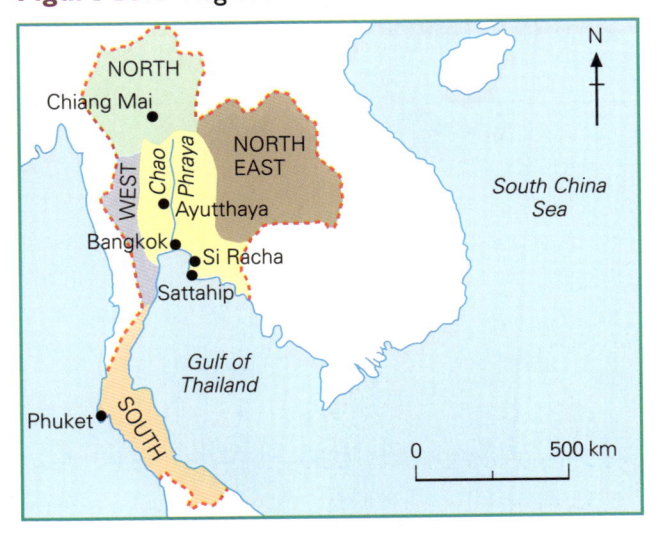

Industrial growth and development   187

3. **Study Figure 25.4. Describe and try to explain the changes in the employment structure of the USA between 1880 and 1990.**
4. **(a) What is the 'multiplier effect' in industrial development?**
   (b) Give an example of the multiplier effect in an industrial region known to you.
5. **How far can the core and periphery regions of the Friedmann Model be recognised in: (i) Thailand; (ii) the UK; (iii) Brazil or Nigeria?**

Industrial growth in Thailand

During the 1990s the kingdom of Thailand has had one of the world's fastest growing economies. It is one of the NICs of South East Asia, along with South Korea, Taiwan, Malaysia, Hong Kong, Singapore and Indonesia. So fierce has been the growth and competition in this region that these countries are sometimes referred to as the 'Young Tigers of Asia'.

Between 1970 and 1995 the percentage of the Thai workforce employed in agriculture declined from 80 per cent to 60 per cent while the percentage employed in manufacturing increased from 5 per cent to 11 per cent. Manufactured goods have grown to dominate Thailand's export earnings (see Figure 25.9).

Figure 25.9 Thailand's export earning, 1970 and 1995

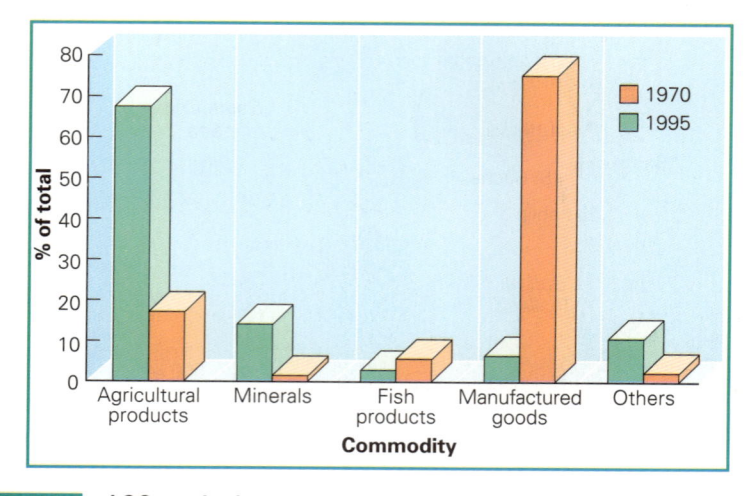

Manufacturing in Thailand has passed through a series of stages of development in a pattern which is familiar in each of the NICs.

- In the 1950s manufacturing was dominated by textiles to meet local demand.
- During the 1960s the textile industry developed overseas export markets.
- Industries such as oil refining, motor vehicle assembly, steelmaking, cement and chemicals were developed during the 1970s in order to replace the imported goods on which the country had depended. Such industrial development is called **import substitution**. It was only possible because the Thai Government placed high taxes on imported goods.
- During the 1980s and early 1990s there was a rapid expansion of the electronics industry and foreign companies were invited to open factories in Thailand. Japanese, Taiwanese and US firms moved in, attracted by Thailand's low wages and strong Government.
- In the early 1990s import duties were cut as the Thai Government tried to speed up a further stage of industrialisation towards more value-added, high-technology industries.

The motor industry in Thailand

Thailand's motor vehicle industry started during the 1970s. The Thai Government was keen for the kingdom to become a car producer of regional importance. Foreign car manufacturers were welcomed with a range of financial incentives such as cash grants and low tax rates. Very high import duties made Thai-assembled cars seem cheap by comparison with imported cars. In 1980, 24 000 cars were assembled in Thailand. Continued growth saw output reach 82 000 by 1990.

In 1991 the high import duties on cars and car parts were slashed as the Government thought that the industry had reached a mature stage of development. They were proved right when car production reached 174 000 in 1994. Today, five Japanese companies dominate production in Thailand and they forecast that production will reach 400 000 by the year 2000.

188 Industrial Change

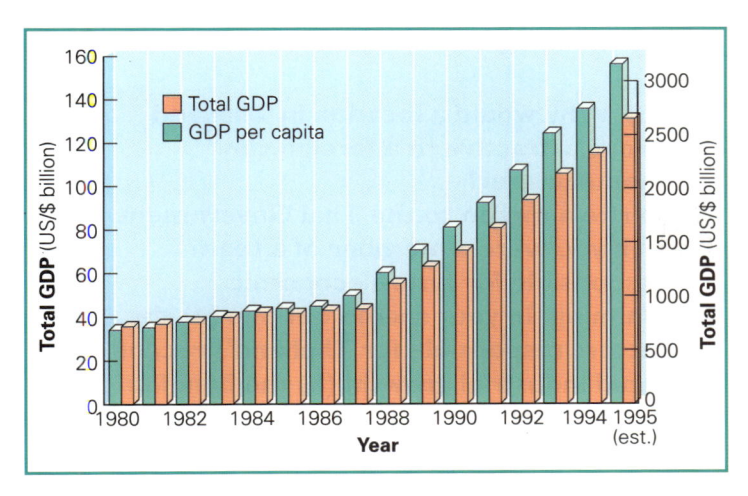

Figure 25.10 Thailand's total GDP and per capita GDP

The effects of rapid industrial development

Thailand's rapid economic growth has brought many material benefits to its people. Total GDP and GDP per capital have grown remarkably quickly (see Figure 25.10). The average wage has increased rapidly, and so has the ownership of consumer goods. By 1995, 86 per cent of Thai households owned a television set and 50 per cent a refrigerator. Industrialisation has forced the Government to improve education and training in order to overcome shortages of skilled labour, and in 1993 the school leaving age was raised from 11 to 14.

There have been some problems, however.

- Rapid industrial growth has brought serious pollution problems to Thailand and especially to Bangkok. Bangkok's air is hot, humid and filthy. Both airborne dust and lead pollution are serious problems. Lead levels in the blood of Bangkok residents are over three times as high as those in the USA and western Europe.
- Bangkok claims to suffer from the world's worst traffic jams. Eleven per cent of Thailand's population live in Bangkok, which has 72 per cent of the country's cars. Each day over 500 new vehicles join the traffic on Bangkok's polluted roads.
- Working conditions in some of Thailand's factories and workshops are poor, with long working hours and very low pay.

Figure 25.11 Traffic congestion in Bangkok, Thailand

- Bangkok and its surrounding area has grown very rapidly. With a population of 7 million it is now 50 times larger than the second largest city, Chiang Mai. However, some remoter regions in Thailand, such as the North East region, have suffered from a lack of development. The North East contains 35 per cent of Thailand's population but produces only 20 per cent of the nation's GDP. It is a region of high agricultural employment but low agricultural production. People have been leaving the North East in large numbers to find work in Bangkok. Forty-three per cent of people migrating to Bangkok come from the North East.

Industrial growth and development

6. Explain the meaning of the phrase 'the Young Tigers of Asia'.
7. Describe and explain the five stages of industrial development through which Thailand has passed since the 1950s?
8. (a) Draw a bar graph to show car production in Thailand in 1980, 1990, 1994 and estimated production in the year 2000.
   (b) How did the Thai Government attract foreign car manufacturers to build assembly plants in Thailand?
   (c) From which country did most of the foreign car manufacturers come?
   (d) Why would a location in Thailand prove attractive to a foreign car manufacturer?
9. Write a memo to the Thai Government as if you were a member of a team responsible for future economic planning. In your memo outline: (a) the factors responsible for Thailand's recent rapid industrial growth; (b) the benefits and problems associated with industrial growth; (c) suitable policies for dealing with the problems.

Summary

- Several models have been developed to help explain industrial growth. When the process is studied in an individual country we can see that there are many benefits and many problems created by industrial growth.

Chapter 26 Industrial location

Why do industries develop where they do?
This unit considers the location of manufacturing industry.

Industry as a system

In order to understand the factors affecting the location of industry it is necessary to understand the way in which industry operates.

All manufacturing industry works as a system with inputs, processes and outputs (see Figure 26.1) at a variety of scales. At the smallest level are workshop and cottage industries which employ very few people. These are usually craft industries, and involve working at home. An example is pottery produced in rural areas of Britain and aimed at the tourist market. In LEDCs, cottage industries are very important. Weaving is a major example (see Figure 26.2, page 192). The village workshop will feature hand looms – simple machines using traditional skills. Such weaving will be aimed mainly at a

Figure 26.1 The industrial system for making chocolate

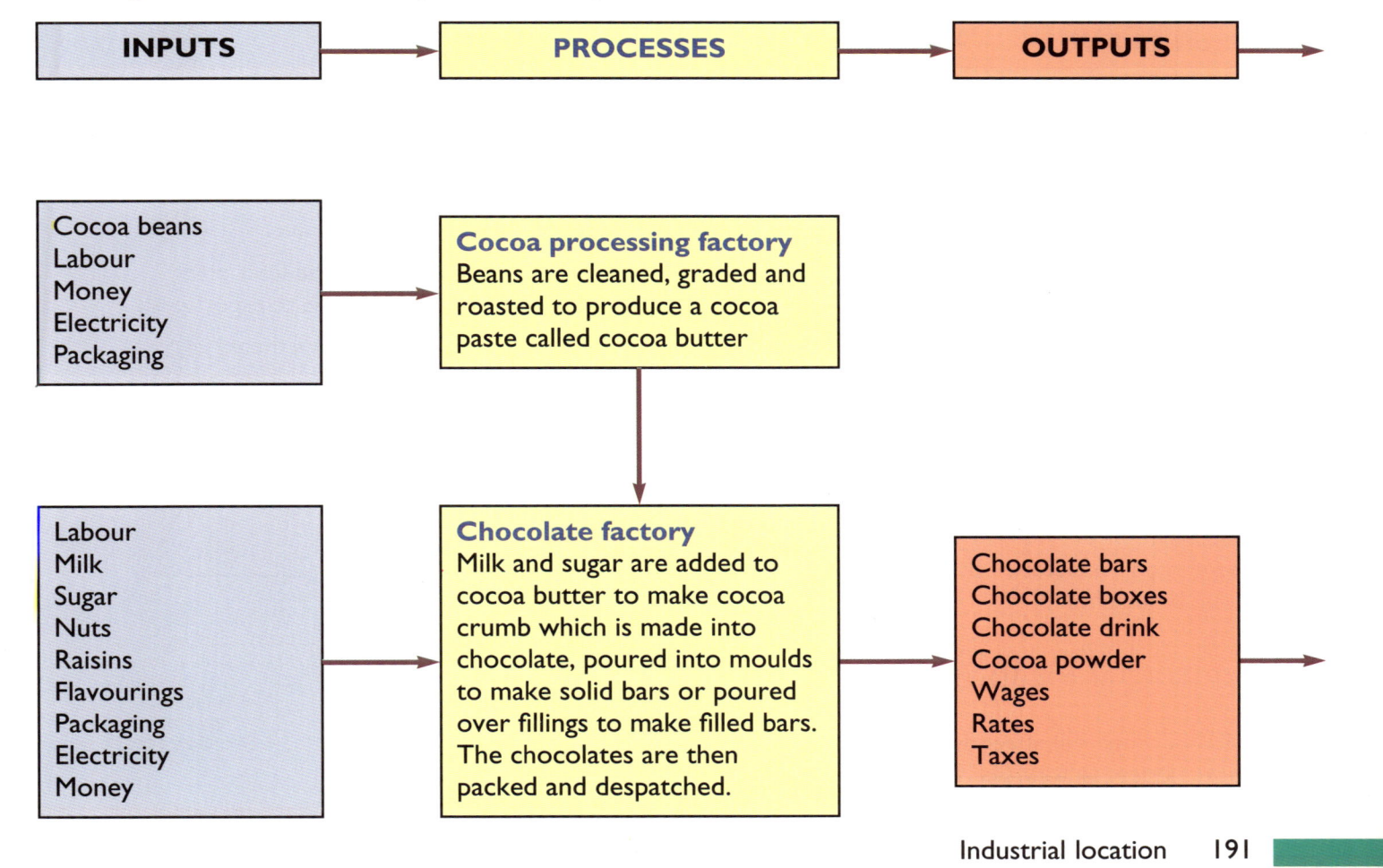

INPUTS	PROCESSES	OUTPUTS
Cocoa beans Labour Money Electricity Packaging	**Cocoa processing factory** Beans are cleaned, graded and roasted to produce a cocoa paste called cocoa butter	
Labour Milk Sugar Nuts Raisins Flavourings Packaging Electricity Money	**Chocolate factory** Milk and sugar are added to cocoa butter to make cocoa crumb which is made into chocolate, poured into moulds to make solid bars or poured over fillings to make filled bars. The chocolates are then packed and despatched.	Chocolate bars Chocolate boxes Chocolate drink Cocoa powder Wages Rates Taxes

Industrial location 191

Figure 26.2 Weavers in Akwete, Imo in Africa

subsistence level to support the weaver and his or her family.

Most manufacturing industry operates a factory system. Large factories first became common during the Industrial Revolution in Britain. After about 1750, the introduction of large steam-powered machines burning coal meant that large factory buildings had to be built to house them.

Factories remain the most important type of manufacturing building today, but their design has changed considerably since the days of the early steam-powered mills with their tall chimneys. Increased automation has meant that fewer people are needed in factories, and in some modern factories almost all the work is done by machine.

Industrial location

Many factors will affect decision about where to locate a new factory (see Figure 26.3). Theories

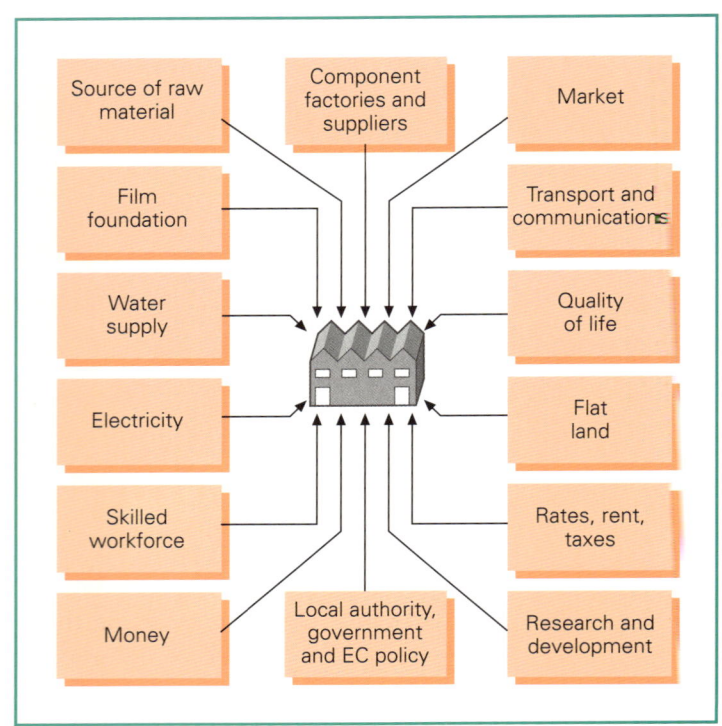

Figure 26.3 Factors affecting industrial location

of industrial location have concentrated on the importance of keeping costs to a minimum, especially transport costs because of the expense of moving bulky raw materials and heavy products. A well known example is Weber's theory. Weber assumed that:

- industry will locate where costs are lowest (the 'least-cost' location);
- transport costs vary with the weight of a product and the distance it is transported;
- there is no political interference.

Weber used triangles to find the least-cost location (see Figure 26.4). In **A** transport costs

Figure 26.4 Diagram of Weber's theory of industrial location

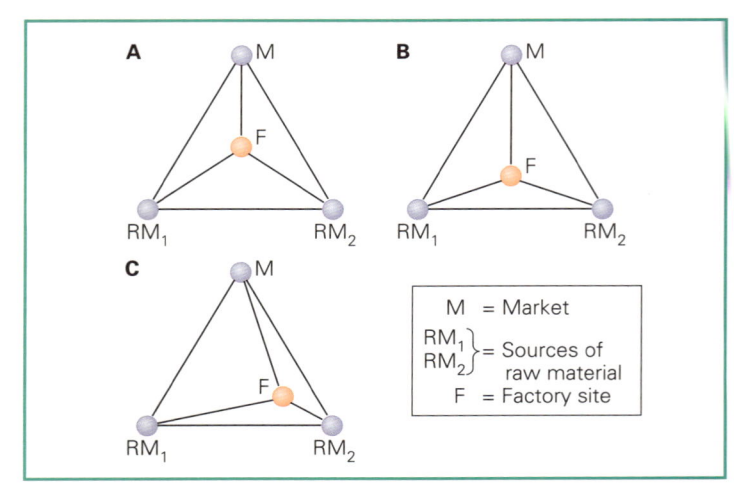

M = Market
$\left.\begin{array}{l}RM_1\\RM_2\end{array}\right\}$ = Sources of raw material
F = Factory site

192　Industrial Change

are equal for raw materials and the finished product – so the factory is located at the centre of the triangle. In **B** the weight of the raw materials is higher than that of the finished product – so the factory is located nearer the raw materials. In **C** one of the raw materials (RM$_2$) is heavier than the other and the finished product – so the factory is located nearer to RM$_2$.

Weber used the material index to discover where an industry would be located:

Material index = $\dfrac{\text{weight of raw materials}}{\text{weight of finished product}}$

An industry with an index of over 1 will be located nearer the raw materials. An industry with an index of under 1 will be located nearer the market. For example, in baking, 1 tonne of flour produces 2 tonnes of bread. Material index is 1 ÷ 2 = 0.5 so baking should be located near the market.

Weber's model has been criticised for several reasons.

- The model places too much importance upon transport costs.
- The model assumes that transport costs increase with weight; this is not always the case – costs may increase with the bulkiness of the goods.
- The model assumes that the least-cost location will also be the place where most profit can be made – this is not necessarily the case.
- Labour, power or land costs may be more important than transport costs.
- Government policy may provide grants and loans which improve the costs of more expensive locations.

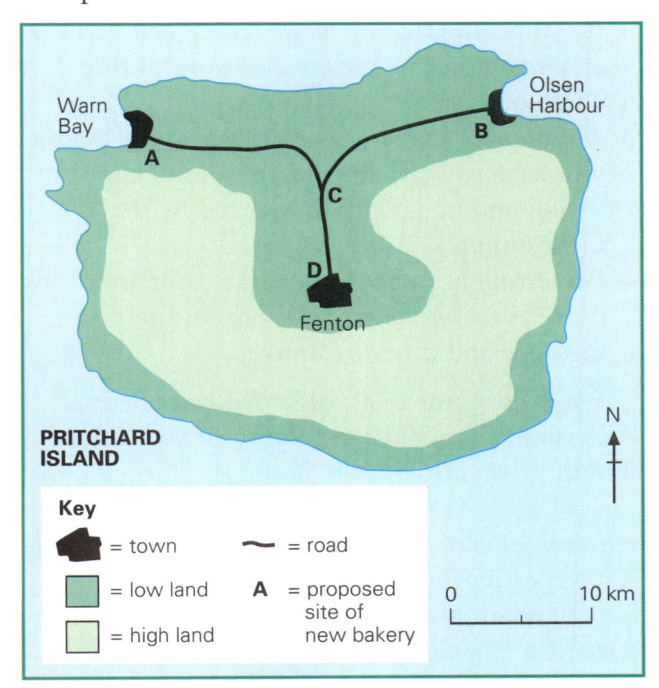

Figure 26.5 Pritchard Island

1. Figure 26.5 shows Pritchard Island where Cassidy Bread plc intends to build a new bakery. The bakery uses flour which is imported to the island through the two ports of Warn Bay and Olsen Harbour. The most important market for bread is the City of Fenton. Cassidy Bread is studying four possible sites for its new bakery, shown as A, B, C and D on the map.
   (a) List the advantages and disadvantages of each of the four sites for the location of a bakery.
   (b) Decide which of the four sites you would recommend for the location of the bakery and give your reasons.
   (c) What other information would it be useful to know about the island and the four possible locations before making a final decision on the site for the new bakery?
2. Draw a system diagram with inputs, processes and outputs and list the following under the correct headings. Wages; raw materials; electricity; rates; products; packaging; taxes; labour.
3. Study Figure 26.4.
   (a) What is the basic idea behind Weber's industrial location theory?
   (b) What are: (i) the least-cost location; (ii) the material index?
   (c) Draw a triangle to show the least-cost location for an industry whose product is twice as expensive to transport as its raw materials.
   (d) How could Weber's theory be criticised?

Industrial location

The geography of the organisation

Recent studies of industrial location have highlighted the importance of the geography of the organisation. This means that locational decisions are made on the basis of the company's own requirements rather than external factors.

- A new company seeking a site for its first factory will be greatly affected by the managers' knowledge of the locations under consideration. They may choose a site which is known personally to them, perhaps near their homes.
- A company with several factories seeking a new site will base its decision upon the market for its products. The new factory will be built to fill gaps in the current locations of the company.
- A company which is controlled by the State will have to consider the interests of the nation and be greatly influenced by the Government.
- Government policy may make some locations more attractive due to the provision of financial and other incentives.

For most companies, older factories dating back more than 30 years tend to be located within urban areas. Such factories can only survive if they are modernised. However, the requirements of modern industry are such that it is often easier for a company to build a new factory on an undeveloped, or 'greenfield', site, because a large area is needed for modern low-rise factories with room for future expansion and access to the regional trunk roads and the motorway system.

Case study – the Ford Motor Company

Ford is a US-owned multi-national company. It was started by an engineer named Henry Ford who lived in Detroit, Michigan. The history of Ford's operations in Europe provides a valuable insight into the geography of the organisation.

- Henry Ford built his first car in 1896 in his garden shed.
- In 1903 he built his first car factory in his home town.
- Having sought a site in Europe, in 1911 Ford chose Trafford Park, Manchester, for his first European factory. At that time, Britain was the largest market in Europe for Ford's cars. The Trafford Park site was beside the Manchester Ship Canal which provided easy access to materials and markets.
- France and Germany were important markets for Ford cars. The company sought a site in both countries, but the French Government refused because it was worried about the effect on French car manufacturers. However, the Germans allowed Ford to open a small factory in Berlin in 1925.
- The Trafford Park factory was too small to introduce assembly line production when this was developed during the 1920s. Ford sought a new site and chose Dagenham in Essex. His new factory opened in 1931. It was close to London, the largest market for cars in Britain. The factory had its own wharf on the River Thames.
- The Berlin factory also proved too small to be expanded. In 1931 Ford opened a new factory at Cologne beside the River Rhine.
- During the 1950s demand for Ford cars grew rapidly. Ford wanted to expand its Dagenham factory but the policy of the British Government prevented this. The Government was determined to force companies to open new factories in areas of high unemployment – 'development areas'. In 1962 Ford opened a new factory within a development area at Halewood near Liverpool.
- The rapid increase in demand for cars in Europe led the Ford company to open two new factories, at Genk in Belgium in 1963 and at Saarlouis in West Germany in 1968.
- During the late 1960s demand for cars increased in southern Europe, especially in Spain and Italy. The demand in these countries was for smaller, cheaper cars. Spain offered an important market but the Spanish Government imposed high import duties on cars. Ford decided to overcome this by building a car factory at Valencia (see Figure

Figure 26.6 The Ford car assembly plant at Valencia, Spain

26.6). Spain had the added advantages of lower wage rates and easy access to the growing markets of southern Europe, north Africa and the Middle East.
- In 1989 the communist regimes of eastern Europe collapsed, opening a large new market to Western car manufacturers. General Motors, Fiat, Volkswagen and Suzuki all opened factories in eastern Europe. Ford decided against building an assembly plant in eastern Europe, but it did open a plant manufacturing electrical components near Budapest in Hungary in 1992. In the early 1990s the low wage rates and eager governments continued to attract the car manufacturers. Eventually standards of living will rise across Europe, creating increased demand, and Ford may think again.

Industrial agglomeration

Once an area develops industries it tends to continue to expand as more industries are attracted in because of those already there. Service and component industries develop to support the manufacturing base. This is called the multiplier effect (see page 186) and **industrial agglomeration** (clustering of industries) results. Some industrial areas gain a reputation for certain types of industry and they attract similar industries as a result.

An example is the high-technology and electronics industrial area in and around Cambridge, known as Silicon Fen. The largest single high-technology site in Silicon Fen is the Cambridge Science Park. Opened in 1973 on 50 ha of derelict land owned by one of the colleges of Cambridge University, the Science Park has thrived on its close links with the university which has given it access to some of Britain's top academic scientists. Easy access to the M11 motorway has increased the site's attractions for high-technology industry. Over 2000 people are employed by over 70 companies. The largest employs 300 people, but half the companies employ less than 20 people. Most of the companies are manufacturing computers, telecommunications and precision instruments. A number of companies are involved in bio-technology, producing drugs and medical instruments and there are several

---

4. (a) What is meant by 'the geography of the organisation'?
   (b) How does the geography of the organisation affect (i) a new company; (ii) an existing company with several factories; (iii) a large multi-national company; (iv) a state-controlled organisation when seeking a new factory site?
5. (a) Why did Henry Ford locate his first car factory in Detroit?
   (b) Why was Trafford Park a suitable location for Ford's first European factory?
   (c) Why was Trafford Park no longer suitable for car production after 1924?
   (d) Explain why: (i) Dagenham; (ii) Halewood were chosen as Ford locations.
   (e) (i) Using an atlas, show the location of Ford's current European car assembly plants on an outline map of Europe.
   (ii) How does the geography of the organisation help to explain Ford's choice of Cologne, Genk, Saarlouis and Valencia as factory locations?

companies concentrating on research and development. Many of the research workers at the Science Park are employed at the university laboratories on a part-time basis.

In the late twentieth century most industries in MEDCs are **footloose**, with few important locating factors. This is because improved transport has reduced the need to be close to supplies of raw materials and electricity and water supplies are now available in most areas. Many companies have chosen to move their factories from the older, congested inner city areas to more spacious locations in country towns. The quality of life available to the company's employees has become an important locating factor. It is no coincidence that Britain's fastest growing industrial areas are the rural regions such as East Anglia and the South West.

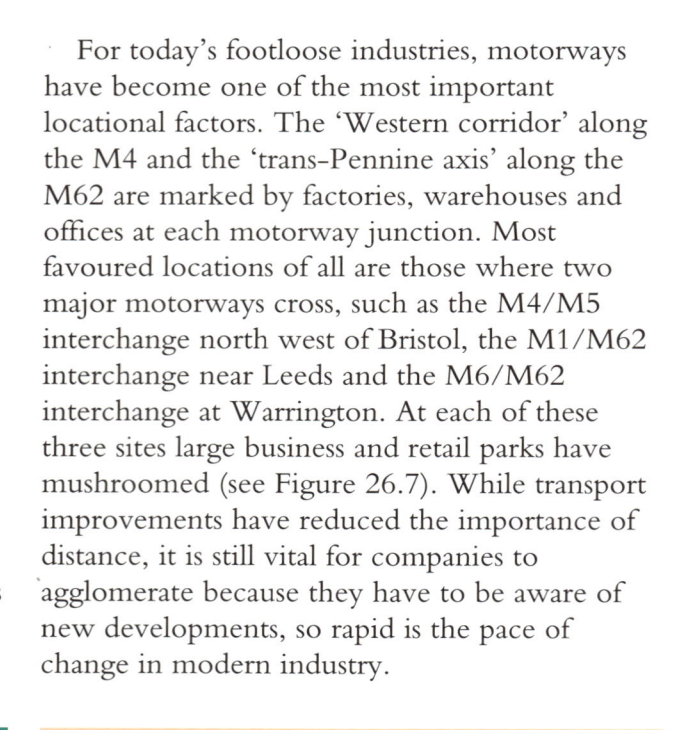

For today's footloose industries, motorways have become one of the most important locational factors. The 'Western corridor' along the M4 and the 'trans-Pennine axis' along the M62 are marked by factories, warehouses and offices at each motorway junction. Most favoured locations of all are those where two major motorways cross, such as the M4/M5 interchange north west of Bristol, the M1/M62 interchange near Leeds and the M6/M62 interchange at Warrington. At each of these three sites large business and retail parks have mushroomed (see Figure 26.7). While transport improvements have reduced the importance of distance, it is still vital for companies to agglomerate because they have to be aware of new developments, so rapid is the pace of change in modern industry.

Figure 26.7 Business park at the junction of the M6 and M62 motorway at Warrington

6. What does 'industrial agglomeration' mean?
7. (a) What is the Cambridge Science Park?
   (b) What are the attractions of a location on the Science Park?
8. Study Figure 26.7. Describe the industrial scene in the photograph and explain why this is a good location for modern industry.
9. (a) Why are many modern industries described as 'footloose'?
   (b) How have transport developments affected recent industrial location in the UK?

Summary

- Many factors affect the location of manufacturing industry, but most industries are now 'footloose' with few vital locating factors.

Changing Urban Environments

27 Housing

What changes have affected the housing in our cities?

Are shanty towns really 'slums of despair'?

This unit uses the case study of Hull to illustrate the changes which have affected many British inner cities. Housing for the urban poor in developing countries is also studied.

1. Study Figures 27.1–27.3. Three contrasting urban housing areas are shown in the photographs.
   (a) Describe the type of housing shown in each photograph.
   (b) In which part of the city would you expect to find the types of housing in the photographs: the inner city; middle class suburbs; or a working class housing estate?

Figure 27.2 Inner city housing, Elephant and Castle in London

Figure 27.1 Suburban housing in East Sussex

Figure 27.3 A council housing estate, London

Housing 197

Hull's inner city

Hull is a sea port and industrial city of 260 000 people on the north bank of the Humber Estuary. During the early nineteenth century, Hull's inner city developed extensive areas of slum housing in the South Myton area. Here the housing consisted almost entirely of closely-packed, back-to-back courtyard housing with tunnel entrances. Hull grew rapidly during the nineteenth century; between 1851 and 1914 the population doubled from 150 000 to 300 000. Much poor quality housing was built at this time.

Between 1919 and 1939 over 10 000 council houses were built in Hull on six large new estates on the edge of the city. Private housing spread along the main roads in extensive **ribbon development**. The inner city was viewed as an unattractive, poverty-stricken area and slum clearance commenced during this period.

During the 1950s the local council undertook extensive slum clearance, replacing the slums with high-rise flats and low-rise maisonettes at a lower density. About half of the affected households were forced to move to the growing peripheral council estates, especially Orchard Park and Bransholme.

Figure 27.4 Hull and its wards

Problems of housing redevelopment

The slum clearances provided more modern, better equipped housing, but they resulted in the destruction of communities. Soon after the new high-rise housing was built a tide of complaints began to flow:

- repairs were frequently necessary;
- there was a lack of neighbourliness and social interaction;
- the design of the tower blocks caused depression amongst some of the inhabitants and elderly residents often felt trapped;
- there was a lack of amenity areas, especially for the young.

The decision was taken in the 1970s to build no more high-rise flats in Hull. An Inner Area Programme was launched in 1977 which aimed to create better housing and housing neighbourhoods, improve social conditions and develop local communities, improve the environment and encourage the growth of industry and commerce. Figures 27.5 and 27.6 show the concentration of deprivation in inner Hull in 1981, when the Inner Area Programme was beginning.

Figure 27.5 Unemployment in the wards of Hull, 1981

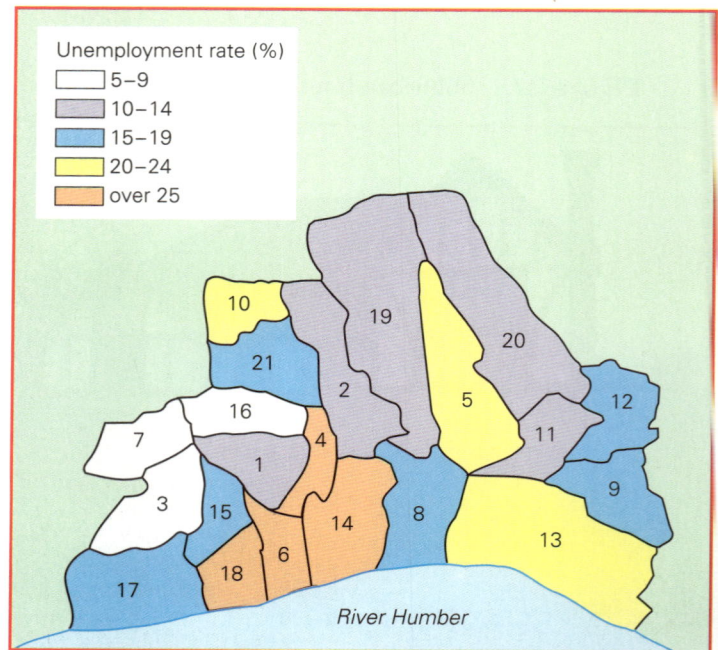

1 Avenue
2 Beverley
3 Boothferry
4 Botanic
5 Bransholme
6 Coltman
7 Derringham
8 Drypool
9 Greatfield
10 Greenfield
11 Holderness
12 Longhill
13 Marfleet
14 Myton
15 Newington
16 Newland
17 Pickering
18 St Andrews
19 Stoneferry
20 Sutton
21 University

Unemployment rate (%)
- 5–9
- 10–14
- 15–19
- 20–24
- over 25

198 Changing Urban Environments

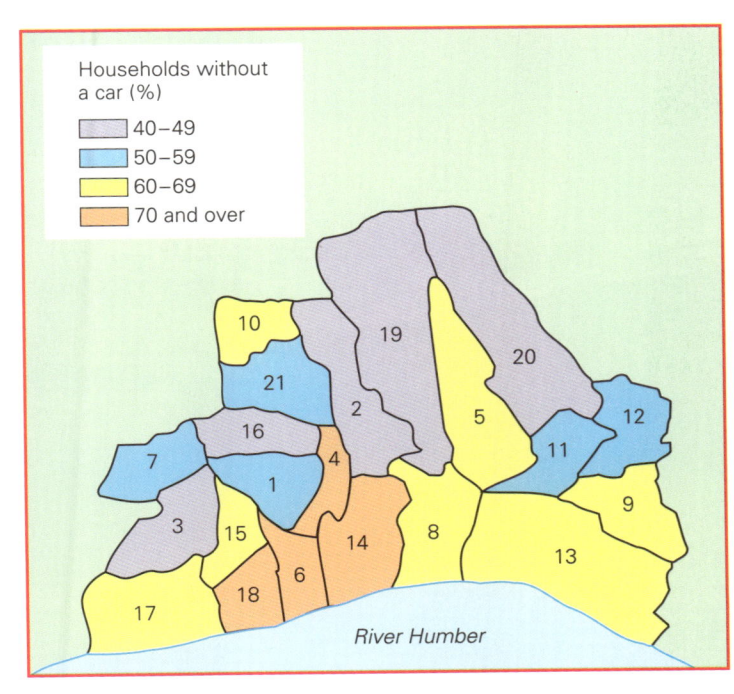

Figure 27.6 Households without a car in Hull, 1981

Where elderly buildings were once demolished, a policy of 'enveloping' was introduced. This involved thoroughly renovating the old homes, repairing and replacing chimneys, roofs, windows, doors and brickwork and improving pavements and road areas. In this way, houses are transformed at a cost of about £15 000, compared with over £50 000 for rehousing each family. Existing communities are not dispersed. The security and privacy of the dwellings is also improved, particularly benefiting the elderly and disabled.

Environmental improvements in the inner city included cleaning, repaving, landscaping and lighting previously neglected areas. A former dock was transformed into an impressive marina with a top class hotel and new houses and apartments (see Figure 27.7). A former warehouse was converted into exclusive flats and

Figure 27.7 Hull marina

Housing 199

Figure 27.8 Prince's Quay shopping centre, Hull

a modern shopping centre was built on stilts above another former dock (see Figure 27.8). All this helped to attract private builders into the inner city. In a £100 million development, 1300 homes were built on the old Victoria Dock site between 1989 and 1996 with the aid of a £17 million grant from the government's Urban Regeneration Grant scheme.

Hull's inner city regeneration has been quite successful. Much of the inner city has been transformed since 1980. However, in the late 1990s much remains to be done. The number of homeless people is increasing and some 8000 households in the inner city still live in pre-1914 dwellings, many in need of major repair.

2. (a) Describe the early nineteenth century houses in Hull's inner city.
   (b) What were the results of the slum clearance programme in the 1950s?
3. What were the aims of the Inner Area Programme?

4. (a) On a copy of Figure 27.4, shade in the wards of Hull according to the key below to show those households lacking their own bath and inside toilet in 1981.

0–4%	5–9%	10–14%	15–19%	20%+
3, 5, 10, 12, 13, 19	16, 21	1, 4, 7, 9, 11	2, 14, 17, 20	6, 8, 15, 18

(b) Use your map and Figures 27.5 and 27.6 to describe the problems facing Hull's inner city dwellers in 1981.
5. What is the policy of 'enveloping' and why was it introduced?
6. (a) Describe the regeneration of Hull's inner city.
   (b) How successful has the regeneration been?

200 Changing Urban Environments

Shanty towns

In LEDCs the inner cities tend to be inhabited by the richer section of the population, living in detached houses, often protected by security guards, and in modern high-rise flats. Much of the housing which surrounds the inner city is older slum housing, inhabited by poorer families. The poorest live in spontaneous settlements, often of self-constructed homes, on the outskirts of the city.

Shanty towns lacking basic amenities are the best known areas of housing for the urban poor in LEDCs (Figure 27.9). Whether they are called *favelas* as in Brazil, *barriadas* (Peru) or *bustees* (India), the shanty towns have many similarities.

- Housing consists of simple shacks made of corrugated iron, wood, straw or even cardboard.
- The houses have mainly been built by the owners themselves, most of whom are squatters – they do not own the land – although some pay a small rent to landlords.
- The shanty towns have not been planned and therefore most lack clean running water, sewerage, electricity and gas.
- The roads within the shanty towns mainly consist of dirt tracks. Very few shanty dwellers own transportation so most depend on limited public transport or have to walk.

In the past, shanty towns were thought to be places of squalor and despair. This idea was accepted by some governments, who bulldozed the shanty towns and displaced the squatters. However, more recently shanty towns have been recognised to be much more hopeful and positive places than was previously thought. The reason for this is that the negative image of the

Figure 27.9 A shanty town in Africa

shanty town is based on short-term observation. Once a longer-term view is taken it becomes obvious that shanty towns pass through a series of stages of development. The early stages do indeed seem to be squalid and chaotic, but they are certainly not hopeless, and the later stages may see the development of well-serviced, well-built suburbs.

Most inhabitants of shanty towns are ambitious, hard-working people who had the drive and initiative to leave their rural homes to travel to the city in search of work. Surveys have shown that the majority of heads of the household are in active employment, for example, 91 per cent in Mexico City shanty towns in Mexico and 84 per cent in Bogota, Colombia. Only about 12 per cent of those are in **informal** jobs such as shoe-shining and cleaning. Thus, a regular wage is coming in to most shanty town households. As time passes, the shanty dwellers are able to buy better building materials and to improve their homes. Thus, a shack can be transformed into a well-built, fully serviced house in a process which may take 20 years.

Now that most governments recognise that shanty towns are not the threats they were once thought to be, they have adopted a new policy, that of self-help. The squatters are capable of building a home for themselves, but they cannot provide the infrastructure. The World Bank and leading charities have funded 'site and services' schemes, where the authorities provide a site, basic building materials and, once the people have built their homes, water and electricity. Roads, clinics and schools may eventually be built as the site develops. In this way, the shanty towns are improved (see Figure 27.10) and a strong community spirit can be created.

Figure 27.10 An example of a 'site and services' shanty town improvement scheme in São Paulo State, Brazil

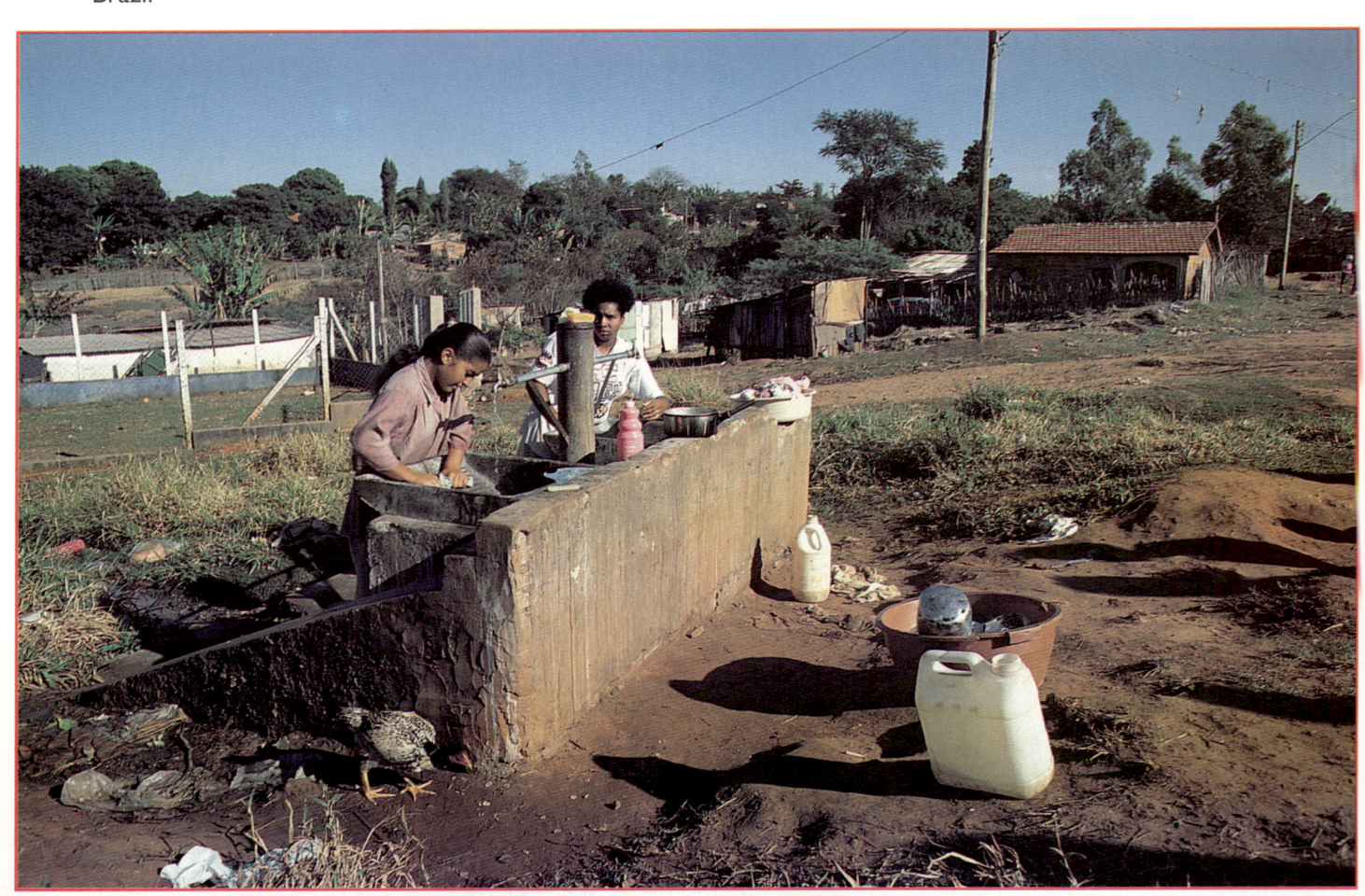

202 Changing Urban Environments

7. Draw a simple model to show the rich and poor housing areas in cities in LEDCs within three concentric circles.
8. Use Figure 27.9 to help you describe the appearance of a shanty town.
9. How and why has the government view of shanty towns changed recently?
10. (a) Explain what is meant by 'site and services' schemes.
    (b) Why have site and services schemes become popular with governments?

Summary

- British inner cities have complex histories of housing development.
- Comprehensive redevelopment programmes have transformed many inner cities. An approach which is more sympathetic to the historical legacy of each area is now being adopted.
- In less economically developed countries shanty towns are no longer thought to be entirely negative.

Chapter 28 Changing communities

Do communities exist in cities?
Do different communities in cities have the same quality of life?

This unit looks at the range of communities to be found in towns and cities. It examines similarities and differences between communities and considers how conditions vary within towns and cities.

Communities in Britain's cities

The population of cities in Britain is made up of many local communities. These communities include people who have moved to the city from other parts of Britain or from other countries. People in all these communities have the same basic needs of shelter, food, clothing, warmth, employment and security.

Britain's Black and Asian population

Until the 1950s, Afro-Caribbean communities were rare in Britain. There were a few earlier Asian communities but only in specific areas like ports. Then during the 1960s Britain encouraged people from India, Pakistan, Bangladesh and the West Indies to migrate to Britain. At the time, Britain had a labour shortage and was keen to

Figure 28.1 An open-air market in Southall

204 Changing Urban Environments

attract workers from Asia and the West Indies. These immigrants helped to rebuild the British economy after the Second World War. However the jobs on offer were often unskilled or semi-skilled and poorly paid. They were usually the jobs that locals were unwilling to do, such as factory work, bus and railway work and cleaning. London, Bradford, Birmingham and Blackburn were four of the main cities to which the newcomers came.

Housing in these cities was in short supply and no extra provision was made for the newcomers, so many of the immigrants and their families were forced to live in run-down, overcrowded conditions. They also faced prejudice both at work and in the community, partly because most British people knew little about the newcomers, their countries of origin and their culture.

Conditions in the 1990s

Now, nearly 40 years later, black and Asian people form just 4 per cent of the total British population. Over 45 per cent of these 2.5 million black and Asian citizens were born in Britain and have never lived anywhere else. Current Government restrictions mean that immigration from Asia and the West Indies is very low (see Figures 28.2 and 28.3).

Many of Britain's black and Asian communities still live in inner city areas, often in poor housing and with inadequate services. However there has been some change in recent

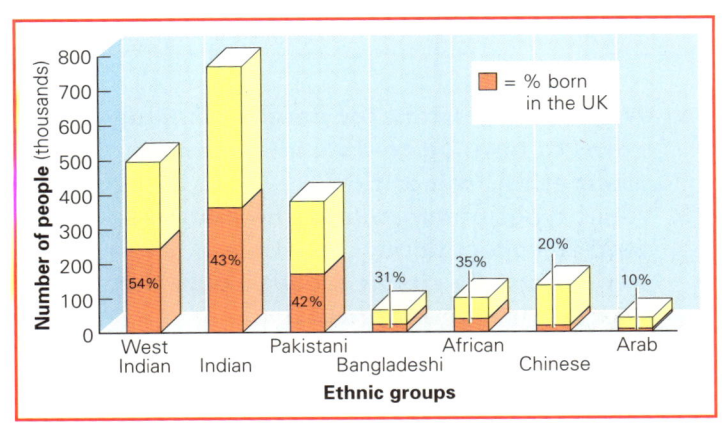

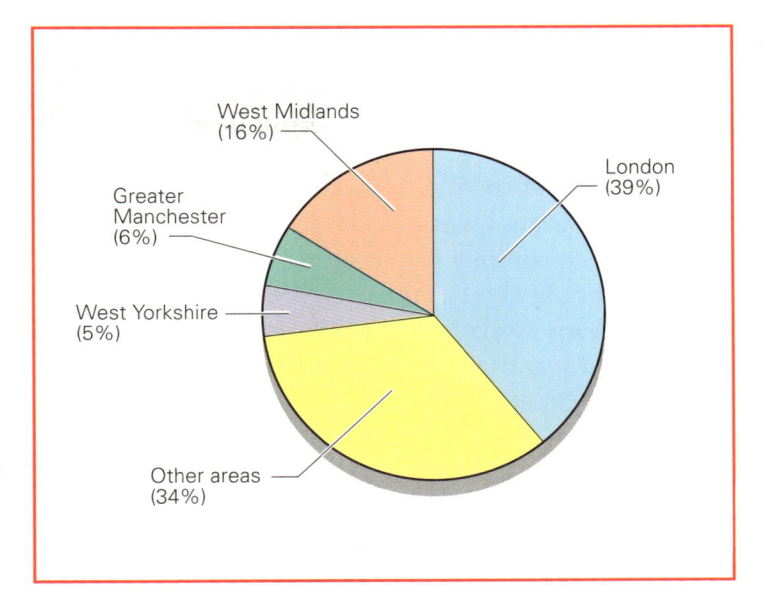

Figure 28.2 Non-white population of Britain in 1993 and the percentage born in the UK

Figure 28.3 The distribution of ethnic minorities in the UK, 1992

years. A number of suburbs in large cities have become multi-racial with generally better conditions and there have also been a few changes in the work place to try and prevent discrimination. For example some companies pursue a policy of positive discrimination in an attempt to redress the balance. There are now a greater number of black and Asian people who have skilled jobs in factories and offices and who work in the professions as teachers, doctors and lawyers.

> 1. Which three cities have the largest percentages of Britain's black and Asian population? Why is this?
> 2. What percentage of black and Asian people live outside the four main conurbations?
> 3. Look at Figures 28.2 and 28.3. Describe the patterns they illustrate.

Eliminating racism?

Although there has been some progress towards 'equal opportunities' in Britain since the 1960s many black and Asian people still do not get equal treatment either at work or in their local area. Figure 28.4, page 206, highlights some of the ways in which racism can still be found operating in Britain, and some suggestions for overcoming these aspects of racism.

Changing communities

Figure 28.4 Some views on racism

'People see me as black and not as a librarian. I was turned down for a job because they told me that not many black people lived in the area! People should be more aware of racism in professions like mine and others such as medicine and teaching.'

'British newspapers like to make headlines out of "race" and "riots". They sensationalise the truth and do not print stories about positive events in the community.'

'Despite laws for equal opportunities there are not enough checks made on employers. In the last 12 months a report said that at least one in four employers discriminates against black people. We need more local businesses to guarantee equal opportunities or even promote positive discrimination.'

'People like to label us a "problem" but they know nothing about us. The real problems are unemployment and poor housing. If more people knew that and supported our claims for better conditions then the government might be forced to do something.'

4. Organise the views in Figure 28.4 into groups concerned with: (a) the media; (b) jobs; (c) housing; (d) violence.
5. Figure 28.4 includes suggestions aimed at combating racism. For each, indicate which groups of people need to be involved (e.g. planners, teachers, health workers, politicians).
6. Why is it important for people planning towns to have up-to-date information about ethnic minorities?
7. What types of information do planners need to collect about the whole population of a city in order to plan the area's future development?

206 Changing Urban Environments

The needs of local communities

Figures 28.5, 28.6 and 28.7 show some of the important aspects of people's lives in different communities in towns. Each photograph highlights the importance of the needs of the community which have to be considered in relation to the future development of the area.

Figure 28.5 Derelict housing in Lambeth, London

Figure 28.6 Mosque in Peckham, London

Figure 28.7 Saltdean Lido, London

8. For each of Figures 28.5, 28.6 and 28.7 write down: (a) what each photograph shows; (b) what each says about the needs of the local community; (c) the related implications for the planners. Give reasons for the statements you make.

Summary

- Communities are vital parts of urban life.
- People in these communities have the same basic needs.
- People in Britain's black and Asian communities often feel discriminated against.
- Attempts are being made to get rid of racism in all aspects of life.
- Local communities have the power to influence changes in their area.

Changing communities

29 Shops and services

- Is there a hierarchy of shopping centres?
- What recent changes have affected our shopping habits?
- What effects have out-of-town shopping centres had?
- How can city centres fight back?

The hierarchy of shopping centres

Over 2 million people in Britain work in shops. Shops can be found in a variety of locations within urban areas. There is a hierarchy of shopping centres which begins with a single shop and is topped by massive out-of-town shopping centres (see Figure 29.1).

The corner shop

Corner shops were a feature of the nineteenth century inner city areas. They sold a wide range of goods and served a few streets, with customers daily walking from their nearby homes. Corner shops can still be found in inner city areas that have not been redeveloped but many corner shops have closed down because they cannot compete with supermarket prices. This affects communities because corner shops provide a valuable service, especially for the elderly and those without cars.

Neighbourhood shopping centres

These small, local shopping centres serve housing estates in the suburbs of towns. They are often in a parade of shops such as that shown in Figure 29.2. Even the smaller parades usually have a range of shops including a newsagent, a post office, a small chain store selling convenience goods, a takeaway food shop and maybe one or two specialist shops such as chemists or electrical shops.

Figure 29.1 Hierarchy of shopping centres

Figure 29.2 A neighbourhood shopping centre in East Sussex

208 Changing Urban Environments

Figure 29.3 The Central Business District in Edinburgh

Main road shopping centres

These centres develop along main radial roads or at major crossroads in the inner city. They often contain 20 or more shops selling a wide range of goods, usually including a small supermarket, a furniture shop, a DIY store, a bank and an estate agent. In addition to serving the surrounding inner city area, main road shopping centres benefit from custom from passing motorists.

The central business district (the CBD)

The central business district (CBD) is the main shopping and commercial centre in a town (see Figure 29.3). There will be at least one large department store and large supermarket, other large chain stores and many specialist shops selling clothes, shoes, books, furniture, consumer goods, etc. The CBD also includes:

- banks;
- building societies;
- insurance offices;
- estate agents;
- solicitors;
- hairdressers;
- cafes and restaurants;
- travel agents.

The CBD is the most accessible shopping centre in a town and may be crowded and congested. Only bigger and wealthier shops can afford to locate there. Large covered shopping precincts, like the Arndale Centre in Manchester, are common in larger CBDs.

1. What is meant by a hierarchy of shopping centres?
2. (a) Why have many corner shops closed?
   (b) How do corner shops provide a valuable service?
3. (a) Describe the shopping centre shown in Figure 29.2.
   (b) Where would you expect to find this type of shopping centre?
4. (a) What is the CBD?
   (b) What types of shops and services would you expect to find in the CBD?
   (c) Why is land very expensive in the CBD?
5. Study Figure 29.4 which shows the results of a fieldwork survey conducted by a group of pupils in two shopping centres in Oxford.
   (a) Calculate the percentages of total shoppers and write these in a copy of the table.
   (b) (i) How do the percentages differ between the two shopping centres?
   (ii) What might be the reasons for these differences?

Figure 29.4 Shopping survey results

Shopping centre	Daily	Two or three times weekly	Once a week	Less than once a week
Rose Hill (% of total)	52	29	26	18
Cowley Centre (% of total)	76	131	85	48

Shops and services

Out-of-town shopping centres

Out-of-town shopping centres are designed to attract motorists from a wide area. They have free car parks and offer easier, less congested shopping than the CBD and are in two forms.

- The retail park, consisting of a number of large warehouse-style shops selling DIY, carpets, furniture, clothing and other goods. A retail park may include one very large shop called a superstore or hypermarket, which provides a wide range of goods.
- The shopping mall, a very large out-of-town shopping centre which serves a regional market. Shopping malls have hundreds of shops and services and feature a limited number of 'anchor' tenants, usually huge department stores, which are strategically sited at the end of long covered malls with rows of smaller shops. The MetroCentre at Gateshead (see Figure 29.5) was the first of the regional shopping malls to be built in Britain. It opened in 1986, a number of other centres have since been built, in Sheffield, Dudley, Leeds, Glasgow and London.

Figure 29.5 The Metro Centre, Gateshead

Case study – Lakeside shopping centre

The Lakeside shopping centre in Thurrock, Essex, was opened in 1990 (see Figure 29.6). It has over 300 shops and provides an example of the trend towards combining retailing with other functions in an integrated development. Lakeside includes a seven-screen cinema, a children's adventure land and a range of restaurants.

Figure 29.6 Inside Lakeside Shopping Centre

Lakeside's location was carefully chosen. The site was formerly a chalk quarry. Its situation is highly accessible, close to junction 30 of the M25 motorway and a new railway station has been opened adjacent to the centre. Lakeside attracts shoppers from Greater London, Essex, Kent, Sussex and Surrey, as well as much further afield, including regular visitors from Europe via the Channel Tunnel and the Channel ferry ports. There are no parking problems and less traffic congestion than in the city centre. Lakeside has over 9000 car parking spaces and has no need for multi-storey car parks which have developed a reputation for being insecure and unattractive.

Why have shopping habits changed?

The development of out-of-town shopping centres has been the result of a number of trends since the mid-1980s.

- There has been an increase in car ownership, and especially in the number of two-car families. This has allowed people to travel further and to carry more, making it easier to shop less often. The second car has allowed people who look after children and the home to shop out-of-town, perhaps while a domestic partner is at work.
- The CBD has become congested and less attractive for shoppers. Out-of-town centres offer all-weather, controlled environment shopping in bright, attractive, air conditioned malls. Security staff make the out-of-town centres safer for families than some city centres.
- Modern shops need large areas for their buildings and car parks, which cannot easily be found in city centres.
- The increasing number of working women has created increased demand for late-night shopping. Lakeside, for example, is open until 8.00 pm every night and until 9.00 pm on Friday. By contrast, most city centre shops are closed after 5.30 pm.

What has been the effect of out-of-town shopping centres?

The development of regional shopping malls has had a number of positive effects.

- They have created employment, for example the Merry Hill centre in Dudley employs 3400 people (two-thirds working part-time).
- They have helped to revitalise areas of derelict land – Lakeside was built on the site of a disused chalk quarry, Merry Hill on the site of a derelict steelworks and the MetroCentre on the site of a waste tip.
- They have proved very popular with shoppers and have provided a safe and attractive environment for family shopping.

However, regional shopping malls have attracted a storm of criticism, especially from people worried about the effect of their success on the traditional town centre CBD. The Merry Hill Centre opened in 1989 and resulted in Dudley town centre's shops losing two-thirds of their market share within four years. Many shops closed and nearby Stourbridge was also badly affected, losing 43 per cent of its market share over the same period. Stourbridge's largest department store closed in 1990 and shop rents fell by 26 per cent. It was estimated that ten other town centres suffered some impact from the opening of Merry Hill.

Out-of-town retailing's share of total retail sales rose from 5 per cent in 1980 to 27 per cent by 1995. Hundreds of superstore developments have contributed to this rapid growth and town centres have been unable to compete. According to a survey carried out for the Department of the Environment and published in 1995, nearly three-quarters of Britain's market towns are stagnant or in decline. The survey showed only 3 per cent to be thriving.

Another drawback of out-of-town retailing is the increased use of cars for journeys to out-of-town shopping centres, causing an increase in air pollution, noise and traffic congestion in suburban areas.

Shops and services

How can city centres fight back?

During the early 1990s, criticism of the adverse effect of out-of-town shopping centres on town centres led the government to change their policy. Previously, planning permission had been easy to obtain for superstores, retail parks and shopping malls in out-of-town locations. Since 1993, planning permission has been much more difficult to obtain. Sainsbury's has stated that, before 1993, it won 70 per cent of its applications for out-of-town superstore sites but since 1993 it has won less than 10 per cent of its applications.

Some experts maintain that the decline of city centre shopping centres cannot be blamed on out-of-town shopping centres. They say that changing social habits and work patterns mean that city centres cannot be revived.

Investment is needed to improve the environment of city centre shopping areas if they are to have a chance to compete with out-of-town centres. In Hull, for example, the city centre streets have been pedestrianised and attractive new street furniture has been provided. Two new enclosed shopping centres have been built at either end of the CBD, new car parks have been opened and dual carriageways constructed to improve access.

As well as efforts to improve the environment, integrated city centre revival schemes have involved building offices and housing as well as shops. The aim is to create new urban communities and ensure that the city centres do not 'die' after shop hours. Birmingham has developed just such an integrated scheme at Brindleyplace.

---

6. What are the two types of out-of-town shopping centre?
7. (a) Where is the Lakeside shopping centre?
   (b) What are the advantages of Lakeside's location?
   (c) Why is shopping at Lakeside attractive to the motorist?
8. Explain how the following have contributed to changing shopping habits: two-car families; controlled environments; security staff; working women.
9. (a) Discuss the effects of out-of-town shopping centres on city centre shopping areas.
   (b) How can city centre shopping areas compete with the out-of-town centres?

Summary

- Increased personal mobility has affected the shopping hierarchy.
- New out-of-town shopping centres have brought both positive and negative effects.
- City centres have faced damaging competition but with increased investment they can fight back.

30 Transport in towns

What are the main problems of transport in towns?
What solutions have been proposed to solve town transport problems?

This unit explores the problems of moving people and goods around towns and cities. It examines some of the steps that have been taken to solve these problems and evaluates their relative success.

Town traffic

Traffic is constantly trying to move around towns and cities as people travel to work or to the shops or on other visits. In most cities there is a clear pattern to this movement which is shown in Figure 30.1.

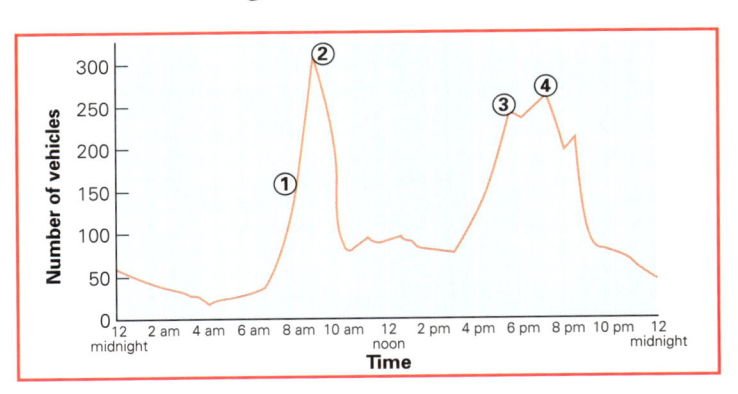

Figure 30.1 Daily traffic flow in Leeds, 1994

1. Look at Figure 30.1. It shows the weekday traffic flow in Leeds, a city of about half a million people. Describe the pattern shown in the graph, and try to explain features such as the steep rise in volume at point 1, the shortness of the peak at point 2, and the longer peaks at 3 and 4.

One of the main elements in the traffic flow of cities is the journey to work. Despite more firms locating in the suburbs and the growth in the number of people working from home, the majority of people still have to travel into a city to work. The changing methods of transport used for the journey to work are shown in Figure 30.2.

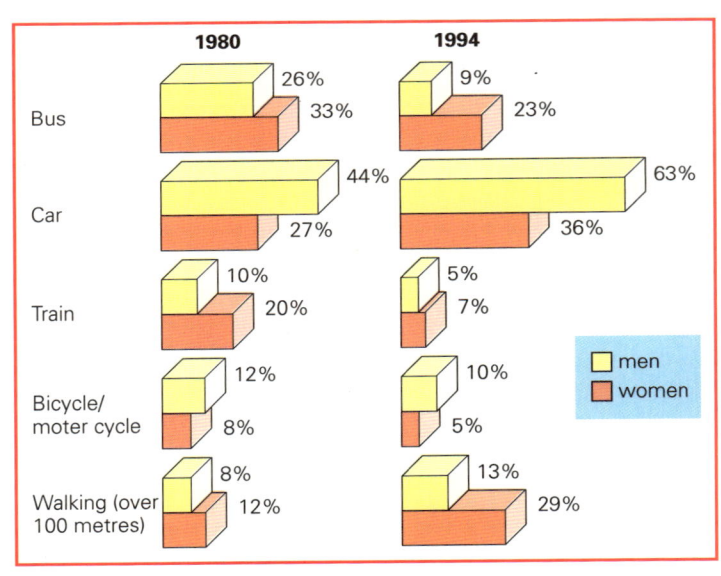

	1980 men	1980 women	1994 men	1994 women
Bus	26%	33%	9%	23%
Car	44%	27%	63%	36%
Train	10%	20%	5%	7%
Bicycle/motor cycle	12%	8%	10%	5%
Walking (over 100 metres)	8%	12%	13%	29%

Figure 30.2 Changing modes of transport to work, 1980 and 1994

2. Look at Figure 30.2.
(a) What percentage of men and of women travelled to work by car in 1980 and in 1994?
(b) Explain what happened to the popularity of each form of transport between 1980 and 1994 and suggest reasons for the changes.

Transport in towns 213

Figure 30.3 Heavy traffic congestion in any large UK town or city

3. Look at Figure 30.4.
   (a) How many vehicles in total travelled into the centre of Leeds?
   (b) What percentage of the total vehicles came from commuter villages and other towns?
   (c) What percentage of the total vehicles came from the inner areas?

Patterns of urban traffic flow

The number of cars, buses, bicycles, vans and lorries travelling into and out of cities varies in different parts of the urban area. Figure 30.4 shows how these flows varied in Leeds between 8 am and 9 am on a weekday.

Problems created by traffic in towns

The increasing numbers of vehicles travelling into cities like Leeds is leading to a series of problems:

- increasing traffic congestion, causing delays;
- an increase in the number of road accidents;
- increasing air pollution;
- increasing difficulty and expense of parking.

Figure 30.4 Traffic flow into Leeds from 8 am to 9 am on a weekday

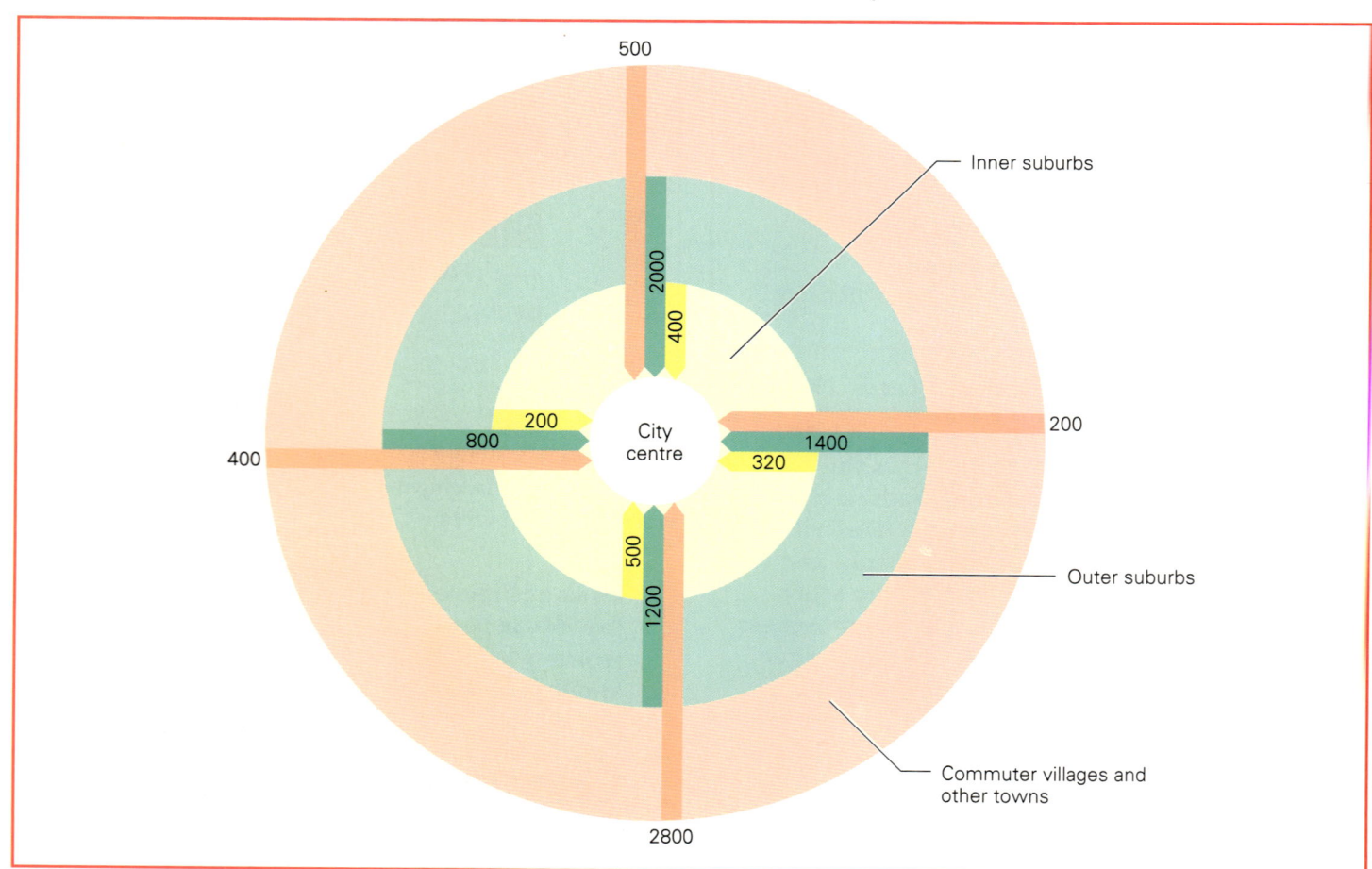

214   Changing Urban Environments

Many of these problems could be solved if more people could be persuaded to use public transport for their journeys to and from work. Figure 30.5 shows some of the relative advantages and disadvantages of different types of transport.

Transport and fuel efficiency

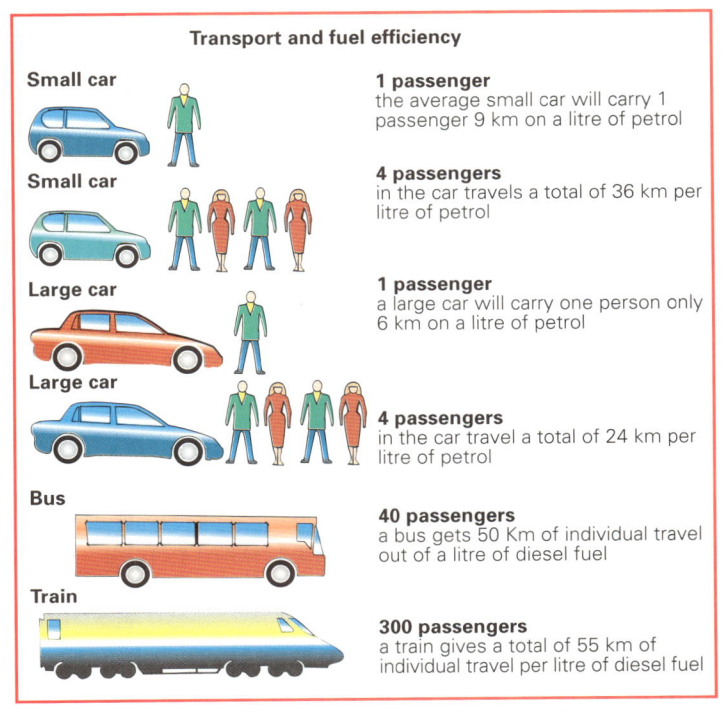

Small car — 1 passenger: the average small car will carry 1 passenger 9 km on a litre of petrol

Small car — 4 passengers: in the car travels a total of 36 km per litre of petrol

Large car — 1 passenger: a large car will carry one person only 6 km on a litre of petrol

Large car — 4 passengers: in the car travel a total of 24 km per litre of petrol

Bus — 40 passengers: a bus gets 50 Km of individual travel out of a litre of diesel fuel

Train — 300 passengers: a train gives a total of 55 km of individual travel per litre of diesel fuel

Figure 30.5 How far on a litre of fuel?

> 4. Figure 30.5 shows how far people can travel on 1 litre of petrol in different types of transport. Draw a graph to show the relative efficiency of the different types of transport.
> 5. Why is it so difficult to persuade more people to use buses and trains?
> 6. Why do more people in London travel to and from work by bus and train?

Moving around in cities

Four main approaches have been adapted to try to solve the problems created by moving people and goods around cities:

- building new motorways and roads;
- introducing **mass transit systems** to provide low-cost transport;
- schemes such as 'park and ride' to reduce or exclude cars from city centres;
- integrating transport systems in order to make them more efficient.

New motorways and roads

Cities like Los Angeles in the USA were designed and built around the car. Huge ten-lane freeways were built in order to allow people to drive everywhere – to shopping malls, to work, to restaurants, etc. As the city expanded to its present 130 km east–west width more freeways were built.

Despite such massive road building programmes, Los Angeles' traffic problems have got worse not better. The freeways are choked with traffic almost all day (see Figure 30.6). Car

Figure 30.6 Traffic jam on Los Angeles freeway

Transport in towns 215

Figure 30.7 Warner World, an edge city in Los Angeles

fumes react in sunlight to create **photochemical smog**, which envelops the city of 14 million people. Parking is still difficult and the freeways have merely encouraged the further outward sprawl of the city. New mini-cities have grown up on the edge of Los Angeles with their own shopping malls, offices and housing developments (see Figure 30.7).

Mass transit systems

Some large cities, like San Francisco, USA, have tried to solve some of their traffic problems by developing mass transit systems. San Francisco built its Bay Area Rapid Transit System (BART) between 1974 and 1978. The system consists of an electric railway which travels both above and below ground, as well as in a tunnel under San Francisco Bay, as Figures 30.8 and 30.9 show.

Figure 30.9 The Bay Area Rapid Transport System (BART), San Francisco, USA

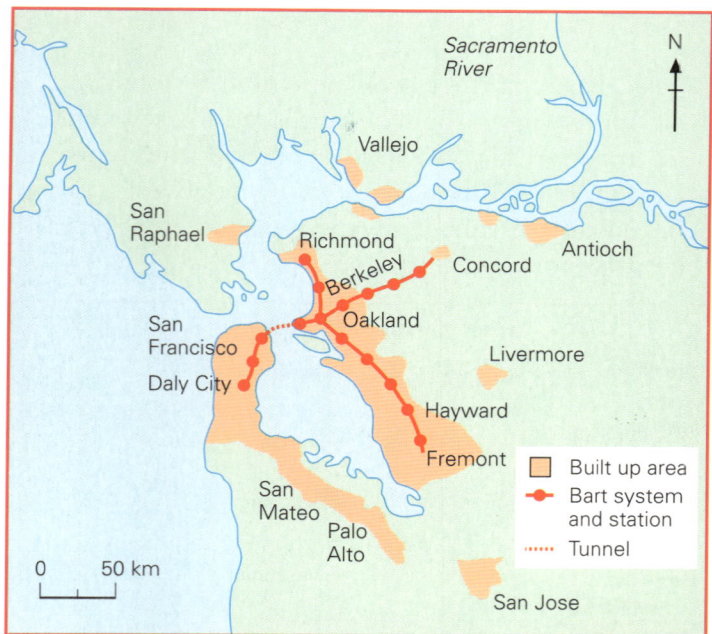

Figure 30.8 Map of the Bay Area Rapid Transport System's service area

The system moves over 350 000 people a day around the city at speeds of up to 110 km per hour. The electric trains do not add to problems of air pollution and at peak times they run every one and a half minutes. The trains are air conditioned and carpeted to maximise passenger comfort and reduce noise. The BART system is also computerised and automatic in order to keep costs below those of buses. However the system does have problems, especially at the suburban stations where there is both traffic congestion and a lack of adequate parking. Despite economies, the system still operates at a loss and many commuters still travel by car. The system partially alleviates the traffic problems but is not an ideal solution.

Park and ride schemes

7. Some British cities like Manchester and Sheffield have developed light railway systems similar to San Francisco's BART in order to reduce congestion and pollution. What are the main advantages and disadvantages of such systems?

216 Changing Urban Environments

Figure 30.10 Oxford's park and ride scheme

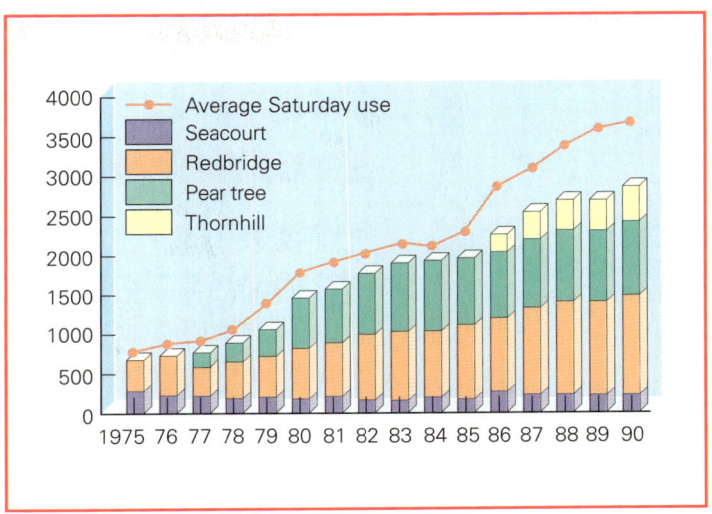

Figure 30.11 The use of park and ride in Oxford

Oxford is one city which has tried to reduce traffic congestion by developing a park and ride scheme (see Figure 30.10). The four main centres for park and ride were built between 1974 and 1985. Since then, there has been a steady increase in the number of people willing to leave their car on the outskirts and travel into the city centre by express bus. Some of the park and ride centres seem to be more successful than others as Figure 30.11 shows.

> 8. Look at Figure 30.11. Which park and ride centres have been most successful since 1985? How do you explain this?
> 9. What factors would you need to consider in selecting a new site for a park and ride scheme on the edge of the city?

Integrated public transport schemes

Merseytravel is an organisation set up in the Liverpool area and responsible for public transport in Greater Merseyside. There are four main types of transport covered by the system – the Mersey tunnels, the Mersey ferries, Merseyrail and Merseytravel bus services. The system centres around the railway system because over 30 per cent of the area's population live within 1 km of a station. The rail system has been modernised with new stations and a new centralised communication and control system. There are also over 30 different bus operators in the area, together with specialised door-to-door buses for disabled people. The ferries are used by both commuters and tourists, whilst road traffic is growing at the rate of 1 million vehicles a year in the tunnels. The aim is to create an integrated system which will speed the movement of people around the area.

Summary

- The movement of traffic in towns causes congestion and pollution.
- Traffic flows vary from day to day and hour to hour.
- Building new motorways only adds to urban traffic problems.
- Mass transit systems are expensive but effective.
- Park and ride schemes have had limited success.
- Integrated public transport systems only operate in limited areas.

Transport in towns

31 New towns

Why have new towns been built?
How successful have new towns been?

This unit looks at the development and aims of new towns, and compares new towns in Britain and Russia.

New towns in Britain

Britain built a series of **new towns** after 1946, with the aim of creating planned communities to relieve the overcrowding and poor housing of large cities like London, Liverpool and Newcastle. Under slum clearance schemes, city dwellers moved to new towns, attracted by the idea of new houses with local jobs, shops and other services in a semi-rural environment. The first generation of new towns (see Figure 31.1) were intended to be self-contained and had planned populations of about 80 000.

Between 1966 and 1970 the second generation of new towns was built. They spread over a wider area of the UK and were mostly **overspill schemes** for large **conurbations** which had high unemployment as well as overcrowding. Craigavon in Northern Ireland and Skelmersdale in Lancashire are examples of these second generation new towns built to help ease the problems in cities like Belfast and Liverpool.

The third generation of British new towns was built after 1970. These are larger than the earlier towns and were designed to be cities with populations of up to 250 000. Like Milton Keynes (see Figure 31.2) and Telford they were envisaged as growth points for their local areas and so were located near excellent communications, like motorways. **Expanded towns** like Ashford in Kent existed before 1970 but were suitable for planned growth and so offered a solution that was cheaper than building completely new towns.

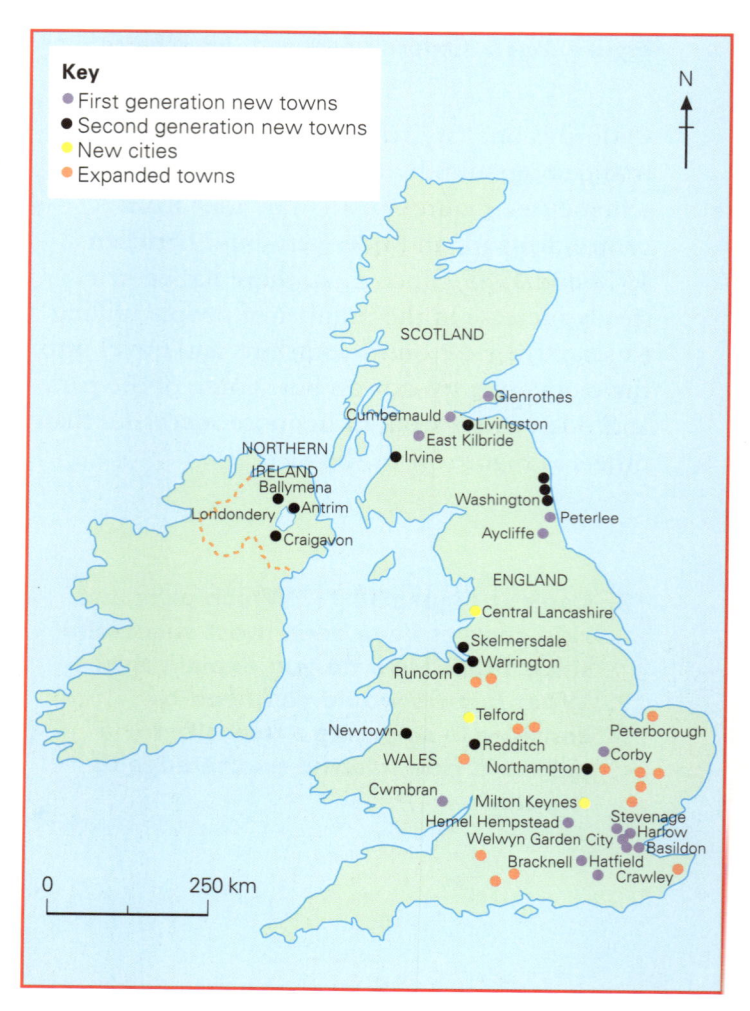

Figure 31.1 New towns in the UK, 1993

1. Trace Figure 31.1 and mark on it the first generation new towns. Label London, Glasgow and Birmingham.
2. Describe and account for the distribution of these new towns.

218 Changing Urban Environments

Figure 31.2 Milton Keynes Station

Figure 31.3 Run-down shopping centre in Skelmersdale

The Skelmersdale example

Skelmersdale new town was built 24 km north east of Liverpool in the 1960s. People were glad to leave the slum houses of Liverpool for the new flats and houses of Skelmersdale. At that time there were jobs in the new factories in Skelmersdale, attracted to the area by government grants. Soon there were large housing estates together with community centres, shops, parks, pubs and other services. However, most of the 42 000 people who live in Skelmersdale now wish they could move to another town, but they are trapped in an environment of deprivation and poverty (see Figures 31.3 and 31.4).

A recent report on Skelmersdale highlighted three main problems.

- Unemployment in Skelmersdale is, in general, higher than the national average and male unemployment has now reached 50 per cent. Factories in Skelmersdale always tended to employ semi-skilled workers, and these

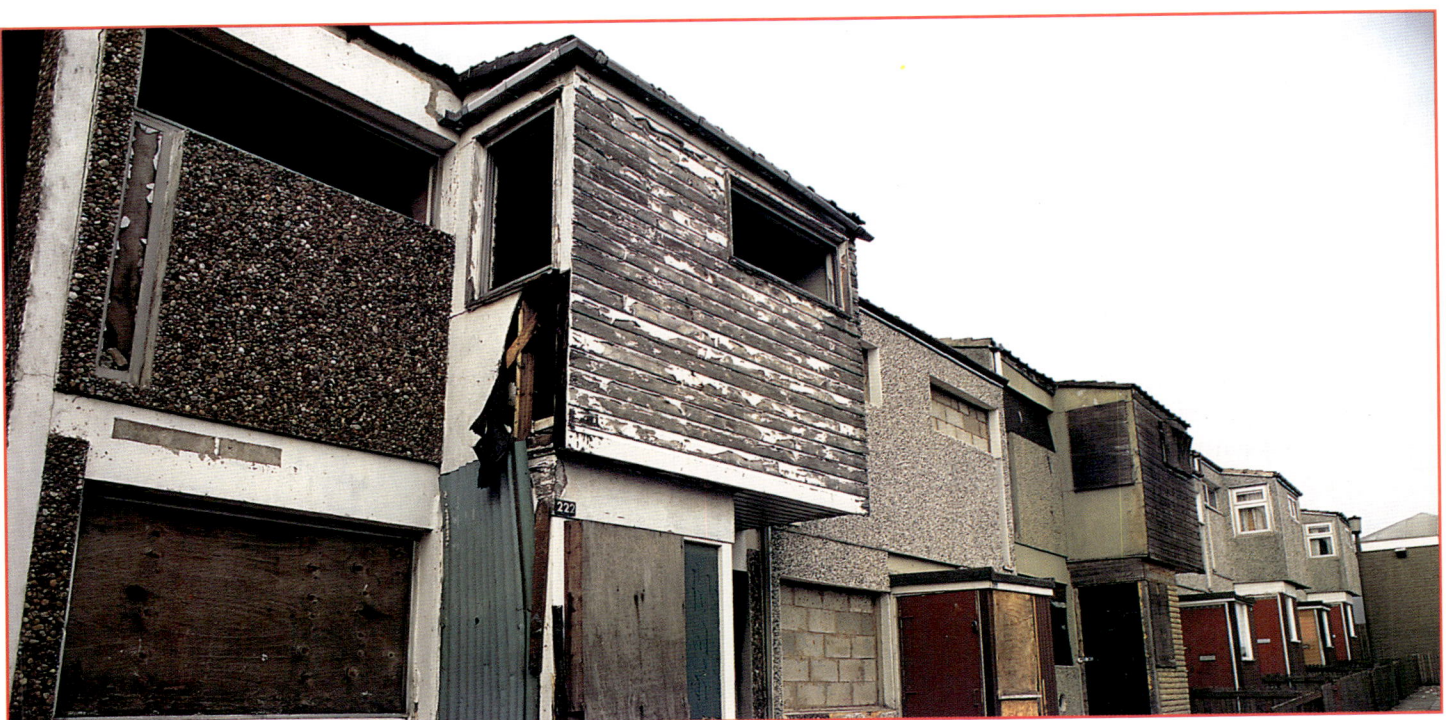

Figure 31.4 Run-down housing in Skelmersdale

New towns

factories were hit hard by the economic recessions of the 1980s and early 1990s. Factories initially attracted by government grants closed when the grants ran out. Skelmersdale was never self-sufficient in jobs and people had to travel to Liverpool, Saint Helens or Wigan for work. But factory closures affected these areas too and so unemployment grew even faster in Skelmersdale.

- Planners in Skelmersdale tried to recreate some of the street structure of the old industrial north. The result, however, is that the view from one house is often the back of another. People also have to walk directly past each others windows and the houses open on to complex warrens rather than on to streets. This encourages crime since it is very hard to police. Most of the houses are poorly built and suffer from damp and rot. Poor planning meant that many houses with flat roofs were built in a region noted for its rain, gales and snow. People in the town feel isolated and trapped because they cannot afford a car to visit other towns. In addition they are a 'captive' population, vulnerable to higher prices. Initial plans for things like a hospital and large stores never materialised, so the town lacks key facilities and fails to attract shoppers and visitors from the surrounding area.
- Standards of living are low. Many children suffer from asthma and other respiratory diseases because of damp houses that people cannot afford to heat. Others suffer from vitamin and other deficiencies as a result of poor diets.

> **3. Imagine that you live in Skelmersdale. Write a letter to your local Member of Parliament pointing out the need for government help to solve some of the town's problems. Describe the background of the town and highlight the main problems for its residents. Prioritise which problems you think the government should tackle first and suggest how they might act.**

New towns world-wide

There are three main types of new town to be found all over the world:

- those built to relieve overcrowding of people and industries in cities (e.g. Skelmersdale and Solnstsevo, near Moscow);
- those built to develop new resources such as timber, minerals, gas or hydro-electricity (e.g. Noyabrsk in Siberia and Tynda in eastern Russia);
- those built to encourage growth in new areas of a country (e.g. Brasilia in Brazil).

Figure 31.5 Tynda, a new town in Russia

> **4. Look at Figure 31.5.**
> **(a) What evidence in the picture shows that this town was planned?**

Problems in planning Tynda, Russia

Tynda is a new town in the eastern part of Russia (see Figure 31.5), which is a region with very few people because of the harsh climate. Winters are long and cold with average temperatures as low as −20°C. At such low temperatures steel in cars can snap, oil may freeze and special machines have to be built to work in the cold conditions. Summers are short but quite hot with temperatures up to 20°C. Much of the ground is affected by permafrost, so

220 Changing Urban Environments

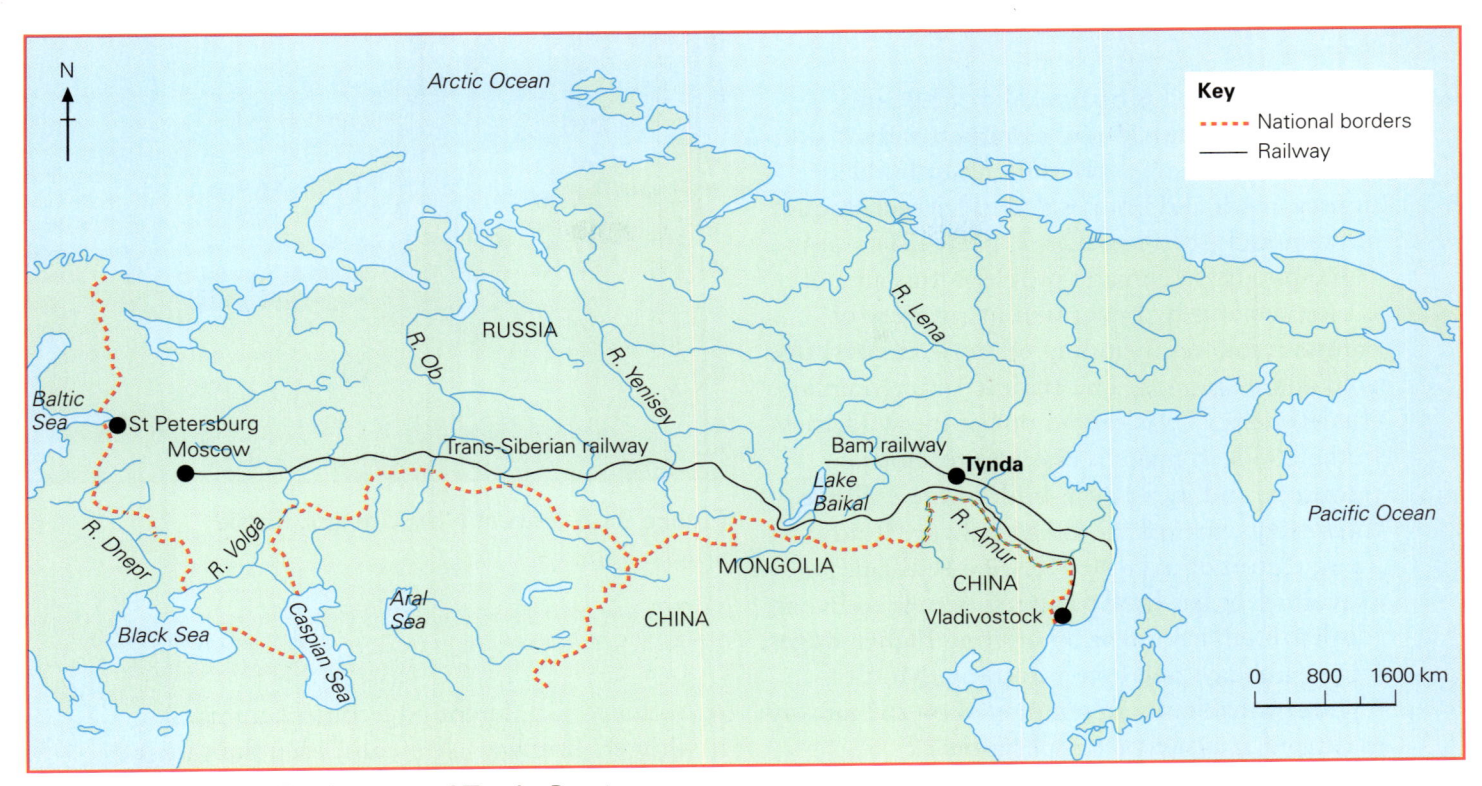

Figure 31.6 The location of Tynda, Russia

Figure 31.7 A house developed for an environment with permafrost

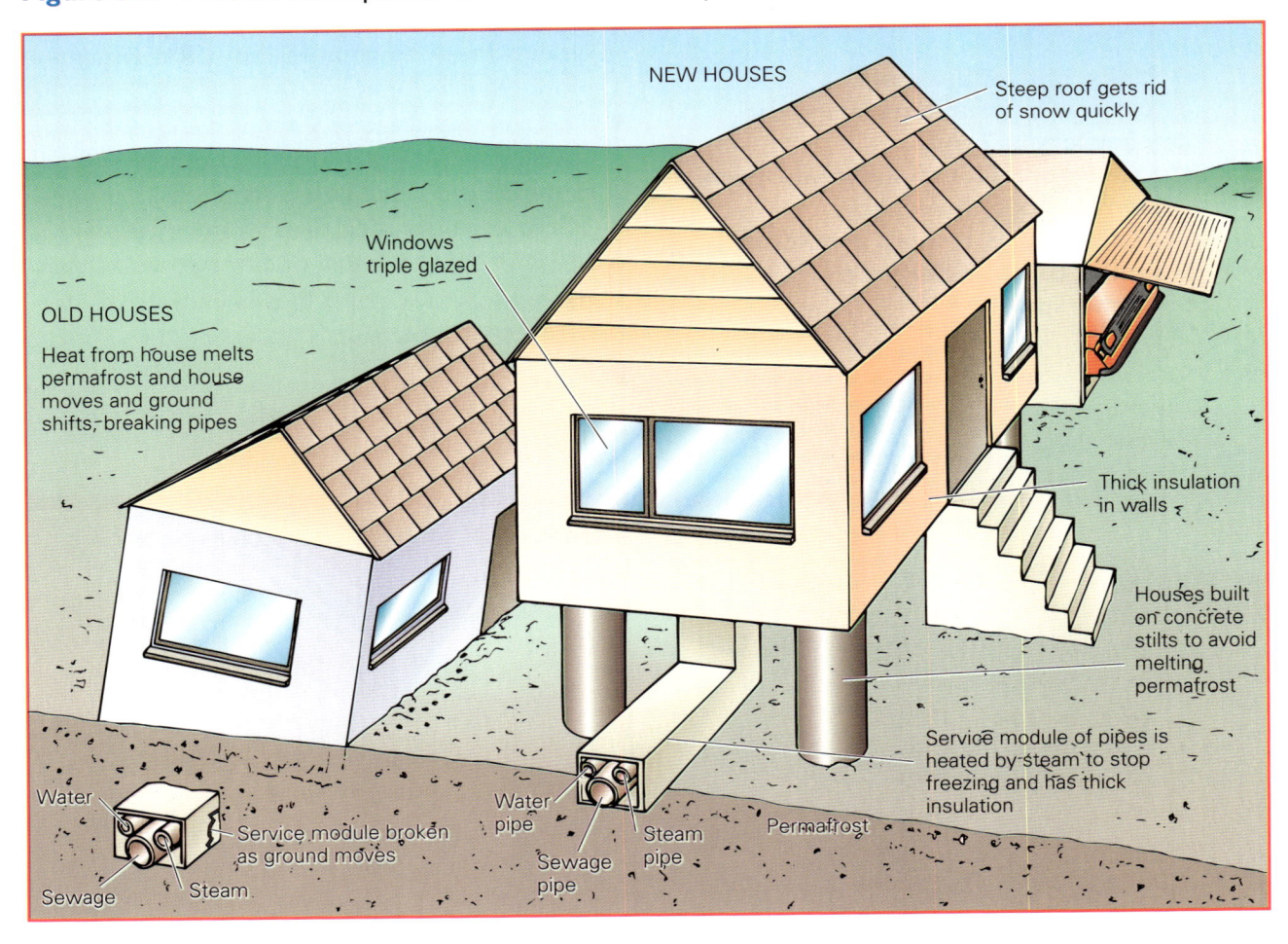

New towns 221

in winter the soil is frozen solid, while in summer only the top few centimetres thaw out. Permafrost makes it very difficult to build houses, roads and bridges and special techniques are required (see Figure 31.7, page 221).

Despite these climatic problems this area of Russia benefits by being rich in a variety of natural resources including oil, coal, timber, firs, gold and diamonds. The Barkal Amur Mainline (BAM) railway was carved out of the wilderness in the 1980s to make it easier to reach these resources, and Tynda was built in the 1970s as the headquarters of the BAM railway. It now has a population of over 30 000. The Russian Government has tried to attract people to live in this harsh environment by offering higher wages, longer holidays and better housing. Most of Tynda's inhabitants are employed on the railway as drivers, maintenance supervisors or construction workers.

Unemployment is not a major problem but the people of Tynda face a number of other difficulties.

Figure 31.8 Flats in New Urengoi, Russia

> 5. (a) **Make a list of the main environmental problems facing the early settlers in Tynda.**
>   (b) **Use Figure 31.7 to show how each problem has been overcome.**
> 6. **In what ways are Tynda's problems:**
>   (a) **similar to;** (b) **different from, those of Skelmersdale?**

- In the past, different government ministries (Power, Railways, Minerals) each built their own blocks of flats in Tynda to house their own workers. There was no co-operation between ministries so there was an overall lack of planning and there are lots of small heating systems in the town instead of a few larger and more efficient ones.
- There is a shortage of some services, such as entertainment, but a surplus of others – for example, there are 50 bakers' shops!
- There are more men than women.
- Many people only stay one or two years, then move back to western Russia because of the harsh environment in Tynda.

Summary

- New towns were built to solve a series of urban problems such as poor housing.
- Different types of new towns were built.
- New towns have been built in many countries.
- New towns generate their own problems.

Chapter 32 Pressures on the urban fringe

What are the pressures on land at the edge of towns?

How are conflicts over land use resolved?

This unit looks at some of the pressures on land at the edge of urban areas, especially in green belt zones. It considers the ways in which green belts are changing and how the demands of different types of land use are reconciled.

Green belts

The continued expansion of towns and cities in to the countryside is a constant theme in many countries. The idea of containing and restraining urban growth was recognised in Britain by people like Ebenezer Howard at the end of the nineteenth century. He proposed a **green belt**, that is an area consisting of *'open and low density land use surrounding existing major settlements where urban extension is to be strictly controlled'*. The green belt around London was designated in the development plan of 1947. Since then, green belts have been created around many UK conurbations as Figure 32.1 shows. The function of greens belts is to:

- check the spread of cities;
- prevent towns merging together in a vast urban sprawl;
- preserve the special character of towns;
- assist urban renewal.

Green belts now cover 12 per cent of England and Wales and within them the construction of new houses, factories, offices and shopping centres is strictly controlled. Green belts face many pressures.

- There is pressure to release land for new housing, especially on the inner edge of green belts.
- There is pressure to release land for the construction of new hypermarkets and shopping malls.

Figure 32.1 The green belts of England and Wales, 1994

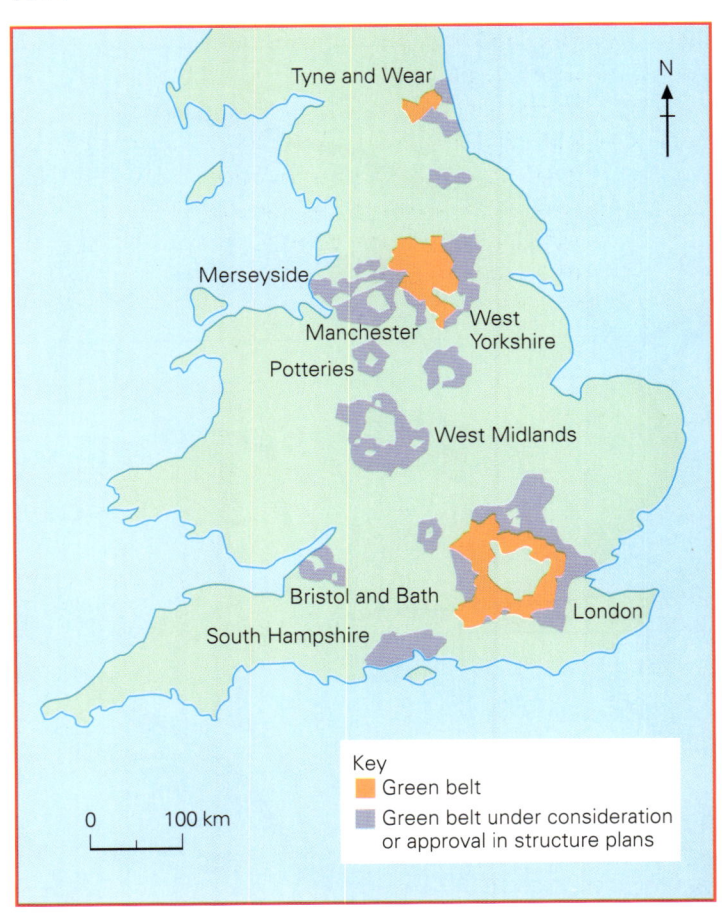

- Many green belts now have new motorways and dual carriageways through them.
- Some land in green belts is not very good agricultural land so has been converted to non-farming uses such as golf courses and riding schools.
- Land in some green belts, like the one around London, has been so damaged that it is really a 'brown belt' and of little environmental value. In these places, green belt land has been used for museums, market gardens, airfields, hotels, hospitals and other developments.

London's green belt

There is exceptional pressure on London's green belt because there is such a huge demand for new houses and roads around the capital. For example, a survey in 1992 argued that London would need 800 000 new homes by 1999. The problem is where to build these estates in an already overcrowded green belt.

The Ordnance Survey map in Figure 32.2 shows part of London's western green belt near Uxbridge. This map can be used as the base for a land use map. Land use maps are important first steps in making decisions about new developments in areas of green belt.

Figure 32.2 Land use map of a green belt area near Uxbridge

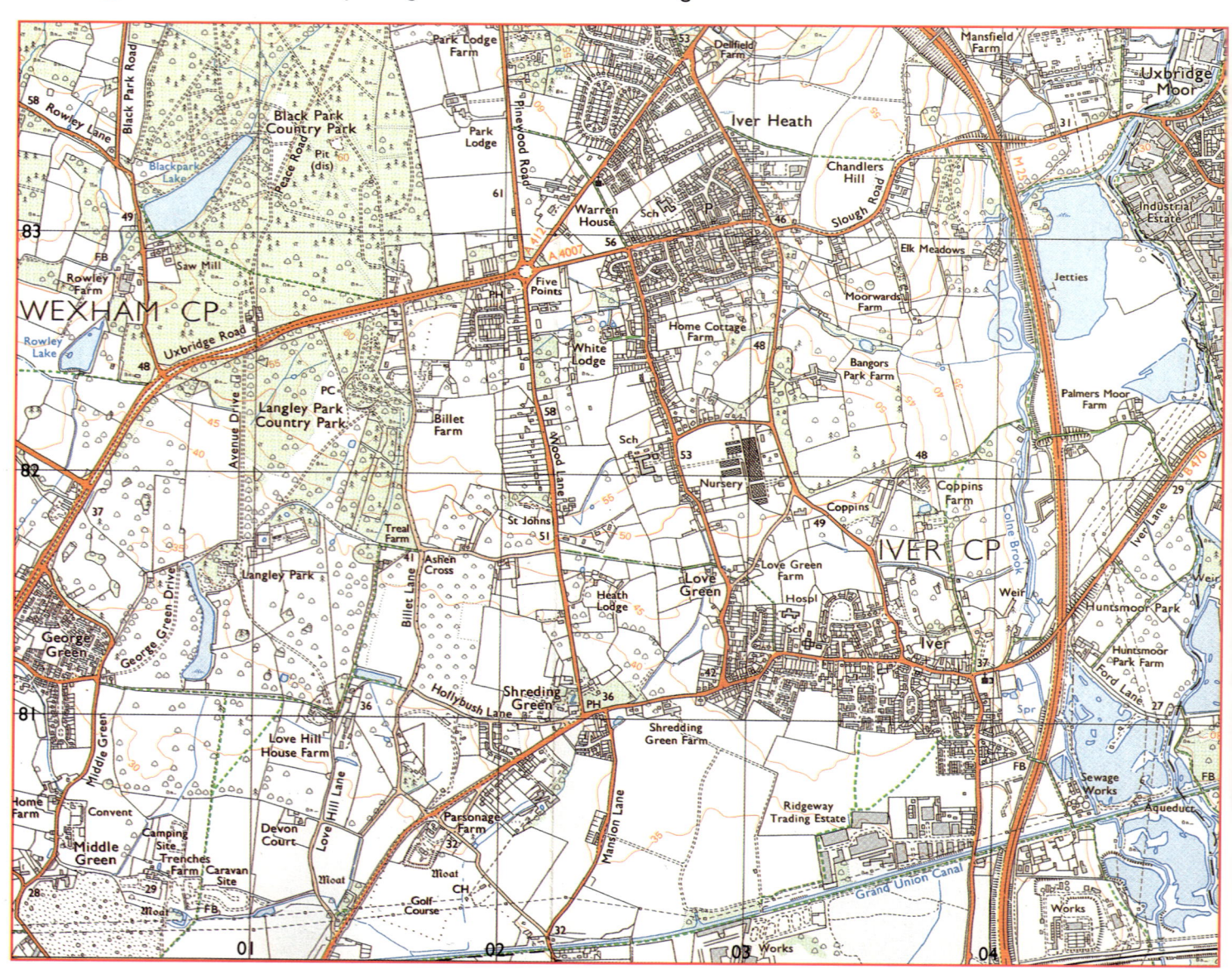

224 Changing Urban Environments

1. Use Figure 32.2 to make and draw a simple land use map of the area. Devise your own symbols to include roads, motorways, woodland, lakes, rivers, farmland, towns and villages and other land uses.
2. Make a list of all the different land uses found in this area of green belt.
3. Divide the list of land uses in to:
   (a) those you think are acceptable in a green belt; (b) those you think are inappropriate in a green belt (e.g. because they create noise, smells, pollution).
4. There is a proposal to extend the settlement of Iver westwards by building houses in grid square 0281.
   (a) What arguments would you advance in favour of this development?
   (b) What arguments would you advance against it?

Summary

- Land on the urban fringe was under great pressure in the first half of the twentieth century.
- Some people want to contain urban growth within green belts.
- Other people believe there is scope for new developments such as housing, leisure, industry or transport in the urban fringes.

The UK

Country fact files

Population

Total (millions)	58.6 (1995)
Density (persons per km²)	239
Birth rate (per 1000 population)	13
Death rate (per 1000 population)	11
Natural increase (per 1000 population)	2
Infant mortality rate (per 1000 population)	9
Per cent urban population	92
Ethnic groups (% of total population)	
White	94
Asian Indian	1
West Indian	1
Pakistani	1

Development indicators

GNP per capita ($US)	17 970 (1993)
Literacy rate (% of total population)	99
Life expectancy (years) Male	74
Female	79
Average	76
Cars (per 1000 people)	497
Telephones (per 1000 people)	473
People per doctor	300

Physical

Area (km²)	244 100
Highest mountain (m)	1344 (Ben Nevis)
Longest river (km)	450 (Thames)
Natural hazards	fog, frost, high winds, floods

Countryside

Agricultural area (% of total area)	64.2
Land use (% of total area) Arable	31
Grass	36
Forest	10
Urban and waste	23
Fertiliser consumption (kg per ha of agricultural land)	137
Number of tractors ('000s)	480
Combine harvesters ('000s)	90
Livestock numbers (millions):	
Chickens	189
Sheep	29.3
Pigs	7.8
Cattle	11.7
Average farm size (ha²)	70
Irrigated area ('000s km²)	1.6
Main crops ('000s ha²)	
Cereals	3931
Fodder crops	11 572
Other herbaceous crops	1196

Resources

Coal:	
Production (million tonnes)	30
World rank	12
Oil:	
Production (million tonnes)	94.2
World rank	11
Natural gas:	
Production ('000 terajoules)	1972
World rank	5
Electricity generation (megawatts)	62 100

226 Country Fact Files

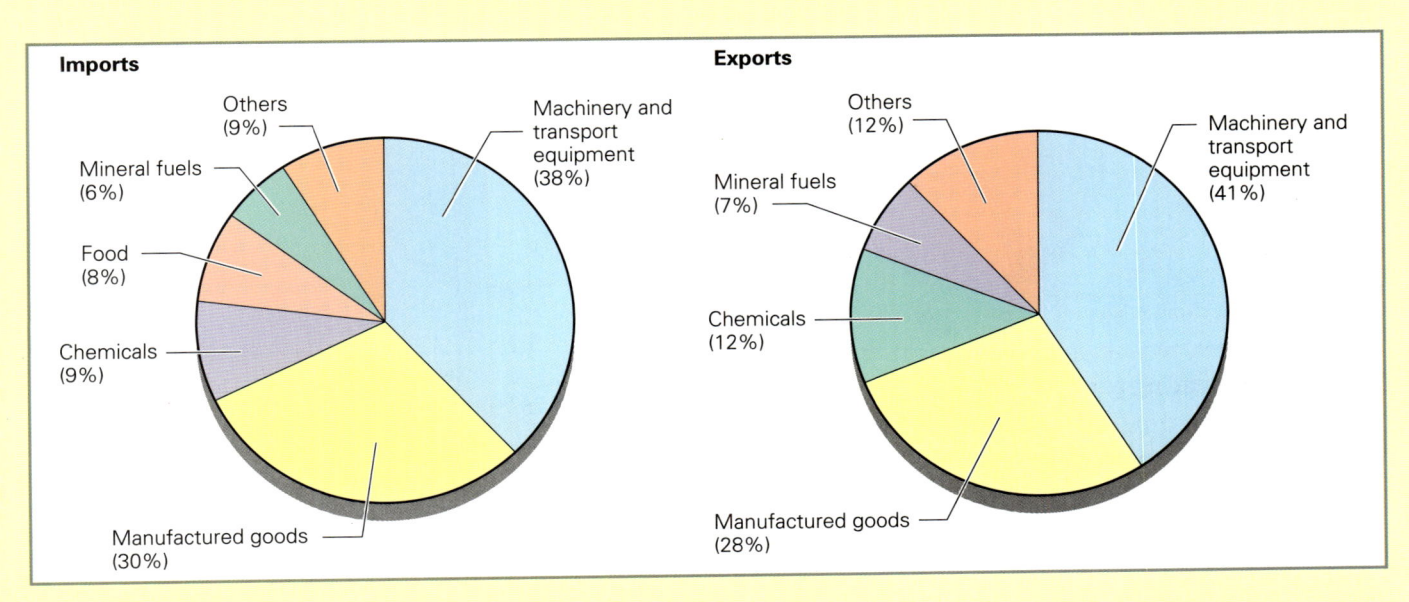

Figure 1 UK imports and exports, 1992

Imports:
- Machinery and transport equipment (38%)
- Manufactured goods (30%)
- Chemicals (9%)
- Food (8%)
- Mineral fuels (6%)
- Others (9%)

Exports:
- Machinery and transport equipment (41%)
- Manufactured goods (28%)
- Chemicals (12%)
- Mineral fuels (7%)
- Others (12%)

Trade and industry

Per cent of workforce involved in:	
Agriculture	2
Industry	28.7
Services	69.3

Trade (1992)
Main imports see graph above
Main exports see graph above
Earnings from tourism ($US, 1992) 13.6 billion
Main tourist attractions London, Scotland, Lake District, Wales, SW England

Industrial production (annual)
Steel (million tonnes) 16.2 (1992)
Cars (millions) 1.2 (1991)
Aluminium ('000 tonnes) 464 (1991)
Petroleum products (million tonnes) 79 (1991)

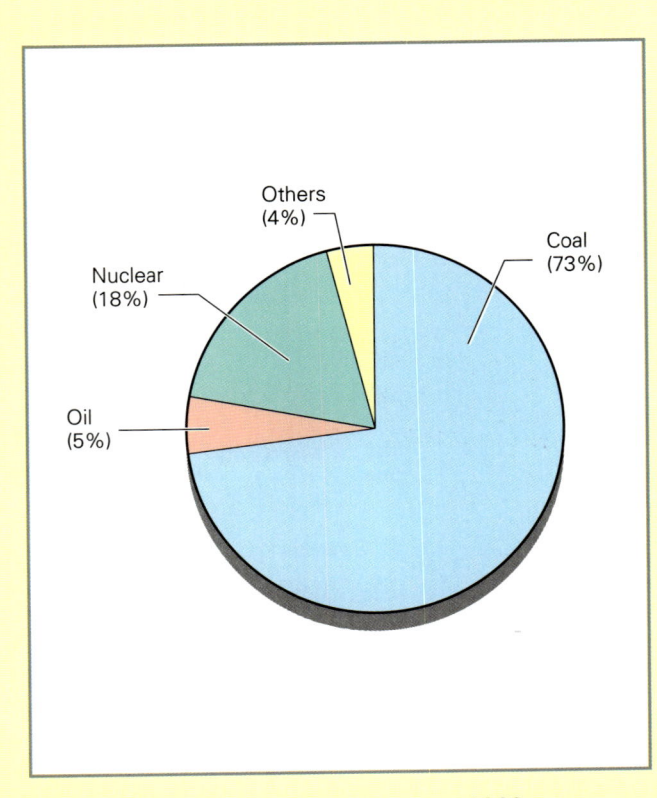

Figure 2 UK electricity generation, 1992

- Coal (73%)
- Nuclear (18%)
- Oil (5%)
- Others (4%)

The UK 227

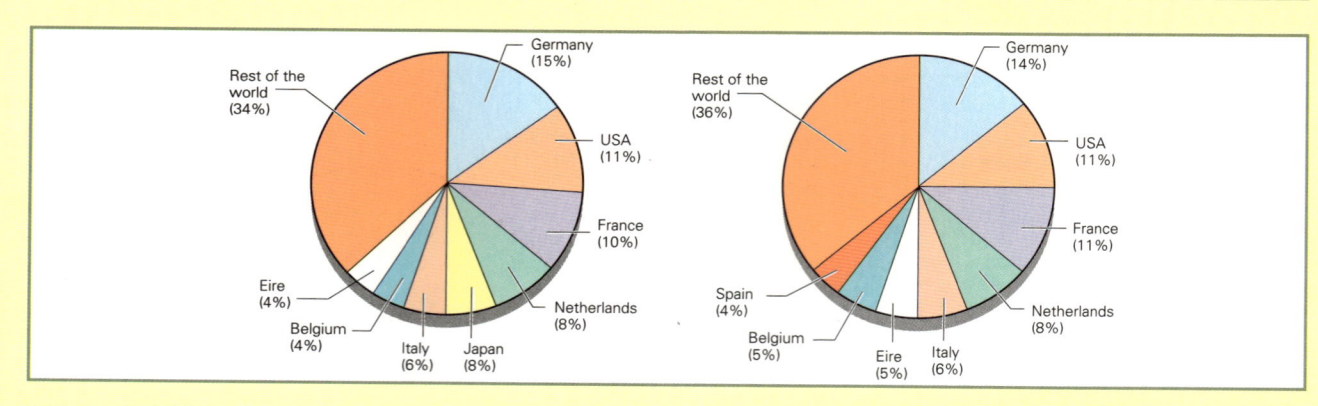

Figure 3 UK trading partners, 1992

Figure 4 A map of the UK

Urban	
Populations of top ten cities:	
London	6.3 million
Manchester	1.6 million
Birmingham	1.4 million
Liverpool	1 million
Glasgow	730 000
Newcastle Upon Tyne	617 000
Sheffield	445 000
Leeds	432 000
Edinburgh	404 000
Bristol	367 000
Teesside	363 000
Roads	
(km per 1000 km² of land)	1476
Motorways (km)	3093
Other roads (km)	376 893
Railway	
(km per 1000 km² of land)	157
(total line length, km)	16 932
Aircraft (over 9 tonnes)	729 (1990)

228   Country Fact Files

Spain

Country fact files

Population

Total (millions)	39.7 (1994)
Density (persons per km²)	80
Birth rate (per 1000 population)	9.7
Death rate (per 1000 population)	8.7
Natural increase (per 1000 population)	1
Infant mortality rate (per 1000 population)	9
Per cent urban population	81
Ethnic groups (% of total population)	
Castilian Spanish	73
Catalan	16
Galician	8
Basque	3

Development indicators

GNP per capita ($US)	13 650 (1994)
Literacy rate (% of total population)	98
Life expectancy (years)	Average 77
Cars (per 1000 people)	336
Telephones (per 1000 people)	358
People per doctor	255

Countryside

Agricultural area (% of total area)	61.2
Land use (% of total area)	Arable 39.9
	Grass 9.5
	Forest 31.9
	Urban and waste 7.7
Fertiliser consumption (kg per ha of agricultural land)	65.2
Number of tractors and combine harvesters ('000s)	756
Livestock numbers (millions):	
Chickens	166
Sheep	24.9
Pigs	18.2
Cattle	4.8
Average farm size (ha²)	15.2
Irrigated area ('000s of km²)	34

Main crops ('000s of ha²)
Cereals	7650
Fodder crops	4600
Other herbaceous crops	3400

Physical

Area (km²)	504 780
Highest mountain (m)	2580 (Inthanon)
Longest river (km)	1010 (Tagus)
Natural hazards	drought

Resources

Coal:
  Production (millions of tonnes) 13.9
  World rank 15
Oil:
  Production (millions of tonnes) 1.1
  World rank 50
Natural gas:
  Production ('000s of terajoules) 55
  World rank 52
Electricity generation (megawatts) 45 200

Urban

Populations of top ten cities (million):

Madrid	3
Barcelona	1.6
Valencia	0.76
Seville	0.69
Saragossa	0.60
Malaga	0.52
Bilbao	0.37
Las Palmas	0.35
Valladolid	0.33
Murcia	0.33

Roads
Metalled roads (km) 150 000
Motorways (km) 7324

Railway (total line length, km) 14 408

Aircraft (over 9 tonnes) 346

Trade and industry

Per cent of workforce involved in:
Agriculture 11
Industry 33
Services 56

Trade (1992)
Main imports   oil, chemicals, motor vehicles, manufactured goods
Imports from (%)   Germany 16
  France 16
  Italy 10
  Benelux 7
  USA 7
  UK 7
Main exports   motor vehicles, machinery, chemicals, plastics, fruit and vegetables
Exports to (%)   France 20
  Germany 16
  Italy 11
  Benelux 8
  USA 5
  UK 8
Earnings from tourism ($US)   17.7 billion
Main tourist attractions   beach resorts, nightlife, scenery, historic sights

Industrial production (annual)
Steel (million tonnes) 12.7 (1994)
Cars (millions) 1.8 (1994)
Aluminium ('000 tonnes) 355 (1994)
Petrochemicals (million tonnes) 45.7 (1994)

Country Fact Files

USA

Country fact files

Population

Total (millions)	263.2 (1995)
Density (persons per km^2)	28
Birth rate (per 1000 population)	15
Death rate (per 1000 population)	9
Natural increase (per 1000 population)	4
Infant mortality rate (per 1000 population)	8
Per cent urban population	75
Ethnic groups (% of total population)	White 85
	Black 12
	Other 3

Development indicators

GNP per capita ($US)	24 750 (1993)
Literacy rate (% of total population)	99
Life expectancy (years)	Male 72
	Female 79
	Total 76
Cars (per 1000 people)	528
Telephones (per 1000 people)	565
People per doctor	420

Countryside

Agricultural area (% of total area)	56.4
Land use (% of total area)	Arable 21
	Grass 26
	Forest 32
	Urban and waste 21
Fertiliser consumption (kg per ha of agricultural land)	43
Number of tractors and combine harvesters ('000s)	4 749 000
Livestock numbers (millions):	
Cattle	3.1
Chickens	272
Sheep	11.2
Pigs	54.5
Average farm size (ha^2)	110
Irrigated area ('000s km^2)	187.7

Main crops ('000s of ha^2)

Cereals	102 701
Fodder crops	91 217
Other herbaceous crops	75 287

Physical

Area (m^2)	9 372 610
Highest mountain (m)	6193 (Mount McKinley)
Longest river (km)	3952 (Mississippi–Missouri)
Natural hazards	earthquakes, hurricanes, tornadoes, floods, avalanches

Resources

Coal:
    Production (million tonnes)   608
    World rank   2
Oil:
    Production (million tonnes)   417
    World rank   4
Natural gas:
    Production ('000 terajoules)   19 322
    World rank   2
Electricity generation   see graph on page 233

Trade and industry

Per cent of workforce involved in:
Agriculture   3
Industry   18
Services   79

Trade (1992)
Main imports   see graph on page 233
Main exports   see graph on page 233
Earnings from tourism ($US, 1992)
    53.8 billion
Main tourist attractions   cities, mountains, beaches, lakes, forests, deserts

Industrial Production (annual)
Steel (million tonnes)   91.5 (1992)
Cars (millions)   5.4 (1992)
Aluminium (million tonnes)   6.5 (1991)
Petroleum products (million tonnes)
    571 (1991)

Urban

Populations of top ten cities (million):
New York   18
Los Angeles   14.5
Chicago   8.1
San Francisco   6.2
Philadelphia   5.9
Detroit   4.6
Boston   4.2
Washington   3.9
Dallas   3.8
Houston   3.7

Roads   612
(km per 1000 km^2 of land)
Motorways (km)   380

Railway   30
(km per 1000 km^2 of land)

Aircraft (over 9 tonnes)   1305 (1990)

Country Fact Files

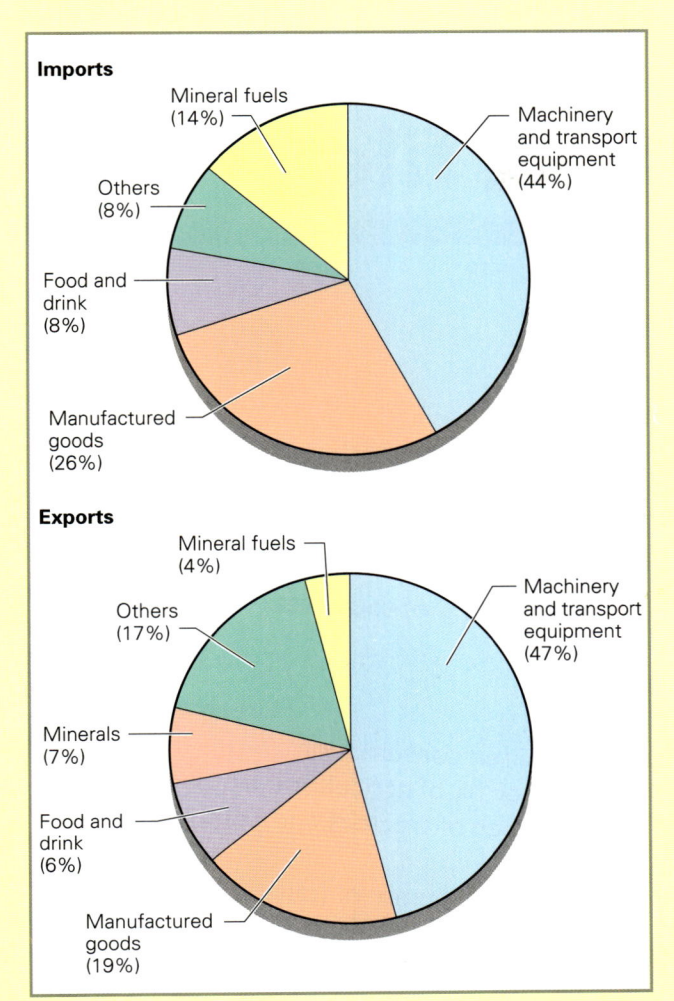

Imports
- Mineral fuels (14%)
- Others (8%)
- Food and drink (8%)
- Manufactured goods (26%)
- Machinery and transport equipment (44%)

Exports
- Mineral fuels (4%)
- Others (17%)
- Minerals (7%)
- Food and drink (6%)
- Manufactured goods (19%)
- Machinery and transport equipment (47%)

Figure 5 USA imports and exports, 1992

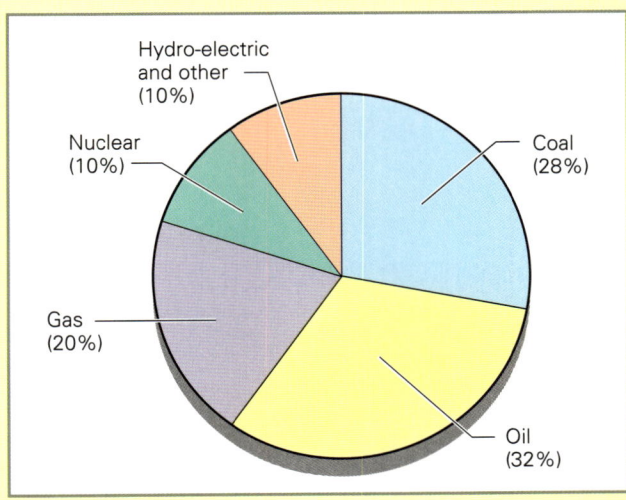

Figure 6 USA electricity generation, 1992
- Hydro-electric and other (10%)
- Nuclear (10%)
- Gas (20%)
- Coal (28%)
- Oil (32%)

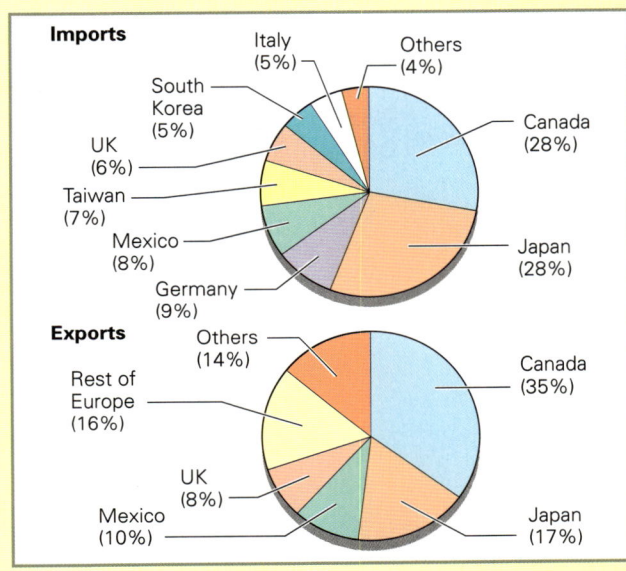

Figure 7 USA trading partners, 1992

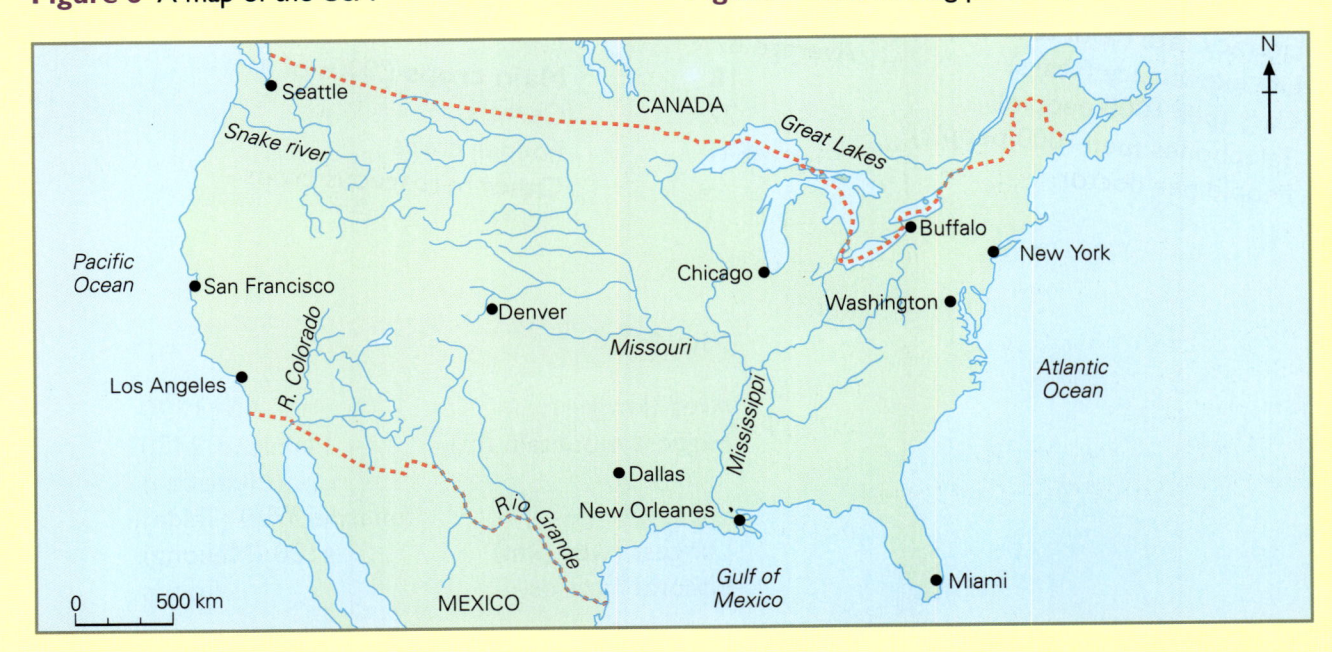

Imports
- Italy (5%)
- Others (4%)
- South Korea (5%)
- UK (6%)
- Taiwan (7%)
- Mexico (8%)
- Germany (9%)
- Canada (28%)
- Japan (28%)

Exports
- Others (14%)
- Rest of Europe (16%)
- UK (8%)
- Mexico (10%)
- Canada (35%)
- Japan (17%)

Figure 8 A map of the USA

USA 233

Thailand

Country fact files

Population

Total (millions)	58.4 (1994)
Density (persons per km²)	114
Birth rate (per 1000 population)	16.9
Death rate (per 1000 population)	4.8
Natural increase (per 1000 population)	12
Infant mortality rate (per 1000 population)	24
Per cent urban population	24
Ethnic groups (% of total population)	Thai 90
	Chinese 8
	Malay 1
	Other 1

Development indicators

GNP per capita ($US)	15800 (1994)
Literacy rate (% of total population)	94
Life expectancy (years)	Average 67
Cars (per 1000 people)	18
Telephones (per 1000 people)	27
People per doctor	4641

Countryside

Agricultural area (% of total area)	40.9
Land use (% of total area)	arable 39.4
	grass 1.6
	forest 26.4
	Urban and waste 25.2
Fertiliser consumption (kg per ha of agricultural land)	37.2
Number of tractors and combine harvesters ('000s)	142
Livestock numbers (millions):	
Chickens	136
Sheep	0.2
Pigs	5.1
Cattle	6.8
Average farm size (ha²)	11.8
Irrigated area ('000s of km²)	44
Main crops ('000s of ha²)	
Cereals	12 800
Fodder crops	3100
Other herbaceous crops	5100

Physical

Area (km²)	513 120
Highest mountain (m)	Mainland: 2480 (Mulhacen)
	Tenerife: 3720 (Teide)
Longest river (km)	4180 (Mekong)
Natural hazards	floods

Resources

Coal:
- Production (millions of tonnes): 15.6 (lignite)
- World rank: —

Oil:
- Production (millions of tonnes): 0
- World rank: 0

Natural gas:
- Production ('000s of terajoules): 280
- World rank: 24

Electricity generation: 6997

Urban

Populations of top ten cities (million):

Bangkok	5.90
Nakhon Ratchasima	0.30
Songkhla	0.25
Nanthaburi	0.23
Khon-kaen	0.21
Chiang Mai	0.17
Nakhon Sauran	0.16
Ubon Ratchathani	0.14
Chon Buri	0.12
Saraburi	0.11

Roads
- Metalled roads (km): 44 409
- Motorways (km): 0

Railway (total line length, km): 4450

Aircraft (over 9 tonnes): 98

Trade and industry

Per cent of workforce involved in:
- Agriculture: 67
- Industry: 11
- Services: 22

Trade (1992)

Main imports: machinery, road vehicles, manufactured goods, chemicals, oil, steel, textile yarn and fibres, fish

Imports from (%):
- Japan 30
- USA 12
- Singapore 7
- Taiwan 7
- Germany 6
- South Korea 4

Main exports: clothing and textiles, rice, rubber, fruit and vegetables, electronic goods

Exports to (%):
- USA 22
- Japan 17
- Singapore 12
- Hong Kong 5
- Germany 4
- UK 3

Earnings from tourism ($US): 4.9 billion

Main tourist attractions: exotic culture and architecture, beach resorts, nightlife, cuisine, scenery

Industrial production (annual)
- Steel (million tonnes): 0.7 (1994)
- Cars (millions): 0.14 (1994)
- Aluminium ('000 tonnes): 0
- Petrochemicals (million tonnes): 11.7 (1994)

Glossary

Chapter 1
Standard of living The quality of life measured in terms of food, clothing, housing and general living conditions.
Undeveloped A 1960s term for poorer countries mostly in Africa, Latin America and South East Asia.
Underdeveloped Countries which still have quite a lot of progress to make towards 'development'.
Third World A 1960s term describing those countries which were not part of the First World (capitalist countries) nor the Second World (centrally planned former communist countries).
Second World A 1960s term for centrally planned, former communist countries.
per capita Gross National Product The value of all goods and services produced by a country divided by the total population.
Physical Quality of Life Index Composite index to measure quality of life made up of life expectancy, infant mortality and adult literacy.
Interdependence A system whereby countries or individuals depend on each other, e.g. The USA depends on Brazil to produce coffee and Brazil depends on the USA to produce computers.

Chapter 2
Birth rate The number of babies born per 1000 of the population.
Death rate The number of deaths per 1000 of the population.
Family planning programmes Projects which aim to help people make decisions about their family size. These projects include educational and publicity materials as well as medical advice.
Population density The number of people living in each km² of a place.

Chapter 3
Demographic transition model A model which describes population change in a country over a period of time. The model assumes countries pass through a series of stages.
Population cycle The changes in the birth rate, death rate and total population of a country over time.

Pro-natalist policy Groups against family planning policies especially those which reduce the birth rate.
Anti-natalist policy Groups in favour of family planning and birth control.
Population structure The number of males and females in the different age groups of a country's population.
Population pyramid A diagram which shows the number of males and females in 5-year age groups e.g. 0–5, 6–10.

Chapter 4
Positive checks Factors described by Thomas Malthus in 1798 such as lack of food and clothing, disease and war which reduced population size.
Preventative checks Factors described by Thomas Malthus in 1798 such as late marriage or abstinence which reduced the birth rate.
Resources Things people find useful, e.g. wood is a resource when people use it in buildings.
Overpopulation The situation when a country or area has too many people to be sustained by its resources at the current state of technology.
Underpopulation The state of a country or area which has too few people for its resources. An increase in population would lead to a rise in living standards.
Population optimum The situation of a country or area in which the size of its population is in balance with its resources.

Chapter 5
International migration The permanent movement of people between countries.
Internal migration The movement of people between different parts of the same country.
Emigrants People who leave an area.
Immigrants People who move into an area.
Push factors Things which encourage people to leave an area such as drought, failure of a harvest or lack of services.
Pull factors Things which attract people to migrate to an area such as available jobs, housing or services.

Chapter 6
Colonies Countries that were once ruled by other countries.
Terms of trade The value of exports and imports expressed in terms of their purchasing power.

Chapter 7
Multilateral aid Aid that goes from richer countries to poorer countries through international organisations such as the World Bank.
Bilateral aid Aid that goes directly from a richer country to a poorer country.

Chapter 8
Multinationals Another name for transnational companies.
Transnational companies Very large companies who have operations world-wide. They usually have their headquarters in a rich country and branches in many other, often poorer, countries.
Supernationals Another name for transnational companies.
Vertical integration Large companies which purchase a range of different types of company in order to control a production process e.g. sugar cane plantations, sugar refineries, road haulage companies, shipping and marketing companies may all belong to one parent company.
Horizontal integration Large companies which purchase very diverse companies in order to spread their investment (and therefore their risks). For example Gulf Oil grows sugar, sells cigars, makes paper and runs a New York ice hockey team.

Chapter 9
Active volcano A volcano which is currently erupting or has erupted in recent times.
Dormant volcano A volcano which, although not recently active, is likely to erupt in the future.
Extinct volcano A volcano which is not likely to erupt in the future.
Plate A very large section of the earth's crust which moves very slowly across the surface of the planet.
Oceanic ridge A range of volcanoes running in a narrow line beneath the ocean; in places the volcanoes break the surface to form islands.
Volcanic bombs Large rock fragments ejected by volcanic eruptions.
Acid lava Thick, slow flowing molten rock.
Focus The point within the earth's crust where an earthquake begins.
Epicentre The point on the surface directly above the focus of an earthquake.
Longitudinal wages (L-waves) Seismic waves moving out from the focus of an earthquake along the surface of the planet.
Rift valley A valley that is formed when the area between two parallel faults subsides.
Magma Molten rock lying under great pressure below the earth's crust; magma becomes lava when it erupts on to the surface.
Mantle The part of the earth between its solid crust and the core. It is about 2900 km thick and rich in silica.
Lava Molten rock which erupts from volcanoes.
Mudflow A slurry of volcanic debris mixed with water which can move at speeds of up to 100 km per hour.
Stratosphere The layer of the earth's atmosphere above the lowest layer, the troposphere; the stratosphere is at heights of between 10 and 30 km above the earth's surface.
Pyroclast Fragments of rock ejected by a volcano – the finest fragments are termed ash, the largest are termed bombs.
Basic lava Runny, easy flowing molten rock.
Tsunami A 'tidal wave' caused by underwater volcanic or earthquake activity.
Caldera Large volcanic craters produced by the collapse, or explosive destruction, of a volcanic cone.
Fault line A crack in a mass of rock caused by earth movements which have displaced the rock on one side relative to the other.
Secondary waves (S-waves) Seismic waves moving out from the focus of an earthquake in all directions, similar in form to light waves; slower moving than P-waves.
Primary waves (P-waves) Seismic waves moving out from the focus of an earthquake in all directions, similar in form to sound waves; the fastest moving earthquake waves.
Fold mountains Mountains formed by earth movements (folding) which crumpled up the layers of rock.
Continental crust The thin, solid, outermost layer of the earth, averaging about 40 km in thickness.

Chapter 10
Weathering The disintegration or decomposition of rock.
Exfoliation The wearing of a rock by peeling off of the surface layers.

Frost shattering The alternative freezing and thawing of water trapped within a crack in a mass of rock. When water freezes it expands and tends to enlarge any crack it is in, which can then hold more water than before, further enlarging the crack on renewed freezing. This weakens the rock and eventually particles break away from the main body of rock.
Scree slope An accumulation of jagged rocks at an angle of around 35° beneath an exposed cliff or free face.
Acid rain Rainwater which has become slightly acidic through dissolving sulphur dioxide gas held in the atmosphere. Sulphur dioxide is discharged into the atmosphere mainly by the chimneys of power stations and factories which burn oil or coal as their fuel.
Hard water Water containing dissolved calcium carbonate.
Joints A crack or fracture in a mass of rock along which there has been no movement of rock.
Bedding plane The boundary between two layers of rock.
Swallow hole A hole in the ground down which a surface stream disappears underground, usually in limestone area.
Cavern A large underground cave formed by the action of water enlarging joints and bedding planes in permeable rock.
Stalactite A long, cylindrical mass of calcium carbonate hanging from the roof of a limestone cavern.
Stalagmite A mass of calcium carbonate projecting upwards from the floor of a limestone cavern.
Gorge A deep narrow section of a river valley with steep sides.
Humus Partially decomposed organic remains left in the soil, especially concentrated close to the surface.
Soil horizon A layer within the soil which is chemically or physically different from the layers above and below.
Soil profile A cross-section through the soil from the surface to the bedrock.
Leaching The downward movement of water through the soil which results in the removal of soluble minerals from the upper horizons and their accumulation lower down the soil profile.
Gully A narrow channel worn into a soil or rock slope by flowing water.
Deforestation The removal of forest for use as fuel or to clear the land for agriculture.

Runoff The flow of water across the surface of the land into stream channels.
Reforestation Re-planting trees in areas where forest has been cleared.
Savanna Tropical grassland.

Chapter 11
Rill A very small channel formed in a soil slope which carries surface runoff downhill to a stream channel.
Flood plain The flat land forming the floor of a river valley. The area is regularly flooded by the river and is usually composed of sediment deposited by the river.
Meander A river bend, often very tightly curving.
Ria An inlet of the sea formed by the flooding of a river valley in a upland area by the sea.
Afforestation The planting of new forests.
Estuary The tidal mouth of a river where it enters the sea.
Deposition The dumping of rock, soil etc which has been eroded by rivers, sea, ice and wind.

Chapter 12
Storm surge Raised sea level caused by low atmospheric pressure.

Chapter 13
Ice sheet A very large, dome-shaped glacier covering a vast area.
Interglacial A warm period during an ice age when the great ice sheets have retreated to be replaced by forest; some interglacial may have been warmer than today's climate.
Ablation The process by which ice or snow is lost from a glacier, by melting, evaporation or by the calving off of icebergs.
Glacier A slow moving mass of ice.
Moraine Glacial sediment – the rocks and other debris carried and deposited by ice; also known as till.
Boulder clay A term still used to refer to sedimentary material directly deposited by a glacier or ice sheet, although it is more correctly termed 'till'.
Till Glacial sediment – the rocks and other debris carried and deposited by ice; also known as moraine.

Chapter 14
Condense The process by which water vapour in the air becomes drops of liquid water.
Solar radiation Energy from the sun.

Stratosphere A layer of the atmosphere extending from approximately 16 km to 50 km above the earth's surface.
Front The vertical boundary in the atmosphere between warm and cooler air.

Chapter 15
Irrigate Controlled addition of water to the land to grow crops.
Evapo-transpiration The loss of moisture from soil and plants by a combination of evaporation and transpiration.
Common Agricultural Policy (CAP) Policy of the European Union designed to reward farmers for their efforts and ensure reliable food supplies for consumers.
European Union Group of European countries which have agreed to join together in order to increase trade and prosperity between member states.
Set aside Policy of not cultivating part of a farm for a fixed period of time. In the European Union farmers are paid to set aside 15 per cent of the land each year.
Quota The amount of a product an individual farmer is allowed to produce.
Intensive (agriculture) Attempts to increase production by the use of more machinery and chemicals.
Aqueducts Structures built to carry water across physical features such as deep valleys or gorges.

Chapter 16
Agro-chemicals Chemicals developed for use in agriculture including pesticides, fungicides and insecticides.
Hybrid A plant or seed produced by cross-breeding two plants or seeds.

Chapter 17
Infrasructure The stock of fixed equipment in a country on which the economy depends including roads, railways, gas, water and electricity supplies.

Chapter 18
Counterurbanisation The movement of people from cities to the surrounding rural areas.
Suburbanisation The movement of people from inner city areas to the suburbs.
Tele-commuters People who work from home but communicate via computer modems, the Internet, faxes, video conferencing equipment with other people elsewhere.
Commuter village A village where many of the inhabitants travel to work in a nearby urban area.

Chapter 19
Non-renewable Usually used to mean a naturally occurring resource such as coal which, once taken and used, cannot be replenished.

Chapter 20
Refining The process of separating the mineral from the rock waste within which it is found.
Aggregate Material used in road construction. Usually this is a rock such as granite or limestone.
Igneous rock Rock formed from volcanic activity millions of years ago.
Enclave Small area within a much larger area. Enclave industries are small areas of modern industry within a largely undeveloped economy.

Chapter 21
Biomass The amount of living plant or animal material in a given area, usually expressed by weight.
Photosynthesis This process by which plants use sunlight to take in carbon dioxide and water to produce complex organic substances such as carbohydrates.
Cycle of nutrients The movement of energy through a system of plants and animals, in which the energy does not leave the system.
Primary producer Basic producers of food. Plants are the main primary producers.
Food chain Movement of energy through a chain of plants and animals.
Ecosystem A community of organisms (plants and animals) which interact with each other and with the environment in order to survive and continue.
Nomadic Moving from place to place. Nomadic herders move their animals from place to place in search of water.
Hydro-electricity Electricity generated by falling water.

Chapter 22
Geothermal energy Electricity which can be generated using the heat from the earth's crust.
Uneconomic Not a viable economic proposition.
Overburden The soil and rocks which overlie a mineral resource and have to be stripped away by excavator in a quarry or open-cast mine.
Colliery Coal mine.
Sound baffle mounds Mounds of soil and rock built up around quarries to reduce the noise and dust.

Tundra The regions lying between the coniferous forests and the permanent polar snow- and ice-fields. They are treeless and marshy areas, usually with permanently frozen subsoil.

Radiation The emission and propagation of energy through material or space by means of electro-magnetic disturbances which display both wave-like and particle-like behaviour. May be damaging to health in large quantities.

radiation electromagnetic waves of energy.

Tidal range The difference between high tide and low tide.

Tidal power Using the rise and fall of tides to generate electricity.

Chapter 23

Contaminant Something which pollutes something else. For example nitrates from fertilisers contaminate some water supplies in the UK.

Dry deposition The deposit of pollutants such as nitrogen oxides and sulphur dioxide in a solid form.

Wet deposition The deposition of pollutants such as nitrogen oxides and sulphur dioxides dissolved in rainwater.

Chapter 25

Multiplier effect The spiral of growth which is created by the establishment of a new or expanded factory or other economic activity.

Import substitution The development of industries in a country whose products will replace those previously imported into the country.

Chapter 26

Cottage industry Traditional craft work which is done on a small scale, often at home or in a small workshop, and does not involve mechanisation or mass production.

Industrial agglomeration The location of several activities in the same place in order to benefit from the sharing of infrastructure and other services and to serve the large market available.

Footloose An industry with no strong raw material or market requirements for its location, usually because transport involves only a very small part of its total costs.

Chapter 27

Ribbon development The building of housing and shops in a line along a main road, extending outwards from a town or city. It was one of the main forms of suburban developing during the 1920s and 1930s.

Shanty town Part of a large town or city, usually in a developing country, where people live in low-cost housing which they may have built themselves from any materials. The inhabitants of shanty towns usually do not own the land they live on, hence the alternative name of squatter settlement.

Site and services A method of building low-cost housing in LEDCs in which the government provides basic facilities such as water and electricity and the people build their own houses.

Informal sector That part of the economy of a country which operates outside official government control including domestic and personal services. Workers in the informal sector do not declare their income and pay no taxes.

Chapter 30

Mass transit systems Transport systems designed to move large numbers of people around towns and cities.

Photochemical smog A mixture of pollutants such as sulphur dioxide, nitrogen oxides and ozone which react together in sunlight to create a brown fog over cities like Los Angeles.

Chapter 31

New towns Towns built from scratch, usually on greenfield sites.

Overspill schemes Housing estates built in smaller towns to accommodate people moving out from cities or conurbations.

Conurbation A very large built-up area which includes at least one major city and often several towns, which have grown together over the years.

Expanded towns Towns which agreed to grow by taking people from nearby overcrowded cities.

Chapter 32

Greenbelt Protected area around a large town or city, designed to prevent the city from spreading without control.